affluence (*AF·loo·unts*, noun)   Having an abundance of possessions and money.

aficionado (*uh·fish·ee·uh·NAH·do*, noun)   A person who truly enjoys and knows a great deal about a particular activity or interest.

avarice (*AV·uh·ris*, noun)   The excessive desire for wealth.

bandwidth (noun)   A measure of how much data can be sent through a transmission medium such as a phone line.

bâte noire (*BET·nwar*, noun)   Someone who is constantly tormenting another person and has therefore become extremely disliked by that person.

bibliophile (*BIB·lee·oh·file*, noun)   A lover or collector of books.

bilateral (*bye·LAT·ur·ul*, adj.)   Describes an agreement that's supported by and binding on two countries.

biotechnology (*bye·oh·tek·NOL·uh·jee*, noun)   The use of biological processes, organisms, or substances to perform specific industrial or manufacturing tasks.

boondoggle (*BOON·daw·gul*, noun)   A frivolous and wasteful project.

boor (noun)   A rude, ill-mannered person.

boot (verb)   To turn on or restart a computer.

codswallop (*KODZ·wol·up*, noun)   Nonsense, rubbish, or drivel.

cognoscenti (*kawg·nuh·SHEN·tee*, noun)   People who are highly knowledgeable about a particular subject.

comestible (*kuh·MES·tuh·bul*, noun)   Something that can be eaten as food.

culpable (*KUL·puh·bul*, adj.)   Describes someone or something that's guilty and deserving of blame or punishment.

cyberspace (*SY·bur·space*, noun)   The virtual terrain created by computers connected to the Internet.

de rigueur (*duh ree·GUR*, adj.)   Required by social convention or current fashion.

dichotomy (*dye·KOT·uh·mee*, noun)   A separation into two contradictory or fundamentally different parts.

disintermediation (*dis·in·tur·mee·dee·AY·shun*, noun)   The trend toward direct interaction between consumers and producers. This reduces or eliminates the need for intermediaries such as wholesalers, retailers, brokers, and agents.

DNA (*dee·en·AY*, noun)   *Deoxyribonucleic* (*dee·ok·see·rye·boh·noo·KLAY·ik*) *acid;* a molecule that carries an organism's genetic information.

domain name (noun)   A name that identifies a specific network or computer connected to the Internet.

download (verb)   To request that a file be sent to your computer.

e-commerce (*ee·KAWM·urs*, noun)   The buying and selling of goods and services over the Internet.

egregious (*i·GREE·jus* or *i·GREE·gee·us*, adj.)   Conspicuously or outrageously bad.

exacerbate (*eg·ZAS·ur·bayt*, verb)   To make a bad situation worse.

expurgate (*EKS·pur·gayt*, verb)   To remove obscene or otherwise objectionable material from a manuscript.

facetious (*fuh·SEE·shuhs*, adj.)   Describes a person who is being playfully humorous or witty, sometimes inappropriately so.

gene (*jeen*, noun)   One or more segments of DNA that determine a specific physical characteristic of an organism.

globalization (*gloh·buh·li·ZAY·shun*, noun)   The trend toward a worldwide, interconnected economy made possible by rapid advancements in communications and transportation and the removal of trade barriers.

hubris (*HYOO·bris*, noun)   Excessive and arrogant pride or presumption.

iconoclast (*eye·KON·uh·klast*, noun)   A person who attacks traditional or popular ideas or established institutions.

inculcate (*in·KUL·kayt* or *IN·kul·kayt*, verb)   To impress something firmly into the mind of another, especially by frequent repetition.

initial public offering (IPO)   The first sale of a company's shares to the public.

internecine (*in·tur·NESS·een*, adj.)   Mutually destructive or relating to a fight within a country or group.

logrolling (*LOG·roh·ling*, noun)   The trading of votes and other political favors between politicians to ensure the passage of legislation favorable to each one.

market capitalization (*MAR·kut kap·i·tul·eye·ZAY·shun*, noun)   The number of shares that a company has outstanding multiplied by the current share price.

microprocessor (*my·kroh·PROS·uh·sur*, noun)   A chip inside a computer that controls most of the computer's functions and performs most of its calculations.

natty (*NAT·ee*, adj.)   Describes a person who is neat, trim, and tidy.

network (*NET·wurk*, noun)   A collection of computers connected via special cables to share files, disks, programs, printers, and other devices.

new economy (*noo iKON·uh·mee*, noun)   An economy in which the fundamental units of production are information and knowledge and in which technology plays a central role in both generating and harnessing that information and knowledge.

obsequious (*ub·SEEK·wee·us*, adj.)   Describes someone who follows the wishes or the will of another person or a group.

pecuniary (*puh·KYOO·nee·air·ee*, adj.)   Of or relating to money.

phlegmatic (*fleg·MAT·ik*, adj.)   Describes a person who is not easily excited or provoked into action.

procrustean (*proh·CRUS·tee·un*, adj.)   Characterized by a ruthless disregard for individual differences or special circumstances; enforcing a merciless conformity.

quid pro quo (*KWID pro KWOH*, noun)   Something given in return for something else.

sleep camel (noun)   A person who gets little sleep during the week and then attempts to make up for it by sleeping in and napping over the weekend.

sophistry (*SOFE·is·tree*, noun)   Argumentation that seems plausible but is actually flawed, especially in a dishonest or fallacious way.

spam (noun)   Unsolicited commercial e-mail messages.

venture capital (*VEN·chur KAP·i·tul*, noun)   Money provided to new businesses or to small businesses with innovative ideas.

windrow (*WIN·droh*, noun)   The pile of snow that a snowplow leaves at the end of a driveway.

ALPHA

Twenty-Five Easily Confused Words

Don't Confuse This Word ...

abbreviation (*uh·bree·vee·AY·shun,* noun)   Any shortened form of a phrase.

abjure (*ab·JOOR,* verb)   To renounce something under oath.

agnostic (*ag·NOS·tik,* noun)   One who believes that it isn't possible to prove God's existence, but who doesn't deny the possibility that God exists.

allusion (*uh·LOO·zhun,* noun)   An indirect or implied reference to something.

artery (*AR·tuh·ree,* noun)   Carries blood away from the heart.

averse (*uh·VURS,* adj.)   Strongly opposed or disinclined to something.

callous (*CAL·us,* adj.)   Describes a person who feels little or no emotion and has no sympathy for others.

complement (*KOM·pluh·munt,* noun)   Something that completes or perfects another thing

comprise (*kum·PRYZ,* verb)   To consist of something; to include or contain.

confidant (*KON·fuh·dahnt,* noun)   A trusted person to whom personal secrets and private matters are revealed.

continual (*kun·TIN·yoo·ul,* adj.)   Recurring regularly or frequently.

deprivation (*dep·ruh·VAY·shun,* noun)   The condition of being without something, especially food and shelter.

diagnosis (*dye·ug·NO·sis,* noun)   The identification of a disease.

disinterested (*dis·IN·tris·tid,* adj.)   Impartial, unbiased, or free from selfish motives.

elicit (*i·LIS·it,* verb)   To draw out something hidden; to cause a reaction.

ensure (*en·SHOOR,* verb)   To make certain that something happens.

flaunt (*flawnt,* verb)   To display something shamelessly or ostentatiously.

horde (*hord,* noun)   A large group.

impractical (*im·PRAK·ti·kul,* adj.)   Unworkable, unfeasible, or not sensible in practice.

loathe (*lohth,* "th" as in "the," verb)   To dislike intensely.

predicament (*pri·DIK·uh·munt,* noun)   An unpleasant, troublesome, or embarrassing situation from which there is no easy way out.

proscribe (*proh·SKRYB,* verb)   To condemn or prohibit.

sadist (*SAY·dist* or *SAD·ist,* noun)   A person who gets pleasure out of inflicting cruelty and pain on others.

stanch (*stanch* or *stawnch*)   To stop the flow of a liquid, especially blood from a wound.

vocation (*voh·KAY·shun,* noun)   A regular occupation, especially one to which a person is particularly well suited.

With This Word ...

acronym (*AK·ruh·nim,* noun)   A word formed by taking the first letter of all or most of the words in a phrase.

adjure (*ad·JOOR,* verb)   To command under oath.

atheist (*AY·thee·ist,* noun)   A person who believes that God doesn't exist.

illusion (*i·LOO·zhun,* noun)   An erroneous or misleading perception or belief, or something that causes such a perception or belief.

vein (*VAYN,* noun)   Carries blood to the heart.

adverse (*ad·VURS* or *AD·vurs,* adj.)   Antagonistic; harmful.

callus (*CAL·us,* noun)   A hard, thickened part of the skin.

compliment (*KOM·pluh·munt,* noun)   An expression of praise or admiration.

compose (*kum·POZ,* verb)   To make up the parts of.

confident (*KON·fi·dunt,* adj.)   Self-assured; undoubting.

continuous (*kun·TIN·yoo·us,* adj.)   Occurring without interruption or change.

depravation (*dep·ruh·VAY·shun,* noun)   The condition of being morally debased or corrupt.

prognosis (*prawg·NO·sis,* noun)   The projection of the likely course and outcome of a disease.

uninterested (*un·IN·tur·es·tid,* adj.)   Indifferent; not interested.

illicit (*i·LIS·it,* adj.)   Not allowed by law.

insure (*en·SHOOR,* verb)   To protect against risk.

flout (*flowt,* verb)   To show contempt for.

hoard (*hord,* noun)   A hidden supply or fund put aside for future use.

impracticable (*im·PRAK·ti·kuh·bul,* adj.)   Impossible.

loath (*lohth,* "th" as in "thin," adj.)   Unwilling to do something.

dilemma (*duh·LEM·uh,* noun)   A situation that requires a choice between two or more equally unsatisfactory alternatives.

prescribe (*pri·SKRYB,* verb)   To order the use of; to set down as a rule or guide.

masochist (*MAS·uh·kist,* noun)   A person who derives pleasure from having abuse inflicted upon himself.

staunch (*stawnch,* adj.)   Loyal, steadfast, and dependable; solidly built.

avocation (*ah·vuh·KAY·shun,* noun)   A hobby or side occupation pursued for enjoyment.

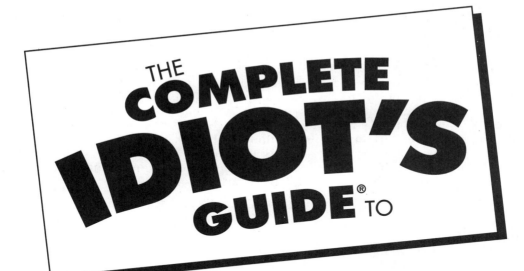

THE
COMPLETE IDIOT'S GUIDE® TO

A Smart Vocabulary

by Paul McFedries

ALPHA

A Pearson Education Company

To word lovers the world over, and to Karen, who is kind enough to laugh at my puns.

Copyright © 2001 by Logophilia Limited

International Standard Book Number: 0-02-863997-9
Library of Congress Catalog Card Number: 2001089684

04   03   02   8   7   6   5   4   3   2

Interpretation of the printing code: The rightmost number of the first series of numbers is the year of the book's printing; the rightmost number of the second series of numbers is the number of the book's printing. For example, a printing code of 01-1 shows that the first printing occurred in 2001.

Printed in the United States of America

For marketing and publicity, please call: 317-581-3722

The publisher offers discounts on this book when ordered in quantity for bulk purchases and special sales.

For sales within the United States, please contact: Corporate and Government Sales, 1-800-382-3419 or corpsales@pearsontechgroup.com

Outside the United States, please contact: International Sales, 317-581-3793 or international@pearsontechgroup.com

Publisher
Marie Butler-Knight

Product Manager
Phil Kitchel

Managing Editor
Jennifer Chisholm

Senior Acquisitions Editor
Renee Wilmeth

Development Editor
Michael Koch

Senior Production Editor
Christy Wagner

Copy Editor
Amy Lepore

Illustrator
Jody Schaeffer

Cover Designers
Mike Freeland
Kevin Spear

Book Designers
Scott Cook and Amy Adams of DesignLab

Indexer
Brad Herriman

Layout/Proofreading
Angela Calvert
Mary Hunt
Daryl Kessler

Contents at a Glance

Contents

Foreword

A person with a rich vocabulary is like an artist with a palette full of colors. One doesn't have to use all the colors in one painting, but it helps to have just the right hue needed to bring out the nuances of a scene. Imagine having to put red where you want to put shades of lateritious (brick-red), incarnadine (blood-red), or russet (reddish-brown) instead.

With a language like English, we are especially fortunate to have such a vast verbal palette. Its fervid proclivity to borrow from other languages has bestowed it with words encompassing all hues of the rainbow. With a vocabulary of some half million words—largest of any language—there is always a word with the right shade of meaning. There is no dearth of expressions to convey the subtle differences in the range of human emotions, thoughts, ideas, feelings, and actions. With the rise of English as the global language, it is increasingly coming in contact with numerous other languages, borrowing from them, and, in turn, lending them words. Science, technology, medicine, trade, and travel are all doing their part in expanding the language by giving it countless new terms. With such an ever-widening spectrum, it is all the more important to be aware of new words.

Language, like any living, breathing creature, is always evolving, shifting, moving. The English that was a few decades ago is not the same English we have today, and what we use today will not be what the next generation will see. With infusion of new words and shift in meaning of other words, a whole new vocabulary takes shape. Today when we check our mail, we don't go out of our house but rather to our computer in the basement office. A few hundred years ago if we called something egregious, we'd be praising it, not condemning it. A misconception among some people is that a richer vocabulary means that one has to use big words on all occasions. Nothing can be farther from truth. Why use deep crimson when all that's needed is a gentle shade of pink? On the other hand, why not employ cachinnate if it is more suitable for the occasion, or maybe cackle, or perhaps titter, or even chortle rather than the plain-vanilla laugh?

I've enjoyed Paul's Word Spy for years and benefited from it. His love of words and language is obvious. He is a true linguaphile. Having written countless books, he knows the importance of using the right words to convey the idea. He is one of the most-suited persons to write a book on improving vocabulary. The book that I have the privilege of writing this foreword for is informative, comprehensive, and colorful.

Delight in the wondrous beauty of language and words. May the music and magic of words always capture your imagination. With *The Complete Idiot's Guide to a Smart Vocabulary,* you'll never be lost for the right words at the right time.

Anu Garg
Founder, Wordsmith.Org

Introduction

"The value of vocabulary is unequivocal. A person with a large vocabulary is able to receive, explore, modify, and express complex ideas and emotions with greater ease and success—and far less frustration and impatience—than the possessor of a small vocabulary. Vocabulary elasticizes a mind."

—Peter Anderson, American writer

Do you want to be successful in school or in your career? Do you want higher marks, a higher income, or a higher position on the corporate ladder? Do you want to improve your relationships with the people around you? Do you want to get the most out of what you read and hear? If so, then here's the secret: *Improve your vocabulary!*

Yes, it *is* as simple as that. Why? Because vocabulary is intimately linked to communication, and study after study has shown that the key to academic, business, and personal success is having above-average communication skills. These skills come in two flavors: expression and comprehension. *Expression* means conveying your thoughts, ideas, and arguments to others by speaking or by writing. If you can express yourself well, other people will be able to follow your train of thought, grasp your ideas, and appreciate your arguments. On the flip side, *comprehension* means understanding the oral and written communications that come your way, which enables you to better relate to other people, appreciate their points of view, and counter their arguments. It also means being better able to learn the ideas and concepts presented in books, articles, and papers, all of which improves your knowledge.

Words are at the heart of both expression and comprehension—one researcher has called words "the tools of thought"—so your vocabulary directly determines the level of your communication skills and therefore your success at school, home, or your job. It sounds unlikely, but it's true. In fact, one study done by the Johnson O'Connor Research Foundation showed that the *only* thing successful businesspeople have in common is a large vocabulary!

Welcome, therefore, to *The Complete Idiot's Guide to a Smart Vocabulary.* My goal in this book is to help you become more successful at whatever you do by helping you increase your vocabulary. I do this not only by taking you through a big collection of words—more than 3,000 are defined in this book—but by taking a different approach than any other vocabulary book:

➤ **This book is organized by subject.** Other vocabulary books just throw a list of words at you in alphabetical order (boring!) or in some random order (confusing!). In this book, I present the words in self-contained chapters, each of which is devoted to a particular subject such as human behavior, business, the stock market, computers, the Internet, and foreign terms.

➤ **This book cares about nuances.** One of the keys to a strong vocabulary is being able to use words precisely. That means knowing the slightly different shades of meaning that one word has over another. For example, do you know the difference between a charlatan and a con man? You'll find out in Chapter 1, "It Takes All Kinds: Types of People."

➤ **This book is conversational.** Few things in this world are as dull as a vocabulary book that simply lists page after page of words and their definitions. To avoid such drudgery, in most of the chapters in this book, I use a relaxed, conversational style to introduce and talk about each main word and the related words.

➤ **This book enjoys words.** I am a *logophile,* a lover of words. For proof, you need look no further than my company name: Logophilia Limited. I've tried wherever possible to inject this love of words into this book's text, and it's my sincerest hope that at least a little of it rubs off on you because an appreciation and curiosity for words is the surest road to vocabulary prowess.

➤ **This book is fun.** Most vocabulary books make you feel as though a furrowed brow and rigidly pursed lips are the only appropriate facial expressions for the serious business of vocabulary study. Well, there will be none of that around here! I aim to prove that having fun and learning new words are *not* mutually exclusive.

Some Tips for Learning Vocabulary

Because you use words all day and every day, learning vocabulary is quite a bit different than, say, learning calculus or biology. This means you need to approach your vocabulary studies in a different way. To help you do so and to help you get the most out of this book, here are a few pointers and tips for learning new words:

➤ Say each word out loud, particularly those that come with a phonetic pronunciation guide. I know it feels silly, but it's the only way to ensure you get the pronunciation right.

➤ Do the exercises that appear at the end of each chapter. Feel free to write your answers directly in the book. (I won't mind, I promise.) That will make it easier to check your answers by referring to Appendix A (which you should do as soon as you've finished the chapter's exercises, to make sure you're on the right track).

➤ Read books, magazines, Web sites, and other media on subjects that interest you.

➤ When you're reading, don't just skip over words you don't recognize, even if you think you can guess the meaning of a word from the context. Instead, take a few seconds and look up the word in a good dictionary.

➤ Consider investing in a good pocket dictionary that you can take with you when you leave the house. This will enable you to look up unfamiliar words as you come across them in your travels.

➤ If you're at a social function and someone uses a word you don't recognize, don't be afraid to ask that person the meaning of the word. Most people enjoy showing off their vocabulary and won't mind your question one bit. If you're too shy, make a mental note of the word and look it up when you get home.

➤ When you learn a new word, try to work it into your writing and conversation as soon as possible and as often as possible.

➤ Don't try to learn too many words at once. For example, instead of trying to learn all the words in a particular chapter at once (50 to 100 words), just work through the chapter one heading at a time (10 to 20 words).

➤ Give yourself some time between sessions. After reading a section, take time to practice the words and work them into your daily routine. When you're comfortable with what you've learned, move on to the next section.

➤ Drop by the home page of this book to find three bonus chapters. One chapter covers words related to medical terminology. Another is devoted to terms from evolution, genetics, and biotechnology. The third chapter lists lots of words related to money to enrich your vocabulary. Here's the address:

   www.mcfedries.com/vocabulary/

➤ If you have a computer and access to the Internet, keep up with the latest lingo by checking out my Word Spy Web site at:

   www.logophilia.com/WordSpy/

This site is devoted to recently coined words, existing words that have enjoyed a recent renaissance, and older words that are now being used in new ways. Each weekday, the Word Spy presents a new word, its definition, and a citation (usually from a major newspaper or magazine) that shows how people are using the word. You also get extra goodies such as background on the word's formation, a list of related words from the Word Spy database, quotations on words and language, and more. Better yet, you can subscribe to the free Word Spy mailing list and get each Word Spy word sent directly to your e-mail inbox. To subscribe, send an e-mail to the following address:

   listmanager@mcfedries.com

In the Subject line of the message, enter the following:

   join wordspy

Learning Some Vocabulary Lingo

Throughout this book, I'll be tossing certain vocabulary-related words your way, so let's take a second now to define these terms so you won't trip over them later (the next section describes the pronunciation scheme I use here):

adjective (*AJ·ik·tiv*)—A word that describes or specifies the characteristics of a NOUN or PRONOUN. For example, in the phrase *the fun book,* the word *fun* is used as an adjective for the noun *book*. Note that I use the abbreviation *adj.* for *adjective* throughout this book.

adverb (*AD·vurb*)—A word that modifies a VERB, an ADJECTIVE, or another adverb. For example, in the sentence *She learns vocabulary quickly,* the word *quickly* is an adverb that modifies the verb *learns*. I use the abbreviation *adv.* for *adverb* throughout this book.

antonym (*AN·tuh·nim*)—A word that has the opposite meaning of another word. For example, *up* is the antonym of *down*.

etymology (*et·uh·MOL·uh·jee*)—The history of a word. For example, the etymology of *etymology* is that it comes from the Greek word *etumologia,* which combines *etumon,* "the true sense of a word," with *logia,* "the study of."

idiom (*ID·ee·um*)—An expression that is peculiar to a particular language and that can't be understood by examining its individual words. For example, to say that someone *has a screw loose* means he's a bit crazy, but of course, he doesn't have an actual loose screw anywhere. So if someone who didn't know English very well came across this idiom, she wouldn't be able to figure out its meaning by looking up each word in a dictionary.

lexicon (*LEKS·i·kon* or *LEKSs·i·kun*)—The entire list of words in a particular language, subject, or profession, or the words that are known by a person.

noun (*nown*)—A word that is the name of a person, place, thing, quality, or action. For example, in the phrase *laugh at the silly author,* the word *author* is the noun.

prefix (*PREE·fiks*)—A group of one or more letters placed at the beginning of a word and used to modify the meaning of the word. For example, the prefix *non-* means "not," so adding it to the word *stop* gives us *nonstop,* "without stopping."

pronoun (*PROH·nown*)—A word that functions as a substitute for a noun. Examples are *I, you, we, they, he, she, myself,* and *anybody*.

root (*root,* rhymes with "boot")—The part of a word that carries the main meaning; the part that remains when the PREFIXES and SUFFIXES have been removed. For example, the root of the word *unhelpful* is the word *help*. (Note that the root isn't necessarily a word in itself.)

suffix (*SUF·iks*)—A group of one or more letters placed at the end of a PREFIX, ROOT, or word and used to create a new word. For example, the suffix *-logy* means "the study of," so adding it to the prefix *bio-,* "life," gives us *biology* "the study of life."

synonym (*SIN·uh·nim*)—A word that has the same or nearly the same meaning as another word. For example, the word *lexicon* is a synonym for the word *vocabulary*.

verb (*vurb*)—A word that expresses action or existence. For example, in the sentence *She opens the book,* the word *opens* is the verb.

A Few More Things About the Book

Just so you know what to expect as you march through the book, here's a list of the various features and knickknacks that I've sprinkled throughout:

➤ **Main words versus secondary words.** The book's *main words* are the ones I devote the most attention to, which means you get one or more of the following: the definition, the pronunciation, the part of speech (noun, verb, and so on), a sample sentence, and the word's ETYMOLOGY. To help you recognize the main words, I've formatted them (and their variations) in **bold**. The *secondary words* are the SYNONYMS and ANTONYMS of the main words; the ROOTS, PREFIXES, and SUFFIXES; and any other related words that fit into the subject under discussion. The secondary words are formatted in *italics*.

➤ **Phonetic pronunciation.** I hate vocabulary books that use obscure pronunciation symbols that you constantly have to look up to figure out how to say a word. I avoid that in this book by using a "phonetic" pronunciation scheme that uses ordinary letters to show you how to say a word. For example, I use *ee* to represent the long "e" sound in a word such as *read*. Here are some notes to bear in mind:

  ➤ I use the symbol · to separate the word's syllables.

  ➤ I use uppercase letters to indicate the syllable that should be stressed. For example, the pronunciation of *syllable* is *SIL·uh·bul,* so you stress the first syllable.

  ➤ English doesn't have any straightforward way to represent the sound made by the *si* in vi*sion*, for example. So I use the letter combo *zh* to fix that, which means the pronunciation of *vision* would be *VIZH·un.*

  ➤ The letter pair *th* can be pronounced either as in *thin* or as in *the*. I'll note which one to use when giving you the pronunciation of words that include *th*. For example, the pronunciation of *athlete* would appear like so: *ATH·leet,* "th" as in "thin."

  ➤ In all pronunciations, the letter *s* is hissed. For example, here's the pronunciation of *once: wuns*. On the other hand, for words that use *s* with a *z* sound, I'll just use *z*. For example, here's the pronunciation of *wins: winz*.

  ➤ Finally, some letter combinations sound different depending on the word. The combo *oo* is a good example if you consider the pronunciations of the simple words *foot* and *root*. For *foot* I'd use *fuht,* but for *root* I'd say "rhymes with 'boot.'"

➤ **End-of-chapter exercises.** Each chapter closes with a series of exercises designed to help you understand and retain some of the words in the chapter. You'll find the answers to the exercises in Appendix A.

➤ **Pointers to related words.** A great way to sharpen your vocabulary is to study related words and see how they differ. To help you do that, I've added "See also" pointers throughout the book so you know that a related word is discussed else-where. Also, if I use a word that's defined somewhere else in the book, I'll for-mat it in small caps, like this: LEXICON.

➤ **Handling gender pronouns.** I use gender throughout this book, particularly in the sample sentences. I have tried as far as possible to alternate gender, so that if one sentence uses a male example, the next uses a female example. Where no specific person is mentioned, I alternate he/him with she/her, which helps me avoid the generic *they* or weirdo constructions such as *his/her* or *s/he*.

Finally, you'll see tons of extra tidbits called *sidebars* positioned on nearly every page. These asides are designed to supply you with extra information, tips, and cautions. Here's what you'll find:

Parts Dept.

This note describes word parts such as ROOTS, PREFIXES, and SUF-FIXES. Note, too, that I provide a long list of common prefixes and suffixes in Appendix B.

You Don't Say

This note warns you about easily confused words that have com-pletely different meanings, im-proper usage, and other vocabulary pitfalls to avoid.

Idiom Savant

This sidebar discusses useful IDIOMS related to a word or subject.

Word Wonders

This sidebar offers up interesting word facts and trivia.

Acknowledgments

I'm not sure what this world would be like without editors, but I can tell you one thing: it would be a *sloppier* world. That's because most writers are just not capable of crossing absolutely every last "t" and dotting every single "i." Not only that, but we can be counted upon to toss commas around with a frightening haphazardness and to dangle participles with an unseemly abandon. We are, in short, very lucky that we have editors who come hard-wired with the requisite amount of fussbudget-ness to transform our slipshod prose into something ready for public consumption.

And I'm particularly lucky to have worked with the top-notch editors at alpha books, who did a remarkable job on this book. So I hereby extend the warmest and most heartfelt thanks to acquisitions editor Mike Sanders, development editor Michael Koch, senior production editor Christy Wagner, and copy editor Amy Lepore. I also want to extend a special thank you to Alpha Books publisher Marie Butler-Knight for giving me the wonderful opportunity to write this book. I had a ball, Marie!

Trademarks

All terms mentioned in this book that are known to be or are suspected of being trademarks or service marks have been appropriately capitalized. Alpha Books and Pearson Education, Inc., cannot attest to the accuracy of this information. Use of a term in this book should not be regarded as affecting the validity of any trademark or service mark.

Part 1

The Good, the Bad, the Ugly, and More: People Words

Have you ever heard the story about how Eskimos have a huge number of words related to snow? It makes sense given the northern climes that Eskimos call home, but it turns out that it's just not true. They use, in fact, about the same number of snow-related words that we do. (An inaccurate bit of information that gets accepted as true only because of constant repetition is called a factoid.)

What is true is that all cultures have many words to describe people. Whether it's describing different types of people or talking about how people act, look, think, or relate to one another, the English language is bursting with people words. Therefore, it will come as no surprise that Part 1 is the longest section of this book with six chapters that cover all aspects of who we are and what we do.

Chum ; Chump

Chapter 1

It Takes All Kinds: Types of People

In This Chapter

➤ People who do good things

➤ People who do nasty things

➤ Friends and enemies

➤ Important and unimportant people

"One forgets words as one forgets names. One's vocabulary needs constant fertilizing or it will die."

—Evelyn Waugh, British novelist

Do opposites really attract, as the old saying tells us? It's probably true for certain kinds of traits. For example, neat and messy, talkative and quiet, and chocolate loving and chocolate hating. I doubt it's true, however, for the opposites you learn about in this chapter. Whether it's good versus nasty, friends versus enemies, or the important versus the unimportant, we're definitely talking oil and water here.

A Few Good Men (and Women)

A good person is someone who performs random acts of senseless kindness and other nice things. I think it's a hopeful sign for the human race that not only are there lots of these good folks around, but they come in many different forms, as this section shows.

An **altruist** (*AL·troo·ist*) is a person who displays unselfish concern for the welfare of other people.

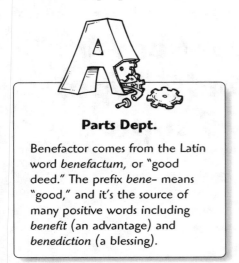

Parts Dept.

Benefactor comes from the Latin word *benefactum,* or "good deed." The prefix *bene–* means "good," and it's the source of many positive words including *benefit* (an advantage) and *benediction* (a blessing).

➤ Only a true **altruist** such as Tim would give up his Thursday night bingo game to teach that "Chess for Newborns" class.

An altruist practices **altruism** and is said to act **altruistically.** You could also call an altruist a *humanitarian* and describe her as *selfless.* The opposite of an altruist is an *egoist,* a person who acts in a *self-centered* way.

See also: CYNIC, EGOCENTRIC, MISANTHROPE.

A **benefactor** (*ben·uh·FAC·tur*) is someone who helps people, organizations, or causes, particularly by giving them money or some sort of gift.

➤ The Center for the Responsible Use of Commas survived thanks to the generous donations of a single **benefactor.**

A female benefactor is called a **benefactress**, and the gift given is sometimes called a **benefaction** (although *donation* is the more common term). A benefactor is also known as a *backer* or a *patron.* If the person is a regular contributor to worthy causes, he's a *philanthropist.* If the person is an older man who is bestowing gifts on a younger woman, he's a *sugar daddy.*

See also: ANGEL INVESTOR.

A **do-gooder** (*DOO·good·ur*) is a humanitarian who sincerely tries to do good deeds but who suffers from naïve and unrealistic expectations.

➤ Can you believe that **do-gooder** of a senator wants to pass a law requiring everyone to volunteer 40 hours per week?

While practicing his **do-goodism**, such a person may also be called a *goody-goody* or a *Goody Two-Shoes,* although both terms have the sense of someone who is overly virtuous in a sickly sweet kind of way. ("Goody Two-Shoes" is the name of the main character in a children's story called *The History of Goody Two-Shoes,* which was published in 1765. She lived most of her life with only one shoe, but when she received a second shoe, she went around yelling "Two shoes! Two shoes!" until nobody could stand the sight of her.)

An **idealist** (*eye·DEE·uh·list*) sees the world as it ought to be (that is, in its ideal state) rather than as it is.

➤ As an **idealist**, Mary believed she would someday live in a world without poverty, disease, or the Macarena.

This person's **idealism** is noble, to be sure, but usually isn't very practical. An **idealistic** point of view can also be described as *quixotic* (*kwik·SAW·tik*) or *utopian* (*yoo·TOH·pee·uhn*), both of which are literary references. The former is from the book *Don Quixote* (*kee·HO·tay*), by Miguel de Cervantes, and carries a hint of foolishness and rashness; the latter is from the book *Utopia*, by Thomas More, and means "impossibly ideal."

See also: IDEOLOGUE.

If you have a **mentor** (*MEN·tor* or *MEN·tur*), then you're very lucky indeed because it means you have a wise and trusted adviser to whom you can turn for help.

➤ When the old "paper-clip-or-staple?" question came up yet again, George knew it was time to ask his **mentor** for advice.

This word comes from Greek mythology, specifically Homer's *The Odyssey*. Mentor was the nobleman who was the most trusted by Odysseus, the hero of the story. **Mentoring** is most often performed in educational and workplace settings, and you may see **mentors** also referred to as *counselors, gurus, tutors,* and even *coaches.* (One of my favorite words of recent vintage is *life coach*, "an adviser who helps a person make decisions or overcome problems in his or her life.")

Idiom Savant

If an idealist makes plans, they will likely be unrealistic, so she'll be said to be making *castles in the air.*

See also: CONFIDANT.

Boors, Tyrants, and Other Nasty Folk

Unfortunately, for every good person in this world there seems to be another half dozen who make your blood boil with their bad behavior. Rather than clenching your fists in rage when confronted with such bad eggs, hurl an insult their way using some of the words I cover in this section.

A **boor** (rhymes with "poor" and "moor") is a rude, ill-mannered person.

➤ Only a **boor** would try to put through 12 items in the "10 items or less" checkout lane.

You definitely wouldn't want to spend a long weekend with someone who exhibits **boorish** behavior. If such an unlucky turn of events comes to pass, remember that you can also call the person a *brute,* a *churl,* a *lout,* or a *vulgarian.*

See also: CRASS, UNKEMPT.

Another real piece of work is the **charlatan** (*SHAR·luh·tun*), a person who makes extravagant but false claims of knowledge or ability.

➤ When he claimed that he knew the Colonel's secret recipe of 11 different herbs and spices, I knew I was dealing with a **charlatan**.

Charlatanic people are clearly not in short supply, as evidenced by the many synonyms we have for them: *faker, imposter, pretender, humbug,* and *four-flusher*. (The latter is a poker term for a player who bluffs his way to a win by having only four out of the five cards needed for a flush.) If this person performs his **charlatanism** in a medical setting, he's a *quack* (short for *quacksalver*) or a *mountebank* (*MOUN·tuh·bank*). If money is involved, he's a *fraud*, a *swindler*, or a *con man*.

Next on the people-not-to-take-home-to-mother list is the **miscreant** (*MISS·cree·unt*), a person who behaves in a criminal or depraved manner.

➤ From window-breaker as a child to leg-breaker as an adult, Tony was a lifelong **miscreant**.

You might also want to call someone engaging in **miscreant** behavior a *villain* or a *reprobate*. If the person's actions aren't overly nasty, try *blackguard* (*BLAG·urd*), *knave* (*NAVE*), or *scoundrel*. If the person's acting more on the mischievous side, have fun with words such as *rascal*, *rapscallion*, or *scallywag* (also *scalawag*).

See also: TOADY.

You Don't Say

Don't confuse a sadist with a *masochist*, a person who derives pleasure from having abuse inflicted upon himself. (An old joke tells us that the difference between a masochist and sadist is that the masochist yells "Hurt me! Hurt me!" and the sadist says "No, I won't.") If a person derives pleasure from simultaneous sadism and masochism, then she's a *sadomasochist*.

Your typical **sadist** (*SAY·dist* or *SAD·ist*) is a person who gets pleasure out of inflicting cruelty and pain on others.

➤ By forcing her guests to listen to her entire collection of Wayne Newton albums, Doris proved herself to be a true **sadist**.

The practice of **sadism** gets its name from a fellow named Count Alphonse François de Sade, or the Marquis de Sade, as he is more familiarly known. He not only was into **sadistic** perversions, he wrote about them as well, thus ensuring his own *infamy* ("evil fame"). He was sentenced to death but escaped and ended up living out his days in an insane asylum.

The word **tyrant** (*TYE·runt*) originally referred to an absolute ruler who wields power without restrictions, but it's now more commonly used for any person in a position of authority who acts in a harsh and oppressive manner.

➤ My boss is such a **tyrant.** Today he ordered me to use the words "SYNERGY" and "PARADIGM SHIFT" in at least one memo every day or he'll fire me.

The **tyranny** of a power-crazed boss or a petty civil servant can be hard to take. To help, also use these words to describe your tormentor: *authoritarian, autocrat, bully,* DESPOT, *ogre,* and *slave driver.*

See also: AUTHORITARIANISM, AUTOCRACY.

Confidants and Cronies: Words for Friends

A friend, somebody once said, is someone who likes you in spite of yourself. To have such a person in your life is a blessing, indeed, and we're also blessed by having lots of different types of friends, as you'll see here.

An **ally** (*AL·eye*) is a person who has entered into a helpful association with another person.

➤ Jones wanted to ban the wearing of Hawaiian shirts on casual Fridays, but he knew he needed at least one **ally** on the board to help him get it through.

When two or more people become **allies,** their association is called an *alliance,* a word that comes from the same source—the Latin word *alligare,* "to bind to"—as ally. (This source also produced the word *alloy,* "a combination of one thing—particularly a metal—with another.") **Allied** people are also called *confederates, partners,* and *associates.*

A **confidant** (*KON·fuh·dahnt*) is a trusted person to whom personal secrets and private matters are revealed.

➤ Her crush on Regis Philbin could only be disclosed to her **confidant.**

If the trusted friend is female, then she's a **confidante** (same pronunciation). Male or female, you can also call your friend an *intimate.*

A **crony** (*KROH·nee*) is a long-time friend or companion.

➤ Mabel and her **cronies** have been getting together every Friday night for more than 30 years to do some sewing and chug a few beers.

You Don't Say

Don't confuse confidant with *confident* (*KON·fuh·duhnt*), which means "self-assured." The two words come from the same root, which is the Latin word *confidere,* "to rely on." However, confidant comes by way of the word *confide,* "to disclose something private." Note, too, that the word *confidence* has two meanings: "that which is confided" and "a feeling of self-assurance."

A crony being the precious thing that it is, there's no shortage of synonyms you can use, including *amigo, buddy* (or *bosom buddy*), *chum,* and *pal.*

See also: CRONYISM.

Sidekick (*SIDE·kik*) is a slang term for a close companion or partner, particularly one who functions as an assistant.

> ➤ Bruce W. and Dick G., his faithful **sidekick**, would often dress up in tights and head out into the night looking for trouble.

No one's quite sure how the word sidekick came about. What seems likely, however, is that it's derived from the criminal slang phrase *side kicks,* "the outside pockets of an overcoat." Perhaps, like these pockets, the criminal's assistant was "by his side" and useful for carrying things.

Adversaries and Antagonists: Words for Enemies

The word *enemy* can be traced all the way back to the Latin word *inimicus,* which combines *in-,* "not," with *amicus,* "friend." (This word is also the source of *inimical,* "hostile or harmful.") I guess that just about sums it up right there, doesn't it? Not quite, as you'll see in this rather unfriendly section.

Idiom Savant

A *fair-weather friend* isn't much of a friend at all. It's someone who acts friendly to another person only when that person is experiencing good times.

An **adversary** (*AD·vur·sair·ee*) is a person who offers formidable opposition to another in a battle, contest, or debate.

> ➤ He knew he was in deep trouble when his Scrabble **adversary** opened the game with the word MUZJIKS to score 128 points.

The key aspect to an **adversarial** relationship is that the other person is seen as being *formidable* ("causing fear, alarm, or dread").

An **antagonist** (*an·TAG·uh·nist*) is a person who offers active and possibly hostile opposition to another in a battle, contest, or debate.

> ➤ The prosecutor was forced to use writs, motions, and the flash of his alarmingly white teeth to combat his **antagonist,** the defense attorney.

The **antagonism** of the other person is active, which means he's constantly trying to defeat his foe. And that person's **antagonizing** may have some *animosity* ("intense dislike") associated with it as well. If the opponents are more or less evenly matched, you can also call them *rivals,* which implies a long-standing history of opposition.

A **bête noire** (*BET·nwar*) is someone who is constantly tormenting another person and thus has become extremely disliked by that person.

➤ Cindy's **bête noire** was the woman in the apartment below who practiced her Dr. Ruth impersonation at the top of her lungs each evening.

A bête noire (which is French for "black beast") is someone who repeatedly makes your life miserable and has become the *bane* ("ruin") of your existence. (It can also be a thing instead of a person.) If the person or thing is not quite so awful, you might prefer to use the cuter terms *bugaboo* or *bugbear*.

A **nemesis** (*NEM·uh·sis*) is an unbeatable opponent or a person who inflicts vengeance or retribution.

Parts Dept.

The *ant–* prefix is a variation of *anti–*, which means "against or opposite." You see *ant–* used when the next letter in the word is a vowel (for example, "antacid" or "antonym").

➤ Pete, the poster boy for mindless optimism, still thought he could beat his old **nemesis** despite having lost to him 52 times in a row.

This word is another refugee from Greek mythology. Nemesis was the goddess of *retribution,* which means "the dispensing of something justly deserved." This usually implies a well-earned punishment, but it can occasionally mean a reward as well. In any case, there was no hiding from Nemesis once she decided to track you down, so that's why her name has also come to stand for an unbeatable foe.

See also: HUBRIS.

Big Shots: Words for Important People

In this section, you learn a few words for people who make the world go around, who do the moving and the shaking, and who are not to be sneezed at.

A **dignitary** (*DIG·nuh·tair·ee*) is a person with a high rank or position.

➤ As a sign of respect, the chef made the **dignitary's** chicken a little less rubbery than everyone else's.

This word is related to *dignity,* "being worthy of esteem or respect," which may be why such a person is also sometimes called a *worthy*. If the person is from the highest rank, feel free to call her a *VIP* (*VEE·eye·pee*), which stands for "very important person." If you want to poke a bit of fun at a nearby dignitary who may be a bit too pleased with his position, call him a *high muckamuck*.

A **luminary** (*LOO·muh·nair·ee*) is a person who has achieved fame or prominence in a particular field.

➤ As the only **luminary** to attend the tractor pull, the movie star paused to let the assembled masses bask in the glow of her celebrity.

9

This word comes from the old French word *luminaire,* or "lamp." Therefore, a luminary can also be any object that gives light, particularly a *celestial* ("from the sky or the heavens") body such as the sun or a star. Human **luminaries** are often described using words related to light, such as *luminous* ("full of light"), *brilliant* ("shining"), or *superstar* ("a hugely popular celebrity").

See also: GLAMOROUS.

A **nabob** (*NAY·bob*) is a person of great wealth or importance.

➤ With his vast riches and power, Andy was a **nabob,** for sure, but was he a happy **nabob?**

Idiom Savant

If the nabob in question seems to have special advantages based on his wealth or power, call him a *fat cat.* However, don't confuse this with a *top dog,* "the person with the highest authority or rank."

Originally, a nabob was a governor in India when that country was part of the Mogul Empire (from 1526 to 1857). This empire also gave us another word for a person of immense wealth and power: a *mogul.* If your local nabob is *pompous* ("showy or pretentious") and tends to abuse his power, then he's a *panjandrum.*

See also: MAGNATE.

A **patriarch** (*PAY·tree·ark*) is the oldest male member of a family or group.

➤ As **patriarch** of the family, Walter demanded respect, attention, and a glass to keep his teeth in when he wasn't using them.

You can also use patriarch to refer to any man who is a father or a founder of a group or enterprise or to describe any *venerable* ("worthy of respect") old man. **Patriarchy** is used loosely to mean the collection of such men and more accurately to mean a social system in which descent is traced through the father's side of the family. If you need to talk about the oldest female member of a family, use *matriarch* instead. Synonyms for patriarch: *dean, elder, paterfamilias, wise man.* For matriarch: *dowager, matron, materfamilias.*

Small Frys: Words for Unimportant People

For every mover and shaker upon high, there are lots of moved and shaken people down below. This section looks at words devoted to these unimportant people.

A **minion** (*MIN·yun*) is a follower or servant.

➤ Instead of barking out orders to his assembled **minions,** the gang leader broke out into a medley of *Fiddler on the Roof* tunes.

The chief characteristic of minions is that they are *servile,* meaning "submissive or slavish." Your average minion isn't exactly plotting to overthrow his boss or start a revolution. There is also a kind of low-man-on-the-totem-pole quality to such a person, which is also reflected in the synonym *hireling*, "a person willing to perform menial tasks." Other words for a person who performs menial labor are *flunky* and *lackey*.

A **subordinate** (*suh·BOR·duh·nit*) is a person of lesser rank or authority than someone else.

➤ "Sorry, Miss Pennypacker, but as my **subordinate**, I believe it *is* your job to massage my ego."

The subordinate person is lower in status than someone else but isn't necessarily servile like a minion. Synonyms that reflect this are *hired hand, junior,* and *underling*. If the person is the lesser of two people, she's a *second banana* or a *second fiddle*. If such a person refuses to submit to the authorities above her, she's guilty of *insubordination*.

A **toady** (*TOH·dee*) is a person who shamelessly uses flattery and favors to gain approval with another.

Parts Dept.

The prefix *sub-* means "below," "less than," or "underneath" and leads off dozens of English words.

➤ After complimenting the boss on the fine shape of his skull, it was clear that Jenkins was turning into a **toady**.

Those who would **toady** to another are looked down upon for obvious reasons, so the language has come up with some not-too-pleasant synonyms for such people, including *bootlicker, brown-noser,* and *lickspittle*. Some less colorful alternatives are *apple-polisher, fawner, sycophant,* and *yes-man*.

See also: OBSEQUIOUS.

Word Wonders

How is a tailless, frog–like amphibian related to a shameless flatterer? Many years ago, certain MOUNTEBANKS would set up shop in fairs and towns to sell supposedly medicinal potions. To demonstrate the healing powers of these "remedies," a young boy (secretly the charlatan's assistant) would swallow a toad, which in those days was thought to be poisonous. The lad would duly keel over, but a quick sip of the medicine would have him back on his feet. Clearly, an assistant like that would do just about anything to gain favor, so over time any such person became known as a "toadeater," which was eventually shortened to toady.

Questions and Exercises to Help Everything Sink In

Here's a list of the main words you learned in this chapter:

adversary	ally	altruist	antagonist	benefactor
bête noire	boor	charlatan	confidant	crony
dignitary	do-gooder	idealist	luminary	mentor
minion	miscreant	nabob	nemesis	patriarch
sadist	sidekick	subordinate	toady	tyrant

1. If you had a personal secret to disclose, which of these people would be the best choice?

2. Fill in the blank: "The guy with the tattoo on his nose is my _____. I've never beaten him."

3. Which word describes a person in a position of authority who acts in a harsh and oppressive manner?

4. Choose the word that refers to a naïve and unrealistic person who sincerely tries to perform humanitarian works:

    a. idealist

    b. do-gooder

    c. benefactor

    d. sadist

5. Choose the word that best describes a *mentor:*

    a. pundit

    b. psychologist

    c. advisor

    d. collaborator

Match the word on the left with the short definition on the right:

6. subordinate   **a.** a person who behaves criminally

7. sidekick   **b.** a person of lesser rank

8. minion   **c.** the oldest male member of a group

9. patriarch   **d.** a follower or servant

10. miscreant   **e.** a close companion

A clique of Curmudgeons

Chapter 2

More People Types

In This Chapter

➤ Words for believers and nonbelievers

➤ Words for fans

➤ Words for grumpy people

➤ Words for groups of people

"I personally think we developed language because of our deep inner need to complain."

—Jane Wagner, playwright

In the right hands, the English language is a tool that can be wielded with an impressive amount of precision. That's not surprising since the language boasts hundreds of thousands of words, so there's bound to be one that articulates the exact meaning you need. This seems particularly true of words related to the types of people we meet and read about every day. As you'll see in this chapter, people can differ in subtly different ways, and the English language is more often than not up to the task of putting a label on these differences.

Ideologues and Apostates: Believers and Nonbelievers

Humans have had belief systems probably for as long as they've had the language to describe those systems. This section looks at a few words for people who believe and for their opposite numbers who don't.

One such person is an **agnostic** (*ag·NOS·tik*), who believes that it isn't possible to prove God's existence but who doesn't deny the possibility that God exists.

➤ Janine's favorite joke was the one about the DYSLEXIC **agnostic** who stayed awake at nights wondering about the existence of Dog.

Agnostic is a combination of the prefix *a-*, which means (in this case) "without," and the word *gnostic* (*NOS·tik*, adj.), "relating to spiritual knowledge."

An **apostate** (*uh·POS·tate*) is a former believer who has since abandoned his religious faith or some other loyalty.

You Don't Say

Don't confuse an agnostic with an *atheist,* a person who believes that God doesn't exist. This word combines the *a-* prefix with *the-ist,* "a person who believes in the existence of God."

➤ Having turned his back on the ruling party, the **apostate** wondered whether he'd still be able to get a date.

In general, you commit **apostasy** (*uh·POS·tuh·see*) when you *renounce* ("reject") any cause—such as a political party or movement—or a set of principles. A religious apostate is also called an *infidel,* while any other type of apostate is also called a *renegade,* a *deserter,* or a *defector.* The opposite of an apostate is an *adherent.*

An **iconoclast** (*eye·KON·uh·clast*) is a person who attacks traditional or popular ideas or established institutions.

➤ A true hockey fan, Alphonse hated those **iconoclasts** who claimed that Wayne Gretzky wasn't the greatest player of all time.

The word iconoclast literally means "image-breaker," and it originally referred to a person who smashed religious images ("icons"). The first iconoclasts weren't antireligious, as you might expect. Rather, they were extremely *devout,* "devoted to religion," and they considered the viewing of religious imagery to be *idolatry,* "the worship of idols."

An **ideologue** (*eye·DEE·uh·log*) is a person who advocates a specific ideology, particularly a political one.

➤ The tycoon accused the senator of being an **ideologue** unconcerned with practicalities such as helping him make fistfuls of money.

An *ideology* is a set of related ideas or principles that form the core of a political, social, or economic system. The ideologue tends to apply these beliefs in a blind or theoretical way without regard to practical considerations.

See also: IDEALIST, PARTISAN.

A **martyr** (*MAR·tur*) is someone who endures tremendous or constant suffering or who makes great sacrifices because of her beliefs or to further a cause. You'd also call someone a martyr who exaggerates her suffering to arouse sympathy.

➤ If Blanche's calculations were correct, another 50 sighs and another 35 groans would make her a **martyr** in her kids' eyes for life.

A Few Fan Words

That all people like certain things more than others will come as no great shock, but there's a wide range associated with the word like. Whether it's simple enjoyment or outright passion, however, the "like-er" is a *fan* of some description, and I offer up some useful fan words in this section.

An **aficionado** (*uh·fish·ee·uh·NAH·do* or *uh·fish·yuh·NAH·do*) is a person who truly enjoys and knows a great deal about a particular activity or interest.

Parts Dept.

The suffix *-logue* means "speaker." We see it in words such as *travelogue*, "a narrated travel film," and *monologue*, "a speech made by one person." Strangely, however, it's now used only rarely to describe people. (Ideologue is one of the few such words left in common use.) The accepted suffixes to describe people are *-logist* (for example, cosmologist) and *-loger* (for example, astrologer).

➤ As an **aficionado** of nude gardening, Connie subscribed to magazines such as *The Naked Pruner* and *Skin and Bulbs*.

Aficionados tend to be very enthusiastic about their pet subjects, so they're often called, naturally enough, *enthusiasts*. You might also call such a person a *buff* or a *devotee*. Note, however, that the aficionado's expertise in his subject is strictly at the amateur level, so don't use this word to describe a professional.

Speaking of amateurs, a **dilettante** (*dil·uh·TAHNT*) is someone who enjoys participating in an activity but only in a superficial or unserious way.

➤ Ted was clearly not serious about his underwater carpentry, so the others considered him a mere **dilettante**.

If you come across a group of such people, call them **dilettanti** (*dil·uh·TAHNT·tee*). If dilettante sounds bit artsy (which wouldn't be surprising since the original Italian word means "lover of the arts"), feel free to substitute the word *dabbler* in its place.

A **fanatic** (*fuh·NAT·ik*) is a person who is excessively and uncritically enthusiastic about a cause or object.

➤ Only a sports **fanatic** such as Tommy would have his home teams' logos tattooed on the inside of his eyelids.

Fanatics are those people you see in sports broadcasts who paint their faces and parade around shirtless in subzero weather. Winston Churchill famously defined a fanatic as a person who "can't change his mind and won't change the subject." The common synonyms testify to the extreme and irrational characteristics of this species: *fiend, freak,* and *nut.*

A **zealot** (*ZEL·ut*) is someone who is extremely passionate about, and who tirelessly pursues, a cause or goal.

> ➤ In his never-ending quest to better the environment, the **zealot** worked all day and all night to perfect his solar-powered flashlight.

Note that, in popular usage, there's an undercurrent of negativity associated with zealot as well as the related words **zealous** (*ZEL·us,* adj.) and **zeal** (*zeel,* noun). In other words, it's common to see the word zealot used as a put-down, usually if a person's devotion to his cause becomes too extreme. So if you admire the person, consider using *champion* or *booster* instead.

Curmudgeons and Other Grumpy People

We've all had to deal with people who, no matter what time of day it is, always seem to have just gotten up on the wrong side of the bed. They're *surly* ("in a bad mood"), *disputatious* ("argumentative"), and *brusque* ("abrupt"). They are, in short, grumpy. You'll meet some of these spoilsports in this section.

The *quintessential* ("most typical") grump is the **curmudgeon** (*kur·MUJ·un*), a bad-tempered, gruff, and stubborn person. They're usually old, but I've met many a middle-aged curmudgeon in my day.

> ➤ The old **curmudgeon** would frown at his grandkids and grumble once again that he used to have to walk to school through six feet of snow, uphill both ways, with the family piano strapped to his back.

As you can see from my definition, there's something about a **curmudgeonly** (adj.) personality that really brings out the adjectives. Here are a few more from the "C" section of the thesaurus: *cantankerous* ("bad-tempered or QUARRELSOME"), *crotchety* ("CAPRICIOUSLY stubborn"), and *crusty* ("gruff and forbidding in manner"). You can also call a grump such as this a *crab,* a *bear,* or a *grouch.*

A **cynic** (*SIN·ik*) is a habitual faultfinder and critic, particularly one who believes that all human behavior is motivated by self-interest.

> ➤ The **cynic** defined *denial* as "the method that an optimist uses to keep from becoming a pessimist."

Cynicism (noun) is characterized by a *scornful* ("contemptuous or disdainful"), *mocking* ("treating with ridicule") attitude that can't help but assume the worst about people and situations. If the cynic's *carping* ("faultfinding") spoils everyone's fun, call him a *killjoy* or a *party-pooper*. If he constantly expresses doubt about generally held beliefs, label him a *skeptic* or a *doubting Thomas*. (The latter comes from Christianity's Saint Thomas, who doubted the resurrection of Jesus and wanted proof.)

See also: ALTRUIST.

Word Wonders

The word curmudgeon was the source of one of the most embarrassing gaffes in the history of lexicography (dictionary making). In his famous dictionary published in 1775, Samuel Johnson claimed that curmudgeon was "a vicious manner of pronouncing *œur méchant*, Fr. an unknown correspondent." That is, he thought the word was from the French words *œur*, "heart," and *méchant*, "evil." Crucially, he used "Fr." as a short form of "from," so he was saying he got this from an anonymous source. A later lexicographer, John Ash, thought "Fr." meant "French," so he wrote "from the French *œur*, unknown, and *méchant*, correspondent." D'oh! Incidentally, Johnson's explanation was wrong, and the origins of the word curmudgeon remain a mystery.

A **malcontent** (*MAL·kun·tent*) is a constantly dissatisfied or rebellious person.

➤ When faced with a new recruit who would not stop complaining, the drill sergeant would tickle the **malcontent** mercilessly.

The prefix *mal-* usually means "bad" or "wrong." In this case, it's used to reverse the meaning of the word *content* (*kun·TENT*), which means "satisfied." If a **malcontent** (adj.) person is habitually complaining about her lot in life, call her a *bellyacher* (*bel·ee·AYK·ur*) or a *sorehead*. If she's rebellious in spirit, call her an *agitator* or, of course, a *rebel*.

The last of our grumps, a **misanthrope** (*MIS·un·thrope*) is a person who hates or mistrusts everyone.

➤ "If I hate all people," the **misanthrope** muttered to himself, "then why do I like myself so much?"

If the person's **misanthropy** (noun) actually extends only to males, she's a *misandrist* (*mi·SAN·drist*) or a *man-hater*. If the person is **misanthropic** (adj.) only to females, he's a *misogynist* (*mi·SOJ·uh·nist*) or a *woman-hater*.

Cadres and Cliques: Groups of People

Human beings are social creatures—*notwithstanding* ("in spite of") the grumps from the previous section—so they seem to enjoy forming their own groups and associations and lumping others into groups as well. In this section, I take you through a few words for these groups.

Let's begin with a **cadre** (*KAH·dray* or *KAD·ree*), a group of highly trained people that forms the core of a larger organization, particularly a political or military organization.

➤ The Corn Roast Society couldn't survive without its **cadre** of members who could shuck a cob in seconds flat.

Parts Dept.

There are lots of prefixes, suffixes, and roots floating around here. Misanthrope marries the prefix *miso-*, "hatred," with *-anthrope*, from the Greek root *anthropo*, "human being." Misandrist combines *miso-* with *-andrist*, which is from the Greek root *andro*, "male." (Think of the male hormone *androgen*.) Misogynist melds *miso-* and *-gynist*, which comes from the Greek root *gyno*, "female." (See GYNECOLOGIST.)

Since the cadre forms the core of the organization, you may also want to call it the *nucleus* (*NEW·klee·us*), which means "the central part around which other parts are grouped." Cadre comes from the Italian word *quadro*, "frame," so cadre is occasionally used to mean "a framework." *Quadro* goes back to the Latin word *quadrus*, "square," but despite this, it's also okay to call a cadre an *inner circle*.

A cadre can also be a group of ZEALOTS that actively promotes the interests of a revolutionary party. (Confusingly, cadre is also sometimes used to denote a member of such a group.) If these revolutionaries are conspirators ("secret planners with intent to do wrong"), call them a *cabal* (*kuh·BAL*).

Current and former high-schoolers will recognize a **clique** (*kleek* or *klik*): an exclusive and usually small group of friends or associates.

➤ The cheerleaders formed their own **clique** and shunned less-perky types who tried to join them.

A clique is also called a *circle* of friends. If these **cliquish** (adj.) folks are hip (or just think they are), they're the *in crowd*. If they have some common interest, it would be fine to call them a *coterie* (*KOH·tuh·ree*). If they're all female, try *sisterhood,* and if they're all male, try *brotherhood*. If these women or men form a social group at a college or university, call it a *sorority* or a *fraternity*, respectively.

The phrase **hoi polloi** (*HOY puh·LOY*) refers to the masses or the common people and has a hint of looking down upon the crowd. This phrase is a bit of a head-scratcher for some people because the original Greek phrase translates as "the many." There-fore, if you say "the hoi polloi," you're really saying "the the many." Hmmm. However, check out how off-kilter things sound when you drop the "the":

➤ At the state fair, Deirdre kept her caviar pancakes under the counter because she didn't want **hoi polloi** eating them.

For this reason (as well as the fact that we're not speaking Greek here), a great many professional writers and language authorities accept "the hoi polloi." If you can't bring yourself to do it, use *the masses* or even *the great unwashed*. If you want to refer to the middle class as a whole, call them the *bourgeoisie* (*boor·zhwah·ZEE*).

The **cognoscenti** (*kahg·nuh·SHEN·tee* or *KAHN·yuh·SHEN·tee*) are those people who are highly knowledgeable about a particular subject.

➤ Blinded by the love of his child, the father asked several art **cognoscenti** to come view his baby daughter's finger paintings.

You Don't Say

Some people mistakenly use hoi polloi to mean "the elite," which is the opposite of its real meaning. It may be that hoi sounds like "high" or because it's reminiscent of HOITY-TOITY.

This now-obsolete Italian word goes back to the Latin *cognoscent*, "to know," from which we get the word *cognition*, "the process of knowing." Although this word is relatively common in the media, you might prefer to use the more common synonym *connoisseur* (*kon·uh·SUR*).

You've probably heard the term **Generation X** quite often, but few people seem to agree on just who is in this *cohort* ("a collection of people in a particular age group"; this word also means "an associate or companion"). Here's the real deal: Generation X refers to those people born in the years 1961 through 1966. This means that **Generation Xers** (plural) comprise the tail end of the *baby boom,* which lasted from 1947 to 1966.

Yes, there certainly is a *Generation Y*. It encompasses people born in the years 1980 through 1995 and is also known in *demography* ("the study of human populations") circles as the *baby boom echo* because they're the children of the baby boomers. Some marketing types have tried to label the generation born since 1995 as "Generation Z," but so far it hasn't caught on. Wondering about those born from 1967 to 1979? Demographers call this group the *baby bust* because so few babies were born in this period.

Questions and Exercises to Help Everything Sink In

Here's a list of the main words you learned in this chapter:

aficionado	agnostic	apostate	cadre
clique	cognoscenti	curmudgeon	cynic
dilettante	fanatic	Generation X	hoi polloi
iconoclast	ideologue	malcontent	martyr
misanthrope	zealot		

1. Which group would you automatically join if you became an expert in something?

2. Choose the word that refers to a person who hates all people:

   a. cynic

   b. iconoclast

   c. zealot

   d. misanthrope

3. Fill in the blank: "Hedging his bet, the _____ said that it's possible God exists, but it can't be proven."

4. Choose the word that best describes an *aficionado*:

   a. amateur

   b. official

   c. novelist

   d. fisherman

5. Which word means "image-breaker"?

Match the word on the left with the short definition on the right:

6. cadre	a.	superficial participant
7. malcontent	b.	highly trained core
8. dilettante	c.	former believer
9. apostate	d.	constant sufferer
10. martyr	e.	habitually dissatisfied person

Oafish

Jolly

Chapter 3

How People Behave, Part 1

In This Chapter

➤ Words for selfish behavior

➤ Words for outgoing behavior

➤ Words for shy and quiet behavior

➤ Words for likeable behavior

➤ Words for unlikable behavior

"My father still reads the dictionary every day. He says that your life depends on your power to master words."

—Arthur Scargill, British politician

The people types you met in the previous two chapters represented a good sampling of the diversity that humanity has to offer, but labeling our fellow humans for who or what they are is only part of the joy of linguistic people-watching. To crank up the fun meter another few notches, you need a vocabulary to describe how people act as well. This chapter gets you started by looking at five basic behaviors, which I categorize as follows: selfish, outgoing, shy, likeable, and unlikable. See Chapter 4, "How People Behave, Part 2," for a second helping of behavioral buzzwords.

I, Me, Mine: Selfish Behavior

It's probably not stretching the truth to say that the bulk of the populace is at least aware that there are other people on the planet. We may not be full-fledged saints, but we treat others with respect and courtesy. Then, on the other hand, there's that small segment of the population that reacts to every situation by asking, "How does this affect *me?*" and that thinks there really is an "I" in "team" somewhere if you just look hard enough. This section is dedicated to them (but they knew that already).

In the broadest terms, what we're talking about here is conduct that's **egocentric** (*ee·goh·SEN·trik*, adj.). This describes behavior that's concerned only with one's own needs or activities.

➤ Horns blared, sirens wailed, and the Four Horsemen of the Apocalypse went galloping by, but **egocentric** Donald just wondered if the traffic would soon clear up.

The core word here is *ego*, "the self," which is combined with the suffix *-centric*, "having a specified object as the center." So the main synonyms for egocentric are, uh, *self*-explanatory: *selfish, self-centered, self-absorbed.*

You Don't Say

Don't use the words egoist and egotist interchangeably. An *egoist* is an ADHERENT of the philosophy of *egoism*, which holds that a person can prove nothing beyond the existence of his own mind. An *egotist* is a self–centered person.

A similar word is **vain** (adj.), which describes an EGO-CENTRIC person who is excessively proud of his appearance or accomplishments.

➤ With its giant neon arrows pointing from all directions, you could tell Paul was a little **vain** about the new deck he'd built.

This over-the-top pride is called **vanity**, and a person exhibiting such behavior is also called *conceited* and *narcissistic* (*nar·suh·SIS·tik*). The latter is another word from the Greek myths. Narcissus was an exceptionally prideful lad whose punishment was to fall in love with his own reflection in a nearby pool. Unable to leave, he wasted away and died.

An **arrogant** (*AIR·uh·gunt*, adj.) person is one who exaggerates her own worth in an excessive, domineering way.

➤ Amy was **arrogant** enough to believe that Brad Pitt ought to beg *her* for a date.

A person displaying **arrogance** (noun) is also said to be *cocky, self-important,* or *overconfident.*

Mix a large amount of VANITY with a generous helping of ARROGANCE and you get an unpleasant concoction called **hubris** (*HEW·bris*, noun).

➤ Figuring he was "the way best cook ever," Todd, in an act of pure **hubris**, went to remove the soufflé a few minutes early.

The **hubristic** (adj.) person's arrogant and excessive pride has been viewed for many ages as the worst of all behaviors. In fact, a person's hubris and his or her subsequent punishment by the goddess NEMESIS forms the basic storyline for most of the Greek myths. That's why, to this day, pride is considered the worst of the seven deadly sins (the others are anger, envy, gluttony, greed, lust, and sloth), and we still remind each other that "pride goeth before the fall."

The last of our selfish behaviors is **hedonism** (*HEE·dun·iz·um,* noun), the philosophy of living life only for the pursuit of pleasure.

> ➤ A beer in one hand, a box of Bac-O-Bits in the other, and *Gilligan's Island* on TV, Hank's **hedonism** was complete.

The **hedonistic** (adj.) human is particularly interested in those pleasures related to the senses, so this philosophy is also called *sensualism.* You can call the **hedonist** (noun) a *bon vivant* (*bon vi·VAHNT*) and describe him as being *self-indulgent* or *pleasure-seeking.*

See also: EPICURE.

Party Types and Talkers: Adjectives for Outgoing People

A person who is outgoing is someone who truly enjoys meeting and talking with people and who wonders why everyone else wants to go home when the party's just getting started. This section looks at a few words that describe these social types.

Outgoing folks come in various guises, but they all have one trait in common: they're **extroverted** (*EK·struh·vur·tid*). This means they're mainly interested in other people or in their surroundings rather than in themselves.

> ➤ The most **extroverted** of the sisters, Jaunita relished her trips downtown to ask people why Jerry Lewis is so popular in France.

If extroverted sounds too clinical, try *gregarious* or *sociable.*

See also: INTROVERTED.

Extroverts are the communications majors of the social world because they all tend to be **talkative** (*TAW·kuh·tiv*), which means they have an inclination to talk and to enjoy conversation.

Parts Dept.

The prefix *extro–* is a variation of the common prefix *extra–,* "outside or beyond." (See EXTRAMARITAL.) The *–verted* suffix goes back to the Latin verb *vertere,* "to turn," and is found in words such as *converted,* "turned into another form," and *perverted,* "turned away from what is proper."

➤ "Boy, Caroline sure is **talkative.** I'll bet that girl could talk the ears off a tin donkey."

If the talker can express herself in clear and effective language, she's *articulate.* If that *articulateness* (noun) comes easily to her, call her *loquacious.* However, if she's insincere or shallow, she slips down a notch to *glib.*

Of course, there are talkers and then there are *talkers.* People who are able to talk at length can be described as *voluble,* but if a person tends to go on and on in a rambling kind of way, he's *garrulous.* If he uses too many words to get his point across, he's *verbose* or *prolix.*

Idiom Savant

The Irish are famed as talkers, and they've come up with some colorful sayings for the long-winded. If a person is *eloquent* ("vividly or forcefully expressive") in a persuasive way, she's said to have *kissed the Blarney Stone.* (Yes, there is an actual stone located in Blarney Castle near Cork, Ireland.) If someone talks incessantly about trivial things, he's said to have *the gift of the gab.*

We all like to eat, but outgoing people are **convivial** (*cun·VIV·ee·ul*), which means they're fond of eating and drinking in good company.

➤ The **convivial** sock repairman loved to ask his best friends to dinner, where he would amuse them with tales about the darnedest things.

Not being, by definition, shy people, the outgoing are often **demonstrative** (*di·MON·struh·tiv*), which means they display their feelings openly.

➤ Byron knew that Wendy was **demonstrative,** but this business of spelling out I-L-O-V-E-Y-O-U with her body every time they met was a bit much.

We say that a demonstrative person readily "expresses" her feelings, so you can also label her as *expressive* (no surprise there). If those emotions just come pouring out of her, feel free to call her *effusive* (from the verb *effuse,* "to flow out").

See also: RETICENT.

Homebodies: Adjectives for Shy and Quiet People

Besides growing up to be used-car salesmen and talk-show hosts, the outgoing members of our species also seem to be the ones who garner most of the attention and most of the appearances on the evening news. Perhaps this is why English has far fewer words to describe those who inhabit the opposite end of the personality spectrum. For example, how come we can say that TALKATIVE and GREGARIOUS people are "outgoing," but we can't say that shy and quiet people are "incoming"? No matter, there are still a good number of words you can wield to describe these people, as this section shows.

There may not be a word that's the opposite of outgoing, but there *is* one that's the opposite of EXTROVERTED. It's **introverted** (*IN·truh·vur·tid*), and it describes a person who's mainly interested in his own self rather than other people or his surroundings.

> ➤ Being **introverted**, Cletus would happily spend many hours fishing around in his own thoughts, but he rarely caught anything.

The **introvert** (noun) is the master of *introspection,* "the contemplation of one's own thoughts and feelings." If he prefers most of the time to stay home and do this, call him *unsociable,* and if his shunning of the outside world is extreme, call him *antisocial.*

Introverts are usually **reticent** (*RET·uh·sunt*), which means they tend to keep their thoughts and feelings to themselves.

> ➤ Margaret was **reticent** to speak for fear that she would expose the desperate and forbidden yearning she felt for Morley Safer.

A person's **reticence** (noun) usually is accompanied by a *restrained* ("held back; kept in check") manner of speaking, so a good synonym for this type of behavior is *reserved.* If this *reserve* (noun) makes the introvert appear emotionally distant, describe her as *aloof* (*uh·LOOF*).

As you can imagine, the reticent person doesn't have much to say. If the person tends to speak only when spoken to, she's *taciturn* (*TAS·uh·turn*). If when she does speak she uses few words, she's *terse* or *laconic* (*luh·KON·ik*).

A common subclass of introverts consists of those souls who are **phlegmatic** (*fleg·MAT·ik*), meaning they are not easily excited or provoked into action.

Parts Dept.

As you might expect, the opposite of the prefix EXTRA– is the prefix *in–,* which means "in, into, or within." It's seen in dozens of words such as *inhale,* "breathe in," and *innate,* "born within." However, there are probably more words that use a second meaning of *in–,* "not." For example, a person who does not speak well is often called *inarticulate* (*in–* + ARTICULATE).

➤ Roused not by touchdowns, taunts, or the exhortations of his peers, **phlegmatic** Phil's cheerleading career was short-lived.

Word Wonders

The word laconic goes back all the way to an ancient Greek people called the Laconians. One day, a fellow named Philip of Macedon threatened to invade Sparta, the Laconian capital city. He sent them a note: "If I enter Laconia, I will level Sparta to the ground." The Laconians returned a single-word reply: "If." Now *that's* laconic!

By the way, history tells us that the residents of Sparta were a self-disciplined bunch who were content to live with only the bare necessities. This has given us the adjective *spartan*, which means "simple; frugal; self-restrained."

If this calm type is coolly unconcerned, describe him as *nonchalant* (non·sha·LAHNT). If he appears to be indifferent to pain or pleasure, he's *stoic* (STOH·ik). If he shows no physical reaction to an event, call him (or his look) *impassive*. If this lump just isn't interested in or curious about anything, file him under *stolid* (STAH·lid).

You Don't Say

Don't confuse demure with *de-mur* (duh·MUHR), which means "object to; take exception to."

Let's close this foray into the world of the INTROVERTED with a quick look at the different ways that people can be **shy**, which describes someone who draws back from or resists contact with others.

➤ Tina was too **shy** to ask Biff to remove her pigtail from the inkwell.

If the shy person draws back out of a lack of self-confidence, describe her as *timid* or *diffident*. She's *bashful* if her **shyness** (noun) is caused by a self-consciousness or awkwardness around other people, and she's *demure* (duh·MYOOR) if it's caused by an inherently modest nature. If, however, she's just pretending to be shy, call her *coy*.

Word Wonders

The word phlegmatic has come down to us through the ages from medieval physiology and its theory of the four "humors" (body fluids): phlegm, blood, yellow bile, and black bile. The relative concentrations of these humors were thought to determine a person's behavior. For example, a predominance of blood was said to make a person courageous and hopeful. The old French word for blood was *sanguin*, which gives us *sanguine*, "confident; optimistic." A tad too much phlegm (*flem*) caused sluggishness and calmness, so that's where we get phlegmatic. Yellow bile was also called choler (*KAW·ler*), and it caused a person to be bad-tempered, from which we get *choleric*, "easily angered." Finally, excess black bile caused low spirits, and it gives us our word *melancholy*, "sadness or depression" (from the French word *melancolie*, "black bile").

Words for People We Like

Nice guys may finish last but not in this chapter. This *penultimate* ("next to last") section concentrates on words related to nice guys and gals and other people whose company we like to keep.

A **genial** (*JEEN·yul*, adj.) person is one who has a friendly or pleasant disposition.

➤ Despite yet another "What's-the-best-direction-to-dispense-toilet-paper?" argument, the **genial** host remaining happy and smiling throughout the meal.

You can also describe friendly folk as being *amiable* (*AY·MEE·uh·bul*), and if they also throw in an eagerness to please, call them *affable* or *agreeable*. The **geniality** (*jee·nee·AL·uh·tee*, noun) expressed by such a good-natured person is also called *cordiality* (*cor·dee·AL·uh·tee*) or *bonhomie* (*bon·uh·MEE*).

A **gracious** (*GRAY·shus*, adj.) person is one who treats other people with kindly consideration and warm courtesy.

Idiom Savant

Some writers with an old-fashioned bent will describe a genial sort as a *hail-fellow-well-met* type of person. This strange construction goes back to a very old phrase that good friends would say when greeting each other: "Hail, fellow. Well met!" The closest translation I can think of in today's terms is "Hey, man, great to see you!"

➤ Always **gracious** winners, Gregg and Lorraine made a point of thanking their opponents after accepting the National Wheelbarrow Race championship trophy.

Those who shine their **graciousness** (noun) with social polish and buff it with a *sophisticated* ("cultured") view of the world can also be called *suave* (*swahv*). (Note, however, that suave is often used as an IRONIC put-down if the person's graciousness is only *superficial*, "shallow.")

If we say that a person has **charm** (noun), we mean that she has some personal quality that fascinates, attracts, or delights us.

➤ The way her eyeballs roll up out of their sockets when she laughs is just one of the many **charms** that make me want to be with her.

If her **charming** (adj.) nature is particularly strong or if she displays the power to lead people or inspire devotion on a large scale, she has *charisma* (*kuh·RIZ·muh,* noun). If her charms are childlike and innocent, describe her as *winsome* (adj.).

Words for People We Don't Like

An old proverb tells us that "you catch more flies with honey than with vinegar." The not-so-nice people in the world probably respond to this by saying, "Yeah, fine, but who the heck wants to catch flies?" This section runs through a few words that describe those people who just don't get it.

The **callous** (*CAL·us,* adj.) individual feels little or no emotion and has no sympathy for others.

➤ The **callous** baby-sitter ignored the children's crying and simply tossed the newly deceased goldfish over the balcony.

The original ancestor of callous was the Latin word *callum,* meaning "hard skin," from which we get the notion of a callous person being hardened emotionally. This hardness is also reflected in a couple of synonyms: *hard-boiled* (used almost exclusively to describe private detectives in crime novels) and *hard-hearted.*

Another person to shun is the **crass** (noun) individual, who is as crude as they come and lacks any kind of discrimination or sensitivity.

➤ The **crass** dinner guest bellowed directly at Robert, "Yo, Bobster! Toss me a coupla &#$@! dinner rolls, will ya?"

You Don't Say

As you may have guessed by now, the Latin term *callum* was also the source of the noun *callus,* "a hard thickened part of the skin." You may also have guessed that it's very easy to confuse callous and callus, so be careful when using either word.

Other names to call such a person are *coarse, gauche,* and *uncouth.*

See also: BOOR, UNKEMPT.

We've all seen (or, shudder, had to deal with) the child acting up in the store while an embarrassed and frustrated parent tries to settle the noisy tyke down. From now on, call such a child **petulant** (*PECH·uh·lunt,* adj.), which describes a person who demonstrates petty and unreasonable irritability or anger.

> ➤ As Nancy watched the **petulant** child rant and rave and refuse to get up off the ground, the thought of becoming a nun suddenly seemed very attractive.

You can also describe that annoying child as *peevish.* (You *will* just say these things in your head, right?)

Idiom Savant

If the petulant person is acting unreasonably angry, a wonderful but somewhat obscure alternative adjective is *shirty.* This comes from the phrase *keep your shirt on,* which means "don't get angry or upset." What does a shirt have to do with anger? One story has it that, in olden times, there lived ferocious Viking warriors called "berserkers." They were quick to anger and, in their fury, would rip off their chain mail shirts and fight bare-chested. So the phrase means that by keeping your shirt on, you avoid a potential battle. (These Norse hotheads also gave us the word *berserk,* which means "destructively frenzied.")

Another (and generally more accepted) story on the original of *keep your shirt on* is that American men in the mid–1800s wore overly starched shirts that were too stiff to fight in. So taking off your shirt was seen as a prelude to fisticuffs.

High on most people's lists of the Top Ten Most *Insufferable* ("impossible to endure") People are the **sanctimonious** (*sank·tuh·MOH·nee·us,* adj.), who act righteous or holy in a showy or pretend way.

> ➤ My **sanctimonious** neighbor is constantly telling me that he gives away half his income to charity, but I just found out he doesn't even have a job!

If this GOODY-GOODY is absolutely certain about his own *piety* ("religious devotion"), call him *self-righteous.* If he acts superior because of it, hurl the insult *holier-than-thou* at him.

Questions and Exercises to Help Everything Sink In

Here's a list of the main words you learned in this chapter:

arrogant	callous	charm	convivial	crass
demonstrative	egocentric	extroverted	genial	gracious
hedonism	hubris	introverted	petulant	phlegmatic
reticent	sanctimonious	shy	talkative	vain

1. Which of these words would you use to describe someone who brags a lot?

2. Fill in the blank: "Our _____ host treated us with the utmost consideration and courtesy."

3. Choose the word that describes a person who likes to eat and drink in an atmosphere of good-fellowship:

    a. convivial

    b. hedonistic

    c. extroverted

    d. phlegmatic

4. Choose the word that best describes *crass:*

    a. angry

    b. quick

    c. crude

    d. pious

Match the word on the left with the short definition on the right:

5. callous   **a.** displaying feelings openly

6. genial   **b.** living for pleasure

7. introverted   **c.** feeling no emotion

8. hedonism   **d.** interested only in oneself

9. demonstrative   **e.** friendly or pleasant

10. Choose the word that's an insulting synonym for *sanctimonious:*

    a. cocky

    b. holier-than-thou

    c. glib

    d. suave

Layabout

Chapter 4

How People Behave, Part 2

In This Chapter

➤ Words for people who are changeable

➤ Words for people who are stubborn

➤ Words for people who are hostile

➤ Words for people who are inactive

➤ Some easily confused behavior words

"I had a linguistics professor who said that it's man's ability to use language that makes him the dominant species on the planet. That may be. But I think there's one other thing that separates us from animals. We aren't afraid of vacuum cleaners."

—Jeff Stilson, comedian

We as a species may not be scared of vacuum cleaners (although I've known some guys who *seem* to be scared of them), but we do exhibit a wide range of other behaviors, some of which seem to effectively eliminate the separation between us and the animals. And, of course, the language is always standing by, ready to document these behaviors, no matter how wacky or way-out they are, with the *mot juste* (*moh ZHOOST;* French for "exactly the right word"). In this chapter, you learn a bunch of words related to four different behaviors: changeability, stubbornness, hostility, and inactivity. I close by giving you the real deal on five behavior words that many people find confusing.

Following the Wind: Words for Changeable People

If someone calls me out for being changeable—say, professing one thing one day and then championing the exact opposite the next—I always trot out my favorite quotation from my favorite philosopher, Ralph Waldo Emerson: "A foolish consistency is the hobgoblin of little minds." Take that! So it's not without at least a little *empathy* ("understanding of another's feelings") that I present in this section a selection of words related to the *changelings* ("changeable people") who walk (erratically!) among us.

A **fickle** (*FIK·ul,* adj.) person is one whose behavior suffers from erratic changeableness and instability.

> ➤ The **fickle** teacher would praise his students' intelligence one minute and then call them "NINNIES and NINCOMPOOPS" the next.

If the person's **fickleness** (noun) seems to be hard-wired into his personality, describe him as *inconstant.* If he changes because of *whims* ("sudden and unpredictable inspirations or ideas"), he's *whimsical* or *capricious* (*kuh·PRISH·us*). If it's his mood or his *temperament* ("manner of thinking and reacting") that changes, he's *mercurial.*

Idiom Savant

In the idiomatic world, changeableness is closely related to the wind. That makes intuitive sense because winds can quickly change direction and speed because of swirls and gusts. So we say that a person who hasn't made up her mind is waiting to see *which way the wind blows.* If she constantly changes her opinion, she *blows hot and cold.* She might even be called a *weather vane* because the direction in which such an object points depends on the wind.

The **protean** (*PROH·tee·un,* adj.) person has talents or tendencies that can assume a variety of forms.

> ➤ Her **protean** musical skills came out during the concert when she did solo pieces for both the double bass and the ukulele.

This word comes from the name of the Greek god Proteus, who could change his shape and form at will. (If you captured Proteus, he would attempt to escape by changing into various forms such as a lion or dragon. If you held on until he returned to his normal shape, he would tell you a prophecy.) A similar type is the *chameleon* (*kuh·MEEL·yun*, noun). This word comes from the animal that's renowned for its unique ability to change color in response to its environment.

An **obsequious** (*ub·SEEK·wee·us*, adj.) person follows the wishes or the will of another person or group.

➤ The **obsequious** new kid didn't think jumping off a cliff was a good idea, but everyone else said they were going to do it.

Someone who is obsequious has no mind of his own and will change his mind based solely on what someone tells him. If he's not into confrontation and goes along with the wishes of the crowd or another person without protest, he's *acquiescent* (*AK·wee·es·unt*). If he does this out of respect or courtesy, he's *deferent* (*DEF·uh·runt*).

See also: TOADY.

To **meander** (*mee·AN·dur*, verb) is to change direction randomly and aimlessly.

➤ He **meandered** through the market, looking for those rare and elusive blue foods.

This word flowed to us from ancient Greek times when there was a river named Meander that followed a twisting, crooked course. Like an old, slow river, **meandering** (present participle) has a leisurely quality to it. If a person's purposeless wandering is a bit more restless and energetic, use the verb *gad* instead, and by all means call them a *gadabout* (noun). If a person's roaming is in search of pleasures or amusements, use the verb *gallivant*.

Immovable Objects: Words for Stubborn People

"Stubborn" is one of those beauty-is-in-the-eye-of-the-beholder words. If you're facing off with a stubborn person, you might describe him using words such as "unreasonable," difficult," and "maddening." If, however, you're the one being stubborn or if you're rooting for someone who's stubborn, then words such as "perseverance" and "persistence" may spring more readily to mind. Whatever side you're on, you'll appreciate the words for various stubborn behaviors that I cover in this section.

People who view stubbornness in a negative light probably enjoy the synonym **obstinate** (*OB·stuh·nit*, adj.), which describes a person who is unreasonably rigid in her opinions, ideas, or actions.

➤ Old Muriel knew the young whippersnappers all thought the world was round, but she was **obstinate** in her belief that it had to be flat because otherwise she'd fall right off.

Word Wonders

Stubbornness and animals are, at least linguistically, closely related. A person whose stubbornness is immune to reason is called *stubborn as a mule, mulish,* or *mule-headed.* A foolish stubbornness is often described as *bullheaded* or *bullish,* while a stupid stubbornness is sometimes described as *pigheaded.* If a person is admirably persistent, you can describe them as *dogged.*

If her **obstinateness** (noun) is also sprinkled with ARROGANCE or ALOOFNESS, she's *stiff-necked.*

A **headstrong** (adj.) person shuns all advice and suggestions in favor of his own way of doing things.

➤ Despite his best man's pleading, the **headstrong** groom insisted that baby blue was the perfect color for their tuxedos.

Parts Dept.

In my earlier Word Wonders sidebar, I mentioned some "mule" metaphors that apply to stubborn people. Mules are also know for kicking things with their hind legs, so it's interesting that recalcitrant combines the prefix *re–*, which means "back" in this case (it also means "again"), and the Latin verb *calcitare,* "to kick."

If he combines a headstrong nature with strong self-will, call him *willful* or *intractable.*

A **recalcitrant** (*ri·CAL·si·trunt,* adj.) person defies authority and resists any form of control.

➤ The principal scolded the **recalcitrant** student who refused to participate in the Wear-a-Chicken-on-Your-Head Day festivities.

Such a person doesn't want to be ruled or governed by anyone else, so you can also describe her as *unruly* or *ungovernable.*

An **incorrigible** (*in·KOR·uh·juh·bul,* adj.) person not only is difficult to control or reform, but is also incapable of being controlled or reformed.

➤ "Oh, you're just **incorrigible**," said the hostess to the guest who wouldn't stop double-dipping his chips.

If you want to emphasize that an incorrigible person can't be reformed from his wicked ways, describe him as *irreformable* or *irredeemable*. If he's an incorrigible criminal, describe him as *obdurate*.

Fightin' Words: A Hostility Lexicon

If a person is hostile (perhaps he's had to deal with one too many stubborn people), he's more likely to communicate with his fists than with words (obscenity-laced hollering notwithstanding). Fortunately, as you see in this section, that doesn't stop us innocent bystanders from conjuring up a word or two to describe the behavior and actions of those whose tempers have long been lost.

Belligerent (*buh·LIJ·uh·runt,* adj.) describes a person who is naturally aggressive and has a tendency to hostile behavior.

> ➤ The **belligerent** salesman got face-to-face with the customer and said, "You'll be the biggest loser of all time if you don't buy this car RIGHT NOW!"

If that **belligerence** (noun) is combined with a desire to fight, the person is *bellicose* (*BEL·uh·kose*) or *pugnacious* (*pug·NAY·shus*). Toss in a dash of defiance and you've got a person's who's *truculent* (*TRUK·yuh·lunt*). If the person will start a quarrel at the drop of a hat, he's definitely *quarrelsome* (naturally enough). If he's always spoiling for an argument, he's *contentious* (*kun·TEN·shus*).

An **irascible** (*i·RAS·uh·bul,* adj.) person is easily angered and prone to outbursts of temper.

> ➤ After another screaming fit, the priest knew he shouldn't be so **irascible** in the confessional, but some of these people were so *stupid*.

The word "temper" figures prominently in any list of synonyms for irascible. Here are a few: *bad-tempered, hot-tempered, ill-tempered, quick-tempered, sharp-tempered,* and *short-tempered*. Strangely, you're also angry if you *lose your temper,* so it doesn't seem to matter if you have a lot of it or none of it. A person's **irascibility** (noun) is also captured by the synonyms *testy* and *short-fused*.

See also: CANTANKEROUS, CHOLERIC.

Umbrage (*UM·brij,* noun) means "offense; resentment," so if a person **takes umbrage** (verb), it means they get angry and upset by a perceived insult.

Parts Dept.

Are the *belli–* prefixes in belligerent and bellicose related? You bet they are. Both hark back to the Latin root *bellum,* "war." Belligerent combines this with the root *gerere,* "to make." Bellicose is from the related root *bellicus,* "warlike."

➤ After asking her boyfriend, "Do I look fat in this dress?" Sarah **took umbrage** over the fact that he hesitated 0.25 seconds before answering.

If the person gets mad at even the slightest of slights, she's *thin-skinned* or *touchy*. At this point, she is likely to experience *indignation* (noun), which means "anger at something unjust or unworthy" (see also IRE), and her *indignant* (adj.) mood is also known as *dudgeon*. (In books—particularly those written in the nineteenth century—people are always running around "in high dudgeon.")

What the BELLIGERENT, IRASCIBLE, UMBRAGE-TAKING person is feeling is anger, of course, and a common (if somewhat poetic) synonym for anger is **ire** (noun).

➤ Jack tried counting to 10, but his **ire** got the better of him at only 3, and he punched a big, honkin' hole in the wall.

If the person's ire is such that he's moved to seek vengeance or some kind of punishment, it's *wrath* (*rath*, "th" as in "thin"), and if he's lost all self-control, he's experiencing *rage*. If you combine wrath and rage, you get *fury*. Luckily, not all anger is so violent, and there are lots of words to express a milder form of anger or annoyance, such as *huff*, *pique* (*peek*), and *vexation* (*VEKS·ay·shun*).

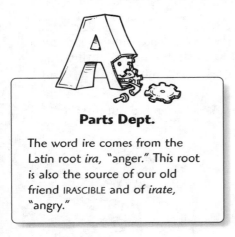

Parts Dept.

The word ire comes from the Latin root *ira*, "anger." This root is also the source of our old friend IRASCIBLE and of *irate*, "angry."

You Don't Say

The word *idyll*, "a picturesque and tranquil scene," has the same pronunciation as idle, so don't get them confused.

Living La Vida Lazy: Adjectives for the Inactive

The English language offers quite a collection of words to describe people who are inactive, and few of these words are complimentary. Unfortunately, you can't ask inactive people what they are because it's just too much work for them to get up off the couch to check the dictionary. Fortunately, you don't have to ask them because I'm up anyway and am happy to pass along the best ones to you here in this section.

The simplest way to describe an inactive person is to label him as **idle** (*EYE·dul*), which means he's not busy or engaged in any activity.

➤ As long as he was **idle** for a few hours, Eric decided to spend the time watching his wife's paint job dry.

If his **idleness** (noun) is caused by a job or another situation that requires him to sit for long periods, describe him (or his job) as *sedentary*. If he's unable to move for some reason, he's *inert*. If his lack of activity is as though he's asleep, call him *comatose* or *dormant*.

Unsurprisingly, inactivity is often the result of laziness, so *do-nothings* are often described as **indolent** (*IN·duh·lunt*), which means they're inclined to avoid activity or exertion or they're habitually lazy.

> ➤ The **indolent** student decided against having the Minute Rice because it just didn't seem worth the effort.

Interestingly, the word indolent is a meeting of the prefix *IN-* and the Latin root *dolere*, "to feel pain." So the lazy person feels no pain, which sounds about right to me. If the person's **indolence** (noun) is particularly notable, go right ahead and describe her as *slothful* or *otiose*.

See also: PHLEGMATIC.

A person who is **lethargic** (*luh·THAR·jik*, "th" as in "thin") lacks energy and vitality and moves extremely slowly, if at all.

> ➤ After finally dragging herself out of bed, Belinda was so **lethargic** that she could only open one eye at a time.

You can also describe such a person as *listless, languid,* or *sluggish*. The person's **lethargy** (*LETH·ur·gee*, "th" as in "thin," noun) also packs a couple of synonyms you should know. If the lethargy is caused by fatigue or sickness, it's *lassitude;* if it's caused by conditions that are *enervating* ("weakening of strength or vigor"), such as a hot, humid climate or the overindulgence of food, drink, and other luxuries, it's *languor* (*LANG·gur*).

Word Wonders

Slugs, being the painfully slow creatures that they are, serve as excellent metaphors for the lethargic. Besides SLUGGISH, other adjectives you can toss around gleefully are SLUGABED and *sluggard* ("a lazy person"). Speaking of slow, my two favorite fun words to describe the unhurried are LOLLYGAGGER and DILLY-DALLIER.

Some Tricky Behavior Words

My goal throughout this book is to show you that the English language has all kinds of nuances that you need to know to make your speaking and writing more precise. I also want to help you avoid common traps that even long-time English speakers fall into, and I normally do this using the "You Don't Say" sidebars. However, I had a long list of tricky behavioral words that I wanted to get to, so I'm just going to devote this entire section to these "gotcha" words.

The first word is **discreet** (*dis·KREET*, adj.), which describes a person who uses good judgement and tact, particularly when speaking.

➤ When giving his toast, Marvin was **discreet** and didn't mention the affair he'd once had with the bride.

The potential trap here is to confuse this word with *discrete* (*dis·KREET,* adj.), which means "separate; individual." It doesn't help matters that the noun associated with discreet is *discretion* (*dis·KRESH·un*), "discernment; judgement," which looks an awful lot like discrete. (In case you're wondering, the corresponding noun for discrete is *discreteness.*) To avoid problems, you might want to take out discreet and substitute *careful, discerning,* or *prudent.*

Next is **disinterested** (*dis·IN·tris·tid,* adj.), which means impartial, unbiased, or free from selfish motives.

➤ The judge, having lost his collection of Michael Dukakis jokes after a program crash, could not be considered a **disinterested** party in the software company's antitrust trial.

A great many people confuse this word with *uninterested,* which means "indifferent; not interested." That's not the least bit surprising because the word *interest* can mean "a state of curiosity" or "a benefit." So the notion of being "without interest" can cut both ways. And, indeed, it does because lots of people now use disinterested to mean "not interested." That's a shame because it means we may be on the verge of losing a useful distinction. Therefore, my advice is to only use disinterested if you can make it clear from the context that you're talking about impartiality instead of indifference.

If a person is being **facetious** (*fuh·SEE·shus,* adj.), she's being playfully humorous or witty, sometimes inappropriately so.

➤ Carla was being **facetious** when she said the deceased person had never looked so good.

Word Wonders

Here's something else that's interesting about the word facetious: it contains all five vowels in order! Another word that has this rare property is *abstemious,* "eating and drinking in a restrained manner."

Some folks think facetious means *disingenuous* (*dis·in·JEN·yoo·us,* adj.), "not sincere or straightforward," or IRONIC. Just remember that you can only use facetious when there's an element of humor involved in what the person said.

A person who is **nonplussed** (*non·PLUST,* adj.) is bewildered and is at a loss as to what to think, do, or say.

➤ **Nonplussed** after glimpsing her thong underwear, the president didn't know what to do next.

Many people think this word actually means the opposite, that the nonplussed individual remains unfazed and composed. I think the reason for this is that the *non-* ("not") prefix makes it sound as though nothing happened ("the guy didn't get plussed"). It doesn't help that the *-plussed* part comes from the Latin root *plus,* which means "more." So the Latin phrase *non plus* means, "no more." The way I remember it is to think of some poor, bewildered soul throwing up his hands and saying "No more! No more!"

To **proscribe** (*proh·SKRIBE,* verb) means to condemn or to prohibit.

> ➤ Wet shaving in the car was high on the list of Larry's **proscribed** activities.

When many people see or hear this word, they think the talker or writer means *prescribe* (*pri·SKRIBE,* verb), which, as luck would have it, has almost the opposite meaning: "to order the use of; to set down as a rule or guide." To avoid this confusion, consider chucking proscribe in favor of *ban, forbid,* or *prohibit.*

Questions and Exercises to Help Everything Sink In

Here's a list of the main words you learned in this chapter:

belligerent	discreet	disinterested	facetious	fickle
headstrong	idle	incorrigible	indolent	irascible
ire	lethargic	meander	obsequious	obstinate
proscribe	protean	recalcitrant	take umbrage	

1. Choose the alternate definition of *idle:*
   a. an object of worship or adoration
   b. capable of moving sideways
   c. lacking substance or basis in fact
   d. able to curl one's tongue

2. Choose the word that means "erratic changeableness and instability":
   a. incorrigible
   b. fickle
   c. obsequious
   d. protean

3. Choose the sentence that uses *disinterested* correctly:
   a. As the only parent without a kid playing in the game, Oscar could be a disinterested umpire.
   b. Tanya hated opera, so she was disinterested in attending the premiere.
   c. As his antique book lay in its dusty heap, Desmond couldn't believe it had disinterested so quickly.

4. Fill in the blank: "She was only being _____, but Maria's crack about the rabbi's funny cap was not appreciated."

Match the word on the left with the short definition on the right:

5. obstinate   a. easily angered

6. lethargic   b. change direction randomly

7. recalcitrant   c. unreasonably rigid

8. meander   d. defiant of authority

9. irascible   e. lacking in energy

10. Choose the word that's a respectful synonym for *obsequious:*

    a. acquiescent

    b. bellicose

    c. bullish

    d. deferent

Chapter 5

How People Think

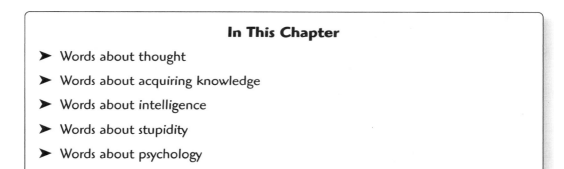

In This Chapter

➤ Words about thought

➤ Words about acquiring knowledge

➤ Words about intelligence

➤ Words about stupidity

➤ Words about psychology

"We have no words for speaking of wisdom to the stupid. He who understands the wise is wise already."

—G. C. Lichtenberg, German physicist and philosopher

Your long-term memories are stored in a chunk of the brain called the *hippocampus*. Psychologists have theorized that these long-term memories are arranged within the hippocampus in various structures that help us retrieve our memories. For example, the storage of words and their meanings (that is, everything you're learning in this book) is organized into something called *semantic memory*. (*Semantic* means "relating to meaning, particularly in language.") This structure also holds the meanings of all the concepts you learn.

This tells us that the concept "semantic memory stores concepts" is itself stored in se-mantic memory. If you get that far, then the concept "semantic memory stores the concept 'semantic memory stores concepts'" is also stored there. Homework question:

Word Wonders

This may come as a bit of a shock, but the word hippocampus implies that you have a sea horse in your head! Let me explain. The word comes to use from the Greek word *hippokampus*, which combines *hippos,* "horse," and *kampos,* "sea monster." It was the name of the creature ridden by the god Poseidon, and it was later applied to the marine animal known as a sea horse. In turn, the hippocampus brain structure got its name from its resemblance to the sea horse.

If you continue to follow this train of concepts within concepts, will your brain eventually become full?

Now that your brain is suitably limbered up (but not scarred for life, I hope), you can now turn its attention to itself. That is, in this chapter, you learn about words and phrases related to thinking, including words about thought, knowledge, intelligence, stupidity, and psychology.

A Thinking Person's Guide to Thought

Thought, as I think you know, is the mental consideration of a subject. It's the act or the process of thinking; it's what goes on in your mind as opposed to your body. But these definitions of thought are far too simple-minded to capture the complexity of our not-at-all-simple minds. This section (and, indeed, this entire chapter) gives you a hint of that complexity by having you think about a few words related to thought.

Let's begin with words related to that organ of thought, the mind. The **intellect** (*IN·tuh·lekt,* noun) is the part of you that formulates thoughts.

➤ The continuing popularity of Cheez Whiz was too much for Roy's **intellect** to grasp.

The intellect is often referred to as a person's *mental faculties* or just his *faculties* (*FAK·ul·tees,* noun) for short. Broadly, a *faculty* is an ability or power, so the intellect is also called the *powers of thought.*

The act of thinking is captured nicely by the word **ponder** (*PON·dur,* verb), which means to think deeply about, reflect on, or weigh in the mind.

➤ Given the seventies, eighties, and nineties, Lillian **pondered** what word we should use for the years 2000 to 2009.

If the person ponders by turning a matter over and over again in her mind, she *ruminates* (*ROO·muh·nates,* verb) or *mulls* (verb). If she ponders carefully and slowly, she *deliberates* (*di·LIB·ur·ates,* verb) or *cogitates* (*KOJ·uh·tates,* verb).

Word Wonders

The word fragment "ough" has no less than eight different pronunciations, as the following sentence shows:

Lost in thought, the tough ploughman hiccoughed and coughed; he then went through the streets of Scarborough looking for cookie dough.

Here, in order, are the "ough" pronunciations from this sentence: aw uff ow up off oo uh oh.

To **conceive** (*kun·SEEV,* verb) is to form an idea or conception in the mind.

➤ Bill took the day off to **conceive** his plan for world domination.

To form an idea is also to *ideate* (*EYE·dee·ate,* verb). If the idea takes the form of a mental image, then you *visualize* (*VIZH·oo·uh·lise,* verb) it or *imagine* (*i·MAJ·in,* verb) it.

To **speculate** (*SPEK·yuh·late,* verb) is to reflect on a matter and come to a conclusion despite lacking all the facts or evidence.

➤ Although she hadn't met the man yet, Tessa **speculated** that her interview with "Killer" Ken Stone would be a tough one.

You *hypothesize* (*hye·POTH·uh·size,* verb) if your **speculation** (noun) produces a suggested explanation for a set of facts. Such an explanation is called a *conjecture* (*kun·JEK·chur,* noun), although this word can also be used as a verb. If you know a lot about the topic at hand, then you're making an *educated guess.*

43

Idiom Savant

Our language is loaded with fun *idioms* for thinking. For example, the verb ruminate has the same Latin root as the word *ruminant,* "an animal that chews cud." (The root is *rumen,* "throat.") Therefore, to think is also to *chew over.* Other idioms include *put on one's thinking cap* and *rack one's brains.* To *brainstorm* means to gather some people and have them contribute ideas spontaneously.

The Search for Knowledge

Philosophers and PSYCHOLOGISTS spend huge gobs of their time trying to figure out how human beings create new knowledge and determine the truthfulness of that new knowledge. All that hard work has paid off in a basic theory that says we use four FAC-ULTIES of the mind: reason, intuition, comprehension, and judgment. This section examines these four mental abilities and the words that surround them.

Reason (*REE·zun,* noun) is the mental ability that enables a person to think orderly and logically.

> ➤ Although his **reason** told him that eating a cake a day would make him fat, Duane thought, "You know, I think I can live with that."

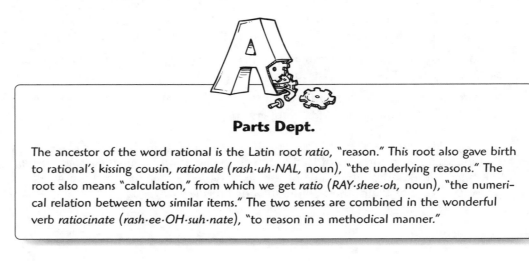

Parts Dept.

The ancestor of the word rational is the Latin root *ratio,* "reason." This root also gave birth to rational's kissing cousin, *rationale* (*rash·uh·NAL,* noun), "the underlying reasons." The root also means "calculation," from which we get *ratio* (*RAY·shee·oh,* noun), "the numerical relation between two similar items." The two senses are combined in the wonderful verb *ratiocinate* (*rash·ee·OH·suh·nate*), "to reason in a methodical manner."

44

You can also describe orderly and logical thought as *rational* (*RASH·uh·nul*), and if the thought is particularly convincing, call it *cogent* (*KOH·junt*). If two or more people seek knowledge by engaging in a **reasoned** (adj.) argument, they're in a *dialectic* (*dye·UH·lek·tik*, noun).

Intuition (*in·too·ISH·un* or *in·tyoo·ISH·un*, noun) is the ability to know something directly without going through a conscious, RATIONAL process (that is, without using REASON).

➤ Thanks to her excellent **intuition**, Priscilla just had to take one look at the new girl they hired, and she knew right away that she would fail spectacularly.

Another word for intuition is *insight* (*IN·site*), and on the verb front, to **intuit** (*in·TOO·it* or *IN·tyoo·it*) something is the same as to *divine* (*di·VINE*) it. The noun intuition also applies to the knowledge itself, and in this context it's also called a *hunch*, a *gut reaction*, and a *feeling in one's bones*.

Comprehension (*com·pri·HEN·shun*, noun) is the ability to fully grasp the meaning or nature of something.

➤ His **comprehension** of the Beanie Baby phenomenon gave Trevor profound insights on the human condition.

There's no problem using the word *understanding* as a synonym for comprehension. If the comprehension takes the form of a deep spiritual INSIGHT, a good word to use for that insight is *enlightenment* (*en·LITE·un·munt*).

You Don't Say

The words "comprehension" and "apprehension" are similar and are often used interchangeably. However, *apprehension* is the weaker word in that it means merely "taking in with the mind." Both words are based on the Latin root *prehendere*, "to grasp." Apprehend came from tacking on a variant of the Latin prefix *ad–*, "to," while comprehend was formed by adding the prefix *com–*, "together."

The final stop on the road to new knowledge is **judgment** (*JUJ·munt*, noun), the ability to form a sound opinion or conclusion after mentally assessing the facts or circumstances.

➤ "In the **judgment** of this court, the attempt by the accused to sell the PLAINTIFF a wind-powered fan represents not only fraud but stupidity as well."

If a person has particularly good judgment, describe her ability as *judiciousness* (*joo·DISH·us·nis*) or *perspicacity* (*pur·spuh·KAS·i·tee*), and if she's wise, call it *sagacity* (*suh·GAS·i·tee*). If this ability leads to unusually sharp intellectual ideas, call it *discernment* (*di·SURN·munt*).

You Don't Say

Don't confuse perspicacity with *perspicuity* (*pur·spuh·KYOO·i·tee*), which means "clarity and precision of expression."

Parts Dept.

The origins of the word *intelligent* lie in the Latin root *intellegere*, "to perceive." This root combines *inter-*, "between, among," with *-legere*, "to choose." This root is also the source of the words INTELLECT, *intellection* ("the process of understanding"), and *intelligible* ("capable of being understood").

Words to the Wise: Terms for Intelligence

It's notoriously difficult to pin down exactly who coined a particular word. Most of the time, they just seem to appear in the language and then assume a life of their own. However, *someone* had to make up each word, and I'm willing to generalize that most of these wordsmiths are smart people. That would partially explain why almost all the words related to intelligence are complimentary, as you'll see in this section.

An **acute** (*uh·CUTE*, adj.) mind is one that is intellectually penetrating and perceptive.

➤ Dora's **acute** mind glimpsed the box of pink slips in her boss's desk and knew there was going to be trouble.

Penetrating means "able to understand the inner significance of something." It conjures up the image of something sharp, and it just so happens that *sharp* is a synonym for acute, as are some other pointy words: cutting, keen, and *incisive* (*in·SYE·siv*). Not only that, but acute comes from the Latin *acus*, "needle," which also gives us *acuity* (*uh·KYOO·i·tee*), "keenness of insight," and *acumen* (*AK·yuh·mun* or *uh·KYOO·mun*), "depth of insight in practical matters."

A person who is **clever** (*KLEV·ur*, adj.) is one who is mentally quick and inventive.

➤ "Mitch is so **clever**. The other day I happened to mention Edam cheese. He said, 'Do you know why Edam is peculiar? Because it's *made backward*.'"

If the person is extraordinarily clever, call him *ingenious* (*in·JEEN·yus*). Clever people are also described as *witty*, where *wit* is the "quick and perceptive mental ability that can find unusual and amusing relationships between things." Finally, adjectives for people who display **cleverness** (noun) often use light as a metaphor: *bright, brilliant* (*BRIL·yunt*), *sparkling.*

A **shrewd** (*SHROOD,* "oo" as in "boot," adj.) person has keen intelligence and awareness in practical matters.

> ➤ As a **shrewd** negotiator, Carly knew the best time to mention her most controversial demand was when her opponent had just taken a bite of his muffin.

If the person's **shrewdness** emphasizes practical matters, call her *savvy* (*SAV·ee*), and if those matters relate to survival in an urban environment, label her *streetwise.* A *canny* (*KAN·ee*) person is one who combines shrewdness and carefulness, while an *astute* (*UH·stoot*) person is shrewd about her own concerns.

Being **learned** (*LUR·nid,* adj.) means having deep and profound knowledge.

> ➤ The **learned** professor was the world's foremost expert on the mating habits of learned professors.

If the person is learned in a scholarly way, he's *erudite* (*ER·yuh·dite* or *ER·uh·dite*). If he's read a great many books, call him *well-read,* and if he has a good background in a specific subject, call him *well-grounded, well-schooled,* or *well-versed.*

Idiom Savant

I mentioned earlier that most intelligence–related words are complimentary to the intelligent. *Most* of them. Here are some colorful idioms that are less–than–complimentary synonyms for "intelligent person": *book-worm, egghead, highbrow, know-it-all, tall forehead type.*

A Fool and His Words: Terms for Stupidity

As further proof that smart people make up most of our words, look no further than the collection of terms we have for those who are, uh, a few sandwiches short of a picnic. As you'll see in this section, there seems to be a barely suppressed glee underlying each of these insults, and that can only mean they were made up by a bunch of smart alecks.

Let's begin with **dull** (adj.), which describes a person who is mentally weak or who is slow in perception or intellect.

> ➤ Petula was so **dull** that her head ached whenever she contemplated the question, "Who wants to be a millionaire?"

As the word implies, this is the opposite of SHARP, and some equally dull synonyms to describe the *dullards* (*DULL·urds*, noun) of the world are *dense* and *thick*. Speaking of opposites, the opposite of ACUTE gives us another synonym, *obtuse*, which comes from the Latin word *obtundere*, "to blunt."

A **witless** (*WIT·lis*, adj.) person lacks intelligence, sense, or understanding.

> ➤ As the most **witless** of the Riker boys, the only job that Derek could handle was to wipe the drool off his brothers' chins.

Witless implies a total lack of WIT, but it's just as insulting to imply that a stupid person's wits just aren't up to snuff, as the following synonyms show: *dim-witted, dull-witted, half-witted, slow-witted, thick-witted*. You might be tempted to think that a truly stupid person doesn't have a brain at all, in which case you might prefer to use the adjectives *mindless* or *brainless*.

If a person is **fatuous** (*FACH·oo·us*, adj.), she's complacently stupid or silly.

> ➤ Velma was being even more **fatuous** than usual when she said "Oh, but my dear I *know* that the earth is flat. Otherwise, we'd all fall off!"

What's often annoying about a fatuous person is that he's *smug*, which means "offensively self-satisfied." In other words, he actually enjoys the qualities that make him appear foolish or stupid to other people. Argh! If someone's **fatuousness** (noun) has a vacant quality to it, describe her as *vacuous* (*VAK·yoo·us*) or *inane* (*IN·ane*), both of which mean "lacking substance or sense."

If you want to say that a person is about a dumb as they come, call him a **moron** (*MOR·on*, noun), which refers to an extremely stupid person.

> ➤ That **moron** took one look at the painting and immediately started trying to teach his dogs to play poker.

However, the **moronic** (*muh·RON·ik*, adj.) person is not quite the lowest of the low on the dumb scale. A bit below is *imbecile* (*IM·buh·sul*), "a person with well below average intellect," which is about on par with a *dolt*. Under that comes the *cretin* (*CREE·tin* or *CRET·in*), a true idiot.

Word Wonders

Donkeys (also known as asses) have a reputation for being as stupid as anything on four legs, so actions and behaviors (rarely people) are sometimes called *asinine* (*ASS·uh·nine*), "completely and utterly stupid or silly."

The Mind Field: Terms from Psychology

So far in this chapter, you've seen thinking words that are generally used by regular folks. But there are plenty of mind-related words used by specialists in the field. Most of these are hopelessly technical and uninteresting to us, but quite a few have slipped the shackles of professional usage and have taken up residence in the mainstream. I walk you through a few of those words in this section.

For starters, you should know that **psychology** (*sye·KOL·uh·jee,* noun) is the science of the mind, mental processes, and human behavior.

> ➤ As a **psychology** major, Meredith knew all about the workings of the human mind, but she still couldn't explain the existence of fruitcake.

Psychologists (*sye·KOL·uh·jists,* noun) usually follow a particular *school* ("a group of people with a common set of beliefs and ideas"). The **psychological** (*sye·kuh·LOJ·i·kul,* adj.) world has dozens of these schools, but here are the ones you'll likely hear about most often:

Freudian psychology—This school emphasizes the influence of the patient's childhood (particularly the relationship with the mother and father) as well as the interplay of the id (the unconscious mind), the ego (the conscious mind), and the superego (the conscience).

psychoanalysis—This is a technique used by the Freudian school. It's a form of therapy that uses dream interpretation, free association, and other techniques to explore the patient's unconscious.

Jungian psychology—This school emphasizes the patient's relationship with the mythological, cultural, and racial inheritances that have contributed to his individuality. It stresses the process of "individuation," or the unification of the self.

depth psychology—This refers to any school or technique (such as the previous three) that emphasizes the role of the unconscious.

behavior therapy—This is a form of treatment that uses standard learning techniques to change problematic behaviors. It does this by replacing a negative response to a given stimulus with a positive response.

group therapy—In this form of treatment, a therapist leads a session attended by several patients who discuss their personal problems.

Psychologists spend much of their day helping individual patients overcome a **neurosis** (*noo·ROH·sis,* noun), a mental or emotional disorder that affects part of the personality and generates symptoms such as anxiety, insecurity, and depression.

You Don't Say

Don't confuse psychology with *psychiatry* (*sye·KYE·uh·tree* or *suh·KYE·uh·tree*), a branch of medicine that deals with the diagnosis and treatment of mental and emotional disorders.

➤ When she began feeling panicky, crying for no reason, and actually enjoying Pauly Shore movies, Rhonda knew her old **neurosis** had returned.

A more extreme problem is a *psychosis* (*sye·KOH·sis*, noun), a severe mental disorder, particularly one that causes loss of contact with reality and impairment of normal social functioning.

You Don't Say

An example of a psychosis is *schizophrenia* (*skit·suh·FREE·nee·uh*, noun), which many people believe means having multiple personalities. Not true. Schizophrenia is a disorder characterized by severe emotional and behavioral disturbances, hallucinations and delusions, illogical thinking, and withdrawal from reality. A patient who exhibits two or more separate personalities has a *multiple personality disorder*.

Many **neuroses** (*noo·ROH·sees* or *nyoo·ROH·sees*, plural) take the form of a **phobia** (*FOH·bee·uh*), an abnormal or irrational fear of an object or situation.

➤ Cliff's Barney the Dinosaur **phobia** caused him no end of trouble on the weekends that he looked after his kids.

The **phobic** (*FOH·bik*, adj.) patient's fear can apply itself to almost anything, from common household objects to everyday situations. Some common phobias have their own names, which are usually formed by taking an appropriate prefix and welding it to the front of "phobia." For example, the prefix *hydro-* means "water," so *hydrophobia* means "fear of water." The following table lists some of these phobias-with-names.

Some Common Phobias

Phobia	Fear of ...	Phobia	Fear of ...
acrophobia	heights	agoraphobia	open spaces
ailurophobia	cats	androphobia	men
bacteriophobia	germs	brontophobia	thunder
cynophobia	dogs	gamophobia	marriage

Phobia	Fear of ...	Phobia	Fear of ...
gynephobia	women	hydrophobia	water
hypegiaphobia	responsibility	lalophobia	public speaking
nosocomephobia	hospitals	ophiciophobia	snakes
phobophobia	fear	pantophobia	everything
scotophobia	dark	technophobia	technology
tridecaphobia	thirteen	xenophobia	foreigners

The fact that you've gotten this far in the book definitely means you don't suffer from *logophobia,* "the fear of words."

Maniaphobia is the fear of going insane, and this brings us to the other common form of **neurotic** (*noo·ROT·ik* or *nyoo·ROT·ik,* adj.) behavior, the **mania** (*MAY·nee·uh,* noun): an exaggerated desire for or obsession with an object.

➤ Estelle's **mania** took the form of being obsessed with just exactly how they got the caramel inside the Caramilk bar.

As with phobias, many manias also have their own names. The following table lists a few of the dozens of manias that exist.

Some Common Manias

Mania	Desire for ...	Mania	Desire for ...
ablutomania	washing	chrematomania	money
dromomania	traveling	egomania	oneself
ergomania	work	hippomania	horses
kleptomania	stealing	logomania	talking
megalomania	power	monomania	one thing
mythomania	lying	nymphomania	sex (in women)
oniomania	shopping	paramania	complaining
pyromania	fire	satyromania	sex (in men)

Questions and Exercises to Help Everything Sink In

Here's a list of the main words you learned in this chapter:

acute	clever	comprehension	conceive
dull	fatuous	intellect	intuition

judgment	learned	mania	moron
neurosis	phobia	ponder	psychology
reason	shrewd	speculate	witless

1. Choose the alternative definition of *reason:*
   - **a.** the basis or motive for an action or decision
   - **b.** a logical outcome
   - **c.** an orderly series of steps
   - **d.** a microorganism carried by the fruit fly

2. Choose the word that means "having deep and profound knowledge":
   - **a.** comprehension
   - **b.** intuition
   - **c.** learned
   - **d.** fatuous

3. Fill in the blank: "Without all the facts, Cosmo could only _____ as to why his jelly doughnut actually contained jam."

4. Choose the word that has the meaning closest to "sharp":
   - **a.** witless
   - **b.** clever
   - **c.** conceive
   - **d.** acute

Match the word on the left with the short definition on the right:

5. ponder   **a.** an irrational fear
6. fatuous   **b.** direct knowledge
7. phobia   **c.** think deeply about
8. intuition   **d.** keen, practical, intelligence
9. shrewd   **e.** smugly foolish

10. Choose the word that's a stronger synonym for *clever:*
    - **a.** ingenious
    - **b.** savvy
    - **c.** discernment
    - **d.** erudite

Chapter 6

How People Look

In This Chapter

➤ Words for attractive people

➤ Words for unattractive people

➤ Words for small people

➤ Words for big people

➤ Fun terms for selected body parts

"Words should be an intense pleasure, just as leather should be to a shoemaker."

—Evelyn Waugh, British novelist

After all that focus on the inner life in the previous chapter, it's time to take the opposite tack and switch into judging-a-book-by-its-cover mode. This chapter does that by taking a surface (but hopefully not *superficial,* "on or near the surface; shallow; trivial") look at the human animal. Here you'll find words and phrases about how people look, arranged in four appearance categories: attractiveness, unattractiveness, smallness, and bigness. I close with a look at the some informal and slang terms for various body parts.

Hale, Hearty, and Hunky: Attractiveness

Despite the fact that many of us are rendered speechless at the sight of an extremely good-looking person, English is chock full of words that describe attractive people. Many of these words are quite common: Women can be *lovely* or *pretty;* men can be *handsome* or *hunky;* and both sexes can be *beautiful* or *gorgeous.* This section looks at a few words that aren't quite so common, and I also cover other elements of attractiveness including neatness, good health, and strength.

An **alluring** (*uh·LOOR·ing,* adj.) person is one who is highly attractive and enticing.

> ➤ She was so **alluring** that when Oscar went up to her to say "Hi," it came out as "shrdlwu."

The verb *allure* made its way into English by way of the French verb *aleurrer,* "to bait." It was originally used by falconers and referred to a device or bait to lure the birds into returning, from which we get the current sense of "enticing." I suppose this means that the person doing the alluring must have to watch the other person like a hawk!

If the alluring person is attractive in a pleasantly wholesome way, call her *comely* (*KUM·lee*). However, if she's sexually attractive, you can say she has *come-hither looks.* If the person is both highly attractive and CHARMING, use the slightly old-fashioned word *fetching.* If you want to describe a woman who is physically attractive, use *shapely, curvaceous* (*kur·VAY·shus*), or one of my all-time favorite adjectives, *pulchritudinous* (*PUL·kri·TOO·di·nus* or *PUL·kri·TYOO·di·nus;* from the noun *pulchritude,* "great physical beauty").

See also: CHARISMATIC, GLAMOROUS, GRACEFUL

If a person is **natty** (*NAT·ee,* adj.), he's neat, trim, and tidy.

> ➤ Johnny Carson, with his trim physique and perfectly tailored suits, was a walking definition of the word **natty.**

The **nattily** (*NAT·uh·lee,* adv.) dressed person would be quite precisely described as *dapper.* If he's *meticulous* (*muh·TIK·yuh·lus,* "extreme, perhaps even finicky, concern for details") about being neat, he's *well groomed.*

Good health can certainly be an attractive trait, so consider **hale** (adj.), which describes a person who is free from disease or INFIRMITY.

You Don't Say

Don't confuse *hearty* with HARDY, which is a synonym for ROBUST.

> ➤ After the exhaustive checkup, Belinda's doctor pronounced her **hale** and ready to resume training for the World Finger Wrestling Championships.

You don't see the word hale alone very often. Instead, it can usually be spotted as part of the phrase *hale and hearty,* which means "healthy and vigorous." If a person's body is free from disease and other defects, describe him as *sound,* a word used most often at the start of wills ("I, Paul McFedries, being of allegedly sound mind and body …").

Having some color in your cheeks is a universal sign of good health, so the hale are often called *rosy-cheeked* or, taking the hue down a notch, *pink-cheeked* or *in the pink*. A healthy red complexion is described as *ruddy* (*RUD·ee*), but if you want to describe someone who has a red face because of his emotional state, use *florid* (*FLOR·id*, "flushed with rosy color").

If a person's cheeks are a particularly nice shade of red, it's probably because they're **fit** (adj.), which means physically SOUND and healthy due to exercise.

➤ With all the swimming, bicycling, and running they'd been doing, Felix and Felicia knew they were **fit** enough to compete in tomorrow's three-legged triathlon.

You can also describe the fit person as being *in good shape* or *in good condition*. (Exercise is also called *conditioning*.) If the person's muscles are well exercised, describe her as *toned*. If all that exercise has given the person the ability to bend or flex easily, call her *limber, lissome* (*LIS·um*), or *supple*.

Another attractive type is the **robust** (*roh·BUST,* adj.) person, who is full of health and strength.

➤ Despite the all-day hike and the mosquitoes as big as his head, Ray was **robust** enough to make it through his company's annual jungle trek and picnic without any problems.

The strength of the robust person is evident from the history of this word. It comes from the Latin *robustus*, which means "as sturdy as an oak tree."

You can also describe such a person as *hardy* (*HAR·dee*). If the person's strength has also made him active and energetic, then he's *vigorous* (*VIG·ur·us*), and we say he's full of *vim* (noun), *vigor* (*VIG·ur*, noun), and *vitality* (*vye·TAL·i·tee*, noun). If the person has a sturdy or strong *constitution* (noun, "physical makeup"), call him *rugged* (*RUG·id*) or *strapping*. Finally, use *stalwart* (*STAHL·wurt*) to describe someone with impressive physical strength.

Idiom Savant

Many fit-related idioms equate a person's **fitness** (noun) with some object or animal: *fit as a fiddle, fit as a flea, sound as a bell, strong as an ox, healthy as a horse.*

Word Wonders

Muscular people are usually big and strong, but you'd never know it from the history of the word *muscle*. It actually goes back to the Latin word *musculus*, which means "little mouse." Huh?! Word historians SPECULATE that the ancients thought a big, rippling, muscle looked something like a mouse. Makes sense, I guess, but it's kind of creepy.

Soft, Scruffy, and Unsightly: Unattractiveness

Sadly, only a small minority of the population qualifies as attractive. Most of us sit somewhere within shouting distance of the middle of the attractiveness scale. But then there's that *other* minority that keeps balance in the world by being decidedly *un*attractive. The ugly, the untidy, the sickly, the soft, and the weak, they're the "wretched refuse" that the Statue of Liberty calls to, and they're all here in this section.

Starting with ugly, a person who is **hideous** (*HID·ee·us*, adj.) is extremely displeasing to look at.

➤ With enough makeup on her face to make Bozo the Clown look plain, Coco looked nothing short of **hideous.**

This extreme ugliness is also captured by *repugnant* (*ri·PUG·nunt*), "arousing disgust, distaste, or intense dislike." If you're forced to look away or avoid the person, that's called *aversion* (*uh·VUR·zhun*, noun, "avoidance caused by disgust or dislike"), and that makes a person *repellent* or *repulsive*. If you need an adjective that's not quite as strong as these, try *unsightly*, "unpleasant to look at," or *homely* (*HOME·lee*), "not good-looking."

The **unkempt** (*un·KEMPT*, adj.) person is untidy, messy, or disorderly.

➤ With her hair flying out in all directions, her face stained with last night's dinner, and her clothes askew, Tracy had the new **unkempt** look down pat.

Unkempt goes back to the Old English word *kemb*, "comb." So unkempt originally described someone who had uncombed hair. (And, in case you're wondering, the word *kempt* is legitimate and means, not surprisingly, "tidy, trim.")

You can also call an unkempt person *blowzy* (*BLOW·zee*, "BLOW" rhymes with "now") or *frowzy* (*FROW·zee*, "FROW" rhymes with "now"). If it's her hair or clothing that unkempt, she's *mussed* (*must*) or *disheveled* (*duh·SHEV·uld*). If it's only her clothing, describe her as *rumpled* (*RUMP·uld*), "wrinkled or creased." If she's dirty (she thinks the phrase "getting cleaned up for dinner" means wiping your hands on her sweat pants), then call her *grungy* (*GRUN·jee*), *grubby* (*GRUB·ee*), or *scruffy* (*SCRUF·ee*).

See also: BOOR, CRASS.

The **peaked** (*PEE·kid*, adj.) person is one who has a sickly appearance.

➤ When even the blind guy on the bus told him he looked **peaked**, Alonzo new he was coming down with something serious.

If he's pale, call him *pallid* (*PAL·id*), *pasty* (*PAY·stee*), or *wan* (rhymes with "on"), but if his complexion has taken on more of a yellowish hue, use *sallow* (*SAL·oh*) or *jaundiced* (*JAWN·dist*). If the person has lost a lot of weight to the point of unnatural thinness, describe him as *cadaverous* (*kuh·DAV·uh·rus*), *emaciated* (*i·MAY·see·ay·tid* or *i·MAY·shee·ay·tid*), or *gaunt* (rhymes with "want"). If he also looks exhausted, then he's in *haggard* (*HAG·urd*) territory.

A person who is **flabby** (*FLAB·ee,* adj.) lacks muscle TONE and may also lack energy.

➤ Elke knew she was too **flabby** when she tried to flex her biceps and the muscle actually dropped *down.*

This lack of firmness is also implied by the synonyms *flaccid* (*FLAS·id* or *FLAK·sid*), *slack,* and *soft.*

Lastly, the **infirm** (*in·FURM,* adj.) person is weak, particularly because of disease or old age.

➤ "Old man Garvey may be too **infirm** to even hold his head up, but that hasn't stopped him repeating the same old stories all day long."

Some synonyms you can toss around are *frail, feeble* (*FEE·bul*), and *debilitated* (*duh·BIL·uh·tay·tid*). If the person lacks VIGOR, describe him as *anemic* (*uh·NEEM·ik*) or *listless.*

Parts Dept.

The prefix *a–* usually means "without or not." In the word *anemia,* it's combined with the Greek work *haâma,* "blood," so the anemic person is weak as though from lack of blood. This is also seen in *anemia,* a disease in which the blood has too few red blood cells, resulting in weakness.

It's a Small Word After All: Terms for the Tiny

The name Paul comes from the Latin word *paulus,* "small," so you'll see in this section whether that gives me some special insight into teeniness. I've divided these words into three not mutually exclusive categories: general smallness, shortness, and thinness.

A good word to start with is **petite** (*puh·TEET,* adj.), which refers to a person (particularly a woman) with a small and slender figure.

➤ Holly was the **petite** girl in the crowd, so she was always the one who had to go into the trunk when entering the drive-in.

This word came from the French word *petit,* "small," which we can also thank for giving us the word *petty,* "trivial; of little or no importance."

You can describe either a man or a woman with a small build using the words *slight, small-boned, puny* (*PYOO·nee*), or *Lilliputian* (*lil·i·PYOO·shun*). A small person who has an aggressive, fighting spirit is sometimes called a *bantam* (*BAN·tum,* noun).

The word **diminutive** (*di·MIN·yuh·tiv,* adj.) describes a person who is small in stature.

➤ Mel was **diminutive,** but you didn't dare tease him about it or he'd bite you in the stomach.

Some not-very-flattering synonyms are *pint-sized* and *runty* (*RUN·tee*), and some equally unflattering nouns are *pygmy* (*PIG·mee*) and *dwarf*. If you prefer to use something less insulting, try *wee*.

A person who is **lean** (*LEEN*, adj.) has little or no fat.

> ➤ Carrie was proud of how **lean** she was, but asking total strangers to see if they could "pinch and inch" was going too far.

If the person's **leanness** (noun) is attractive, you can call her *svelte* (*svelt*). If you combine lean with strong and muscular, you get *sinewy* (*SIN·yoo·ee*) or *wiry* (*WIRE·ee*). If the person is overly thin, describe her as *scrawny* (*SKRAW·nee*) or *skinny* (*SKIN·ee*), and if she's unhealthily thin, she's *anorexic* (*an·uh·REX·ik*) or *skeletal* (*SKEL·uh·tul*). Here are some metaphors you might like to use: *beanpole* (noun), *stringbean* (noun), *reedlike* (adj.), and *wasp-waisted* (adj.).

A Lexicon for the Large

This section delves into words related to big people. As with the small-related words in the previous section, I've tried to divide these words into three semisensible sections: generally big, tall, and overweight.

A **burly** (*BUR·lee,* adj.) person (it's almost always a man) has a big, strong body.

> ➤ With the company's biggest-ever loss in the books and his biggest-ever bonus in the bank, Simpkins hired a **burly** bodyguard for protection at the shareholders' meeting.

For synonyms, use *beefy* (*BEE·fee*), *big-boned*, *brawny* (*BRAW·nee*), and *husky* (*HUS·kee*). If the person has a big upper body, describe him as *barrel-chested* or *broad-shouldered*, whichever is most appropriate.

There are many words for tallness, so let's start with **statuesque** (*stach·oo·ESK*, adj.), which describes a woman who is tall and shapely.

> ➤ The **statuesque** model would look down upon (literally and figuratively) the men who ogled her as she walked past.

If the person is tall because of long legs, call her *leggy* (*LEG·ee*). If she's tall, strong, and aggressive, she's an *amazon* (*AM·uh·zon*, noun). If the person is tall, thin, and awkward, describe her as *gangly* (*GANG·glee*), *gangling* (*GANG·gling*), or *lanky* (*LANG·kee*). On the other hand, if she's tall, slender, and graceful, then she's *willowy* (*WIL·oh·ee* or *WIL·uh·wee*).

A **corpulent** (*KORP·yuh·lunt*, adj.) person is extremely fat.

> ➤ Although he knew his enormous size made it inevitable, the **corpulent** businessman still hated being called a "fat cat."

A more common adjective you can use is *obese* (*oh·BEECE*). If the person is just a little fat, describe him as *plump, pudgy* (*PUJ·ee*), or *tubby*. If you're talking about a full-figured woman who is healthily plump, use *buxom* (*BUKS·um*) or *zaftig* (*ZAF·tig* or *ZOF·tig*). If the person is sturdy, compact, but a bit on the heavy side, use *heavyset, stocky,* or *thickset.* A couple of polite terms are *portly* and *stout* (*STOWT*).

Slang Terms for Various Body Parts

I'm going to close this chapter with something a little different. We humans seem to revel in coming up with fun nicknames and informal synonyms for the various parts of our bodies. To celebrate that, here's a list of the words people use for a dozen different body parts:

Head	Bean, belfry, block, coconut, conk, dome, gourd, nob, noddle, noggin, noodle, nut, pallet, pate, poll, sconce, upper story
Face	Kisser, mug, phiz, puss, visage
Eyes	Headlights, lamps, orbs, peepers, windows of the soul, winkers
Nose	Beak, bugle, proboscis, schnoz, schnozzle, schnozzola, smeller, sneezer, snoot, snout
Mouth	Chops, gob, kisser, mush, muzzle, orifice, trap, yap
Teeth	Choppers, crumb crunchers, fangs, ivories, pearly whites
Heart	Clocker, pump, ticker
Stomach (general)	Belly, breadbasket, gullet, gut, maw, middle, midriff, midsection, tummy
Stomach (big)	Bay window, beer belly, paunch, pot, potbelly, spare tire
Hands	Claws, dukes (fists), flippers, mitts, paws
Legs	Drumsticks, gams, hams, pegs, pins, shanks, stems, stilts, stumps, wheels
Feet	Dogs, hooves, tootsies

Questions and Exercises to Help Everything Sink In

Here's a list of the main words you learned in this chapter:

alluring	burly	corpulent	diminutive
fit	flabby	hale	hideous

infirm	lean	natty	peaked
petite	robust	statuesque	unkempt

1. Choose the alternative definition of *peaked:*
   a. took a quick look
   b. ending in a point
   c. stimulated one's curiosity
   d. had excessive nose hair

2. Choose the word that describes someone with a small and slender figure:
   a. petite
   b. lean
   c. natty
   d. hale

3. Fill in the blank: "Herman put on his Halloween mask and became so _____ that people gagged at the mere sight of him."

4. Choose the word that best describes *alluring:*
   a. lovely
   b. winsome
   c. charming
   d. enticing

Match the word on the left with the short definition on the right:

5. diminutive   a. healthy and strong
6. robust   b. tall and shapely
7. statuesque   c. messy
8. unkempt   d. with little fat
9. lean   e. small in stature

10. Choose the word that's a more polite synonym for *corpulent:*
    a. stout
    b. obese
    c. soft
    d. strapping

Part 2

And Now, Some Words from Our Culture

From the title of this section, I may have you believing that the five chapters in Part 2 are the culture section of the book. If so, then please accept my humble apologies and virtual slap-on-the-forehead for leading you astray. To understand why, you need to know that culture is, broadly, "the sum total of human knowledge, beliefs, behaviors, and anything else that's the product of human thought and effort and that's transmittable to subsequent generations." That covers a lot of ground!

So you see it isn't possible for a word to exist outside the culture. Therefore, this entire book is about culture words. So why am I calling Part 2 the culture words section of the book? Simple: I couldn't think of anything else to call it! Nevertheless, I hope you enjoy these words about food, drink, TV, books, and newspapers.

Chapter 7

A Few Food Words to Chew On

In This Chapter

➤ Some general food terms

➤ Eating verbs

➤ Cooking verbs

➤ Some restaurant terms

"The difference between the almost right word and the right word is really a large matter—'tis the difference between the lightning bug and the lightning."

—Mark Twain, American novelist and humorist

At first blush, eating seems to be the most straightforward of activities. You slap together a meal, pour yourself a cold one, and then try not to spill any of it on yourself. What's the big vocabulary deal? Ah, but there's always someone who'll come along and try to lift a particular aspect of the culture to some rarefied height, either as a performer or as an AFICIONADO. Cooking, and appreciating that cooking, is an example.

The difference, though, is that unlike high-level activities such as brain surgery, rocket science, or professional roller derby, cooking and eating are chores that we mere mortals do every day. Therefore, it's inevitable that we're going to come across some fancy-schmancy terminology that the food elite have foisted upon an unsuspecting world. This chapter takes you through a few of these words so you'll know what all those food fanciers are talking about.

A Cornucopia of Food Words

The word *cornucopia* (*kor·nuh·KOH·pee·uh* or *kor·nyuh·KOH·pee·uh*) means, literally, a *horn of plenty* (which is a synonym), and it's defined as "an abundance, particularly an abundance of food." This section gets you started with a cornucopia of food words.

A **comestible** (*kuh·MES·tuh·bul,* noun) is an item that can be eaten as food.

> ➤ After picking up bread, meat, cheese, and a few other **comestibles**, Deirdre was ready for the weekend-long *Three Stooges* festival.

This word, which today is used most often in a humorous or ironic sense, comes from the Latin *comedere,* which combines *com-,* "altogether," with *edere,* "to eat." Strangely, the word completely disappeared from English for about 150 years before reentering the language via French in the early nineteenth century.

Some synonyms (each of which almost always shows up as a plural) are *consumables* (*kun·SOO·muh·buls*), *edibles* (*ED·uh·buls*), *foodstuffs, viands* (*VYE·unds*), and *victuals* (*VIT·uls*). If you're talking about a supply of food, use *provisions* (*pruh·vizh·uns*) or *rations* (*RASH·uns* or *RAY·shuns*). If the comestible in question is one that sustains life (such as chocolate cake), call it *sustenance* (*SUS·tuh·nunce*). Slang terms for stuff you can eat include *chow, eats, grub, vittles,* and if the food is particularly bad, *swill.*

A **cuisine** (*kwi·ZEEN,* noun) is a style of cooking as well as the food cooked in that style.

> ➤ His local restaurant was supposed to specialize in French **cuisine**, so Sean wondered why they didn't serve french fries.

Fusion (*FYOO·zhun*) *cuisine* is a cooking style that uses techniques and ingredients from a variety of ethic or regional cuisine. *Haute* (*ote*) *cuisine* is an elaborate and highly skilled style of cooking, particularly French cooking. *Nouvelle* (*noo·VEL*) *cuisine* is a style that uses light ingredients (little flour or fat) and fresh vegetables and tries to bring out the natural flavor of foods.

An **appetizer** (*AP·uh·tye·zur,* noun) is food or drink that's served before the main meal and is meant to stimulate the appetite.

> ➤ A slow eater, Karen was only halfway through her salad **appetizer** when the waiter showed up with the main course.

A synonym is *hors d'œuvre* (*or·DURV*), a French phrase that translates as "outside work," meaning that the appetizer is "outside" of the regular meal. (In English, the word *oeuvre* (*OO·vruh*) means "an artist's body of work.") An alcoholic drink that acts as an appetizer is an *apéritif* (*ah·per·i·TEEF*).

Word Wonders

An example of an appetizer is a *canapé* (*KAN·uh·pay* or *KAN·uh·pee*), a small cracker or piece of toast covered with some kind of *savory* (*SAY·vuh·ree*, adj., "pleasing to the taste") spread or topping. Unfortunately, it's a little *unsavory* to consider that this word's origins are mosquito related! It goes back to the Greek word *konopion*, "a mosquito net," which turned into the English word *canopy*, "a curtain that encloses a bed or sofa." The French call the enclosed sofa a *canapé,* and the inventor of the above dish thought the cracker or toast acted as a kind of sofa for the topping, so—voilà!—the *canapé* was born.

An **epicure** (*EP·uh·kyoor,* noun) is a person with sophisticated tastes, especially when it comes to food and wine.

➤ Being able to tell beef stroganoff from beef Wellington and a Bordeaux from a Beaujolais convinced Dominic that he was quite the **epicure.**

This word comes from a Greek philosopher named Epicurus, who lived from 341 to 270 B.C.E. He believed that pleasure was the highest aim of human life, but he viewed pleasure as the absence of pain and difficulty. This meant that one must practice self-restraint and moderation and forego such obviously painful activities as marriage, children, and dealing with other people! His followers eventually twisted this philosophy into self-gratification and lazy indulgence, but the word gradually took on its current meaning over the past 400 years or so.

Someone with **epicurean** (adj.) tastes is also a *connoisseur* (*kon·uh·SUR* or *kon·uh·SOOR;* although this word also applies to a person with refined taste in any field) or a *gourmet* (*GOOR·may*).

See also: HEDONISM.

You use the phrase **à la mode** (*al·uh·MODE,* adj.) to describe a dish that's served with ice cream.

➤ Give her a big spoon and a piece of apple pie **à la mode** the size of her head, and Moira had her own little slice of heaven.

You Don't Say

Don't confuse a gourmet with a *gourmand* (*GOOR·mahnd* or *GOOR·mund*), a person who is merely fond of good food, often excessively so.

This is French, and its translation in that language—"in the manner or style of"—provides a second definition of the phrase in English.

A shortened form of the phrase—*à la*—is also often used to mean "in the manner or style of" (for example, "a thriller à la Stephen King"). The masculine form of à la is *au* (*oh*), and we see both used in the following adjectives:

> *à la carte* (*al·uh·KART*)—Food items in a restaurant are chosen from and priced individually on the menu.

> *à la king*—Served in a cream sauce with mushrooms and either green peppers or pimiento.

> *au fromage* (*oh·fraw·MAZH*)—Served with cheese.

> *au gratin* (*oh·GRAH·tin*)—Cooked with a light coating of grated cheese or bread crumbs.

> *au jus* (*oh·ZHOO*)—Served in its natural juices.

> *au naturel* (*oh·nach·uh·REL*)—Cooked plainly.

Verbs for Eating

Eat, drink, be merry; with these three simple verbs, you could probably construct a whole philosophy of life. In the absence of that, there's no point restricting yourself to just these three, so in this section, you'll learn lots of other action words for eating. (I discuss drinking verbs in the next chapter. You're on your own for the being merry verbs.)

To **ingest** (*in·JEST,* verb) is to take food into the body.

> ➤ Not at all hungry, but also unwilling to displease his wife, Mr. Tortellini **ingested** her spaghetti with grim determination.

If ingest feels a bit too much like something a scientist might say, there are plenty of fun alternatives including *break bread, chow down, dig in, fall to,* and my personal favorite, *strap on the (old) feedbag.* Note, too, that it's perfectly okay to use *breakfast* and *lunch* as verbs but not dinner or supper (although *sup* is okay).

To **inhale** (*in·HAYL,* verb) is to eat quickly or greedily.

> ➤ "I bent down to tie my shoe and her cake was gone by the time I straightened up, so she must have really **inhaled** it."

The idea here is that the person appears to take in food just as quickly as she takes in air when she breathes (and with about as much chewing). There must be a lot of speed-eaters around because there's no shortage of synonyms for this verb, including *bolt, gobble up, gulp down, wolf down,* and *scarf.*

To **gorge** (*gorj*) is to eat an excessive amount of food.

➤ They had PROVISIONS for three days, but Wendel **gorged** himself and ate almost everything in one sitting.

Engorge means the same thing, as do *pig out, pork out,* and *stuff your face.*

To **nosh** (*nawsh*) is to eat a light meal or a snack.

➤ Wanda would guiltily **nosh** on a pepperoni stick before going in to her vegetarian cooking class.

When eating a small meal, you may just *nibble* (*NIB·ul,* "to take small, quick, or cautious bites") at the food, and that's appropriate because nosh comes from the German word *naschen,* "to nibble." If you eat many light meals or snacks throughout the day instead of full meals, use the verb *graze* (*grayz*).

Verbs for Cooking

Cooking is one of those skills that many people can do, but very few people can do really well. My personal theory on the good-cook shortage is that cookbook instructions can be awfully hard to follow. The verbs, in particular, are a bit much. What's the difference between "blending" and "folding" or between "dicing" and "mincing"? What's all this about "parboiling" or "braising"? So, as a public service, this section runs through a few verbs that are popular in today's cookbooks.

Let's start with verbs for combining ingredients, including **blend,** which means to combine ingredients into a single substance (that is, so that the individual ingredients are no longer distinguishable).

➤ "Add one scoop each of vanilla, chocolate, strawberry, and mango ice cream, **blend,** and then enjoy."

Here are four more combining verbs to keep straight:

beat—To MIX rapidly.

fold—To combine an ingredient by gently lifting it with a spoon or other tool so that it's enclosed without being MIXED.

mix—To BLEND ingredients evenly.

whip—To BEAT into a froth or foam.

For cutting things, first consider **mince** (*mintz*), "to cut into very small pieces."

➤ "**Mince** the onion, red pepper, and mango so that they will mix easily with the hamburger meat."

Here are a few other verbs that describe various ways of reducing an ingredient to smithereens:

chop—To cut into small pieces

cube—To cut into cube-shaped pieces

dice—To cut into small cube-shaped pieces

grate—To reduce to short, thin strips or pieces

grind—To crush or reduce to a powder using friction

purée (PYOO·ray)—To rub through a sieve or strainer or put through a blender to make into a paste

shred—To cut or tear into long, thin, irregular strips

On the boiling front, to **parboil** means to cook partially by boiling.

➤ "Before barbecuing pork ribs, **parboil** them in mango-flavored water for about 45 minutes."

There are plenty more where that came from:

blanch (rhymes with "ranch")—To boil briefly

boil down—To boil until reduced in volume

fricassee (FRIK·uh·see or frik·uh·SEE)—To cut up poultry or meat and then STEW in gravy

hard-boil—To boil an egg in the shell until both the white and yolk are solid

poach—To cook in a boiling or SIMMERING liquid

scald (SCAWLD)—To bring to a temperature just below the boiling point

simmer—To cook in liquid that is just below the boiling point

soft-boil—To boil an egg in the shell until both the white and yolk are a soft consistency

stew (STOO or STYOO)—To cook by boiling or SIMMERING slowly

Finally, let's look at some frying verbs including **sauté** (*soh·TAY*), "to fry quickly using a small amount of fat."

➤ "Add a teaspoon of butter to a hot frying pan, add the chopped shallots and mango, and then **sauté** for three minutes."

Here are more verbs for frying:

braise (*BRAYZ*)—To cook by first BROWNING in fat and then SIMMERING in a covered container with only a little liquid

brown—To cook something until it turns brown

deep-fry—To cook by submerging in hot fat or oil

pan-fry—To cook in a frying pan using a small amount of fat

stir-fry—To fry quickly over high heat in a lightly oiled pan or wok while stirring continuously

Fine Word Dining: Restaurant Terms

The word *restaurant,* "a business where meals are served," comes to us from the French verb *restaurer,* "to restore." In other words, a restaurant is a place where you go to eat and drink and thereby restore your energy and good spirits (and not have to worry about all those cooking verbs from the preceding section). This section looks at a few restaurant-related words that you'll need to know when dining out.

Restaurants come in all kinds of shapes and sizes. For example, a **bistro** (*BEE·stroh* or *BIS·tro*) is a small, informal restaurant.

➤ The casual atmosphere of their neighborhood **bistro** seemed like the perfect place to tell Candice that he was going to run for president.

There are several explanations floating around about the origin of this word. One story is that, after the defeat of Napoleon in 1815, Russian soldiers hanging out in Paris would go into restaurants and shout "Vee-stra, vee-stra!" which is Russian for "Hurry, hurry!" The French took up the word as *bistro* and associated it with small restaurants where you could get a meal quickly.

If the restaurant has a good selection of beer, it may call itself a *brasserie* (*brass·uh·REE*). If it specializes in steaks or chops, it's likely a *steakhouse* or *chophouse,* and if it exists mainly to feed people's caffeine addictions, it's a *coffeehouse* or a *café* (*ka·FAY*). An Italian restaurant is commonly called a *trattoria* (*truh·TOH·ree·uh*) or, if it specializes in pizza, a *pizzeria* (*PEET·suh·REE·uh*). A cheap restaurant is a *beanery* (*BEE·ner·ee*) or *hash house,* while a cheap and sanitarily challenged establishment is a *greasy spoon.*

Restaurants have their own lingo that the rest of us would do well to learn. For example, **du jour** (*duh·ZHOOR,* adj.) is a fancy French phrase meaning "of the day."

➤ Vickie usually just ordered the daily specials, but today's soup **du jour**—cream of Cream of Wheat—didn't sound very appetizing.

Here are a few other restaurant terms you should know:

al dente (*al·DEN·tay*)—Cooked so as to be firm, not soft (particularly pasta)

alfresco (*al·FRES·koh*) *dining*—Eating outside

antipasto (*an·tee·PAS·toh*)—Italian appetizers, particularly sliced meats and marinated vegetables

blue plate special—A main course offered at a special low price

continental breakfast—A breakfast consisting of tea or coffee and an assortment of breads

plat du jour (*PLA·duh·ZHOOR*)—The daily special

prix fixe (*pree·FEEKS*)—A complete meal offered at a fixed price

table d'hote (*TAH·bluh·DOTE*)—A PRIX FIXE meal served at a specific time

Restaurants employ all kinds of people, many of whom have very strange titles. Take, for example, the **maitre d'** (*may·truh·DEE* or *may·tur·DEE*, noun), who is the head of the dining-room staff.

➤ Before starting his new job as the **maitre d'** of an upscale restaurant, Pierre spent an hour in front of the mirror perfecting a look of utter disdain.

You Don't Say

Don't confuse dessert with the verb *desert* (*di·ZURT*), "to abandon," which is pronounced identically. Another way these two words get confused is in the idiom *just deserts*, "a due punishment or reward." If this is all a bit much for you to handle, just remember that "stressed" is desserts spelled backward.

This is short for **maitre d'hotel** (*may·truh doh·TEL*), which means "master of the house." If your French accent isn't ready for public consumption, use the word *headwaiter* instead. Some other restaurant workers:

busboy (*BUSS·boy*)—A restaurant employee who clears and sets tables and assists a waiter or waitress

chef (*shef*)—The chief cook (from the French *chef de cuisine*, "head of the kitchen")

pastry chef—A cook who specializes in pastries and other desserts

prep cook—A kitchen assistant who prepares the ingredients used by the CHEF

saucier (*saw·see·AY*)—A cook who specializes in sauces

sous chef (*SOO shef*)—The cook who is second in command behind the CHEF

sommelier (*soh·mel·YAY*)—The waiter responsible for recommending and serving wine (also called a *wine steward*)

Questions and Exercises to Help Everything Sink In

Here's a list of the main words you learned in this chapter:

à la mode	appetizer	bistro	blend	comestible
cuisine	du jour	epicure	gorge	ingest
inhale	maitre d'	mince	nosh	parboil
sauté				

1. Choose the word that means "to combine ingredients into a single substance":
    a. sauté
    b. parboil
    c. blend
    d. inhale
2. Fill in the blank: "On Fridays, the sandwich _____ was halibut on rye."
3. Choose the word that did not come originally from French:
    a. bistro
    b. à la mode
    c. sauté
    d. maitre d'

Match the word on the left with the short definition on the right:

4. gorge   a. something edible
5. parboil   b. a style of cooking
6. comestible   c. cook partially by boiling
7. cuisine   d. with ice cream
8. à la mode   e. eat excessively
9. Choose the word that's a fun synonym for *ingest*:
    a. pig out
    b. graze
    c. break bread
    d. purée

10. Choose the word that's not a synonym for *inhale:*

    a. pig out

    b. wolf down

    c. scarf

    d. bolt

Chapter 8

Drink Words on Tap

In This Chapter

➤ Drinking verbs

➤ Words related to beer

➤ Words related to wine

➤ Words related to coffee, liqueurs, and whiskey

"This is one of the disadvantages of wine, it makes a man mistake words for thoughts."

—Samuel Johnson, lexicographer

I hope the food words I covered in the preceding chapter were enough to *whet* ("stimulate") your linguistic appetite. However, as with any good meal, you need to something to wash everything down with, and food for thought is no exception. This chapter does just that by examining a pitcherful of words related to drinks, including drinking verbs and words that deal with five of our favorite liquids: beer, wine, coffee, liqueur, and whiskey.

Taking a Swig: Verbs for Drinking

Drinking is as natural to us as breathing (it is, after all, one of the first things we do when we come into this world), so perhaps that's why we've come up with so many ways to describe what is, in the end, a relatively simple act.

Let's start with **imbibe** (*im·BIBE,* verb), which means to drink, particularly an alcoholic beverage.

➤ As usual on a Sunday afternoon, Helen's plan was to **imbibe** a few glasses of wine while ogling the cute butts of the football players.

The origin of this word is the Latin verb *bibere,* "to drink," which is also the source of *beer, beverage, bib,* and *bibulous* (*BIB·yuh·lus,* adj), "relating to the consumption of alcoholic drinks." Alternative verbs people use for drinking alcohol are *tipple* and, more rarely, *tope.*

To **quaff** (*kwoff,* verb) is to drink quickly or with enthusiasm.

➤ Mickey was so thirsty that he **quaffed** the entire jug of water in 10 seconds flat and then let out a loud "Aaaaah!" which greatly annoyed the other people in the sauna.

Here are some other verbs for fast or hearty drinking: *chug* (or *chug-a-lug*), *drain, gulp, swig,* and *drink like a fish.*

To **guzzle** (*GUZ·ul,* verb) is to drink greedily.

➤ Unwilling to share her precious milk with anyone, Samantha **guzzled** the entire carton so that her parents would have none to leave for that Santa Claus guy.

Word Wonders

You may be wondering if the noun SWILL (mentioned in the preceding chapter) and the verb *swill* are related. Why yes, they are as a matter of fact. "Swill" was originally the table scraps and other kitchen refuse that was fed to the hogs. That explains swill the noun ("unpalatable food"). Swill the verb comes from eating or drinking "quickly and greedily," which is what a hog would do.

You can substitute the word *swill* for the greedy downing of any liquid, but if it's alcohol that's going down the hatch, try *hit the bottle, liquor up, tank up,* or *souse.*

To **slake** (*slayk,* verb) is to satisfy a need or craving, particularly a thirst.

➤ Hot and parched after his shift at the brewery, it's ironic that Morley would choose prune juice to **slake** his thirst.

This word is almost always used as part of the phrase, *slake one's thirst*. The word comes our way via an Old English word *slacian*, "to make slack; to diminish." The more common verb is *quench* (*kwench*).

A Draft of Beer Words

I mentioned earlier that the word *beer* comes from the Latin *bibere*, "to drink," which shows, to my mind at least, that beer is an essential part of a balanced diet. (As an interesting aside, note that an even earlier form of the Latin *bibere* eventually became our words *potable*, "fit to drink," and *poisonous*, "unfit or dangerous to drink [or eat, or whatever]." It also gave us *symposium* [*sim·POH·zee·um*], "a conference for the discussion of a topic," but that word's original Latin meaning was "drinking party"!)

This section runs through a half a dozen popular beer and beer-like varieties.

Ale is a beer-like beverage brewed by slow fermentation from malt and flavored with hops.

➤ **Ale** drinkers such as Maury look down upon those who drink mere beer, although no one really knows why.

Bock (*bawk*) is a strong, dark, sweet beer that's brewed a relatively short time and is usually the first taken from the vats in the spring.

➤ In the springtime, Sonya's fancy turned to thoughts of the three b's: baseball, boys, and some wickedly strong **bock**.

Lager (*LAH·gur*) is a light, mellow beer made with a small quantity of hops and brewed by slow fermentation.

➤ While chopping down trees, Lloyd liked to keep cool by drinking a refreshing **lager** or two, hence his nickname: the **lager** logger.

Pilsener or **pilsner** (*PILZ·nur* or *PILS·nur*) is a pale-colored LAGER with a strong hop flavor.

➤ "Why," Dolores wondered, "would anyone drink a watered down, tasteless light beer when there were easy-drinking, tasty **pilseners** in the world?"

Porter is a heavy, dark brown, and bitter beer brewed using malt that has been partially charred or BROWNED.

Idiom Savant

Small beer refers to something that's trivial or unimportant. (The phrase originally referred to beer that was weak or of inferior quality.) If someone you know is goofing off or not owning up to his responsibilities, tell him that *life isn't all beer and skittles*, meaning that life isn't just a game. (In Britain, *skittles* is a game much like bowling.)

➤ Everyone was blown into the air by the hurricane-force winds except Dean, who was suitably weighed down from all the **porter.**

Stout (*stowt*) is a strong, full-bodied, dark beer or ale with a distinctive malt flavor.

➤ Knowing that their chests would be plenty hairy, Mary would only date men who drank **stout.**

There are also lots of slang terms for beer, including *amber brew, barley broth, brew, brewski* (or *brewsky*), *froth, suds,* and, *wobbly pop.*

The Message on the Bottle: Wine Words

Most people enjoy a glass of wine, but only a few go on to understand why one wine is superior to another. The problem is that the wine industry and wine CONNOISSEURS like to go out of their way to make this seem like a dauntingly complex subject. (And what's with all the spitting?) To help you get past all that, let's look at some common wine terms. My goal here is to run through the terms you're most likely to trip over when reading the label on a bottle of wine.

Let's begin with **finish** (noun), which is the taste that remains in the mouth after the wine has been swallowed. Better wines have a finish that lasts longer (*lingers* in the lingo) and exhibits multiple flavors (it's *complex*).

➤ With its lingering, complex **finish,** Erica knew her latest batch of Vin de Cul-De-Sac would be a hit with the swirl-and-spit crowd.

The finish is also called the *aftertaste.*

The **nose** (noun) is the overall smell of a wine.

➤ The wine's **nose** reminded him, not unpleasantly, of a wet dog.

Idiom Savant

Trying to put *new wine in an old bottle* is a bad thing. It means you're trying to take a new idea and fit it into an old framework that will ruin it.

The nose is actually a combination of two things:

aroma (noun)—The component of a wine's overall smell that's contributed to by the grapes and the FERMENTATION process

bouquet (*boo·KAY*, noun)—The smell of an AGED wine

The **body** (noun) is the overall texture or "weight on the tongue" of the wine in the mouth.

➤ The wine had so much **body** that Corinne thought she might actually be able to start chewing it.

Wines with a lot of body are called *full-bodied, big,* or *robust.*

Fermentation (*fur·mun·TAY·shun,* noun) is the chemical process by which grape juice combines with yeast to form alcohol.

> ➤ Vito knew the **fermentation** process was the most crucial for making good wine, but he had to admit that his favorite part was stomping on all those grapes.

Here are some other wine process terms you might come across:

> *age* (verb)—To store a bottled or barreled wine in a cellar or other suitable area until it develops its full taste and character (which may take several years)
>
> *barrel-aged* (adj.)—Describes a wine that was stored in a barrel after FERMENTATION
>
> *barrel-fermented* (adj.)—Describes a wine that went through FERMENTATION stored in a barrel

A **balanced** (adj.) wine is one that has the three major components—acids, fruits, and tannins—in a pleasing combination in which no one component dominates.

> ➤ Not too tart, not too sweet, not too bitter; yup, Valerie's Chateau Hackensack was a nicely **balanced** wine.

Here's a bunch of back-of-the-bottle words that relate to a wine's balance and taste:

> *acid* (*ASS·id,* noun)—The component that gives a wine tartness and helps it AGE.
>
> *buttery* (*BUT·ur·ee,* adj.)—Describes a wine with the taste or smell of butter or a wine that feels smooth or creamy in the mouth. (The latter quality is also described as *silky* or *velvety.* You get the idea.)
>
> *crisp* (adj.)—Describes a wine (typically a white wine) with a pleasant tartness. The opposite of SOFT.
>
> *fruity* (*FROO·tee,* adj.)—Describes a wine that has an AROMA and taste of fruit.
>
> *oaky* (*OH·kee,* adj.)—Describes a wine (such as a Chardonnay) that has received a vanilla-like scent and a woody taste from being stored in an oak barrel. The newer the barrel, the more oaky the wine.
>
> *soft* (adj.)—Describes a wine that has low acidity and is not very TANNIC.
>
> *spicy* (adj.)—Describes a wine that has spice flavors such as pepper, cinnamon, cloves, or nutmeg.
>
> *tannin* (*TAN·in,* noun)—A natural preservative found in grape skins, seeds, and stems, it provides the "bitter" component of a wine's taste.

Mixed Drinks: Miscellaneous Liquid Refreshments

To complete this chapter, this section presents some words related to three beverage types: coffee, liqueur, and whiskey.

The word *coffee* comes from the Turkish word *qahveh* (*KAH·vay*), which in turn came from the Arabic word *qahwah*, which means either "wine" or "stimulating," depending on which source you believe. One type of coffee that's gaining popularity in North America is **espresso** (*ess·PRESS·oh,* noun), which is a rich, strong coffee brewed by using steam pressure to force water through darkly roasted, finely ground beans.

➤ After his second cup of **espresso**, Harland felt like he could conquer the world and still have time left over to watch *Seinfeld*.

Espresso means "pressed out" in Italian, and this is more or less how the coffee is made. It sounds as though it means "fast," so many people mispronounce it as "expresso." Here are some other coffees that are made with espresso:

café au lait (*ka·FAY·oh·LAY*)—Espresso coffee mixed half-and-half with steamed milk and then topped with a thin layer of steamed milk froth

cappuccino (*KAP·uh·CHEE·noh*)—Espresso coffee mixed with equal parts steamed milk and steamed milk froth

latte (*lah·TAY*)—One part espresso coffee mixed with two parts steamed milk and then topped with a thin layer of steamed milk froth

A **liqueur** (*li·KYOOR* or *li·KUR,* noun) is a sweet, strongly flavored alcoholic drink made by combining a flavoring ingredient (such as fruits, nuts, or spices) and a spirit (such as brandy, rum, or WHISKEY).

➤ After dinner, Hector liked to kick back with a nice **liqueur**, a good cigar, and the sound of hacking and coughing at the nearby tables.

Here are some common liqueurs:

amaretto (*am·uh·REHT·oh*)—A rich Italian liqueur flavored with almonds.

anisette (*an·i·SET*)—A clear, licorice-tasting liqueur made with anise seeds. *Anise* (*AN·is*) is a herb that grows in the Mediterranean and produces sweet-smelling seeds.

curaçao (*KYOOR·uh·sow* or *KOOR·uh·sow*)—A liqueur flavored using the dried peel of a sour orange.

Grand Marnier (*grand MAR·nyay*)—A liqueur that combines *cognac* (*KON·yak* or *KONE·yak;* a brandy distilled from white wine) and orange extract.

Kahlua (kah·LOO·uh)—A liqueur made from coffee and clear spirits.

sambuca (sam·BOO·kuh)—An Italian liqueur made from elderberries and flavored with ANISE.

Southern Comfort—A liqueur made from BOURBON, peaches, and apricots.

Whiskey (*WISS·kee,* noun) is a strong—typically 40 to 50 percent alcohol by volume—liquor distilled from a fermented MASH of grain such as barley, corn, or rye.

➤ Crystal loved the taste of a fine **whiskey** but refused to drink it on dates because it made her, well, you know, *loose.*

Mash is crushed malt or grain meal steeped and stirred in hot water so it can ferment. The word whiskey comes to use from the Gaelic word *uisge beatha,* which means "water of life" (a fact that whiskey-lovers will no doubt appreciate). Note that, generally speaking, the spelling is "whiskey" in the United States and "whisky" in Britain. There are many different kinds of **whiskies** (plural), but here's a list of the most common ones:

blended—A whiskey combination that includes at least 20 percent straight whiskey. The remainder consists of either straight whiskey or *neutral spirits* (near-pure alcohol with no discernible taste or smell).

bourbon (BUR·bun)—A whiskey distilled from a mash that contains at least 51 percent corn plus some malt and rye.

Canadian—A whiskey distilled using a high percentage of rye as well as barley, corn, and wheat.

Irish—Usually a BLENDED whiskey in which malted barley, unmalted barley, and other grains are used.

rye—A whiskey distilled from a mash that contains at least 51 percent rye.

Scotch—A whiskey distilled in Scotland and made from malted barley as either a SINGLE-MALT or a BLENDED.

single-malt—A whiskey made only from malted barley and produced in a single distillery.

Questions and Exercises to Help Everything Sink In

Here's a list of the main words you learned in this chapter:

ale	balanced	bock	body	espresso
finish	guzzle	imbibe	lager	liqueur

nose   pilsener   porter   quaff   slake
stout   whiskey

1. Choose the alternative definition of *porter:*

   a. a bartender

   b. a baggage carrier

   c. a dock worker

   d. a snake wrangler

2. Choose the word that means "the overall texture or weight of a wine":

   a. body

   b. balanced

   c. nose

   d. finish

3. Fill in the blank: "The wine's _____ made her think of rotting leaves on Halloween night."

Match the word on the left with the definition on the right:

4. bock   **a.** beer-like beverage brewed slowly from malt and flavored with hops

5. lager   **b.** pale-colored beer with a strong hop flavor

6. stout   **c.** strong, dark, sweet beer with a short brewing time

7. ale   **d.** strong, full-bodied, dark beer with a distinctive malty flavor

8. pilsener   **e.** light, mellow beer brewed slowly with a small quantity of hops

9. Choose the drink that's not made with *espresso:*

   a. café au lait

   b. latte

   c. cappuccino

   d. Kahlua

10. Choose the word that's not a *whiskey:*

    a. rye

    b. barley broth

    c. single-malt

    d. blended

Screen Gems: Television Words

"Every word carries its own surprises and offers its own rewards to the reflective mind."

—George A. Miller, American psychologist

Television is a universe in which the old "a picture is worth a thousand words" formula is the law of the land. With its relentless focus on the visual, words get shoved into the background so they won't get in the way of the optical onslaught and its goal of ever-higher JPMs (jolts per minute). Not that this is always a bad thing. I'm sure even the most literate among us doesn't mind the occasional morsel of *eye candy* ("pleasing images"). Moreover, despite its preoccupation with imagery, TV has still managed to create quite a lexicon for itself, as you'll see in this chapter.

Words You Should Know If You're Buying a TV

It used to be that purchasing a TV was a happily simple affair. You just decided what size you could afford, plunked down the plastic, and you were watching *The Brady*

Bunch before you knew it. These days, however, buying a TV has become almost as complex as buying a computer. The problem, as is usually the case when things get complex, is the terminology. Whereas before the only crazy abbreviations and words you had to deal with were TV manufacturer names (RCA, Zenith, and so on), now they're TV feature names: HDTV, aspect ratio, horizontal resolution, and many more. To help you out, this section runs through a few of these newfangled TV terms.

The phrase everyone seems to be tossing about willy-nilly these days is **digital TV (DTV)**, television that's broadcast using a signal that chops up the images into tiny bits (called, uh, *bits*) as opposed to a signal sent using an electromagnetic wave, which is what the current *analog* sets accept.

In the United States, Congress has mandated that all stations broadcast a digital signal by 2003 and that stations must broadcast both digital and analog signals until 2006. (Canadian broadcasters expect to be 18 to 24 months behind the United States.) So a TV set that understands only analog signals should work until 2006 (and perhaps for a few years after). Eventually, however, you're either going to have to get a set that knows how to deal with digital TV, or you're going to have to get a **set-top box** that converts digital signals into something your analog TV can handle. Most digital sets can also display analog signals, so you can take the plunge anytime you like.

Your new digital set may also support **HDTV** (**high definition TV**), a new broadcast format that supports better picture and sound quality. HDTV replaces the old **NTSC** (**National Television System Committee**) sets that we've used up until now.

One of the reasons HDTV is better involves the **aspect ratio**, the width of the screen in relation to its height. NTSC has a 4:3 aspect ratio, which means that if the screen is four units wide, it's also three units tall (say, 40 inches wide and 30 inches tall). HDTV use a 16:9 aspect ratio, which is called *wide screen*. This is the same aspect ratio that's used in the movies, so that's why you often see the following disclaimer when watching a movie on TV:

> "This film has been modified from its original version. It has been formatted to fit your screen."

What they mean is that the movie has been altered so that it fits a screen with a 4:3 aspect ratio. If they didn't do this, the picture would be shrunk to fit the width of the screen, leaving black areas on the top and bottom, a format called *letterbox*. Since HDTV uses 16:9, movies are displayed in their original format, meaning they don't get chopped off on the sides to fit a 4:3 screen or squished into the letterbox display.

The other thing that HDTV improves upon is the **resolution**, which determines how sharp the picture will appear. The keys here are the *pixels* (short for "picture elements"), which are the thousands of teeny pinpoints of light that make up the picture display. Each pixel shines with a combination of red, green, and blue, which is how they produce all the colors you see.

The important figures when buying a TV are the **horizontal resolution** and the number of **scan lines.** The horizontal resolution is the number of pixels there are across the screen. The scan lines are the horizontal lines created by these pixels. The number of scan lines is also called the *vertical resolution.* Basically, the higher these numbers are, the better the picture will be.

NTSC sets have a horizontal resolution of 720 pixels, and they have 486 scan lines. This is often written as 720×486, and multiplying these numbers together, it means the set has 349,920 total pixels to display each frame. The highest quality HDTV broadcast is 1920×1080, which multiplies out to 2,073,600 pixels, or about six times the NTSC value. That, in a nutshell, is why HDTV looks so much better than NTSC. A second HDTV format is 1280×720, which is still much better than NTSC.

Other terms related to resolution that TV sales types bandy about are **interlaced scanning** (or just *interlacing*) and **progressive scanning.** Both refer to how the set "draws" each video frame on the screen. Inside the set is an electron gun that shoots a beam that runs along each scan line and lights up the pixels with the appropriate colors. With interlaced scanning, the beam first paints only the odd-numbered scan lines and then starts again from the top and does the even-numbered lines. With progressive scanning, the beam paints all the lines at once. In general, progressive scanning is better because it produces a more stable picture.

A set that supports interlaced scanning over 1,080 scan lines is called **1080i capable,** while a set that supports progressive scanning over 720 scan lines is called **720p capable.** If you see a set advertised as **HDTV capable,** it means it supports both formats.

Sound is an important component of any modern TV, so let's look at some of the audio lingo. First, **surround sound** provides more than the usual two channels (left and right) of audio information so that you feel surrounded by the sound.

There are lots of TLAs (three-letter abbreviations) in the audio world that you have to know how to interpret. First, **SRS** (sound retrieval system) improves the true-to-life qualities of the sound by extending the sound field beyond the speakers (so a sound can appear to have come from behind you, for example). **SAP** (separate—or second—audio program) is a separate audio signal (such as a translation into another language) that's broadcast along with the main audio signal. **MTS** (multichannel television sound) **stereo** accepts and decodes broadcast stereo signals.

Finally, **automatic volume control** keeps the volume at a preset level, which is handy when switching to and from commercials (which tend to be obnoxiously loud).

To close our look at words for the would-be TV buyer, here's a short list of some other jargon you may see:

> **direct view**—The picture is created directly from a picture tube within the set. These sets have the sharpest picture, but the maximum size is 40 inches.

rear projection—The picture is projected onto the back of a translucent screen. The picture isn't as sharp, but the screen can grow to 50 or 60 inches or more.

picture-in-picture (PIP)—The set has two or more tuners, one of which displays a channel on the screen as a whole, and the other(s) shows another channel in a smaller window. Some sets even support a split-screen view that shows two channels side by side.

scan velocity modulation (SVM)—The electron beam is accelerated or slowed down if the set detects sharp changes from dark to light, which gives sharper definition to those areas but may distort the picture quality (for example, a dark area on a light background may appear larger than it should).

comb filter—A doodad that separates black and white signals from color signals, giving better quality and reducing weird color patterns. A *digital* comb filter is good, and a *3D Y/C* comb filter is the best.

adaptive video noise reduction—A filter that recognizes and eliminates interference in the incoming signal, giving a cleaner and more consistent picture.

high-contrast, dark-tint—The screen has been treated so that it absorbs more ambient light and displays blacker blacks, thus improving the contrast.

The Ratings Game: TV Programming Words

Programming—putting shows on at strategic times and then getting people like you and me to watch them—is a strange science that few nonnetwork types ever really understand. In this section, I'll take you through a few words from this arcane art that may give you a better appreciation of what it's all about.

Network executives spend countless hours arranging and rearranging each show's **time slot**, which is the day of the week and hour of the day when the show is broadcast.

➤ Terry knew that 8:00 on a Saturday night was the wrong **time slot** for *Mall Cops: Life on the Escalators.*

The show immediately preceding another show is called the *lead-in.* The theory is that people are too lazy to change the channel, so the first show will lead them into the second show. Along similar lines, a time slot between two established, popular programs is a *hammock.* This is a coveted spot, particularly for a new show, because the two solid shows "support" the time slot, and any show that gets in there will just have to sit back and rake in the viewers.

Counterprogramming is when a time slot is scheduled with a program that's designed to lure or prevent people from watching another program in the same slot.

A show that's programmed to run in the same time slot every day (or every weekday) is a *strip show* or an *across-the-board show*. These are usually shows that have gone into *syndication*, which means selling old episodes for rebroadcast.

Networks pay attention to the transition from one show to another because they don't want you to *channel flip* (verb, "to use your remote to run through a number of stations to see what else is on"). A **segue** (*SEG·way,* noun) is a smooth and seamless transition from the end of one show to the beginning of the next.

➤ The **segue** from *Surfin', Cleveland-Style* to *Old People Swimming Laps* was as smooth as they come.

A *squeeze and tease* is the process of squeezing a TV show's closing credits into one third of the screen width and using the remaining space for promoting upcoming shows and events. If they don't want you leaving the current show during a commercial, they'll insert a *bumper* just before the first commercial: "*When Good Hamsters Go Bad* will be right back!"

Networks and local stations want you to know what you're watching. One way they do this is with the **station identification,** a brief segment in which the network or local station identifies itself.

Parts Dept.

Segue comes to us via the Italian word *seguire*, "to follow," which has been traced back to the Latin *sequi*, "to follow or come after."

➤ "We now interrupt *It's a Scrabble, Scrabble World* for this **station identification.**"

A local station usually identifies itself by providing its channel number and *call letters,* the four-letter symbol unique to each station. If a network program cuts away to its *affiliates* (local stations associated with the network), it's a *station break.* Many networks now display a small logo in the lower right corner of the screen, and it's called a *burn.* The last station identification of the day before broadcasting stops is called the *sign off.*

The purpose of all this is to increase **Nielsen ratings,** a measure of how many people watch a given show based on a sampling of the viewers. The sampling is done by the A.C. Nielsen Company, so that's where the name comes from. It's measured in *rating points,* where each point represents one percent of the total TV households, and in *share,* the percentage of TVs actually turned on that watched the show.

➤ The **Nielsen ratings** are in and *Who Wants to Be a Legionnaire?* generated only a 1.5 rating and a 5 share.

The period each fall, winter, and spring when the ratings are used to set advertising rates is called *sweeps* (or sometimes *sweeps week* or *sweeps month,* depending on how long they last). More informally, the people watching a given show are called *eyeballs.*

Docudramas, Infomercials, and Other TV Programs

TV programs are usually described by their general content: drama, comedy, news, documentary, variety, and so on. In this section, I tell you about a few special categories of shows.

For example, there's the **pilot**, a program created either as a prototype for a proposed new show or as the first episode of a new show.

> ➤ The **pilot** for *Mary Hart's Legs and Nothing but Mary Hart's Legs* got boring after about five minutes, so the project was cancelled.

If the pilot is successful and the show enjoys a long life, one or more characters may get their own show, called a *spin off*.

A documentary is a program that aims to present political or historical subjects in a factual manner. A slightly different take on this genre is the **docudrama**, a documentary that dramatizes certain scenes or events.

> ➤ The **docudrama** *The Secret Lives of the Maytag Repairmen* depicts paper folding, solitaire cheating, and other depraved acts of the mind-numbingly bored.

Word Wonders

Other members of the docu-mentary family are the *rocku-mentary*, a documentary about a rock band, and the *mockumen-tary*, a fictional show filmed to look like a documentary.

If the documentary's goal is purely entertainment or sensationalism, it's *docutainment*. A reality-based show that contains footage of accidents and violence is a *shockumentary*. A documentary that stalks or attempts to find a person is a *stalkumentary*.

One of the concerns that people have with modern television is the increased blurring of information and advertising or entertainment. An example is the **in-fomercial**, an ad (usually on late at night) that runs the same length as a regular program (a half hour or even an hour) and is produced so that it looks like a talk show, variety show, or documentary.

> ➤ As the two men sat there discussing chest hair implants, it was a couple of minutes before Clark realized he was watching an **infomercial**.

If the show is designed to look like a newscast, it's an *advertorial* ("advertisement" combined with "editorial"). If the newscast only discusses the entertainment industry (think of *Entertainment Tonight*), it's *infotainment* (although this term also applies to shows that are both informative and entertaining). *Newszak* is a program containing mostly fluff pieces and gossip (especially from the entertainment industry) but for-matted to resemble a news broadcast.

Situation comedies are commonly called *sitcoms,* and there are various types including the **warm-edy**, a sitcom that features warm-hearted, family-oriented content.

➤ *The Widower with the Three Unrealistically Cute Kids* was a decent **warmedy**, but the title needed some work.

A show that combines aspects of both a drama and a comedy is a *dramedy*. Note that these shows usually don't include a *laugh track,* recorded laughter played at appropriately comic moments, also called *canned laughter*. If the show is a series of *skits* ("short, comic performances"), it's a *skitcom*.

Parts Dept.

Newszak is a blend of "news" and "Muzak," the dull and inoffensive "music" piped into grocery stores, dentist offices, and elevators (hence the synonym, *elevator music*).

Kickers and Stand-Ups: Television News Terms

TV has many subcultures, and one of the things that subcultures do is create words and phrases that reflect who they are and what they do. The subculture of television news is *rife* ("abundant") with jargon words and phrases, just a few of which I present here.

I think it's appropriate that I should start with the **lead** (*leed,* noun), the first—and therefore usually the most important or sensational—story of the newscast.

➤ They had tape of the man actually biting the dog, so that story would be the **lead** in tonight's newscast.

Many news organizations try to attract a particular class of viewer by showing lots of crashes, murders, and general blood and gore. The unofficial motto of such news organizations is *If it bleeds, it leads.*

Other story genres are *hard news*—serious events of national or international significance—and *soft news*—relatively minor events of local import. The latter are also called *human-interest stories*. A short item that deals with a secondary aspect of a story is a *sidebar,* while a story that's read *verbatim* ("word for word") from a wire service item is a *rip and read*. Finally, the cute or funny story that closes many a newscast is called a *kicker*.

An individual story within a newscast is called a *segment*. Let's look at a few segment-related terms starting with **stand-up**, a portion of a segment in which the reporter stands in front of the camera and runs through a report.

➤ While Sharry did a **stand-up** in front of the White House, you could see the President behind her with his forefinger and thumb extended on his forehead to make the "loser" sign.

If the reporter walks while giving the report, it's called a *walk and talk.* If the stand-up acts as a transition from one part of the story to the next, it's a *bridge.* The newscaster's introduction to the segment is known as a *lead-in,* while the newscaster's comments after the segment are called the *tag.* Often a longer segment will require a longer tag, which is usually called an *outro* (the opposite of an intro).

Video plays a big part of any newscast. For example, it's a rare segment that runs without any **B roll**, which is video footage used to illustrate a news story.

> ➤ With the Apocalypse now underway, the producer wanted some **B roll** of what the Four Horsemen were up to.

If the footage is really just filler (such as those goofy clips of the subject walking down the street), it's called *wallpaper.* Video footage of interviews or stand-ups is called *A roll.* A *nostril shot* is unflattering footage caused by poor lighting or a bad camera angle. If the angle is from well below the subject, it's an *up-the-nostril shot.* During an interview, two popular techniques are the *reversal shot*—a clip that shows a reporter's reaction to an answer—and a *reversal question*—a clip that shows a reporter asking a question. In both cases, the shots are usually taken after the interview is over and the subject has left.

Newscasters often don't get much respect from either reporters or the technical staff, and this is reflected in the insulting lingo that's often directed their way. For example, a **twinkie** is a newscaster with an attractive physical appearance but little journalistic experience.

> ➤ "That **twinkie** needs to learn that 'perky' is not the appropriate tone when discussing a plane crash."

Another not-so-nice term is *meat puppet,* a newscaster who is the intellectual equivalent of a puppet. The *news team* consists of all the on-air personalities including the newscaster, sportscaster, and weatherperson. They're often called the *HINT*—happy idiot news team—because that's what they become when they have to fake their way through some light-hearted banter either between segments or to fill time at the end of the broadcast.

From Boob Tube to Couch Potato: TV Slang

Much of what you've seen so far would qualify as TV slang ("hammock" and "squeeze and tease," to name just two), and there are lots more where that came from, as you'll see in this section.

Probably the most common slang term for television is the **boob tube.**

> ➤ Winston would tell everyone that only idiots watch anything on the **boob tube**, but then he would go home and secretly watch *Hee Haw* for hours on end.

Here, a *boob* is used in the sense of a dumb or foolish person, which shows you what the people who come up with these terms think of TV. In fact, most of the slang terms for TV are *pejorative* ("belittling"), as you can see for yourself from the following list: *idiot box, brain drain, thought vampire, one-eyed monster, plug-in drug, vast wasteland, chewing gum for the eyes.* One of the few terms that's not an insult is *small screen* (the opposite of *big screen,* which is used for movies shown in theaters).

A **couch potato** is a lazy person who spends far too much time on the couch watching TV.

> ➤ When she decided against going out on Saturday night because they were showing 10 consecutive episodes of the *Partridge Family,* Eustace knew she'd officially become a **couch potato.**

You can also call such a person a *sofa spud.* If the couch potato is a woman, call her a *couch tomato* (*tomato* is a slang term for an attractive woman). A TV sports addict is a *spec-tater,* and a fan of a certain sitcom (or, more generally, sitcoms with sophisticated humor) is a *M*A*S*H potato.* Finally, a person who likes to watch TV while high on drugs is a *baked potato.*

A **Bambi** (*BAM·bee*) is a game show contestant or other nonactor who freezes up on-camera.

> ➤ With the woman staring wide-eyed and slack-jawed at the camera, the horrified producer realized he had another **Bambi** on his hands.

This term comes from the fact that such people are frozen *like a deer caught in headlights,* and Bambi is the name of a famous Walt Disney deer.

Almost as bad is the contestant who is *dead wood,* meaning he shows little enthusiasm or reaction to good or bad events on the show. The opposite is the *cheerleader* who is very enthusiastic and lively. Finally, the hostess who leads contestants on and off the game show set is called an *elbow grabber.*

Questions and Exercises to Help Everything Sink In

Here's a list of the main words you learned in this chapter:

1080i capable	720p capable	adaptive video noise
reduction	aspect ratio	automatic volume control
B roll	boob tube	comb filter
couch potato	digital TV (DTV)	direct view
docudrama	HDTV	HDTV capable

high-contrast dark tint	horizontal resolution	infomercial
interlaced scanning	lead	MTS stereo
Nielsen ratings	picture-in-picture	pilot
progressive scanning	rear projection	resolution
SAP	scan lines	scan velocity
modulation	segue	SRS
stand-up	station identification	surround sound
time slot	twinkie	warmedy

1. What does the "i" in *1080i capable* stand for?
2. Choose the word that means "video footage to illustrate a story":
   a. A roll
   b. B roll
   c. lead
   d. segue
3. Fill in the blank: "All stations must broadcast _____ signals by 2003."
4. Choose the word that describes how sharp a TV's picture will be:
   a. aspect ratio
   b. resolution
   c. SRS
   d. direct view

Match the word on the left with the short definition on the right:

5. segue   a. first news story
6. aspect ratio   b. family-oriented comedy
7. lead   c. a seamless transition
8. pilot   d. width versus height
9. warmedy   e. prototype show

10. Choose the word that's a longer synonym for *tag:*
    a. outro
    b. bumper
    c. spin off
    d. sign of

The Book Nook: Book and Publishing Terms

"If words, as Samuel Johnson said, are the 'dress' of rational thought, a good vocabulary is the Wonderbra of intellect."

—Hilary Bower, English professor

Authors sometimes jokingly refer to themselves as "tree-killers" because of the great numbers of trees that go into the making of their books. However, from a historical point of view, they could also get away with calling themselves "tree-makers." That's because the word *book* can be traced back to Anglo-Saxon times when scribblers used to scribble on chunks of bark from the beech tree. Their name for this tree was *boc,* and eventually that also became their name for the slabs of beech bark–based writings that they would bind together. That word eventually changed to *book* and stuck around even when the beech-bark slabs were replaced by printed pages.

To celebrate this most enduring of mediums (recent electronic book developments notwithstanding), this chapter looks at a host of book- and publishing-related words.

From Bluestockings to Bookworms: Book Folk

People tend to be passionate about books. It may be a book buff with her nose constantly buried inside some *tome* ("large or scholarly book") or a book basher with his nose constantly out of joint about the uselessness of "book learning." The language has words for book people, both pro and con, as you'll see in this section.

First up is the **bluestocking** (noun), a woman with pretentious literary interests.

> ➤ Ever the **bluestocking,** Winnifred held up her copy of *War and Peace* so that everyone on the bus could see she was reading it.

The story behind this curious word is that around 1750, a Mrs. Elizabeth Montagu, who looked down on the less-refined entertainments of the day, organized a series of get-togethers in which the object was literary conversation. Although most of the attendees were women, one regular was a man named Benjamin Stillingfleet who, rather than wearing the black silk stockings that were considered fashionable and proper at the time, wore "vulgar" blue worsted stockings. The gatherings were soon mockingly nicknamed the Blue Stocking Society, and the short form *bluestocking* has been applied to the literarily pretentious ever since.

One whose literary interests aren't mere affectation is the *littérateur* (lit·ur·uh·TUR, noun), a person who studies or writes literature. If things get out of control and the person ends up with an excessive desire to write for publication, she's a *typomaniac.*

A **bookworm** (noun) is a person who spends an exceptional amount of time reading.

> ➤ "My boyfriend the **bookworm** refused to go out with me on Saturday night," complained Hilary. "He said he was just getting to the 'good part' of *The Lord of the Rings.*"

This word is sometimes used as a mild insult hurled at *bookish* (adj., "fond of books; studious; reliant on book learning") people by antibook types. The origin of the insult is no doubt based on the *real* bookworms, which are insect larvae that feast upon the bindings and pages of books.

A **bibliophile** (*BIB·lee·oh·file*, noun) is a lover or collector of books.

> ➤ Toni knew she'd become a **bibliophile** when she could no longer remember the color of her walls thanks to all the bookshelves.

You can also call such a person a *bookwoman* or a *bookman.* If her love of books is a tad over-the-top, she's suffering from *bibliolatry* (see also IDOLATRY). If the person is cursed with an excessive desire to own or acquire books, she's a *bibliomaniac.* If she expands her collection by stealing books, she's a *bibliokleptomaniac* (or just a *biblioklept*). The opposite of all these people is the *bibliophobe,* a person who is scared of books. People who hate books so much that they destroy them are *tomecides.* (You can also use this word to describe the process of destroying a book.)

A **bookseller** (noun) is a person who sells books (no surprise there).

➤ His business plan in place, Curtis was set to become a **bookseller,** but he wasn't sure if *Throwing the Book at You* was the best name.

If the person sells rare or old books, he's a *bibliopole,* a *bibliopolist,* or an *antiquarian bookseller.*

Parts Dept.

I've thrown out lots of prefixes and suffixes in this section, so let's take a second to catch up. First, *biblio–* means "book" and comes from the Greek word *biblios,* "the inner bark of papyrus." So the root words for both *book* (mentioned at the beginning of the chapter) and *biblio–* are bark-related! The other prefix I should mention is *klepto–,* which means "thief." As for the suffixes, *–phile* means "one who is a lover of," *–phobe* means "one who fears," *–cide* means "killer," and *–pole* means "seller or dealer."

From Manuscript to Galley: Book Editing

The book you hold in your hands existed for most of its life as a relatively well-ordered collection of electrons. That is, I composed it on my computer, sent the results to my publisher electronically, and the editors whipped it into publishable shape on *their* computers. It didn't see the light of day as a physical, tangible *thing* until the printer coughed up the fully bound and ready-to-read copies.

That all-electronic process is a bit unusual in publishing (although it's becoming less so), but the basic write-it-edit-it-print-it cycle is almost as old as the printing press itself. This section looks at a few words related to this cycle.

Everything starts with the **manuscript** (*MAN·yuh·script,* noun), the author's draft of the book submitted for publication.

➤ After pulling a week's worth of all-nighters to complete the **manuscript,** Bianca staggered into bed and slept for 48 hours.

It used to be that a manuscript was a physical product such as a handwritten or typed document. Now, with computers and e-mail, it's more accurate to think of a manuscript as just the "raw text" that the author has composed.

93

Manuscript comes from the Latin phrase *manu scriptus,* "handwritten." (*Manu* is from *manus,* "hand," and *scriptus* is from *scribere,* "to write.") This phrase explains why you often see manuscript abbreviated as either *ms* or *MS* (or as *ms.* or *MS.*). The abbreviations *mss* and *MSS* (or *mss.* and *MSS.*) refer to the plural.

If the publisher didn't ask the author for the submission, it's called an *unsolicited manuscript,* and it's said to come in *over-the-transom.* (A *transom* is a small, hinged window above a door.) All such manuscripts end up in the *slush pile,* rarely to be read.

Word Wonders

Slush is a slang term for *maudlin,* "excessively sentimental," which is what many unsolicited manuscripts tend to be. One notable exception was J. K. Rowling's manuscript of the first *Harry Potter* book, which was rescued from the slush pile of a literary agent!

Once the manuscript is in the publisher's hands, the editors all have a good laugh and then set to work fixing it. For example, if the text is overly long, the editors may **abridge** (*uh·BRIJ,* verb) it, which means they'll shorten the manuscript or make it more concise.

➤ When he saw that the editor had **abridged** his 2,000-page manuscript down to 150 pages, Ernest felt as though he'd had several limbs chopped off.

This is the same as to *blue-pencil* (*bloo·PEN·SIL,* verb) a manuscript, which comes from the blue lead pencils once used to mark corrections, particularly deletions. To *redact* (*ri·DACT,* verb) is to revise or rearrange existing material for publication. To *emend* (*i·MEND,* verb) is to correct the faults in a manuscript.

To **expurgate** (*EKS·pur·gayt,* verb) is to remove obscene or otherwise objectionable material from a manuscript.

➤ Doreen didn't think "fiddlesticks" and "fuddle-duddle" were swear words, but she **expurgated** them anyway, just in case.

If the **expurgation** (*eks·pur·GAY·shun,* noun) is *prudish* ("excessively proper or modest"), the better verb is *bowdlerize* (*BODE·luh·rize* or *BOWD·luh·rize*). This comes from Dr. Thomas Bowdler, who in 1818 published *The Family Shakespeare* in which he had expurgated from the works of William Shakespeare all those words that, as he put it, "cannot with propriety be read aloud in a family."

You Don't Say

The verb *amend* (*uh·MEND*) is sometimes used interchangeably with emend, but amend has the more general sense of "to change something in order to improve it."

After the manuscript has been poked and prodded and generally made somewhat presentable, the publisher produces a **galley** (*GAL·ee,* noun), a test printing with the text typeset as it will appear in the final book.

➤ Earl's job was to take the **galley** of *A Few Geese Shy of a Gaggle* and give it the old once-over.

If the galley is given covers and a spine (that is, a BINDING), it's called a *bound galley.* (Bound galleys are often sent out as advance copies to book reviewers.) Galley is short for *galley proof,* in which a *proof* is a test sheet of printed material used for corrections and revisions, and that's generally what a galley is for. The editor who checks the galley for problems is called the *proofreader.*

The Book Look: Book Parts and Pages

With the manuscript written, edited, checked, and now (fingers crossed!) error-free, it's shipped off to the printer where it's assembled into its final form. In this section, you learn most of the components that go into that form.

The **binding** (*BINE·ding*) is the combination of materials that hold the book together, including the front and back covers, the SPINE, and the ENDPAPERS. Bindings come in two general flavors: the *hardcover* (also called *hardback, hard-bound,* or *case-bound;* the hard covers themselves are called the *boards*) and *paperback* (also called *softcover* and *paper-bound;* see also MASS-MARKET PAPERBACK).

The **spine** is the part of the book to which all the pages are glued and that, on the outside, joins the two covers and usually shows the name of the book and the author. (Books displayed on the shelf where you can only see the spine are said to be *spine out.*)

An **endpaper** is a folded sheet of heavy paper, half of which is pasted to the inside front (or inside back) cover of a book and the other half of which is pasted to the base of the first (or last) page.

A *perfect binding* is a binding in which the SIGNATURES are cut along the inside edge (called the *binding edge*), roughened along that edge, and then glued to the cover spine. (Most paperbacks are perfect-bound.) A *lay-flat binding* is a perfect binding in which the glued edges of the pages aren't joined to the cover spine; this enables the book to lay flat when opened.

A **flyleaf** (*FLY·leef*) is the blank or nearly blank page that appears immediately after the front ENDPAPER (or immediately before the back ENDPAPER). Here are some other pages that appear at the front of most books:

frontispiece (*FRUN·ti·speece*)—An illustrated page that appears before the TITLE PAGE. Also called a *front plate.*

half-title—A page that contains only the title of the book.

card page—A page listing the author's previous books, usually appearing opposite the TITLE PAGE.

title page—The page that contains the book's title, publisher's name, and the author's name.

copyright page—The page that lists the book's copyright notice, printing history, and Library of Congress cataloging data. (*Copyright* is the legal right to reproduce, publish, distribute, and sell copies of a book or other work. It's usually designated with the © symbol.)

All these pages are part of the book's **front matter**, the material that appears before the book's main text. Front matter also includes some or all of the following:

table of contents—A listing of the book's chapter titles and possibly also the main headings within each chapter.

acknowledgments (*ak·NOL·ij·munts*)—The author's expressions of thanks and appreciation for those people who helped create the book.

dedication—A note inscribing the book to another person, organization, or cause as a mark of affection or respect.

epigraph (*EP·uh·graf*)—A page that contains one or more quotations that the author uses to suggest the overall theme or spirit of the book.

foreword—An initial statement about the book, usually written by someone other than the author.

introduction—A note describing the book and usually including material about the book's goals or intentions and its structure.

preface (*PREF·is*)—A note that is similar to and shorter than, but usually appears in place of, an introduction.

Idiom Savant

The enormous role of the book in people's lives is evidenced by the sheer number of book-related idioms in the English language. I'll highlight these idioms throughout this chapter, but here are a few to get you started: *To go by the book* is to follow the rules strictly. The opposite is to *throw the book away* (or *out the window*). If someone is an expert in a field, we say she *wrote the book* on that subject.

As I'm sure you can guess, the **back matter** is the material that appears after the book's main text. The following items may appear in the back matter:

epilogue (*EP·uh·log*)—Additional notes or commentaries by the author. Also called an *afterword.*

appendix—Supplementary material related to the book's main topic.

bibliography (*bib·lee·OG·ruh·fee*)—A listing of the books, articles, and other sources consulted or recommended by the author.

glossary (*GLOS·uh·ree*)—A listing of terms used in the book along with their definitions.

addendum—Supplementary material composed after the book's initial publication and bound into a subsequent printing, usually at the back of the book.

colophon (*COLL·uh·fon*)—A short note describing facts about the book's publication materials and methods.

index—An alphabetical listing of the book's unique names, facts, ideas, and terms and the pages on which they occur.

errata (*uh·RAT·uh*)—A loose page that contains a list of the known errors in the book. This is also called an *errata sheet* or an *errata slip.* Errata is the plural of *erratum,* which comes from the Latin *errare,* "to lead astray." This root is also the source of err, error, erratic, and aberration.

Idiom Savant

To *take a leaf out of someone's book* is to perform the same actions as another person or to generally imitate that person. To *turn over a new leaf* is to reform one's conduct for the better.

A **leaf** (*LEEF*) is a single sheet in a book. Of the two pages that represent a single leaf, the one that appears on the right-hand side when the book is open is the *recto* and is usually odd-numbered (from the Latin *rectus,* "right"). The one that appears on the left-hand side when the book is open is the *verso* and is usually even-numbered (from the Latin *vertere,* "to turn").

A **signature** (noun) is a group of pages (usually 16 or 32) that have been printed on a single, large sheet, folded so that they appear in page-number order, and then cut along the inside edge for attachment to the spine.

Word Wonders

No discussion of book words would be complete without at least a mention of *blurb*, "comments or notes about the book that appear on the book's dust jacket." This fun word was coined in 1907 by Gelett Burgess, who later described the blurb as "abounding in agile adjectives and adverbs, attesting that this book is the 'sensation of the year.'" Mr. Burgess is also famous for coining a word that never caught on but certainly deserved to: *tintiddle*, "a witty retort, thought of too late."

The Business of Publishing

The business side of publishing, by which I mean the relationships between a publisher and its customers and authors, is loaded with interesting and useful lingo, as this section attests.

Up front there's the **frontlist** (noun), a publisher's collection of new or soon-to-be-published books.

> ➤ "At Self-Helpless Books, our fall **frontlist** includes the title *The Seven Habits of Highly Ineffective Couch Potatoes.*"

These books are called frontlist because they always appear at the front of the publisher's seasonal catalogs. The *backlist* (noun) is the collection of books published before the current frontlist season and still designated as *in print* (adj., "available for sale").

Whether it's a frontlist or backlist book (both terms can be used as adjectives), the publisher has to decide on a *print run,* which is the total number of printed copies of a book (also called the *press run*). To *reprint* (verb) is to send the original book back to the printer to make more copies. Publishers sometimes incorporate minor edits and corrections during a reprint. If the book requires major changes, it will usually be published as a *new edition* with a new ISBN. (*ISBN* stands for International Standard Book Number and is a 10-digit number—although the last "number" is sometimes an "X"—that uniquely identifies the book's title and publisher.)

A **mass-market paperback** (noun) is an inexpensive, small-format version of a book that's sold not only in bookstores but also in grocery stores, variety stores, and other high-volume outlets.

> ➤ The **mass-market paperback** *How to Get a $10 Haircut with a 50¢ Head* was sure to be a bestseller in barber shops and hair salons.

Such a book is also called a *rack edition* or a *pocket book.* Mass-market books are recognizable by their *trim size* (height and width), which usually is a little more than four inches wide and a little less than seven inches high.

A *trade paperback* is a SOFTCOVER edition of a book with a trim size that's larger than a mass-market paperback but smaller than a HARDCOVER. They're usually about twice the price of a mass-market title and about half the price of a hardcover. Since the paper in a trade paperback is of higher quality than a mass-market book, they're also called *quality paperbacks.* (In the publishing industry, *trade* is short for *book trade,* which means the bookstores and book clubs; that is, vendors who specialize in books.)

Idiom Savant

To be in someone's *bad (or good) books* means "to be out of (or in) favor with someone." *In my book* means "to my way of thinking," and a *closed (or open) book,* means "something about which one has little (or a lot of) knowledge."

The **discount** (noun) is the percentage the publisher takes off a book's suggested retail price when selling to a vendor (such as a bookstore).

> ➤ The fourteenth book in the *Harry Potter* series—*Harry Potter and the Oppressive Mortgage*—was sold initially at a 50 percent **discount.**

The percentage usually varies according to the quantity of books purchased, but the average is 40 to 50 percent. That's for a *long discount,* the discount given to bookstores, distributors, and other vendors who will resell the books. (A *distributor* is a wholesale company that buys books in bulk quantities, warehouses them, and then sells them to BOOKSELLERS and other retailers.) A *short discount* is the discount given to libraries, colleges, and other vendors who will not resell the books to the public. This discount is always under 40 percent.

When a book stops selling in stores, the publisher's leftovers usually become **remainders** (noun), copies of the book that are auctioned off or sold at a huge DISCOUNT.

> ➤ *Sylvester Stallone's Greatest Soliloquies* sold poorly, so no one was surprised to see **remainders** on sale for $3.99.

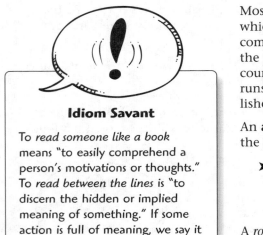

Most remainders are books that are no longer in print, which is to say they're *out of print* (or *OOP*). They also come from *overstock,* excess copies of an old book that the publisher can no longer sell at the regular discount. Overstocks are created from overconfident print runs, poor sales, or *returns,* books sent back to the publisher from vendors for full credit.

An **advance** (noun) is money the publisher pays to the author prior to the book's publication.

➤ Wilma was ecstatic to get a $5,000 **advance** until she realized that was all she had to live on for the next six months.

A *royalty* is money paid to authors, usually as a percentage of the publisher's net receipts for the books sold over a given period. (Net receipts refer to the suggested price of the book less the DISCOUNT.) A *work-for-hire* agreement means the author accepts a flat fee and assigns all rights to the book to the publisher. A *reserve* is a percentage of royalties held back by the publisher to allow for future returns.

Questions and Exercises to Help Everything Sink In

Here's a list of the main words you learned in this chapter:

abridge	acknowledgments	addendum	advance	appendix
back matter	bibliography	bibliophile	binding	bluestocking
bookseller	bookworm	card page	colophon	copyright page
dedication	discount	endpaper	epigraph	
epilogue	errata	expurgate	flyleaf	
foreword	front matter	frontispiece	frontlist	
galley	glossary	half-title	index	
introduction	leaf	manuscript	mass-market	
paperback	preface	remainders	signature	
spine	table of contents	title page		

1. In which part of a book would you include the introduction?

2. Choose the word that means "a woman with literary pretensions":
   a. colophon
   b. bluestocking
   c. bookworm
   d. galley

3. Fill in the blank: "The generous _____ meant the author could finally quit his job at Chuck E. Cheese."

4. Choose the word that best describes the materials that hold a book together:
   a. spine
   b. endpaper
   c. flyleaf
   d. binding

Match the word on the left with the short definition on the right:

5. frontlist   a. to remove obscene material
6. signature   b. new books
7. expurgate   c. the author's draft
8. manuscript   d. a voracious reader
9. bookworm   e. a group of pages

10. Choose the word that's a more prudish synonym for *expurgate*:
    a. bowdlerize
    b. proof
    c. reserve
    d. blurb

Chapter 11

The Lexical Enquirer: Newspaper Words

"I have never met a person who is not interested in language."

—Steven Pinker, Canadian psycholinguist

The writer Marguerite Duras described journalists as "the manual workers, the laborers of the word." That's no insult. On the contrary, I believe she meant that journalists have a duty to be accurate, honest, and ruthlessly truthful about the subjects they cover. This makes them wizards of the practical word, verbal artisans constructing solid, well-crafted, and occasionally even beautiful word works.

This is particularly true of newspaper journalists and their daily dealings with the people, events, and ideas that govern our lives. I'm a great admirer of newspapers and the people who run them, and I agree with the playwright Arthur Miller, who said that "A good newspaper … is a nation talking to itself." Good newspapers only rarely talk about *them*selves, but when they do, they often fall into jargon (called *journalese*) that's mysterious to the uninitiated. This chapter gives you the scoop on that jargon by running through various terms related to newspapers, editors, journalists, and their stories.

Newspaper Odds and Ends

Let's get warmed up with a few general newspaper words, beginning with **broadsheet** (*BRAWD·sheet*), the name given to a larger-format (some would say standard-format) newspaper, typically measuring 13 to 14 inches across and 21 to 22¹/₂ inches high. By contrast, a **tabloid** is a smaller-format paper, usually about half the size of a broadsheet (that is, about 10 to 11 inches across and about 14 to 18 inches high).

Parts Dept.

The *-oid* suffix in tabloid means "resembling or having the form of." Strangely, the *tabl-* prefix is short for *tablet,* one definition of which is "a small, flat pellet of medicine." It turns out that the original meaning of tabloid was a trademarked name for a pill–like medicinal substance invented and sold in the late 1800s! However, another meaning of *tablet* is "a small piece of material for writing," and that's probably where the newspaper form of tabloid came from.

Besides the difference in size, there is also a difference in journalistic philosophy and attitude between these two types. Broadsheet papers tend to be more traditional and formal, with an emphasis on current events and longer stories. Tabloids tend to be flashy and highly graphical, with a cheeky, sometimes sensational approach and a focus on local news and shorter stories.

The **nameplate** is the name of the newspaper as it appears at the top of the front page. (Why is it a "plate"? In printing lingo, a *plate* is a surface created from a page of movable type and from which the actual paper page is printed. The front-page nameplate is created from a separate plate that includes just the paper's name. Just so you know, a plate that contains a single item—such as a name—is called a *logotype*.) The nameplate is also called the *flag*.

The spaces to the left and right of the nameplate are called **ears**, and they're used for ads, the weather, jokes, or small pictures and text (sometimes called *teasers*) that point to stories inside the paper.

Within the paper, the **news hole** (or *newshole*) is the space left over after all the ads have been placed on each page. It is, in other words, the space where the news stories appear. Stories are measured by the **column inch**, which is an area of text or space that's one column wide and one inch high. The white space around each story is called **air,** and the lines you see separating stories are called **rules** (or *column rules* if they separate one column from another within a story). The white space on the inside of each page is the **gutter.**

The **editorial page** is where the paper presents its *editorials,* short articles or columns written by an editor or manager and used to outline newspaper policy or to express the opinion of the newspaper's management or ownership. The editorial page usually also includes letters to the editor and an editorial cartoon.

The editorial page is also the usual location of the **masthead** (*MAST·hed*), a box that includes the name of the paper, the names and positions of the paper's senior managers and editors, and other data such as addresses, phone numbers, and the paper's motto.

You Don't Say

Don't confuse the masthead with the NAMEPLATE, above. It used to be that the front-page title was called the masthead, which accounts for FLAG being the alternate name for the title because, on a ship, the masthead *is* where the flag *is* displayed.

The **Op-Ed** (*AWP·ed*) **page** is opposite the editorial page, and it's used for articles by guest writers and the paper's columnists, although sometimes letters to the editor appear here as well.

When the paper is done, you say it has been **put to bed** and is ready to roll off the presses. (The *bed* is the part of a printing press on which the paper lies.) The first edition that comes out is called the **bulldog edition** (or sometimes the *street edition*). (Bulldog edition can also refer to an edition of the paper printed outside of its regular schedule, but the term *extra* is more commonly used for this.)

Editors and Their Departments

An **editor** prepares a story for publication. This entails many tasks including correcting errors, revising text for better readability, checking facts, cutting text to fit the space allotted, and making sure the story adheres to the paper's *stylebook.* (The style book is a collection of rules that all stories must follow to ensure uniform treatment of things such as spelling, punctuation, capitalization, and abbreviations.) Editors also assign stories to reporters, approve (or disapprove) story suggestions, and work with reporters to develop stories. Many editors also have writing duties, which may include writing news stories, columns, or EDITORIALS.

Word Wonders

You might think that the verb *to edit* ("to prepare text for publication") came first and then the noun "editor" followed. Nope. It seems editor existed for a good 80 years before someone chopped off the "or" to create the verb. In linguistic circles, this process of creating a simpler word from a more complex one is known as *back-formation.*

The Big Kahuna of the editors is the **editor in chief,** who is responsible for the paper's overall editorial policy and its operations. She's also called the *executive editor* or sometimes just the *editor.*

Next in line is the **managing editor,** who traditionally supervises the senior editors and coordinates all the paper's editorial activities. (At some papers, the managing editor does more COPY editing than anything else.)

Below that there are all kinds of editors for sections (for example, the *sports editor*), broad topic areas (for example, the *national editor* for national news), and even individual pages (for example, the *editorial page editor* and the *Op-Ed page editor*).

We normally think of a desk as a piece of furniture with drawers and a flat top somewhere under all those papers and files. At a newspaper, however, a *desk* is a department with a specific operational focus. Here are three common newspaper desks:

copy desk—This is where *copy* ("written material intended for publication") is edited and headlines are written. A person who does this is a *copy editor* (or sometimes a *copy reader*).

city desk—This is where the *city editor* and his staff assign, write, and edit stories about local news events. It's also called the *metro desk.*

rewrite desk—This is where a reporter in the field phones in the basic facts of a story to an editor who then writes the story.

Similar to a desk, a **bureau** (*BYOOR·oh*) is a separate department that covers a specific news topic (such as a level of government) or a geographical area. (For the latter, the bureau is usually located somewhere in the geographical area.) The *bureau chief* is the editor in charge of the bureau.

Idiom Savant

If you're going to pay close attention to details, you say you're going to *dot the i's and cross the t's.* If you're going to be on your best behavior, you say you're going to *mind your p's and q's.* (This is from the printing world where the letters p and q are mirror images of each other and need to be typeset carefully.)

Newspaper Journalism and Journalists

Journalism (*JUR·nuh·liz·um*) is the gathering, writing, editing, and presenting of news stories through a medium such as a newspaper, a magazine, a radio or television broadcast, or a World Wide Web site. This diversity of media means that there are many different types of journalism and many different types of journalist. However, to keep with the central theme of this chapter, this section looks at just newspaper journalism and journalists.

Word Wonders

The origin of yellow journalism goes back to a newspaper called the *New York World,* in which a cartoon strip called "The Yellow Kid" featured a child in a yellow dress. This was in the late 1800s, so it was one of the first times color had been used in a newspaper. At the time, the paper was also printing sensational and exaggerated stories about Spanish atrocities against rebels who were fighting Spanish rule in Cuba. It was these stories combined with the yellow print gimmick that produced the term yellow journalism.

Yellow journalism is a sensational form of newspaper journalism that exaggerates or distorts the news to create publicity and increase circulation.

This is similar to **sensationalism** (*sen·SAY·shuh·nuh·liz·um*), the attempt to increase reader interest by arousing an intense but usually short-lived emotional response, often by using *lurid* ("shocking or gruesome") details. Newspapers that make their living on these kinds of stories are called the **gutter press.**

If this sensationalism is focused on exposing misconduct and corruption in prominent individuals or institutions, it's called **muckraking** (*MUK·ray·king*).

Investigative (*in·VES·tuh·gay·tiv*) **journalism** provides in-depth coverage of a news story, often involving the uncovering of previously hidden or unknown information. This is usually considered the highest form of the journalist's craft.

Anniversary journalism covers the anniversaries of important events. This type of coverage is often scorned because it rarely deals with current events.

Civic (*SIV·ik*) **journalism** solicits increased citizen feedback and then uses this feedback to attempt to frame public debate in ways that are reflective of people's concerns. (This is also known as *public journalism*.)

Horse-race journalism is coverage that focuses on poll results and political battles instead of policy issues. The increased scrutiny given to the candidate who is currently ahead in the polls is sometimes called *frontrunneritis* (*FRUNT·run·ur·eye·tis*).

The standard title for a newspaper journalist is **reporter.** If the reporter covers news in an area away from the newspaper's head office, she's a **correspondent** (a *foreign correspondent* if the news is outside the country).

Idiom Savant

A *source* ("a person who supplies information related to a story") can tell a reporter that some or all of their conversation *is off the record,* which means "not for publication." (If the source just doesn't want to be identified, the conversation *is not for attribution.*) Information that's okay to publish *is on the record.*

A **cub reporter** is a young reporter or a reporter who is just starting out. (*Cub* is the name given to the off-spring of certain animals such as wolves, lions, and bears.)

A **stringer** is a reporter who freelances or only works part-time for the newspaper. He usually covers only a specific subject or geographical area and is most often paid by the COLUMN INCH. (This also gives the origin of the word: To get paid, the reporter would paste all his clippings together to form a string, and an editor would measure the string to find the total number of column inches.)

The press as a whole is sometimes called the **fourth estate.**

A **beat** is a reporter's regular area of coverage, usually either a topic (such as crime or national politics) or a geographical area. CUB REPORTERS are often given **general assignment,** which means they cover a variety of areas. **Bummer beat** is journalists' slang for an assignment covering a tragic news story such as a murder, accident, or natural disaster.

See also BEAT SWEETENER.

Word Wonders

In Britain, the three "estates of the realm" are the Lords Spiritual (senior bishops who sit in the House of Lords), the Lords Temporal (peers who sit in the House of Lords), and the elected members of the House of Commons. A story has it that a British parliamentarian from the eighteenth century named Edmund Burke once pointed to the reporters' gallery and called them "a Fourth Estate more important far than they all."

Thumbsuckers and Tick-Tocks: Words for News Stories

Although most newspapers contain a variety of writing—including columns, editorials, and commentaries—the *news story* is the essence and the bulk of what a newspaper does. It makes sense then that there are many different types of stories, and I'll tell you about some of them in this section.

An **exposé** (*eks·poh·ZAY*) is a story that reveals (exposes) hidden corruption or a scandal. It's often written in the format of a **feature** (*FEE·chur*), a major article that provides timely coverage of a topic with a focus on either the background of the story or the human-interest angle. If the topic is particularly large, it might be called a **thumbsucker** (or, less colorfully, a *think piece*). This type of story should be distinguished from **hard news,** a shorter story that provides a factual account of a current news topic.

A **tick-tock** is a news story that recounts events in chronological order. This type of story is often a **notebook dump,** an article that is dense with facts but light on story, as though the writer simply copied everything that was in his notebook.

Any good reporter's day is made if he comes up with a **scoop,** a major story discovered and published before any other paper. A scoop sometimes falls under the category of **muffin choker,** a bizarre or unbelievable news story. This comes from the reaction one would supposedly have after reading about such a story in the morning newspaper.

It's a bad reporter who writes a **puff piece,** a flattering, noncritical profile of a public figure. If the profile is written by a reporter whose regular beat includes coverage of that person, it's a **beat sweetener.**

Newspapers have many smaller stories scattered around their pages. For example, a **sidebar** is a secondary story that appears alongside a larger story and provides supplementary or supporting details or facts. It's also called a *shirt tail.* A **reefer** (*REE·fur*) is a small article on the front page of a newspaper that refers the reader to a larger story inside the paper. A **squib** (*skwib*) is a short news item used to fill in space in the NEWS HOLE. (You can also called such a story a *filler.*) A **brite** is a light-hearted or humorous story. An **obit** (*OH·bit*), short for *obituary* (*oh·BICH·oo·air·ee*), is a notice of a person's death, often accompanied by a short biography of that person. Many newspapers keep *canned obits,* prewritten obituaries of prominent, living people.

The *really* bad reporter might write a **Danny Boy,** a news story or column that contains fabricated data. Writing such a story is called **piping.** Either way, it usually leads to a **retraction,** a short notice that corrects an error made in a previously published story.

Idiom Savant

A person who is a problem or causes trouble is often described as *bad news*. If a person becomes newsworthy, we say he has *hit the papers* or *made the headlines*. If it's favorable, he's gotten *good press*; if it's unfavorable, it's *bad press*. (Although public relations types will tell you that "there's no such thing as bad press," meaning that any publicity is good publicity.) If someone tells you something trivial, a good sarcastic rejoinder is to say, "*I'll alert the papers.*" *Stop the presses* means "hold everything because some important new information has just come up."

The Anatomy of a News Story

Newspaper stories seem simple enough, but they're actually composed of many different parts, the goal of most of which is to help the reader make it from start to finish.

The start of any story is the headline, of which there are several different varieties. For example, a **banner** is a large, front-page headline that extends the width of the page. This is also called a *streamer* (although this can also apply to a large headline anywhere in the paper that doesn't quite span the width of the page). If the banner runs across the page above the NAMEPLATE, it's a *skyline*. If the headline is sensational, it's a **screamer**, and it's usually composed in **Second Coming type**, an extremely large type size.

You Don't Say

Some newspapers use the ancient spelling "lede" instead of "lead," for reasons that remain mysterious. Stick with "lead."

A **deck** is a sentence or two that appears below the headline and gives a slightly longer description of the content of the story. A **kicker** is a word or short phrase that appears above the headline.

The **byline** is the name of the reporter or reporters who wrote the story, and it's often accompanied by the **dateline**, which includes the place from which (and occasionally the time when) the story originated.

The **lead** (*LEED*) is the first paragraph or two of the story, the purpose of which is usually to outline the central idea of the story (in which case it's called a *hard lead*; in contrast, a *soft lead* uses an anecdote or other device to arouse the reader's interest).

Following the lead is usually the **nut graph,** a paragraph that details the story's main themes (it's also called a *focus graph*). In journalese, *graph* (or sometimes *graf*) is short for "paragraph."

A **subhead** is a heading that's smaller than a regular headline but larger than the article text and that appears throughout the article to identify sections or just to break up a long article. A special type of subhead is the *run-in head,* which consists of the first few words of a paragraph, usually formatted in bold type.

A **pull quote** is a quotation culled from the story and displayed in larger type as a way of breaking up the text and catching the reader's attention. A pull quote is often a **money quote,** a quotation from a SOURCE that perfectly captures the essence of the story.

To **jump** (verb) is to continue a story on another page. The **jump line** is text that appears at the bottom of a column that directs the reader to jump to the remainder of the story.

Thirty, written as "-30-" marks the end of a story.

Newspaper photos have their own parts. For example, the **caption** is text that appears underneath a photo and describes the content of the image. It's also called a *cutline.* If a small headline appears above the caption, the headline is called a **catchline.** An **overline** is a heading that appears above a photo. Finally, the **credit line** is text that identifies that photographer who took the picture or the organization that supplied the picture. -30-

Questions and Exercises to Help Everything Sink In

Here's a list of the main words you learned in this chapter:

air	anniversary journalism	banner	beat
beat sweetener	brite	broadsheet	bulldog edition
bummer beat	bureau	byline	caption
catchline	city desk	civic journalism	column inch
copy desk	correspondent	credit line	cub reporter
Danny Boy	dateline	deck	ears
editor	editor in chief	editorial page	exposé
feature	fourth estate	general assignment	gutter
gutter press	hard news	horse-race journalism	investigative journalism
journalism	jump	jump line	kicker
lead	managing editor	masthead	money quote

muckraking	muffin choker	nameplate	news hole
notebook dump	nut graph	obit	Op-Ed page
overline	piping	puff piece	pull quote
put to bed	reefer	reporter	retraction
rewrite desk	rules	scoop	screamer
Second Coming type	sensationalism	sidebar	squib
stringer	subhead	tabloid	thirty
thumbsucker	tick-tock	yellow journalism	

1. What is the standard unit of measurement in a news story?

2. Choose the word that means "a department that covers a specific news topic":

    a. beat

    b. copy desk

    c. bureau

    d. correspondent

3. Fill in the blank: "When she found out the congressman was out of town during the drug bust, the editor knew they'd have to print a _____."

4. Choose the type of journalism that provides in-depth coverage:

    a. investigative

    b. horse-race

    c. civic

    d. anniversary

Match the word on the left with the short definition on the right:

5. stringer		a.	story that reveals corruption
6. exposé		b.	regular area of coverage
7. bulldog edition		c.	short news story
8. beat		d.	freelance reporter
9. squib		e.	first papers printed

10. Choose the word that's a specific type of *ear:*

    a. teaser

    b. filler

    c. extra

    d. obituary

Part 3
Lexiconomics: Words from the Economy

Did you ever take a class called "home economics" in school? If so, then, at least etymologically speaking, you would have been well within your rights to just call it "economics." That's because the word economy comes from the Greek word oikonomos, which combines oikos, "house," with nemein, "manage." When this word first drifted into English about 500 years ago (as "yconomie"), it meant "the management of a household, especially the household finances." Over time, the word branched out and became not only economical, "thrifty; efficient," but also the economy, "the production and management of material wealth in a country or area." It's this latter sense that we celebrate here in Part 3. These four chapters take you through words related to job titles, business, economics, money, and the stock market.

Chapter 12

Words at Work: Job Titles and Professions

In This Chapter

➤ Some general words for occupations

➤ Business titles

➤ Jobs from the movies

➤ Names for the jobs that tradespeople do

➤ Titles for doctors and other medical types

"Don't use words too big for the subject. Don't say 'infinitely' when you mean 'very'; otherwise you'll have no word left when you want to talk about something really infinite."

—C. S. Lewis, British novelist

At cocktail parties and receptions, the second most popular question (after "Where's the bar?") is "So what do *you* do for a living?" We're fascinated by other people's occupations, probably because most of us spend a good 40 or 50 percent of our waking lives on the job. In that sense, your work defines a big chunk of who you are (which may be a scary thought for some people), so it's a good place from which to launch a conversation with a total stranger.

Unfortunately, not all jobs are immediately recognizable by their titles. If someone says he's a writer or a secretary or a bullfighter, you pretty much know what he does all day. But if he calls himself a chief technology officer or a wainwright or a gastroenterologist, you may not be so sure. This chapter takes a look at some words related to occupations. After a short look at some general terms, I then cover job titles in business, the movies, the trades, and medicine.

General Job Jargon

Let's kick things off on an easy note by looking at a few nonspecific words related to jobs.

A **vocation** (*voh·KAY·shun,* noun) is a regular occupation, especially one to which a person is particularly well suited.

➤ Rip and grin, rip and grin. It all came so naturally to Gwen that she knew "movie theater ticket-taker" was the **vocation** she'd been searching for.

Word Wonders

I also talked about some restaurant-related jobs in Chapter 7, "A Few Food Words to Chew On," TV news jobs in Chapter 9, "Screen Gems: Television Words," and newspaper editors in Chapter 11, "The Lexical Enquirer: Newspaper Words."

This word goes back to the Latin verb *vocare,* "to call." An earlier (Middle English) version of the word was *vocacioun,* which meant "a divine calling to a religious life." The word took on a more general sense over the years, but the word *calling* is still a synonym. Any job for which one is well suited is called a *métier* (*meh·TYAY* or *may·TYAY,* noun). More generally, if you have a talent or skill that you consider to be your strong point, call it your *forte* (*FOR·tay* or *fort*).

Blue-collar (*BLOO·kawl·ur,* adj.) describes manual laborers, industrial workers, or any wage earner whose job requires wearing work clothes.

➤ As a **blue-collar** guy, Archie felt it was important to ask the manicurist to leave the dirt under his fingernails.

The opposite, in a sense, is *white-collar,* which describes nonmanual laborers, especially office workers. The collar color (or material) of some jobs has become a whimsical way of describing certain workers. Here are a few such words:

dog-collar worker—A graphic artist or designer. (So-called because, at least from a management point of view, most artists and designers have a vague or overt "punk" look, which stereotypically includes the wearing of a dog collar.)

open-collar worker—A person who works at home.

pink-collar worker—A female executive.

steel-collar worker—A robot used in manufacturing.

You Don't Say

Don't confuse vocation with *avocation,* a hobby or side occupation pursued for enjoyment. In this case, the *a-* prefix mans "away from," so this word literally means "to call away from."

An **intern** (*IN·turn,* noun) is an advanced student or recent graduate working under supervision to gain practical experience.

➤ When the medical **intern** first saw the emergency room, she said, "Blood!? No one told me there would be *blood!*"

In the trades or professions, such a person is called an *apprentice* (*uh·PREN·tis,* noun). In some cases, the apprentice is under legal obligation to work for an employer for a specified amount of time in return for instruction in a trade or business.

The word **emeritus** (*i·MAIR·uh·tus,* adj.) describes a person, especially a professional, who is retired from active service but who retains the title used before retiring.

➤ Tal Forehead, professor **emeritus** from Wiseacre University and now full-time gardener, had the curious habit of addressing his plants as "Mister" or "Miss."

This word comes our way via the Latin *emereri,* "to earn by service."

Gaffers, Grips, and Best Boys: Movie Workers

The film's just ended, and you're sitting there wondering why on earth they ever let *Saturday Night Live* cast members make movies. But then your attention is drawn to the credits crawling up the screen, and here comes the usual cast of show business characters: the *gaffer,* the *key grip,* the *clapper-loader,* and everybody's favorite, the *best boy.* You think "Who the heck are these people, and what exactly is it that they do?"

It's a distressingly common scenario, so it's time to end the mystery and explain what these and other movie workers do to earn their paychecks.

The **best boy** is the GAFFER's assistant and is in charge of the other electricians (called *juicers* in the biz) and the electrical equipment. Sometimes the best boy is given the longer title *best boy electrician* to differentiate him from the *best boy grip,* who is the KEY GRIP's assistant and is in charge of the other GRIPS and the grip equipment. In both cases, the best boy's job is to find out what the film needs in terms of people and equipment and then make sure those needs are met. Most best boys are men, but there are some female best boys, and they'll sometime use the title *best girl* instead.

The **cinematographer** (*sin·uh·muh·TOG·rah·fur*) is responsible for the overall look of the movie. To get the look he wants, he sets up the lighting for each scene, chooses the lenses and film for the cameras, and helps the DIRECTOR frame each shot. This person may also be called the *director of photography* (or DP, for short).

The **clapper-loader** has two jobs. The "clapper" part means she operates the *clapboard,* which is a small board that displays data identifying each shot, including the working title of the movie, the scene and take numbers, and the date and time. It has a hinged stick on top that she "claps" down to start each take, which is used to help synchronize the audio and video. The "loader" part means she also loads film magazines into the camera (although this job is often given to the *film loader* or the *assistant cameraman*).

117

The **director** (*di·REK·tur*) oversees all the creative aspects of the movie by guiding the actors, consulting with the writer, selecting the camera angles, and translating the script scenes into the film's images.

The **dolly grip** is the GRIP responsible for handling the *dolly*, which is a wheeled vehicle that run on tracks and holds the cameras and the camera crew.

The **focus puller** is the member of the camera crew that adjusts the focus of the camera during shooting.

The **Foley** (*FOH·lee*) **artist** integrates special sound effects (such as footsteps, creaking doors, or punches) into the movie's soundtrack. *Foley* is the craft of creating such sound effects. Both terms are named after Jack Foley, a movie sound pioneer who added the first music and sound effects to movies in the 1930s.

Word Wonders

If you ever see the name Alan Smithee listed as the director of a movie, chances are the movie was downright awful. That's because Alan Smithee (or sometimes Allen Smithee) is the name that a director uses in place of his own when he realizes that he's made an absolute turkey of a film and doesn't want his real name anywhere near it.

The **gaffer** (*GAF·ur*) is the head electrician and the person responsible for gathering, placing, and directing the movie's all-important lights. The gaffer reports directly to the CINEMATOGRAPHER.

A **grip** is a person who moves equipment, especially lights, and sets up camera supports such as scaffolding. Grips are also used as general handypersons and will tackle any odd job that crops up. There's an old saying in the movie business that "if no one else will do it, a grip will." Reflecting this can-do philosophy, the term *extra hammer* refers to a standby grip who helps out as needed.

The **key grip** is in charge of all the grips and reports to the CINEMATOGRAPHER.

The **location scout** spends her day looking for sites that would be suitable for individual scenes.

The **producer** arranges the financing of a film and then supervises the production of the film from start to finish.

The Corporate Ladder: Some Top Business Titles

If you've ever seen an *organization chart* (a tree-like graph that shows the relative positions of each employee in a company; often shortened to *org chart*), then you know the titles used by elite executives and corporate officers. But what do these titles really mean? You'll find out in this section.

Starting at the top, the **CEO** (*SEE·ee·oh*) is the chief executive officer. She's the highest-ranking executive and the person responsible for the overall administration of the company and for carrying out the policies dictated by the BOARD OF DIRECTORS. Here are some other "C-something-O" abbreviations:

> **COO** (*SEE·oh·oh*)—The chief operating officer; the executive responsible for all of the company's day-to-day operations. The PRESIDENT usually holds this title.

> **CFO** (*SEE·eff·oh*)—The chief financial officer; the executive responsible for all of the company's financial operations.

> **CTO** (*SEE·tee·oh*)—The chief technology officer; the executive responsible for all of the company's computer and technology operations.

The **board of directors** is a group of people who are elected by the company's shareholders and who collectively manage the company's operations. The day-to-day responsibility for these operations is usually *delegated* ("officially given to") the CHAIRPERSON. The board also appoints the company's top-level management team, including the CEO and PRESIDENT.

The **chairperson of the board** is the company's top corporate officer and is responsible for all of the company's high-level affairs. The chairperson (or *chair* or *chairwoman* or *chairman*) is appointed by the BOARD OF DIRECTORS and presides over their meetings. The chairperson is also usually the CEO.

The **president** (*PREZ·uh·dunt*) is the second-highest ranking corporate officer (behind only the CEO) and is the one responsible for running the company day to day. The president is usually also the COO.

The **controller** (*kun·TRO·lur*) is the executive responsible for the company's accounting activities.

You Don't Say

You'll occasionally stumble upon the word *comptroller* (for example, the comptroller general of the United States) and may be tempted to pronounce it *komp·TROH·lur*. Don't! It's pronounced exactly the same as controller, and it means the same thing as well. Why does comptroller even exist, in that case? To answer that, you first need to know that controller comes from a combination of the Latin *contra*, "counter," and *rotulus*, "roll." That *is*, the original controllers kept a "counter-roll" to double-check the accounting. However, *contra* became *compte* in French, and some overly ZEALOUS scribe thought controller ought to be spelled comptroller.

Here are a few general words to describe businesspeople:

A **proprietor** (*pruh·PRY·uh·tur*) is a person who owns or operates a business.

You Don't Say

Some people pronounce magnate exactly the same as *magnet*, so don't get them confused.

A **rainmaker** (*RAIN·may·kur*) is an executive with an excellent record of bringing in new clients and generally increasing sales and profits. This word was originally used for the member of a tribal community who would use (or would claim to use) magic to bring rainfall, which would help the crops grow and bring prosperity to the tribe.

A **magnate** (*MAG·nayt* or *MAG·nit*) is a rich, powerful, and influential businessperson. You can also call such a person a *tycoon* (*tye·KOON*).

See also NABOB, MOGUL.

Smiths, Wrights, and Other Tradespeople

A *tradesperson* is someone who is proficient in a job that requires a particular skill (such a job is called a *trade*). They're the people who build, maintain, and repair most of the stuff you see around you. This section celebrates these indispensable members of our community by talking about what they do.

In general, a **wright** (*rite*) is a person who constructs or repairs something. This comes from the Old English word *wyrhta*, which means "worker; maker." You don't usually see wright on its own, however. It's usually preceded by the object that the person builds or works on. Here are some examples: *boatwright, bookwright, candlewright, gatewright, playwright, plowwright, shipwright, tilewright,* and *wheelwright.* Here are a few more that aren't so obvious:

> *cartwright*—A person who builds or repairs carts and wagons.
>
> *millwright*—A person who builds or repairs mills and mill machinery.
>
> *pitwright*—A person who builds or repairs mine equipment.
>
> *wainwright*—A person who builds or repairs wagons.

A **smith** is a person who works with metal, but it can also be a person who makes a particular thing. Once again, you rarely see smith flying solo. Instead, like WRIGHT, it has the noun for whatever metal or thing the smith works with riding up front, as in these examples: *anvilsmith, arrowsmith, bladesmith, boilersmith, clocksmith, coppersmith, goldsmith, gunsmith, hammersmith, ironsmith, knifesmith, locksmith, metalsmith, sawsmith, scissorssmith, silversmith, stonesmith, swordsmith, tinsmith,* and *toolsmith.*

Here are some that aren't as clear-cut:

blacksmith—A smith who works with iron, which is also known as *black metal*.

songsmith—A person who writes the music or lyrics (or both) for songs. You can also call such a person a *songwriter* or a *songster*. If the person writes popular music, she's a *tunesmith*.

whitesmith—A smith who works with tin, which is also known as *white metal*.

wordsmith—A skillful and *prolific* ("abundantly productive") writer. This also applies to a word expert or to someone who forges new words.

Here's a list of some other tradespeople you should know:

A **boilermaker** makes or repairs boilers.

A **bookbinder** makes book BINDINGS.

A **brazier** (*BRAY·zhur*) works with brass.

A **cabinetmaker** makes finely crafted wooden furniture.

A **chandler** makes or sells candles. This comes from the Latin *candela,* "candle," which is also the source of *chandelier.*

A **cobbler** makes or repairs shoes.

A **cooper** makes or repairs wooden barrels and casks.

A **die maker** makes *dies,* devices used to cut, shape, or stamp material.

A **glazier** (*GLAY·zhur*) makes glass and cuts and fits glass for installation.

A **joiner** is a CABINETMAKER who specializes in constructing furniture by joining pieces of wood (which is called *joinery*).

A **miller** operates or owns a mill.

A **steeplejack** constructs or maintains steeples or chimneys.

A **stonecutter** cuts or carves stone.

A **stonemason** builds structures using stones.

A **tanner** tans animal hides (that is, he converts them to leather by treating them with tannin).

A **tinker** is a traveling craftsman who mends household utensils such as pots, pans, and kettles.

Idiom Savant

The phrase *not worth a tinker's damn* means "useless or worthless." One explanation of this curious phrase is that the original tinkers apparently swore a lot, so a single curse didn't mean much. Others believe it's a corruption of *tinker's dam,* a wall (that is, a dam) made of dough or clay and placed around a spot where the tinker needed to pour solder. This dam would then be thrown away once the solder dried.

Medicine Men and Women

To close this look at occupations, this section runs through a long list of professions from the medical community.

An **anesthesiologist** (*AN·is·thee·zee·OL·uh·jist,* where the "th" is the same as in "thin") is a physician who studies the theory and practice of *anesthesia* (*AN·is·thee·zee·uh*), the total or partial loss of sensation in some part of the body. In this case, the patient's anesthesia is induced by breathing in or being injected with an *anesthetic* (*AN·is·thet·ik;* an example is nitrous oxide, otherwise known as laughing gas). See also -LOGIST.

An **anesthetist** (*uh·NES·thuh·tist*) is a person who specializes in administering anesthesia to a patient before surgery.

An **audiologist** (*aw·dee·OL·uh·jist*) studies hearing and evaluates and treats hearing disorders. The prefix *audio-* means "hearing."

A **cardiologist** (*kar·dee·OL·uh·jist*) studies the heart and diagnoses and treats heart problems. The prefix *cardio-* means "heart."

A **chiropractor** (*KYE·ruh·prak·tur*) manipulates the spinal column and other body structures to improve the functioning of the nervous system. This word combines *chiro-,* "hand," with the Greek *praktikos,* "practical."

A **dermatologist** (*dur·muh·TOL·uh·jist*) studies the skin and provides a diagnosis and treatment of skin disorders. The prefix *derma-* means "skin."

A **gastroenterologist** (*gas·troh·en·tuh·ROL·uh·jist*) studies the digestive system (including the stomach and intestines) and diagnoses and treats digestive disorders. This word includes *gastro-,* "stomach," and *entero-,* "intestine."

A **gerontologist** (*jer·un·TOL·uh·jist*) studies the aging process and diagnoses and treats age-related diseases. The prefix *geronto-* means "old age."

A **gynecologist** (*guy·nuh·KOL·uh·jist*) provides routine physical care for, and treats the diseases of, the female reproductive system See also GYNO-.

A **homeopath** (*HOH·mee·uh·path*) treats a disease by administering small doses of drugs that in much larger amounts would produce the symptoms of the disease. This word combines *homeo-*, "similar," with *-path*, "practitioner."

An **internist** (*in·TUR·nist*) is a specialist in *internal medicine,* the diagnosis and nonsurgical treatment of diseases related to the body's internal organs.

A **naturopath** (*NAY·chur·uh·path*) treats a disease not with drugs or surgery but with natural remedies such as diet, massage, and sunshine.

A **neurologist** (*noo·ROL·uh·jist*) studies the nervous system and the brain and evaluates and treats nervous system and brain disorders. The prefix *neuro-* means "nerve."

An **ob-gyn** (*OH·bee·jee·why·EN*) is an OBSTETRICIAN-GYNECOLOGIST.

An **obstetrician** (*ob·stuh·TRISH·un*) cares for women during pregnancy, childbirth, and the recuperation period after delivery. This word is built from the Latin *obstare*—which combines *ob-* "opposite" and *stare*, "to stand"—and the suffix *-ician,* "skilled person."

An **ophthalmologist** (*off·thul·MOL·uh·jist*) studies eyes and provides the diagnosis and treatment of eye-related diseases. The prefix *ophthalmo-* means "eye."

An **orthodontist** (*or·thuh·DON·tist,* "th" as in "thin") examines teeth for irregularities and prescribes corrective measures (such as braces). The prefix *ortho-* means "straight," and the fragment *dont* means "tooth."

An **orthopedist** (*or·thuh·PEE·dist*) prevents and corrects injuries and diseases of the skeleton and its attached muscles, ligaments, and joints. The *ped* part means "child," which comes from the fact that this type of physician used to work only on children.

An **osteopath** (*AWS·tee·uh·path*) views diseases as being caused by problems in the muscles

Word Wonders

There are many nicknames for medical practitioners. Here are a few of my favorites: *baby catcher* (OBSTETRICIAN), *bonesetter* (ORTHOPEDIST, especially an orthopedic surgeon), *gasser* (ANESTHESIOLOGIST), *blade* or *sawbones* (surgeon), *plumber* (UROLOGIST), and *shadow gazer* (RADIOLOGIST).

and skeleton (the *musculoskeletal system*) and treats the diseases by manipulating those parts and administering conventional remedies (such as surgery or drugs). The prefix *osteo-* means "bone."

An **otolaryngologist** (*oh·toh·lair·ing·GOL·uh·jist*) studies the ear and throat and evaluates and treats ear and throat disorders. The word combines *oto-,* "ear," and *laryngo-,* "larynx" (the upper part of the windpipe).

An **otorhinolaryngologist** (*oh·toh·rye·noh·lair·ing·GOL·uh·jist*) studies the ear, nose, and throat and evaluates and treats ear, nose, and throat diseases. Here, *rhino-* means "nose."

A **pediatrician** (*pee·dee·uh·TRISH·un*) studies and treats childhood diseases.

A **periodontist** (*pair·ee·uh·DONT·ist*) treats diseases related to the bones, tissue, and other structures that surround and support the teeth. The prefix *peri-* means "around; enclosing."

A **podiatrist** (*puh·DYE·uh·trist*) studies the foot and evaluates and treats foot-related injuries and diseases. The prefix *pod-* means "foot."

A **radiologist** (*ray·dee·OL·uh·jist*) studies the theory and practice of using x-rays and other radioactive substances in the diagnosis and treatment of diseases. The prefix *radio-* means "radiation."

A **urologist** (*yoo·ROL·uh·jist*) studies the urinary tract and provides diagnosis and treatment of urinary tract diseases. The prefix *uro-* means "urine."

Questions and Exercises to Help Everything Sink In

Here's a list of the main words you learned in this chapter:

anesthesiologist	anesthetist	audiologist	best boy
blue-collar	board of directors	boilermaker	bookbinder
brazier	cabinetmaker	cardiologist	CEO
CFO	chairperson of the board	chandler	chiropractor
cinematographer	clapper-loader	cobbler	controller
COO	cooper	CTO	dermatologist
die maker	director	dolly grip	emeritus
focus puller	Foley artist	founder	gaffer
gastroenterologist	gerontologist	glazier	grip

gynecologist	homeopath	intern	internist
joiner	key grip	location scout	magnate
miller	naturopath	neurologist	ob-gyn
obstetrician	ophthalmologist	orthodontist	orthopedist
osteopath	otolaryngologist	pediatrician	periodontist
pharmacologist	podiatrist	president	producer
proprietor	radiologist	rainmaker	smith
steeplejack	stonecutter	stonemason	tanner
tinker	urologist	vocation	wright

1. Choose the word that describes a manual laborer:
    a. grip
    b. blue-collar
    c. wright
    d. chiropractor

2. Choose the tradesperson who makes leather:
    a. tanner
    b. chandler
    c. cobbler
    d. cooper

3. Fill in the blank: "Roberta's brought in 10 new clients in two weeks. She's quite a _____."

4. Choose the doctor who works with the brain:
    a. cardiologist
    b. neurologist
    c. podiatrist
    d. urologist

Match the word on the left with the short definition on the right:

5. magnate   a. brass-worker
6. gaffer   b. well-suited work
7. vocation   c. teeth-straightener
8. brazier   d. wealthy and powerful businessperson
9. orthodontist   e. head electrician

125

10. Choose the word that's a type of grip:

   a. dolly
   b. extra hammer
   c. apprentice
   d. tradesperson

Chapter 13

Terms from Business and Economics

In This Chapter

➤ Words from economics

➤ Words for business practices

➤ Business finance terms

➤ Words from the new economy

"You must bring out of each word its practical cash-value, set it at work within the stream of your experience."

—William James, American psychologist and philosopher

With all the newspapers and magazines I read and all the news shows I watch on TV and listen to on the radio, I think I do a pretty good job of keeping *abreast of* ("up to date with") the latest developments in the world. One thing I've noticed over the past few years has been the slow but steady increase in the amount of coverage given to business stories. Now it seems that MERGERS, profit reports, stock movements, and other business-related news has become just plain, old *news*.

What I find truly brow-furrowing about this is that the reporters and newscasters who bring us these stories seem content to toss out all kinds of business lingo without so much as a how-do-you-do. Apparently, they just expect us to know what the NATIONAL DEBT is or what the MONEY SUPPLY is all about. As an antidote to this business monkey business, this chapter takes you through a few of the common economic- and business-related terms that you might come across in your media travels.

Supply-Siders and Keynesians: Words and Phrases from Economics

Economics has been called "the dismal science," and I'm sure there's many an economics undergraduate who would agree with that sentiment. It's a discipline that exults in reducing complex human interactions into soulless graphs and equations, all of which assume, laughably, that "people act rationally." Well, dismal or not, our society spends a heck of a lot of time talking about economic concepts, so let's see if we can knock some sense into some of them.

I'll begin with **supply-side economics**, which holds that government policies—such as removing regulations and lowering tax rates, especially for corporations and high-income earners—lead to a greater incentive to invest, which boosts productivity and stimulates economic growth (an increase in the supply of goods), therefore increasing income throughout the system.

A person who believes in this theory is called a *supply-sider,* and he might also call this *trickle-down economics.* (Note, however, that the latter's more general meaning is that the more governments can do to help businesses flourish and be profitable, the more those profits will trickle down to the rest of the economy.)

Reaganomics—the economics as practiced during the administrations of U.S. President Ronald Reagan—was a combination of supply-side economics, reduced government spending on social programs, increased government spending on the military, and a restriction of the MONEY SUPPLY.

The opposite argument is *demand-side economics,* which says that a portion of the overall demand for goods and services is controllable by the government. So during severe economic downturns (too little demand), the government should institute policies that boost demand; during overheated economic booms (too much demand), the government should institute policies that decrease demand. This is also called *Keynesian economics*, which is named after the economist John Maynard Keynes who championed these ideas in the 1930s.

Idiom Savant

The word "business" does big business in the idiom trade, and I'll run through some of them in this chapter. To get you started, there's *to mean business,* "to have serious intentions," and *mind your own business,* "attend to your own affairs and keep out of mine."

The **inflation rate** is the percentage increase in the price of goods and services over a period of time, usually one year. The *consumer price index* (CPI) measures inflation by tracking the cost over time of a "basket" of basic goods and services that includes certain foods, housing, electricity, and transportation. This is also called the *cost of living index.* This brings us to the term *cost of living allowance* (COLA), which is an annual increase in wages that matches the increase in the inflation rate.

If prices go down, it's called *deflation* (or sometimes *disinflation*).

There are actually a number of different types of inflation, including *stagflation,* a high rate of inflation combined with a stagnant economy. (Normally, high inflation and economic growth go together.) Since poor economic growth usually means a high unemployment rate, stagflation always leads to a high *discomfort index,* the combined rates of inflation and unemployment.

Creeping inflation is a small but persistent increase in inflation, and *galloping inflation* is a sudden, quick, and uncontrollable rise in inflation. If things get totally out of hand, you end up with *hyperinflation,* in which the country's currency essentially becomes valueless.

Fears of inflation lead to a fixation on the **money supply,** the total supply of money in the country's economy at a given time.

Monetarists are economists who believe the money supply is the most important economic statistic. To see why, you need to know the fundamental rule of economics: *Supply and demand* determines the market price of a product. *Supply* is the total amount of a product available, and *demand* is the amount of the product consumers are willing to buy. If supply exceeds demand, manufacturers drop the price so that they can sell their inventory. If demand exceeds supply, the price rises because people are competing for the product. Eventually, the price settles at a point where supply and demand are balanced, and that price is "what the market will bear."

Idiom Savant

To have *unfinished business* is to have a score still to be settled with someone. To have *no business* doing something or being somewhere is to have no right to do that or be there.

Monetarists believe that more money in the system means the supply of money exceeds the demand, so prices—that is, interest rates—go down. (You get the same result if you force interest rates down: the money supply will increase.) This means that investment increases and the economy is stimulated. If there is less money in the system, demand exceeds supply, so interest rates rise and the economy slows down. So a monetarist will tell you that you can regulate the economy by changing the money supply. This *monetary policy* has two basic forms:

> *Tight monetary policy*—Increasing interest rates and reducing the money supply (for example, by issuing *bonds*—a loan in the form of certificates that are purchased with the guarantee that the money will be repaid with interest—so that the money is returned to the government). This policy is designed to slow down an economy that appears to be growing too fast and so the risk of excessive inflation is high.

129

Loose monetary policy—Decreasing interest rates and increasing the money supply (for example, by paying off BONDS so that the money is returned to the economy). This policy is designed to stimulate economic activity and decrease unemployment.

The ideal is to create a *soft landing* for the economy, meaning that it doesn't fall into a *recession.* This is an extended decline in the country's economic output, generally defined as two consecutive *quarters* (three-month periods) of decline in the *gross domestic product.* (The GDP is the total market value of all the goods and services that a country produces in a year. Add the money that the country's residents make in the year from foreign investments, subtract the money that foreigners make in domestic investments, and you have the *gross national product*—the GNP.) An extended recession is called a *depression.*

There is much talk from politicians these days about the **budget surplus,** which is the amount by which the government's tax revenues exceed its expenditures. If, on the other hand, the government spends more than it takes in, it has a *budget deficit.* To finance that deficit, the government borrows money from the public, for example, by issuing *bonds.* A bond is a form of debt in which the government is given a sum of money and agrees to pay back that money—the PRINCIPAL—along with some interest at a specified time.

The *national debt* is the sum of all the budget deficits. That is, it's the total amount of PRINCIPAL the government still owes to bondholders.

Word Wonders

Grubstake goes back to about the mid-1800s when it was used to mean a supply of food (otherwise known as *grub*) and other equipment that a wealthy investor would give to gold prospectors in exchange for a share of whatever gold was found.

The Business of Business

The day-to-day operations of businesses may be more in the open now, but that doesn't make many of them any less mysterious. In this section, you'll get the scoop on some of the words that seem to be on everyone's lips these days.

Many businesses begin with an investment of **venture capital,** money provided to new businesses or to small businesses with innovative ideas. *Venture capitalists* (*VCs*) invest in firms that can't get money from a bank or by selling shares to the public (more on this in a second). This is usually because the business is just too new, too small, or its ideas too risky. In return for taking a chance on the business, the VCs get a portion of the company and some role in managing the company.

Most VC money goes to new businesses, which are called *startups.* However, sometimes a startup's money comes from a wealthy individual, who is called an *angel investor.* The initial money provided to a startup is also called *seed money* or a *grubstake.*

Once the business gets going, its main goal is probably to increase its **market share**, the percentage of the total sales of a product, service, or industry attributable to a single company.

One way companies do this is by building their *brand*, which is a distinctive name, symbol, or catchphrase that uniquely identifies a company or product. If the brand is officially registered with the government so that its use is legally restricted to the company, it's a *trademark* (and is denoted with the ™ symbol). If the company has a unique invention, it can apply for a *patent,* which gives it the exclusive right to make, use, and sell the product for a certain amount of time. (See also COPYRIGHT.)

If the company wants to grow, one way to do so is by **acquisition** (*ak·wuh·ZISH·un*), the purchase of another company using cash, borrowed funds, or shares. If borrowed money is used (especially if the collateral for the loan is the assets of the company to be purchased), it's called a *leveraged buyout* (LBO).

If the assets of the purchased company are fully integrated into the buying company, it's called a *merger*. If the two companies are (or, I guess, were) competitors with similar products or services, then it's a *horizontal merger*. If the purchased company is a supplier for the purchasing company, it's a *vertical merger*.

An acquisition or a merger is also known as a *takeover,* and they come in two flavors: A *friendly takeover* occurs when both companies agree to the acquisition; a *hostile takeover* occurs when the company to be purchased is against the deal. In this case, the company may seek out a *white knight,* an individual or business that the management of the besieged company would prefer to make the purchase. Alternatively, the company may create a *poison pill,* a tactic that makes the company less attractive to a hostile bid. For example, it might issue stocks that give SHAREHOLDERS the right to cash in their SHARES at an increased value after the takeover.

Idiom Savant

A bankrupt company that no longer exists is said to have gone *belly–up.*

When a company can no longer pay the debts it owes to its creditors (that is, it's *insolvent*), it declares **bankruptcy**, which is a court proceeding in which the company's remaining assets are sold off (*liquidated*) and the proceeds used to pay off the creditors as far as possible. The company is then off the hook for any remaining debts.

Rather than liquidating its assets, the company can go into *receivership,* which means it reorganizes and is run by a court-appointed trustee who manages the assets to best protect the creditors. Alternatively, the company can file for a *Chapter 11* bankruptcy, which enables the company's existing management to work with creditors to reorganize. (Chapter 11 is a section of the U.S. Bankruptcy Code.)

Business Finances: From Balance Sheet to Cash Flow

Businesspeople just love to bandy buzzwords about (see Chapter 14, "Business Buzzword Buster," for lots of examples), and most of them are pure gobbledygook. However, one area that *sounds* like gobbledygook but really isn't is business finance. This stuff is jargonish in appearance, but there's some sense lurking underneath everything, particularly for anyone looking to invest in stocks or corporate bonds. This section helps you out by looking at business finances from the point of view of three important reports: the balance sheet, the profit and loss statement, and the cash flow statement.

A **balance sheet** is a summary of a company's financial condition on a particular date. The "balance" part means that the report shows that the company's "assets" equal the sum of its "liabilities" and "equity":

> A company's **assets** are the items it owns that have monetary value. *Tangible assets* include cash on hand, bank accounts, *accounts receivable* (invoices that customers have been sent but have not yet paid), product inventory, furniture and equipment, vehicles, real estate, and so on. *Intangible assets* include TRADEMARKS, PATENTS, and *goodwill* (the company's reputation, BRANDS, employee morale, and relationships with the customers and community).

> A company's **liabilities** are the debts that it owes. *Current liabilities* are debts that must be paid within one year, and they include credit card charges, government taxes owed, short-term loans, and *accounts payable* (invoices that the company has received but not yet paid). *Noncurrent liabilities* are debts not due to be paid within one year. These might include long-term loans, mortgages, and bonds.

> The difference between the company's assets and its liabilities is the **equity** or *net worth* of the company. This equity is composed of two things: the money invested in the company by the owners (including the SHAREHOLDERS) and the retained EARNINGS.

The idea of "earnings" brings us to the second report, the **profit and loss statement**, which tells you whether the company made or lost money over a specified period of time. The P&L (as it's familiarly known) is also called the *income statement* or the *earnings report*. By whatever name, it's composed of three values:

> The company's **revenues**, which are the total number of dollars the company received during a given period for the goods and services it provided. (Also known as *sales*.)

> The company's **expenses**, which are the operating costs such as rent, payroll, utilities, and supplies, and the longer-term costs such as *depreciation* (an allowance for the loss in value of an asset; in each year, you expense the total

cost of the asset divided by the number of years of usable life you expect from that asset).

The company's **earnings,** which are calculated by subtracting the expenses from the revenues. Other names for the earnings include *income* and *bottom line.* If the company made money, the earnings are called *profits,* and the company is said to be *in the black;* if the company lost money, the earnings are called *losses,* and the company is *in the red.* (Since the earnings always fall on one side or the other, why isn't it called a profit *or* loss statement?) Finally, once the company pays its taxes, what's left is called the *net earnings.*

Oh, and the *retained earnings* that I mentioned earlier are the net profits that remain in the company after the DIVIDENDS have been paid.

The final (and, to some people, the most important) report is the **cash flow statement**, which measures how cash has moved into and out of the company over a period of time. The cash flow statement essentially shows the company's NET EARNINGS plus DEPRECIATION, AMORTIZATION, and other noncash charges against income. Why is cash flow so important? Many analysts don't trust the earnings number because it's possible to manipulate it, but a company can't hide how much cash it has. The old saying is that "profits are a matter of opinion, but cash is a matter of fact." Also, cash is important because that's what the company uses to pay its employees, suppliers, and SHAREHOLDERS (DIVIDENDS).

New Words from the New Economy

When humans begin any new enterprise, it almost seems as though the first thing they do is form some kind of committee to come up with a few dozen new words specifically designed to confuse the heck out of everyone else. The new economy is no exception because it seems to generate new words and phrases on the hour, and they can be real mind-benders.

A good example is the phrase **new economy** itself. What does it *really* mean? It seems that any person you ask has a different answer, but a good basic definition is "an economy where the fundamental units of production are information and knowledge and where technology plays a central role in both generating and harnessing that information and knowledge." With that in mind, this section looks at a few other new economy terms.

One of the most popular terms is **e-commerce,** which is the buying and selling of goods and services over the Internet. Don't confuse this with *e-business,* which is the conduct of business over the Internet, including buying, selling, marketing, and distribution.

You can also use e-business to refer to an Internet-based business, although *dot com* may be the more common term (*netco* is another). If the business is an Internet-based retail operation, call it an *e-tailer.*

Along similar lines, a **clicks-and-mortar** (adj.) business is one that combines an online e-commerce operation (the "clicks" part) with a traditional retail operation (the "bricks" part). This phrase is based on the old phrase *bricks-and-mortar,* which describes something that has a physical presence in the real world (as opposed to a virtual presence in the online world). Bricks-and-mortar is often abbreviated as BAM, so the Internet version of a traditional bricks-and-mortar retailer is sometimes called a *dotbam.*

Lots of new economy companies specialize in **disintermediation,** the trend towards direct interaction between consumers and producers, which reduces or eliminates the need for intermediaries such as wholesalers, retailers, brokers, and agents. This is also called *friction-free capitalism* because it helps buyers and sellers find each other easily, interact directly, and perform transactions with only minimal overhead costs. Of course, the Internet is so huge and the possibilities so complex that we're now seeing intermediaries making a comeback to help people sort through all the data. Not surprisingly, this process is called *reintermediation.*

A special type of e-commerce is **B2B** (adj.), which stands for business-to-business and describes transactions in which one company sells a service or product directly to another company. There are many variations on this theme:

B2C—Business-to-consumer; describes transactions in which a company sells a service or product to a consumer.

B2B2C—Business-to-business-to-consumer; describes transactions in which a business sells a service or product to a consumer using another business as an intermediary.

C2C—Consumer-to-consumer; describes transactions in which a consumer sells a service or product directly to another consumer. This is also called *P2P,* short for *peer-to-peer.*

C2B2C—Consumer-to-business-to-consumer; describes transactions in which a consumer sells a service or product to another consumer using a business as an intermediary.

Finally, **globalization** is the trend towards a worldwide, interconnected economy made possible by rapid advancements in communications and transportation and the removal of trade barriers. A related idea is *glocalization,* the creation of products or services intended for the global market but customized to suit the local culture.

Questions and Exercises to Help Everything Sink In

Here's a list of the main words you learned in this chapter:

acquisition	assets	B2B	balance sheet
bankruptcy	budget surplus	cash flow statement	clicks-and-mortar

134

disintermediation	earnings	e-commerce	equity
expenses	globalization	inflation rate	liabilities
market share	money supply	new economy	profit and loss statement
revenues	supply-side economics	venture capital	

1. Choose the word that wouldn't be found on a *balance sheet:*

    a. liabilities

    b. equity

    c. market share

    d. assets

2. Choose the word that means "dollars received for products and services sold":

    a. equity

    b. revenues

    c. market share

    d. money supply

3. Fill in the blank: "_____ prescribes lower taxes and decreased regulation to stimulate the economy."

4. Choose the word that's not related to the *new economy:*

    a. e-commerce

    b. disintermediation

    c. budget surplus

    d. globalization

Match the word on the left with the short definition on the right:

5. liabilities   **a.** increase in prices

6. disintermediation   **b.** operating costs

7. inflation rate   **c.** revenues exceed expenditures

8. expenses   **d.** direct transactions

9. budget surplus   **e.** debts owed

10. Choose the word that's not related to the others:

    a. recession

    b. money supply

    c. goodwill

    d. soft landing

Chapter 14

Business Buzzword Buster

In This Chapter

➤ Buzzword verbs such as empower, grow the business, and incent

➤ Buzzword nouns such as paradigm shift, low-hanging fruit, and synergy

➤ Buzzword adjectives such as mission-critical, 24/7, and win-win

"Obscurity is the refuge of incompetence."

—Robert A. Heinlein, American novelist

Back in 1994, the cartoon *Dilbert* (that dead-on deflator of business stupidity and pretentiousness) ran a strip in which one character offered another a "buzzword bingo" card as they were entering a meeting. He explained that if the boss uses a buzzword listed on the card, it gets checked off, and the goal, as in regular bingo, is to get five in a row. A couple of years later, a programmer named Tom Davis created a little application that would create random buzzword bingo cards. He handed out the cards to his colleagues, and before long, the game spread like wildfire. *The Wall Street Journal* ran a front-page story about the game in 1998, and it became a full-fledged phenomenon.

Buzzword bingo is appealing not only because most business meetings are deadly dull, but also because you get the feeling that most of the people spouting these buzzwords are doing it only to sound important. (That is, in fact, the definition of a *buzzword*: "an often-used word or phrase that sounds more important than it really is, used primarily to impress other people.") My goal in this chapter is to run through an alphabetical list of some common buzzwords and show you what they really mean.

Buzzwords I: "24/7" to "Buy In"

24/7 (adj., pronounced *twenty-four seven*) describes something that's open or available all the time; that is, 24 hours a day, 7 days a week.

➤ "We're having so many problems with the new electric moustache waxers that we need to keep Customer Service running **24/7**."

If the thing is open on holidays as well, you can make sure people know this by using *24/7/365*, which means "24 hours a day, 7 days a week, 365 days a year." (It's up to you if you want to change this to 24/7/366 during leap years.)

An **action item** (noun) is a task or to-do list item that requires immediate attention.

➤ "So we're all agreed that agenda item #3, 'Purchase office espresso machine,' is an **action item**?"

A manager will often ask someone to *take ownership* of an action item (or any project), which means the employee takes full responsibility for the completion of the item (as well as for its success or failure!). Some gung-ho workers are *proactive,* which means they deal with the item in advance or anticipate a problem and take steps to prevent it. Such a person is called a *team player* because he works well within the system and is focused on helping the company as a whole (as opposed to just advancing his own career.)

The **big picture** (noun) is the overall view of something, as opposed to its details.

➤ Barricaded in his office with his mutinous employees outside threatening bodily harm, Carlson wondered if he'd been too focused on the **big picture**.

If you want to see the details instead, then you *drill down* (verb).

To **buy in** (verb) is to commit wholeheartedly to an idea or proposal.

➤ "Dinkins, I need to you to **buy in** to this 'underwater hairdryer' concept so that you can sell it to our customers."

Idiom Savant

Seeing *the forest instead of the trees* is the same as seeing the big picture. If you drill down and find that an idea or concept is missing some details, then you say you have to *put some pants on it.*

Idiom Savant

An employee who becomes a firm believer in the goals of the company is said to have *drunk the Kool-Aid.* (This is a reference to the 1978 "Jonestown massacre" in which members of the Peoples Temple cult committed suicide by drinking cyanide-laced Kool-Aid.)

You can also *get on board* (verb) the idea or proposal. If you want other people to buy in or get on board, then you must first *champion* the idea, which means you fight strongly for it.

Buzzwords II: "Core Competencies" to "Exit Strategy"

A company's **core competencies** (noun) are those skills, products, or areas of knowledge that the company excels in and that are central to its business. When you hear a company say it wants to "focus on our core competencies," this is a sure-fire sign that the company is struggling because it has had its fingers in too many pies. It wants to turn things around by concentrating on just its best pies.

> ➤ "After two years of unsuccessfully trying to sell rubber pantyhose, we need to focus on our **core competencies** of dollhouse doorstops and wheelbarrow tires."

This is the same thing as saying a company wants to *leverage its* ASSETS. Similarly, *best practices* are those techniques and skills that employees use to get good results (close the sale, work more efficiently, and so on). "Implementing best practices" means that the company educates the rest of the staff so that they, too, can use these skills.

Customer relationship management (noun; usually abbreviated as CRM) is the practice of keeping current customers by keeping them happy. This means nurturing relationships with customers by providing them with goodies such as top-notch service and easy access to information about products.

> ➤ "The average time spent on hold is 47 minutes!? Sounds like we need to implement some **customer relationship management**."

The theory behind CRM is that it's easier (and costs less) to sell to an existing customer than to a new customer, so a company should never lose a customer. CRM also focuses on a company's best customers since they generate most of the revenue. This is the basis of the *80/20 rule,* which states that 80 percent of a company's sales come from 20 percent of the customers. Finally, the goal of CRM is to increase the company's *mind share* with each customer. This is based on MARKET SHARE, and it loosely means the percentage of time the customer thinks about your company instead of your competitors. If you can get your customers to think of your business first, then your company is said to be *top-of-mind.*

Idiom Savant

To *open the kimono* is to open a company's accounting books for inspection or, more generally, to expose something previously hidden.

The modern manager seeks to **empower** (*em·POW·ur*, verb) her employees, which means she gives them responsibility for projects and the authority to make the decisions necessary to be successful.

➤ Brimson wanted to **empower** O'Donoghue, so she gave him control of the entire "tin foil handkerchief" project.

On a broader scale, empowering means giving people tools and information that help them reach their full potential. If the **empowerment** (*em·POW·ur·munt*, noun) takes the form of making it easier (or even possible) to perform a particular task, then it's called *enabling* (*en·AY·bling* or *en·AY·bul·ing*) or *facilitating* (*fus·SIL·uh·tay·ting*). (A person who does this is called an *enabler* (*en·AY·blur* or *en·AY·bul·ur*) or a *facilitator* (*fus·SIL·uh·tay·tur*). The opposite, in a sense, is *raising the bar,* which means boosting the minimum expectations or standards that an employee must meet to complete a task or to be considered successful. (This idiom comes from track and field. In the high jump and pole vault events, the bar that the jumper must clear is raised in each round.)

An **exit strategy** (noun) is a plan of action to be put into effect when it's time for the company to leave a project or venture.

➤ When the time came to get out of the deal with Square Screw Industries, Burns knew they needed a better **exit strategy** than "lock all the doors and take the phone off the hook."

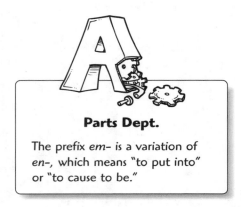

Parts Dept.

The prefix *em–* is a variation of *en–*, which means "to put into" or "to cause to be."

The exit strategy may be executed in the normal course of business (that is, the company planned to use it all along), or it may be forced upon the company in the event that the project turns sour. When planning the exit strategy, smart managers will run through a project's expected sequence of events, and they'll consider the sequence that leads to the most unfavorable outcome. This is called the *worst-case scenario.* More generally, the verb *net out* refers to how things are going to wind up in the end, so it's similar to *net result.* In both case, the "net" part is a reference to NET EARNINGS, which is the profit you end up with when all expenses and taxes have been paid.

Buzzwords III: "Going Forward" to "Litmus Test"

The phrase **going forward** (noun) means moving ahead from some current situation. It has elements of both time and progress to it. That is, the company is here now, then it goes forward, and it ends up not just in the future but also improved in some way.

➤ "**Going forward,** we here at Rickles, Inc. must strive to reduce customer insults by a full 50 percent!"

The goal going forward might be a *go-date,* a date on which a product, service, or project will be launched. If the product or service will have some kind of "audience" (that is, customers, suppliers, or other employees who will use it), then you can also say that the go-date is when you *go live* with it. The time between the original idea for the product or service and its go-date is the *time to market.*

To **grow the business** (verb) is to make the business bigger in some way, including increasing REVENUES, getting more MARKET SHARE, adding customers, reinvesting PROFITS to expand operations, or adding new businesses by ACQUISITION.

➤ Needham, disgusted with his measly six-figure salary, knew he had to **grow the business** if he hoped to get into the seven-figure range.

If the company has success in an area, it is said to have *traction* (that is, it's no longer *spinning its wheels*). This is similar to saying that an idea or project has *legs,* meaning that it has the ability or momentum to advance (go forward!) on its own.

To **incent** (*in·SENT,* verb) means to offer a reward as a way of motivating an employee or customer.

➤ "Do you think the offer of a lifetime supply of our nonslip ski wax will **incent** customers to visit the new store?"

This verb was invented by chopping off the last three letters of the noun *incentive,* "a reward that motivates." You won't find it in many dictionaries, but businesspeople just love it. They also love *incentivize,* which means the same thing but has double the syllables (see also MONETIZE). Note, too, that incent will occasionally be used in the sense of threatening a punishment to induce a particular behavior. The alternative here is the verb to *disincent* (which, again, is nonstandard).

Idiom Savant

To *put wood behind the arrow* means to provide a product or company with money and other resources. Similarly, to *put skin in the game* means to take an active interest in a company or undertaking by making a significant investment or financial commitment.

A **litmus test** is a test in which a single factor is used to determine the action taken. (This phrase comes from chemistry, where the litmus test tells you how acidic or alkaline a solution is.)

➤ Winthorp's pogonophobia (fear of beards) meant that the presence of facial hair was her **litmus test** for hiring new male employees.

141

A similar phrase is *smell test,* a metaphorical test used to determine the legitimacy or authenticity of a situation (from the idea of smelling food to see if it has gone bad). That is, if something doesn't "pass the smell test," it means you have your suspicions about it. Then there's the *reality check,* which tests an assumption or theory by plugging in real-world numbers or concepts to see if it still works as expected.

Buzzwords IV: "Low-Hanging Fruit" to "Paradigm Shift"

A **low-hanging fruit** (noun) is a task that's easily accomplished, an opportunity that's easily seized, or a goal that's easily met. The idiomatic idea here is that if you come across a fruit tree, the easiest fruits to pick are the low-hanging ones because you don't have to stretch or get a ladder.

> ➤ "Let's consolidate the e-mails of the people begging to buy our product and pluck that **low-hanging fruit** first."

These sorts of tasks are also called *easy pickings.* A truly lazy employee may go for a *low-lying fruit,* which is an even easier to task or goal. (In this case, you're supposed to think of fruit lying around on the ground so that you don't even have to go to the bother of picking it.) If you're given various options to choose from and you choose only the best ones (for example, the easiest, most prestigious, and so on), then you're *cherry picking* (and, to pile on the fruit metaphors, these choices are described as *plum* jobs, or assignments, or whatever).

Idiom Savant

An aggressive company's mission statement might have the goal of being on the *leading edge* of a trend or movement. This means the company is at the forefront of that trend and so is in a position to influence the trend or take best advantage of it. In technology circles, the leading edge is a sharp one that can hurt a company if it makes a wrong move (such as relying on new and untested technology or going with a company that doesn't last). In this case, the forefront of the trend is called the *bleeding edge.*

Mission-critical (adj.) describes something that is indispensable for the proper functioning of a company, department, or product.

➤ With his business in ruins, Newman realized the turning point was when he put the **mission-critical** Web site in the hands of that kid who said he could "build ya one real purty-like."

Something that's mission-critical absolutely must exist or the *mission*—the overriding goal or purpose of the company, department, or product—will fail. Any modern company absolutely loves to have a mission, so much so that its managers will spend endless hours in meetings coming up with a *mission statement*, a declaration of the essential purpose, goals, and philosophy of the company.

To **monetize** (*MON·uh·tize,* verb) is to calculate the cash value of something.

➤ "We've got to **monetize** the amount of time our employees are spending on the Internet looking at dirty pictures."

Monetize also means "to get money out of something." This can be as simple as selling something ("Let's monetize our chastity belt division") or cashing in an investment ("I'm going to monetize the SHARES I have in Teflon Brake Pads Ltd."). A similar verb is *productize,* which means to take an existing research project or idea and turn it into a product that can be sold to customers.

A **paradigm** (*PAIR·uh·dime*) **shift** (noun) is a radical change in the assumptions, theories, models, and beliefs that form the basis of how something is done.

➤ Harvey Luddite, president of Head-in-the-Sand Typewriters, Inc., knew the Internet was a **paradigm shift** in business sales and marketing but couldn't figure out how to apply it to *his* business.

Parts Dept.

Business types and other jargon-spouters just can't seem to resist turning nouns into verbs by sticking the suffix *-ize,* "to cause to become," on the end. There's nothing inherently wrong with this. In fact, it's been a common method of constructing verbs over the centuries: baptize, civilize, humanize, politicize, and hundreds more. Problems arise when the new verb is ambiguous. Monetize is a good example because its meaning depends on the context: Is it the cash value or the cash itself? You get the same this–or–that ambiguity with many other new "-ize" words, including securitize, strategize, and prioritize.

143

This is probably the most famous business buzzword, and it's likely the most mocked as well because it tends to be used incorrectly. That is, managers trying to sound impressive will use it for relatively trivial changes in their business environment. Always remember that a paradigm shift is something big that forces a company to rethink most if not all of the ways it does business. Note, too, that if a particular item—an external or internal force or a piece of information—causes the shift, that item is the called a *change agent*.

Buzzwords V: "Solution Provider" to "Win-Win"

A **solution provider** (noun) is a technology company that offers software and/or hardware packages that are customized to solve specific problems faced by each customer.

➤ "As a **solution provider** in the fields of photocopying and electrified fences, we think we've come up with a way to prevent your employees from photocopying body parts."

This is one of those phrases that has pretty much become meaningless thanks to overuse. Part of the problem is that the underlying idea is ridiculously broad in scope. After all, how many companies invest in new software or hardware *without* the goal of solving a problem? Therefore, isn't *every* software and hardware company a solution provider by definition? The key to keeping this a useful phrase (if that's still possible) is to remember that *real* solution providers provide a package with one or both of the following characteristics: It combines different software and/or hardware components, and it's customized for the customer. In this context, note that this package is often called a *solution*. If you're the customer, you hope it's not a *Band-Aid solution*, a temporary fix that doesn't solve the underlying problem. Instead, you'd prefer that the solution is *robust,* meaning it's well constructed and able to function under any circumstances.

Idiom Savant

A good solution provider (or manager or employee) will *think outside the box,* which means she solves problems or comes up with creative ideas by thinking along nontraditional lines.

Synergy (*SIN·ur·jee,* noun) is the combined effect created by two or more cooperating groups that is greater than the total effect created by the groups working separately.

➤ "We're convinced that the merger of Acme Needle Co. and Hoosier Haystacks Ltd. will create a remarkable **synergy**."

Synergy, in other words, is just a fancy-schmancy way of describing a situation in which the whole is greater than the sum of its parts. Synergy is most often used nowadays as the justification for two companies to combine forces via a MERGER. (Don't confuse synergy with *synthesis,* the combination of separate elements to form a new and distinct element.)

To **touch base** (verb) is to reestablish communications with someone.

➤ "When you get to Hoboken, we need to **touch base** so we can come up with a marketing strategy for this new dead-fish scented deodorant."

Someone who wants to contact you might also suggest that the two of you *dialogue* (DYE·uh·log, verb), "discuss," or *interface* (verb), "interact." If he wants you to *liase* (LEE·ayz, verb) between two departments, it means he wants you to act as a go-between. He may tell you that he wants your *feedback,* which means he wants your response, criticisms, or comments about something.

Parts Dept.

The prefix *syn–* means "together." In synergy, it combines with – *ergy,* which comes from the Greek *ergon,* "to work." In synthesis, it combines with *–thesis,* which comes from another Greek word *tithenai,* "to put."

Win-win (adj.) describes a mutually beneficial situation in which both parties involved come out ahead.

➤ "With these sponge-rubber hammers, we save money and your maintenance crew has less noise to deal with. It's **win-win!**"

Win-win is also used to describe a situation in which the company benefits in two different ways. ("We get the sale *and* avoid the lawsuit. It's win-win!") If the company won't benefit in any way, it's a *no-win* situation. If the situation is such that if one party wins another party loses the same amount, it's a *zero sum game.*

Questions and Exercises to Help Everything Sink In

Here's a list of the main words you learned in this chapter:

24/7	action item	big picture	buy in
core competencies	customer relationship management	empower	exit strategy
going forward	grow the business	incent	litmus test
low-hanging fruit	mission-critical	monetize	paradigm shift
solution provider	synergy	touch base	win-win

1. Fill in the blank: "The ejection seat is a _____ part of the new helicopter design."

2. Choose the word that means "a skill essential to run the business":

    a. big picture

    b. core competency

    c. synergy

    d. action item

3. Fill in the blank: "Hensley, the new logo is an _____, so put down that mirror and get on it."

4. Choose the word or phrase that best describes *going forward:*

    a. walking

    b. moving ahead

    c. going faster

    d. being bold

Match the word on the left with the short definition on the right:

5. incent   a. radical change

6. win-win   b. always open

7. big picture   c. offer a reward

8. paradigm shift   d. mutually beneficial

9. 24/7   e. overall view

10. Choose the word that's not related to *customer relationship management:*

    a. mind share

    b. liase

    c. 80/20 rule

    d. top-of-mind

Chapter 15

Bulls, Bears, and Blue Chips: Stock Market Words

In This Chapter

➤ General stock terms

➤ Words for stock market ups and downs

➤ Words for buying and selling stocks

"Good words are worth much and cost little."

—George Herbert, British poet and clergyman

Look in any good-size dictionary and you'll likely find at least a couple of dozen different definitions of the word *stock.* (In the massive *Oxford English Dictionary,* there are well over a hundred!) Ranging from the inventory of a store to a liquid used as an ingredient for soups, stock is well stocked with meanings.

In this chapter, you'll concentrate on just one of the word's meanings: the kind of stock that you buy and sell on a stock market. You'll learn what a stock is in this sense, different types of stocks, words for stocks that go up and down, and terms for buying and selling stocks.

Stock Talk: Some General Stock Words

I scratched my head for quite some time trying to come up with a good definition for the type of stock we're talking about in this chapter. The problem, I soon realized, is that different people talk of stock in different ways. The key, however, is **capital**

(*KAP·uh·tul*), the accumulated wealth of a company in the form of money, equipment, and property. This gives us two ways to take stock of **stock:**

➤ From the point of view of the company, stock is the outstanding capital of the company.

➤ From the point of view of an individual investor, stock is the ownership of some fraction of the company's outstanding capital.

Idiom Savant

To *take stock in* means "to believe in; to attach importance to," just as though you were buying stock in something. To *take stock of* means "to think carefully about something."

In both cases, the company's capital is given a value (see INITIAL PUBLIC OFFERING), and the stock is divided into a number of **shares,** each of which represents a single unit of ownership. For example, suppose a company starts out with $1 million of capital. If a company sells 100,000 shares, then each share is initially worth $10. If you own 1,000 of those shares, you own one percent of the company. A person who buys shares is a **shareholder.**

This ownership position—that is, the sum of the shares a person owns in a company—is called **equity** (*EK·wuh·tee*), and for that reason, in everyday use, the words *stocks* and *equities* are synonymous. (A similar word is *securities,* which refers to government-regulated investments that include not only stocks but also bonds and MORTGAGES.)

One of the two main types of stock is called **common stock,** which refers to ordinary shares that entitle the holder to vote on company decisions (usually one share equals one vote) and sometimes to receive dividends. The second main type is **preferred stock,** which refers to shares that usually have no voting rights but that have two advantages over common stock: Dividends are distributed to preferred stockholders first, and if the company LIQUIDATES, preferred stockholders get first claim on the assets.

A **blue chip** is a big-time company with a long track record of steady growth in REVENUES and PROFITS and the payment of DIVIDENDS. That the safe and solid blue chip companies aren't much of a gamble makes it ironic that the phrase "blue chip" comes from poker, where of all the chips, the blue ones are usually the most expensive. Here are two related (and fairly recent) terms:

new chip—A relatively young technology company.

red chip—A publicly traded Chinese company.

Blue chips usually have a high **market capitalization,** which is the number of outstanding shares multiplied by the current share price. For example, if the company has a million shares outstanding and the current price is $20, then the company's market capitalization is $20 million. Capitalization is often abbreviated as *cap,* and the biggest companies are described as *large-cap* (or are just called *large caps*); relatively small companies are described as *small-cap* (or are called *small caps*). (The market capitalization threshold where a small cap turns into a large cap varies, but $1 billion is the most common value.)

Idiom Savant

Poker chips are the source of several common idioms. To *cash in one's chips* (as you'd do at the end of a poker game) is a euphemism for "to die." To *chip in* (as you'd do at the start of a poker round) means to contribute money to a gift or other expense. *When the chips are down* (in poker, when all the bets have been made and it's time to show the cards) means "a critical moment."

A **growth stock** is stock from a company that has above-average potential to increase revenues and profits and therefore increase its share price. These companies often don't distribute dividends, preferring instead to invest all profits to fuel growth. The opposite end of the stock scale is the **income stock**, which is stock from a stable company that produces regular dividends. A **penny stock** is one with a share price under $1.

Stock options give a person the right to purchase (or sometimes sell) shares at a particular price on or before a specified date. Here are some terms related to stock options:

golden handcuffs—Attractive financial benefits, particularly UNVESTED stock options, that an employee will lose if she resigns from the company.

optionaire—A millionaire whose net worth is composed of, or was created by, stock options.

strike price—The price at which an employee can purchase his company stock options.

underwater options—Stock options in which the STRIKE PRICE is higher than the current share price.

unhirable—An employee who can't be persuaded to join another company because he would lose a large portfolio of UNVESTED stock options from his current job.

unvested—Stock options that have not yet been converted into shares.

What Goes Up ...: Words for Stock Market Movements

An old proverb tells us that one shouldn't "sell the bear's skin before one has caught the bear." This is a pessimistic viewpoint because it assumes you might not catch the bear (well, I guess it's not *that* easy, at least for the average person), so your bearskin contract could become worthless. It's this proverb, with its inherent pessimism that prices could drop, that most linguists agree was probably the source of **bear**, a person who is pessimistic about share prices and believes they will fall.

If the bears are right about an individual stock, it may end up as a *single-digit midget*, a stock with a share price below $10, or it may end up as a *fallen angel,* a company whose once-sky-high share price has come down to earth. A *falling knife* is a stock whose price is currently undergoing a steep or long-standing decline. This term comes from an old Wall Street adage: "Never try to catch a falling knife." It means that it's both dangerous and foolhardy to buy a stock that's falling because, chances are, it's falling for a reason and will likely continue to do so.

If the stock market as a whole is going down, there are a number of words to describe this downward trend, and they depend on what has caused the drop and how long it has lasted. Here's a list of these words, more or less in order of severity, from mildest to strongest:

correction—A short-lived movement of the market (or an individual stock) in the opposite direction of the general price trend. The usual meaning here is that a market (or stock) has become either overvalued or undervalued, so the price needs to be corrected by moving down or up.

profit-taking—Selling stocks to take advantage of higher prices and therefore lock in profits that have been made.

sell-off—Widespread selling in the market as a whole or in a specific sector.

shakeout—A decline in price of a number of stocks that leads to a decline in the market as a whole.

slump—A medium-term reduction in share prices.

bear market—A long-term reduction in share prices.

crash—A quick, sharp decrease in the price of a stock or market.

The drop in prices might lead to *statement shock,* which is the shock a person experiences when he sees a large drop in the value of his investment portfolio. A similar emotion is *ticker shock,* the anguish experienced by an investor who sees the value of his portfolio diminish when the stock market goes down. If the share price goes down far enough, the shareholder might turn into a *stuckholder,* someone who owns stock he can't sell. In the end, this might generate *trade rage,* anger generated by personal stock market losses.

Your average investor much prefers to see prices go up, making him a **bull**, a person who is optimistic that share prices will rise. If the stock market as a whole moves up over a relatively long period, it's called a *bull market.* A short-term increase in either an individual stock or the stock market as a whole is called a *rally.* If an individual company's share price increases dramatically (especially after an INITIAL PUBLIC OFFERING), the stock is called a *moon rocket.*

However, bulls need to beware both the *dead cat bounce,* a temporary recovery from a major drop in a stock's price, and the *sucker rally,* a short-lived gain in the price of a stock or of the stock market as a whole.

Buy Low, Sell High, Talk Funny: Buying and Selling Terms

Buying and selling is what the stock market is all about. That's what's happening when you see all those people yelling at each other on the trading floor. To help you make sense of what's going on, this section runs through a list of the buy and sell words used by stock marketeers. (You'll be no doubt relieved to know that yelling the words is optional.)

Arbitrage (*AR·buh·trazh*) is the buying of securities on one market and the immediate reselling of the securities on another market to make a profit from the small (and usually short-lived) price difference between the two markets. Such an investor is called an *arbitrageur* (*AR·buh·trah·zhoor*) or sometimes just an *arb* for short.

A **capital gain** is the positive difference between how much a stock is sold for and how much it was bought for. If the stock is sold for less than what it was bought for, it's a *capital loss.*

See also: DAY TRADING

Parts Dept.

The word *market* has been traced back to the Latin word *mercari,* "to buy," and *merc-* (or *merx*), "merchandise." These roots were also the source of our words merchant, commerce, mercenary, and mercy.

Day trading is Internet-based stock market trading in which individual investors quickly buy and sell equities to take advantage of short-term trends and then sell most if not all of their holdings before the end of the day.

A **dividend** is a payment set by a company's BOARD OF DIRECTORS and given to the shareholders as a percentage of the company's EARNINGS. If you buy shares after a dividend has been declared, you may not be eligible to receive the dividend. In this case, the shares are said to be offered *ex-dividend*.

The EARNINGS **per share** value is the EARNINGS of a company divided by the number of outstanding shares.

If the company becomes successful enough or if it needs a large amount of cash to build the company, it will set up an **initial public offering (IPO)**, which is the first sale of shares to the public. This is also known as *going public,* and it means the company's stock will be listed and traded on a stock exchange (that is, *publicly traded*). A *stag* is an investor who purchases shares in an initial public offering with the intention of quickly selling them after the price has risen. Some companies decide later on that they prefer not to be traded publicly. If this is the case, they can *buy back* of all their outstanding shares, which is called *going private*.

Trading on margin means borrowing money from a brokerage to buy stocks. The *margin* is cash or stocks deposited with the brokerage to cover losses on the margined stock. If the value of that stock drops, the brokerage may issue a *margin call* that requires the investor to deposit more money or securities or risk having the stock sold to cover the loss.

A **market order** is an order to immediately buy or sell a stock at the current price. Here are some other order terms:

> *limit order*—An order to buy or sell a stock at a specific price or better. If the person is buying, for example, the limit order will be placed only if the stock can be purchased at the specified price or lower.

> *open order*—An order to buy or sell a stock at a specified price, it remains in effect until it is either placed or cancelled.

> *stop order*—An order to buy or sell a stock that is only placed once the stock hits a specified price. A *stop buy* is a buy order that's placed as soon as the stock moves up to or exceeds the specified price; a *stop loss* is a sell order that's placed as soon as the stock moves down to or goes below the specified price.

The **price-earnings ratio (p/e ratio)** is the current price of a stock divided by the company's most recent annual EARNINGS PER SHARE. This is also called the *multiple*.

To **sell short** is to borrow stock from a brokerage, sell it, and then buy it back at a later date to repay the loan. This is done when the investor expects the stock's price to go down because it means she profits by selling the borrowed stock at a higher price and then buying it back later (to repay the brokerage) at a lower price.

To **split** is to divide the value of a company's outstanding shares and to increase the number of shares by the same multiple. For example, a 2-for-1 split reduces the value of each share by half but gives each shareholder double the number of shares.

Questions and Exercises to Help Everything Sink In

Here's a list of the main words you learned in this chapter:

arbitrage	bear	blue chip	bull
capital	capital gain	common stock	dividend
earnings per share	equity	growth stock	income stock
initial public offering	market capitalization	market order	penny stock
preferred stock	price-earnings ratio	sell short	shareholder
shares	split	stock	stock options
trading on margin			

1. Choose the type of stock that produces regular dividends:
    a. common
    b. income
    c. growth
    d. penny

2. Choose the term that means "borrowing money for a stock transaction":
    a. selling short
    b. day trading
    c. trading on margin
    d. arbitrage

3. Fill in the blank: "Angelina was sure the share price of Bedroom Electronics, Inc., would fall, so she decide to _____."

4. Choose the word that means "the sum of the shares a person owns in a company":
    a. dividend
    b. capital
    c. arbitrage
    d. equity

Match the word on the left with the short definition on the right:

5. share   a. accumulated wealth of a company

6. capital gain   b. a payment to shareholders

7. market capitalization   c. unit of ownership

8. capital   d. stock profit

9. dividend   e. shares multiplied by share price

10. Choose the word that's the most similar to *golden handcuffs*:

    a. arbitrageur

    b. stuckholder

    c. fallen angel

    d. unhirable

Part 4

The System: Words for How the World Works

Romantics may insist that love makes the world go 'round, but that honor more likely goes to the battalions of lawyers, politicians, and diplomats who march into work each morning. That's because we live within a hideously complex system that requires an array of specialists to keep things working at least relatively smoothly and to keep our naturally chaotic tendencies at bay. As we know by now, specialists always have specialized language, so the three chapters in Part 4 celebrate the language used by lawyers, politicians, bureaucrats, diplomats, spies, and military types.

Chapter 16

Legal Lingo

In This Chapter

➤ Words for lawsuits and charges

➤ Words for judges and juries

➤ Words for trials

➤ Words for verdicts and judgments

"Why is it that our tongue, so simple for other purposes, becomes obscure and unintelligible in wills and contracts?"

—Michel de Montaigne, French philosopher

Not so long ago, you could get a quick and cheap laugh by mocking the absurdly inflated and pretentious language—otherwise known as *legalese*—spouted by the world's lawyers. Just throw out a "heretofore" or a "forthwith" or a "party of the first part," and you'd have them rolling in the aisles. Unfortunately, jokes about lawyerly language have become passé (although jokes about lawyers themselves are a booming business). The good news is that the jokes were around long enough for the legal profession to take notice and decide to do something about them. There's a movement afoot in legal circles to write contracts and laws using plain English words instead of all those holdovers from the nineteenth century. That's something to look forward to, but it's my guess that it won't happen soon. So, in the meantime, this chapter presents plain English definitions of some legal lingo.

"I'll See You in Court": Lawsuits and Charges

This section kicks things off by looking at various words associated with hauling someone into court.

This could happen, for example, due to **complicity** (*kum·PLIS·i·tee*, noun), involvement in an illegal act.

➤ Murphy's **complicity** in the donut heist was obvious from the powdered sugar and jelly that stained his clothes.

This word comes from the Latin *complex* or *complicem*, "closely connected," which combines *com-*, "together" and *plic*, "to fold." This same root sprouted another word, *complice*, which means "an associate in crime," and that later became our word *accomplice* (*uh·KOM·plis*, noun; strangely, no one knows why or how the *ac-* prefix got tacked onto the front). The accomplice's job is to *abet* (*uh·BET*, verb), "to help," someone else commit a crime.

You Don't Say

The verb *aid* and the verb *abet* both mean "to help," but abet should only be used when talking about a criminal situation. Since the words have the same meaning, the next time you hear a legal eagle accusing someone of "aiding and abetting" a crime, know that you're hearing a *tautology*, "a needless repetition of different words that mean the same thing." Other legal tautologies include "null and void" and "ways and means."

To **litigate** (*LIT·uh·gate*, verb) is to subject someone to, or to engage in, legal proceedings.

➤ With her tongue scalded, Bertha knew she had no choice but **litigate** the stupid restaurant that had the nerve to actually make their hot chocolate hot.

This verb's parents are the Latin terms *lit-*, "lawsuit," and *agere*, "to do; to lead." So litigate literally means "to initiate a *lawsuit*" (*LAW·soot*, noun), a court case in which one party seeks justice from another. Synonyms for lawsuit are *action* and *case,* and the word lawsuit is often shortened to just *suit,* especially when describing specific types of lawsuits. An example is a *civil suit,* a lawsuit between private parties (also called a *civil action* or a *civil case*). Someone who initiates a lot of lawsuits can be described as *litigious* (li·TIJ·us, adj.). To *contest* (kun·TEST, verb) is to challenge or dispute using **litigation** (noun).

A **claim** (klaym, noun) is a legal case in which one party demands something that is rightfully theirs but is possessed by someone else.

> ➤ Conrad figured he needed *both* kidneys, so he filed a **claim** against the hospital that had accidentally removed one of them.

If that someone else disagrees, he may bring a suit against the first person. This is called a *counterclaim*.

A **writ** (rit, noun) is a court order.

> ➤ The deputies arrived at the door with a **writ** ordering them to seize Zelda's collection of Phyllis Diller memorabilia.

Here are three common writs:

subpoena (suh·PEE·nuh, noun)—A writ requiring a person to a appear in court and testify.

habeas corpus (HAY·bee·us·KOR·pus, noun)—A writ requiring that a prisoner be brought to the court to determine whether he is being imprisoned legally. This is Latin phrase that means "to have the body."

warrant (WOHR·unt, noun)—A writ authorizing a police officer to search a location, seize property, or arrest a suspect. The latter is also called a BENCH *warrant*.

An **indictment** (in·DITE·munt, noun) is a formal charge against a party for the commission of a crime, drawn up by a prosecutor after presenting evidence at a preliminary hearing or to a GRAND JURY.

> ➤ A federal **indictment** has charged Vinnie "Rutabaga" Corleone with five counts of assault with a deadly vegetable.

An indictment is handed down (or sometimes handed up) usually only for a *felony* (FEL·uh·nee, noun), a serious crime—such as murder, rape, robbery, burglary, or arson—punishable by at least a year in prison. A *misdemeanor* (miss·duh·MEE·nur, noun) is a relatively minor crime—such as drunk driving, disturbing the peace, or petty theft—that carries a sentence of less than one year in prison.

An **arraignment** (uh·RAIN·munt, noun) is the initial appearance before the court in which the charges are read and a plea—guilty or not guilty—is entered.

> ➤ Matilda's lawyer didn't think that "eeny, meeny, miney, mo" was the best method to determine how she'd plead at tomorrow's **arraignment.**

In general, a participant in a suit is called a *party,* but the two sides have their own special names:

The **plaintiff** (*PLAYN·tif,* noun) is the party who initiates a lawsuit. You can also call her the *complainant, claimant, litigant,* or *accuser.*

The **defendant** (*di·FEN·dunt,* noun) is the party against whom a lawsuit is initiated. You can also call him the *respondent* or the *accused.*

"All Rise": Judge and Jury Words

A *judge* (*juj,* noun) is a public official who hears and decides cases in a court of law. The term comes from the Latin word *judice,* which combines *jus,* "law" and *-dicus,*

Idiom Savant

To be *as sober as a judge* means to be exceptionally serious and solemn (as judges are reputed to be).

Idiom Savant

To *lay down the law* means to forcefully, even arrogantly, state an opinion. To stay *within the letter of the law* means to follow the rules or laws precisely while violating their spirit. To *take the law into one's own hands* means to seek justice without involving the courts.

"speaker." So a judge is one who literally "speaks the law."

The same Latin root also produced **judicial** (*joo·DISH·ul,* adj.), which describes anything related to the courts, judges, or the administration of justice.

➤ Having had his first arrest at age eight and having been in and out of courtrooms ever since, Rufus knew full well how the **judicial** system worked.

Another form of the Latin *jus* was *juris,* "law," from which we get the following:

jurist (*JOO·rist,* noun)—A person with thorough knowledge of and long experience with the law.

juridical (*joo·RID·i·kul,* adj.)—Describes anything related to the administration of justice. The *-dical* suffix goes back to the Latin *dicere,* "to say."

jurisdiction (*joor·is·DIK·shun,* noun)—The authority and right to interpret and apply the law, especially within set limits or a territory. The *-diction* suffix means "declaration."

jurisprudence (*joor·is·PROO·dunce,* noun)—The science or philosophy of law. The *-prudence* part comes from the Latin *prudentia,* "knowledge."

Yet another Latin law word is *jurare,* "to swear an oath." This became *juree* in French and then our word **jury** (*JOO·ree,* noun), a group of people sworn to hear a case and hand down a verdict.

➤ Sheena was so egotistical that she figured there was no way they'd be able to select a **jury** of *her* peers.

A *grand jury* is a jury that weighs evidence presented in a private session by a prosecutor and then determines whether the accused should face formal charges (an INDICT-
MENT). To *sequester* (*suh·KWES·tur,* verb) means "to keep separate or segregated." In
high-profile court cases, sequestering means isolating the jury in a separate place
(such as a hotel) so that they won't be influenced by news media accounts of the
trial. A trial that includes a jury is called, not surprisingly, a *jury trial;* a trial in which
there's no jury—that is, the judge will render the verdict—is called a *bench trial.*
(*Bench* means not only where the judge sits but also the office or position of a judge.

"Order in the Court": Trial Terms

Anyone who has visited a courtroom is well aware of the *motley* ("varied") collection
of lawyers, PLAINTIFFS, DEFENDANTS, and hangers-on that always congregate there. It's
much like a farmyard with its motley collection of animals. Too much of a metaphorical stretch, you say? Perhaps, but it's not all that much of an etymological stretch.
That's because the word *court,* "the room in which
law cases are heard," goes back to the Latin word
cohors, meaning "farmyard." It eventually became
the French word *court,* which meant "the king's
lands or residence." Since this is where the king
also made JUDICIAL decisions, *court* eventually came
to mean what it does today. This section looks at a
few words you might hear while attending court to
watch a trial.

You Don't Say

Don't confuse abjure with *adjure,* "to command under oath."
Remember that *ab–* means
"away" and *ad–* means "toward."

To **abjure** (*ab·JOOR,* verb) is to renounce something under oath.

➤ Despite the "H-A-T-E" and "K-I-L-L" tattoos
on his knuckles, Leo **abjured** violence while
on the witness stand.

This word combines *ab-,* "away," and the Latin *jurare,* "to swear an oath." A more
commonly used synonym is *forswear* (*for·SWARE,* verb). To *abnegate* (*AB·nuh·gate,* verb)
means to renounce a right, claim, or privilege. This word brings together *ab-,* "away,"
and the Latin *negare,* "to deny." To renounce a right or claim is to *disclaim* (verb).

An **affidavit** (*af·uh·DAY·vit,* noun) is a written statement composed under oath.

➤ While the **affidavit** containing her confession was read in court, Grace was hor-
rified to realize they'd been talking about "Dolly May" instead of Molly Day.

An example of an affidavit is a *deposition* (*dep·uh·ZISH·un*, noun), a written testimony made under oath, especially one that is made during *discovery*, a pretrial fact-finding process in which both sides request documents and testimony from each other.

Perjury (*PUR·juh·ree*, noun) is a crime in which a person deliberately provides false information while under oath.

> ➤ His explanation for not having filed taxes for 10 years—"the dog ate my returns"—was both silly *and* grounds for **perjury**.

This comes from the Latin *per-*, "to destroy," and *jurium*, "oath." To *suborn* (*suh·BORN*, verb) is to induce a person to commit perjury.

"We Find the Defendant ...": Verdicts and Judgments

Earlier I mentioned that the etymology of the word *judge* told us that the word literally means a person who "speaks the law." The word *verdict*, "the decision of a jury in a trial," has a related past. It combines the Latin *ver*, "true," with *dit*, "speech." So someone rendering a verdict literally "speaks the truth." This section covers words related to verdicts and *judgments* ("decisions made by a court generally").

To **annul** (*uh·NUL*, verb) is to cancel or declare void.

> ➤ They had barely even looked at each other after getting married in front of millions of people on TV, so the judge found that there were sufficient grounds to **annul** their marriage.

You Don't Say

Abrogate is sometimes confused with *arrogate* (*AIR·uh·gate*, verb), to claim or seize without right or justification.

If you want a more official-sounding word, use *abrogate* (*AB·ruh·gate*, verb).

The word **culpable** (*KUL·puh·bul*, adj.) describes someone or something that's guilty and deserving of blame or punishment.

> ➤ The judge was more certain than ever that the defendant was **culpable** in the EMBEZZLING scheme after his offer to buy the judge's wife "something nice for Christmas."

The source of this word is the Latin *culpa*, "fault; blame," from which we get the common Latin phrase *mea culpa* (*MAY·uh·KUL·puh* or *MEE·uh·KUL·puh*), "my fault."

Word Wonders

You may think that the word *culprit*, "a person accused or guilty of a crime," is related to *culpable*. If so, you're right but probably not in the way you think. Hundreds of years ago, after a prisoner had pleaded "not guilty," the Clerk of the Crown would then say, "*Culpable: prest d'averrer nostre bille*," a French phrase that means: "Guilty: ready to prove our charge." (In those days, court proceedings were conducted in French.) This would be recorded in short form as *cul. prit.* (*prit* being a variation of *prest*). Later, when French was no longer used, people thought *cul. prit.* referred to the prisoner, and so the word *culprit* passed into the language by, as the *Oxford English Dictionary* cheekily puts it, the "fortuitous or ignorant" combining of these two words.

To **acquit** (*uh·KWIT*, verb) means to free from an alleged charge or accusation.

➤ Their decision to **acquit** Joe "Jury Killer" Kowalski came as no surprise to anyone.

Here are some synonyms you can use: *absolve, exonerate, exculpate,* and *vindicate.* The opposite is *convict* (*kun·VIKT*, verb). If a person is convicted, the judge can show *clemency* (*KLEM·un·see*, noun), "mercy toward an offender," which usually means a reduced sentence. In this case, the judge is said to *commute* (*kum·YOOT*, verb) the sentence. *Amnesty* (*AM·nus·tee*, noun) is a general pardon, especially for political crimes. A judge can also *set aside*, "ANNUL or override," a jury's verdict. If a verdict is set aside because the judge deems there to be insufficient evidence, he will *quash* (*kwosh*, verb) the verdict.

A guilty party may have to give **restitution** (*res·tuh·TOO·shun*, noun), the restoration of something (or its equivalent) that was taken illegally.

➤ Since she'd stolen $1,000 worth of Tickle-Me Elmos, the judge ordered her to pay the store the same amount in **restitution.**

Alternatively, the court may ask for *reparation* (*rep·uh·RAY·shun*, noun), payment for the damages or harm caused to another. This is also called *damages. Punitive damages* are damages that exceed what's necessary to compensate the wronged party, and they're levied as a punishment to the offender.

Questions and Exercises to Help Everything Sink In

Here's a list of the main words you learned in this chapter:

abjure	acquit	affidavit	annul	arraignment
claim	complicity	culpable	defendant	indictment
judicial	jury	litigate	perjury	plaintiff
restitution	writ			

1. Which word comes from the Latin word meaning "to swear an oath."

2. Choose the word that means "to subject to legal proceedings":
    a. annul
    b. abjure
    c. litigate
    d. claim

3. Fill in the blank: "The grand jury handed down an _____ against the President for lying under oath."

4. Choose the word that means "lying under oath":
    a. perjury
    b. restitution
    c. culpable
    d. abjure

Match the word on the left with the short definition on the right:

5. culpable   a. payment for a thing taken illegally
6. plaintiff   b. statement written under oath
7. restitution   c. involvement in an illegal act
8. affidavit   d. one who initiates a lawsuit
9. complicity   e. guilty and deserving of punishment

10. Choose the word that's not a synonym for *acquit*:
    a. exculpate
    b. exonerate
    c. abrogate
    d. vindicate

Chapter 17

Weasel Words from Politics and Government

"The politician is trained in the art of inexactitude. His words tend to be blunt or rounded, because if they have a cutting edge they may later return to wound him."

—Edward R. Murrow, American journalist

More than any other group (with the possible exception of lawyers; see Chapter 16, "Legal Lingo"), politicians are criticized for the words they use. For example, Theodore Roosevelt disliked their use of *weasel words,* which are those words that someone uses to make a statement sound ambiguous. (In the same way that a weasel sucks the life out of an egg and leaves only the shell, a weasel word sucks the life out of the words around it.) Another charge leveled at politicians is that they have a *rhinestone vocabulary,* which means they use words or phrases chosen only because they appeal to a particular person or group. Others have complained that *pols* (an acceptable short form of *politicians*) use *plastic words,* words or phrases that normally have a specific meaning but are used by politicians to say whatever the audience wants to hear. Examples are "change" and "family values."

In this chapter, I'll try to avoid all such words and concentrate only on a few useful terms related to elections, candidates, governing, corruption, and political philosophies.

Stump to Stalking Horse: Election Words

An elected politician is someone who the people have picked out to lead them and to take care of the affairs of government. It's this notion of picking someone out that lies at the heart of the word *elect,* "to choose by vote for a political office." It comes from the Latin word *eligere,* which combines *ex-,* "out," and *legere,* "to pick." This section looks at a few words related to elections.

A **candidate** (*KAN·duh·dayt* or *KAN·duh·dit,* noun) is a person who seeks political office. From a political party's point of view, the candidate is their *nominee* because she was nominated to represent the party.

Word Wonders

If you're the least bit cynical about politicians, you'll no doubt be surprised to learn that the word *candidate* comes from the Latin word *candidatus,* which means "clothed in white." What's up with *that?* The story is that, in ancient Rome, people who aspired to political office wore white togas to symbolize the purity of their motives. The same Latin root—*candere,* "white; glistening"—also gave us *candid,* "open and sincere," and *candor,* "honesty and sincerity of expression."

An **incumbent** (*in·KUM·bunt,* noun) is the candidate who currently holds the office. The **challenger** (*CHAL·un·jur,* noun) is the person trying to defeat the incumbent. If there's no incumbent, you say that it's an *open seat.*

The **slate** is the list of all the candidates running for office at one time from a single political party. It's also called the *ticket,* although in the United States, *ticket* also refers to a party's presidential and vice-presidential nominees.

A **stalking horse** is a candidate put forward either to split the vote with an existing candidate or to conceal the candidacy of another person. (This is a hunting term that refers to a horse behind which a hunter would hide while stalking his quarry.)

To **barnstorm** (verb) is to campaign by making numerous brief stops in small towns and rural areas. The **hustings** (*HUSS·tings,* noun) is a general term for the places where the candidate gives speeches (you usually say the candidate is "on the hustings"). This is also called the *stump,* and if the candidate gives the same basic speech at each stop, it's called her *stump speech.* More generally, the **campaign trail** refers to all the places the candidate goes and all the events the candidate attends.

In day-to-day usage, a **whistle stop** is a small station or town at which a train would stop only if signaled. During a campaign, it's a brief appearance by the candidate in a small town, especially if the candidate appears on the back observation platform of a train. A **rally** is a large gathering intended to arouse enthusiasm for the candidate, party, or *platform* (the policies and principles put forth by a candidate or party). While at whistle stops or rallies, politicians are often accused of **glad-handing,** which means giving warm but not completely sincere greetings.

A **political action committee (PAC)** is a group with a pet cause. The committee raises money for and contributes money to the campaigns of candidates who support that cause. See also SPECIAL INTEREST GROUP.

A **fundraiser** is a social event designed to raise money for a candidate or party. Most fundraisers are meals and most of those meals feature chicken, the least controversial of the main-course meats. If a candidate finds himself attending many such events (and it's a rare candidate these days who doesn't), you can say he's on the **rubber-chicken circuit** (a joshing reference to how overcooked the chicken is on some of these occasions). If the candidate is particularly good at raising funds, he'll end up with a **war chest,** a large fund *earmarked* ("reserved") for a campaign (or some other purpose).

When the votes have been counted, the candidate hopes she has received an **absolute majority,** which means more than 50 percent of the votes cast. If she really impressed the voters and garners much more than 50 percent of the tally, call it a *landslide.* Failing that, she'd like at least a **plurality** (*PLOO·ral·i·tee,* noun), which means less than 50 percent of the votes but more than anyone else.

Word Wonders

Why a *stump* of all things? Because in days of yore, candidates rarely had official podiums from which to regale their audiences. So, instead, they would climb onto a nearby tree stump and hold forth from there.

Idiom Savant

A *straw poll* (also called a *straw vote*) is an unofficial, quick-and-dirty vote taken to assess public opinion. It's a "straw" poll because a piece of straw thrown into the air will tell you which way the wind is blowing.

If the INCUMBENT loses, he becomes a **lame duck**, the holder of a political office between the election date and the date when the successor is **inaugurated** ("inducted into office"). The implication is that, although he still holds office, he's "lame" because he can no longer wield the power of that office.

Word Wonders

Why is a lame duck a duck and not some other animal? No one really knows for sure. The most plausible explanation I've seen is that a duck that's lame would not fly as well as the healthy ducks, so it would soon fall behind, which is sort of what happens to a defeated incumbent. Others believe it's a play on the phrase *dead duck,* "a doomed person." In this case, the loser isn't officially "dead" until his term ends, so between the election and then he's merely "lame."

Government Words of the People, by the People, for the People

I'd like to take this opportunity to clear up a linguistic mystery that has been confounding people for a very long time. First, we need to take a look at the history of the word *govern* (GUV·urn, verb), "to create and administer public policy and affairs of the state." The source is the Greek word *kubernan,* "a person who steers a ship." This became *gubernare* in Latin, then *governeur* in French, and then it passed into English as *governor* (noun) and *govern* (verb). No surprises there. However, *gubernare* also became the old English word *gubernator,* "ruler; governor," which led to the adjective *gubernatorial,* "of or relating to a ruler or governor." So *that* is why you hear things related to governors (especially the governors of U.S. states) described a "gubernatorial."

With that off my chest, let's look at a few other words related to government. No government official's day would be complete without at least one meeting with an **interest group**, a group of people working to further a cause (such as an industry, a specific piece of legislation, or a segment of society), especially by influencing public officials. You can also call these people a *pressure group,* a *special interest,* or a *lobby* (from the Lobby, the entrance hall to the British House of Commons where people used to be able to talk to—and presumably influence—members of Parliament). Because of the latter term, a person who works for an interest group is often called a *lobbyist.*

Idiom Savant

To *jump (or hop) on the bandwagon* means to join a popular movement. It's used for all kinds of rages and crazes nowadays, but it was first popularized in political campaigns. A hundred years or so ago, politicians running for office would literally put a band on a wagon and ride around a town to advertise their candidacy and whip up enthusiasm. Local officials who wanted to show their support for the candidate would jump onto the moving bandwagon.

The word **partisan** (*PART·uh·zun*, adj.) describes avid support for a political party, cause, idea, faction, or group. You can also use this word as a noun to refer to someone who acts this way. Similarly, the word *bipartisan* (*BYE·part·uh·zun*, adj.) describes support that comes from two parties. In the United States, for example, you'll occasionally hear of a bill or resolution having "bipartisan support," meaning it has supporters from both the Democratic party and the Republican party. If the support comes without any party affiliation strings attached, you can say the support is *nonpartisan*.

See also: IDEOLOGUE.

To **spin** (verb) is to provide information, particularly to reporters, in an attempt to put a more favorable interpretation on a politician's ideas, actions, or policies. A person who spins is a *spin doctor,* and the language he uses is sometimes called *spinnish.* Spinning is a high art in political circles as evidenced by *Zen spin,* which means to spin a story by not doing any spinning at all.

A **filibuster** (*FIL·uh·bus·tur*, noun) is an exceptionally long speech designed to delay or obstruct legislative action. Feel free to use this as a verb as well. As an aside, note, too, that *dilatory* (*DIL·uh·tor·ee*, adj.) describes any action that's intended to cause delay.

Speaking of speeches, a **stem-winder** is a stirring political speech. (This comes from the stem-winding watch, the kind you wind by turned a small knob on the side. When these watches first came out in the latter half of the nineteenth century, they became instantly popular, and the adjective *stem-winding* was soon used to refer to anything that was first-rate, such as a particularly good speech.) Here are some other words for speeches:

> *allocution* (*al·uh·KYOO·shun*, noun)—A formal, authoritative speech.

> *diatribe* (*DYE·uh·tribe*, noun)—A bitter and abusive speech.

harangue (*huh·RANG,* noun)—A ranting, scolding speech.

philippic (*fuh·LIP·ik,* noun)—A harsh, bitter, denunciation.

rodomontade (*roh·duh·mawn·TAYD* or *ro·duh·mawn·TAD,* noun)—A bragging, blusterous speech.

screed (noun)—A long, monotonous HARANGUE.

tirade (*TYE·rayd* or *tuh·RAYD,* noun)—A long, angry, highly critical speech.

Word Wonders

The word filibuster has a strange history that would probably take a filibuster or two to describe. The condensed version is that it comes from the Dutch word *vrijbuiter,* "freebooter," which is another name for a pirate (*vrijbuit* literally means "free booty"). This word then passed into French (*flibustier*) and Spanish (*filibustero*) before arriving on English shores as *filibuster,* and it referred to any marauding pirate who sought to encourage revolutions in Central America. It was the obstructionist warfare of these pirates that gave politicians a good word for the obstructionist verbal warfare waged by some of their colleagues.

When Good Politicians Go Bad: Corruption Words

Despite the lack of white togas (see CANDIDATE), most of today's candidates for office are honorable people who are driven to serve their country, state, or whatever. There are, of course, bad apples in every bunch, so it won't shock you to hear that some *politcos* (yet another variation of *politician*) are *venal* (*VEE·nul,* adj.), meaning they're open to BRIBERY or corruption. This section looks at a few of the things these bad political seeds do when we're not looking.

Cronyism (*KROH·nee·iz·um,* noun) refers to political favors granted to old friends without regard to their qualifications. (See also CRONY.) A similar ethical lapse is **nepotism** (*NEP·uh·tiz·um,* noun), political favors granted to relatives (from the Italian word *nepote,* "nephew").

Logrolling (*LOG·roh·ling,* noun) is the trading of votes and other political favors between politicians to ensure the passage of legislation favorable to each one. This is also called *vote trading.*

Influence peddling occurs when a politician uses the influence of her authority to grant or obtain favors for someone in return for cash or other favors.

See also: KICKBACK.

To **gerrymander** (*JAYR·ee·man·dur,* verb) means to adjust voting districts to favor one party over another. Of course, voting districts get adjusted all the time to reflect changing populations (especially after a census). The legitimate forms are called either *redistricting* or *reapportionment.*

Pork barrel refers to government legislation or projects that provide jobs and other benefits to a politician's district. This is now more commonly abbreviated to just *pork.* Originally, a pork barrel was exactly that: a barrel in which pork was kept. How full the barrel was became a symbol of a person's wealth, so eventually pork barrel came to mean simply "wealth" or "a supply of money." The cynical politician who wanted to remain on good terms with his constituents would pass legislation enriching his district or, figuratively, filling their pork barrels.

A pork barrel project may end up as a **boondoggle**, a frivolous and wasteful project.

Word Wonders

As weird as it may sound, it was the combination of the last name of Elbridge *Gerry*, a former governor of Massachusetts, and *salamander* (a small lizard-like amphibian) that gave us the word gerrymander. This strange beast was formed when Governor Gerry re-shaped his state's voting districts to favor his party. One such district looked suspiciously like a salamander and was drawn as such in an editorial cartoon by Gilbert Stuart. His editor immediately dubbed the creature a *Gerry-mander*, and the name stuck. (Some trivia: Stuart was the same man who painted the portrait of George Washington that appears on the U.S. $1 bill.)

Some Political "-isms"

The suffix *-ism* has several meanings including "characteristic behavior or quality" (as in *patriotism*), "action" (see CRONYISM), "prejudice" (as in *racism*), and "state or condition" (as in *gigantism*). It also means "a doctrine; a system of principles," and that's what I want to concentrate on in this section. Here's a list of a dozen of the most influential and common political "-isms" and what they stand for:

authoritarianism—The concentration of power in the hands of a leader or group not constitutionally responsible to the people.

colonialism—The control of one state or people by another.

communism—A system of government in which the state plans and controls the economy with the goal of having all goods owned and shared by the people.

conservatism—A political philosophy based on respect for traditional and exist-ing institutions, social stability, and a preference for gradual rather than abrupt change.

despotism—A system of government in which a ruler (a *despot*) exercises unlimit-ed and absolute power.

fascism—A system of government in which power is centralized under a dicta-tor, opposition is suppressed using censorship and terror, social and economic activities are rigidly controlled, and the nation or race is exalted above the indi-vidual.

federalism—A system of government in which power is shared between a nation-al (federal) government and smaller local governments (for example, at the state or provincial level).

feudalism—A European political system in place from about the ninth to the fif-teenth century in which various lords owned all property and vassals lived on and worked the property.

liberalism—A political philosophy based on the inherent goodness of people, the autonomy of the individual, and the protection of civil and political liberties.

pluralism—A doctrine that embraces cultural diversity and in which members of diverse cultural groups (including ethnic, racial, social, and religious groups) participate in the decision-making process.

socialism—A political system in which the means of producing and distributing goods are owned collectively or by the government.

totalitarianism—A system of government in which the state exercises total and absolute authority over all aspects of life and in which the individual is com-pletely subject to the will of the state.

Government by, Well, Whoever You Want

While we're on the subject of suffixes, this section looks at two more. First there's the suffix *-cracy*, which means "government; rule." It comes from the Greek word *kratos*, "power; authority." Second is the suffix *-archy*, which also means "government; rule," but it comes from the Latin *archein,* "to rule." Combine these with the appropriate prefixes and you get words that mean "government by" or "rule by," as shown in the following table.

Word	Government/Rule By	Word	Government/Rule By
anarchy	No one	*mobocracy*	A mob
aristocracy	The best citizens	*monarchy*	A hereditary ruler
autocracy	One person	*oligarchy*	A few people
democracy	The people	*plutocracy*	The wealthy
duarchy	Two people	*stratocracy*	The military
gerontocracy	Old people	*technocracy*	Technicians, scientists
gynocracy	Women	*theocracy*	Church officials
meritocracy	Talented people	*triarchy*	Three people

Questions and Exercises to Help Everything Sink In

Here's a list of the main words you learned in this chapter:

absolute majority	barnstorm	boondoggle	campaign trail
candidate	challenger	cronyism	filibuster
fundraiser	gerrymander	glad-handing	hustings
inaugurate	incumbent	influence peddling	interest group
lame duck	logrolling	nepotism	partisan
plurality	political action committee	pork barrel	rally
rubber-chicken circuit	slate horse	spin	stalking
stem-winder	war chest	whistle stop	

1. Fill in the blank: "She doesn't agree with us right now, but I think I can _____ her to see our point of view."

2. Choose the word that means "to adjust voter districts in a biased manner":

    a. gerrymander

    b. inaugurate

    c. barnstorm

    d. influence peddling

3. Fill in the blank: "To seal this election, we need to _____ across the entire state."

4. Choose the word that means "having the most votes but less than 50 percent":

   a. absolute majority

   b. lame duck

   c. incumbent

   d. plurality

Match the word on the left with the short definition on the right:

5. boondoggle   a. induct into office

6. stem-winder   b. obstructionist speech

7. incumbent   c. stirring speech

8. inaugurate   d. frivolous, wasteful project

9. filibuster   e. candidate currently holding office

10. Choose the word that's a stronger synonym for *absolute majority:*

    a. plurality

    b. dilatory

    c. landslide

    d. platform

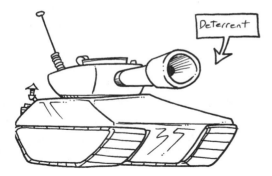

Deterrent

Chapter 18

War and Peace: Military, Spying, and Diplomatic Terms

In This Chapter

➤ Words about war

➤ Military ranks and units

➤ Words from the world of espionage

➤ Words from the world of diplomacy

"A language is a dialect with an army and a navy."

—Max Weinreich, Yiddish linguist and scholar

The linguist Eric Partridge once said that war "has ever been an augmentor of vocabulary." He meant that the terminology and jargon of war seems to slip easily into everyday use. So now you hear executives talking about using a *scorched-earth policy* ("destroying everything in your path as you retreat to leave nothing for the enemy"), you hear politicians talking about a *barrage* ("overwhelming outpouring") of criticism, and you hear marketers talking about *outflanking* ("outmaneuvering or outwitting") their competitors. This chapter examines a few other war words, some of which have broader uses in everyday life, and it also looks at military ranks and units. To keep things in balance, I also run through a few words from the fields of espionage and diplomacy.

A War of Words

It may be a truism that "an army travels on its stomach," but could it travel on sausages in particular? I ask because of the surprising fact that the words *war* and *wurst* (a sausage such as bratwurst or liverwurst) share a common history. War goes way back to the root *wers-*, "to confuse; to mix up." This became *weera*, "confusion, strife" in Old High German, and then the "strife" part took over and eventually became our word *war*. Meanwhile, *wers-* also became *wurst*, "sausage," because a sausage is "mixed-up meat." Confused? Exactly.

The word **martial** (*MAR·shul*, adj.) describes anything related to war. (For example, *martial law* is a temporary authority that the armed forces wield over the civilian population.) This word comes from Mars, the Roman god of war. A synonym you can use is *warlike*.

Military (*MIL·i·tair·ee*, adj.) describes soldiers or the armed forces in general. (You can also use this word as a noun.) It comes from the Latin *miles*, "soldier," and it has lots of offshoots:

Parts Dept.

In paramilitary, the prefix *para-* means "alongside; near." It can also mean "beyond" (as in *paranormal*); "subsidiary; assistant" (as in *paralegal*); and "faulty; abnormal" (as in *paresthesia*).

militant (*MIL·i·tunt*, adj.)—Aggressive or combative, especially when fighting for a cause or movement.

militarism (*MIL·i·tuh·riz·um*, noun)—The policy of being aggressively prepared to wage war.

militarize (*MIL·i·tuh·rize*, verb)—To prepare for war.

militate (*MIL·i·tate*, verb)—To have weight or influence against something.

militia (*muh·LISH·uh*, noun)—An army that consists of ordinary citizens instead of professional soldiers. You can also describe such a group as paramilitary (pair·uh·MIL·i·tair·ee, adj.).

See also: BELLICOSE.

Infantry (*IN·fun·tree*, noun) refers to soldiers trained and equipped to fight on foot. For some reason, the soldiers who make up the infantry seem to attract more than their share of slang terms. Here are just a few of them: *blisterfoot, dogface, doughboy, foot, foot soldier, G.I.* (government issue), *ground-pounder, grunt, line dog, paddlefoot.*

Internecine (*in·tur·NESS·een* or *in·tur·NEE·sun*, adj.) means mutually destructive or relating to a fight within a country or group. Speaking of fights, there are many different kinds, as shown here:

combat (*KOM·bat*, noun)—An armed fight. You can also use this as a verb, in which case it's pronounced *kum·BAT*. Either way, the word combines the prefix *com-*, "with," and the Latin *battuere*, "fight." Combat has nonmilitary uses as well, as do the following synonyms: *clash, fray, melee,* and *strife*. If you're talking strictly about a fight in the military sense, use *conflict* or *warfare*.

skirmish (*SKUR·mish*, noun)—A minor battle, usually between two small forces.

176

pitched battle—Officially, it's an intense, closely fought battle in which both sides are arrayed in a predetermined formation. Unofficially, it also means any fierce and bitter battle.

blitzkrieg (*BLITS·kreeg, noun*)—A swift and surprising military offensive that uses combined air and ground forces to overwhelm the enemy. This is a German term that brings together *blitz,* "lightning," and *krieg,* "war."

Word Wonders

If you're thinking that the "infant" part of infantry couldn't possibly have anything to do with children, think again! The story is that, although we generally think of an infant as a young baby, in the Middle Ages, the word was used for any young person (equivalent to what we would call a "minor" today). In Italy, a youngster was also expected to perform military duties, and in that capacity, he was called an *infante.* As a group, they were called the *infanteria.* From there, it was only a short march to the English word *infantry.*

The **front line** is the point of contact between two armies. It's also called the *battle-front* or just the *front.*

Materiel (*muh·teer·ee·EL, noun*) is a general name for the equipment, weapons, ammunition, and other supplies of a military force. This is from the French word *matériel,* and you sometimes see it spelled with the accent over the "e" (this is called an *acute* accent). If you just want to refer to the weapons and ammunition, use *ordnance* (*ORD·nunce, noun*).

You Don't Say

Don't confuse *ordnance* with *ordinance,* "a statute or regulation, especially one issued by a local government."

An **armistice** (*AR·muh·stis, noun*) is an agreement to stop fighting. An armistice can be temporary, but in that case it's better to use either *truce* (*troos, noun*) or *ceasefire* (*SEES·fire, noun*). In war (and, indeed, elsewhere in life), you don't want a *Pyrrhic victory,* which refers to a victory that comes at the cost of overwhelming losses. (The source of this metaphor is the Greek King Pyrrhus of Epirus who, in 279 B.C.E., defeated the Romans at Asculum but suffered staggering losses.)

An Aside on the Suffix "-cide"

War and killing are unfortunate blood brothers, so it makes sense to briefly consider the suffix *-cide*, which means the killing of something. The following table runs through a few words that use this suffix.

Word	Killing of a ...	Word	Killing of a ...
filicide	Daughter or son	*parricide*	Parent
fratricide	Brother	*patricide*	Father
genocide	National, political, cultural, or racial group	*regicide*	King
homicide	Person	*sororicide*	Sister
infanticide	Infant	*suicide*	One's self
mariticide	Husband	*tyrannicide*	Tyrant
matricide	Mother	*uxoricide*	Wife

Idiom Savant

To *pull rank* is to use one's higher position in an organization to overrule a subordinate or gain an advantage. To *close ranks* is to unite in defense against a common enemy or for a common cause. The opposite is to *break ranks*, to fail to remain unified.

U.S. Military Ranks

The word **rank** originally referred to a row or line, and it's still occasionally used in that sense today. However, its more common meaning is "a relative position in an organization, especially the military." However, unless you've been in the armed forces, the relative ranks can be confusing (for example, who's higher, a First Sergeant or a Master Sergeant?). To help dispel this confusion, the following table presents the military ranks from highest to lowest for the U.S. Army, Marines, Air Force, and Navy.

Officer Ranks

Army	Marines	Air Force	Navy
General	General	General	Admiral
Lieutenant General	Lieutenant General	Lieutenant General	Vice Admiral
Major General	Major General	Major General	Rear Admiral (Upper Half)
Brigadier General	Brigadier General	Brigadier General	Rear Admiral (Lower Half)
Colonel	Colonel	Colonel	Captain
Lieutenant Colonel	Lieutenant Colonel	Lieutenant Colonel	Commander
Major	Major	Major	Lieutenant Commander
Captain	Captain	Captain	Lieutenant
First Lieutenant	First Lieutenant	First Lieutenant	Lieutenant Junior Grade
Second Lieutenant	Second Lieutenant	Second Lieutenant	Ensign
Master Warrant Officer	Chief Warrant Officer 5		
Chief Warrant Officer 4	Chief Warrant Officer 4		Chief Warrant Officer 4
Chief Warrant Officer 3	Chief Warrant Officer 3		Chief Warrant Officer 3
Chief Warrant Officer 2	Chief Warrant Officer 2		Chief Warrant Officer 2
Warrant Officer	Warrant Officer		

Enlisted Ranks

Army	Marines	Air Force	Navy
Sergeant Major Army	Sergeant Major Corps	Chief Master Sergeant Air Force	Master Chief Petty Officer Navy
Command Sergeant Major	Sergeant Major		
Sergeant Major	Master Gunnery Sergeant	Chief Master Sergeant	Master Chief Petty Officer
First Sergeant	First Sergeant	Senior Master Sergeant	Senior Chief Petty Officer
Master Sergeant	Master Sergeant	Master Sergeant	
Sergeant First	Gunnery Sergeant	Technical Sergeant	Chief Petty Officer Class
Staff Sergeant	Staff Sergeant	Staff Sergeant	Petty Officer 1st Class
Sergeant	Sergeant	Senior Airman	Petty Officer 2nd Class
Corporal Specialist	Corporal	Airman First Class	Petty Officer 3rd Class
Private First Class	Lance Corporal	Airman	Seaman
Private	Private First Class		Seaman Apprentice

U.S. Military Units

Almost as confusing as the ranks are the various units such as brigade and division. The following table clears the air by listing each unit, the approximate number of personnel in each unit, its composition based on the next smallest unit, and the rank of the commanding officer.

Unit	Personnel	Composition	Commander
Army	100,000	2 or more corps	General
Corps	20,000 to 40,000	2 or more divisions	Lieutenant General
Division	10,000 to 16,000	3 brigades	Major General
Brigade	3,000 to 5,000	3 or more regiments	Brigadier General
Regiment	1,000 to 3,000	2 to 3 battalions	Colonel
Battalion	300 to 1,000	4 to 6 companies	Lieutenant Colonel
Company	60 to 200	3 to 5 platoons	Captain
Platoon	4 to 16	2 to 4 squads	Lieutenant
Squad	8 to 16		Sergeant

Spies, Spooks, and Sleepers: Espionage Words

Espionage (*ES·pee·uh·nahzh,* noun) is spying to obtain secret information about another country's political or military operations. (This word has also filtered into other contexts. For example, businesses that spy on each other are engaged in *corporate espionage.*) The secret information obtained is called *intelligence* (*in·TEL·uh·juhnts,* noun).

Idiom Savant

The word *muster* (*MUS·tur,* verb) means to gather troops together. You see it in the idioms *pass muster,* "to pass inspection," and *muster up one's courage,* "to summon one's courage."

Counterespionage is spying designed to thwart the espionage activities of an enemy (such as another country). This includes preventing the enemy from obtaining secret information, supplying the enemy with misleading information, and preventing sabotage and *subversion* ("the overthrow or undermining of a government"). Information gleaned from counterespionage activities is called *counterintelligence,* and the misleading information sent to an enemy is called *disinformation.*

All espionage activities can be described as **covert** (*koh·VURT,* adj.), meaning they're concealed, disguised, or unacknowledged. A similar word is *clandestine* (*klan·DES·tin,* adj.), secrecy and deception to conceal an improper or even illegal action. A *safe house* (noun) is a secret and secure location where agents

180

can safely stay and meet. To *burn* (verb) means to deliberately expose a secret agent or operation.

A person who works for an intelligence agency is called a **spy**, an *agent,* an *operative,* or a *spook*. Here are some other terms to consider:

> *double agent*—An agent who pretends to work for one country while actually working for another country.

> *mole*—A double agent who works for the intelligence agency of another country.

> *sleeper*—A double agent who emigrates to another country, spends many years living a normal life under an assumed name, and then begins spying once she has worked her way up to a sensitive government or corporate post.

> *counterspy*—A spy who works in a COUNTERESPIONAGE operation.

Word Wonders

If a vote was held on the most unlikely starting point for a word's etymology, *sabotage* (*SAB·oh·tahzh,* verb)—"damage inflicted in secret to impair an enemy's ability to fight"— would be a "shoe"-in for the top 10. That's because it comes from the French verb *saboter,* "to walk noisily in wooden shoes"! (See what I mean?) Opinions vary on how this verb was transformed, but the most reasonable path is that it eventually came to mean "clumsiness" and then "to work badly" and then "to destroy machines deliberately."

The Art of the Deal: Some Words from Diplomacy

Somebody—no doubt a cynic—once defined **diplomacy** (*di·PLOH·muh·see,* noun) as "lying in state." A nicer definition is "the skill and practice of conducting relations between countries." More broadly, diplomacy is the use of *tact* ("a keen sense of what is right and proper") in dealing with difficult people or delicate situations. Here are some specific **diplomatic** (*dip·luh·MAT·ik,* adj.) types:

> *dollar diplomacy*—Diplomacy that aims to increase a country's economic power in other countries.

> *gunboat diplomacy*—Diplomacy that involves the use or threat of military force.

181

shuttle diplomacy—Diplomacy between multiple, usually hostile, countries that's conducted by an intermediary traveling back and forth between the countries involved.

A diplomatic **mission** is a permanent diplomatic office established in a foreign country. Note that this can also refer to all the diplomats assigned to the foreign country. See also DIPLOMATIC CORPS.

Diplomatic immunity is the freedom from prosecution and taxation granted to diplomatic workers living in a foreign country.

A **diplomat** (*DIP·luh·mat,* noun) is a person sent to a foreign country as a representative of a government and charged with conducting relations between the two countries. Note, too, that people who officially represent a country in international organizations (such as the United Nations) are also considered diplomats. Here's a field guide to the many different kinds of diplomats at large in the world:

ambassador (*am·BAS·uh·dur,* noun)—The highest-ranking diplomat assigned to a foreign country.

ambassador-at-large (noun)—An ambassador who isn't assigned to a particular country.

chargé d'affaires (*shar·ZHAY·duh·FAIR,* noun)—A diplomat who fills in for an absent ambassador or who runs a mission for which no ambassador is assigned.

attaché (*at·uh·SHAY* or *uh·TASH·ay,* noun)—A nondiplomatic expert assigned to work with a mission in a specific capacity. (For example, a *military attaché* is an officer in the armed forces who covers the military aspects of diplomacy.)

envoy (*EN·voy* or *AHN·voy,* noun)—A diplomat sent on a specific mission.

consul (*KON·sul,* noun)—A diplomat who resides in a foreign country and acts as a representative for the commercial interests of his own country's businesses and citizens. A consul lives or works in a *consulate.*

consul general (noun)—The highest-ranking consul and the one in charge of all the other consulates in a particular country.

courier (*KOOR·ee·ur* or *KUR·ee·ur,* noun)—A diplomat who acts as a messenger.

diplomatic corps (*kor,* noun)—The diplomatic staff assigned to a country. See also DIPLOMATIC MISSION.

Diplomats like to reach an **accord** (*uh·KORD,* noun), which is an agreement between countries. A synonym is *concord* (*KON·kord,* noun), although this is often used to mean a TREATY that establishes peaceful relations between countries.

An **entente** (*ahn·TAHTN*, noun) is an agreement between countries that establishes a friendship or an alliance and that usually stipulates some common course of action. This is similar to *détente* (*day·TAWNT*, noun), a lessening of tensions between rival countries.

A **treaty** (*TREE·tee*, noun) is a formal, negotiated agreement between countries. You can also call it a *compact* (*KOM·pakt*, noun) or simply a *pact*.

A **bilateral** (*bye·LAT·ur·ul*, adj.) agreement is one that's supported by and binding on two countries.

Questions and Exercises to Help Everything Sink In

Here's a list of the main words you learned in this chapter:

accord	armistice	bilateral	counterespionage
covert	diplomacy	diplomat	diplomatic immunity
entente	espionage	front line	infantry
internecine	martial	materiel	military
mission	rank	spy	treaty

1. Choose the word that describes soldiers or the armed forces:
    a. martial
    b. infantry
    c. rank
    d. military

2. Choose the word that describes an agreement supported by two countries:
    a. accord
    b. bilateral
    c. counterespionage
    d. diplomacy

3. Fill in the blank: "He arrived at the _____ and could see the enemy position only a few hundred yards away."

4. Choose the word that means "a friendship agreement":
    a. entente
    b. accord
    c. treaty
    d. bilateral

Match the word on the left with the short definition on the right:

5. internecine
6. diplomacy
7. espionage
8. accord
9. rank

a. spying to obtain secret information
b. relative position in an organization
c. an agreement between countries
d. mutually destructive
e. conducting relations between countries

10. Choose the word that's not a synonym for an *infantry* soldier:

   a. grunt

   b. dogface

   c. G.I.

   d. spook

Part 5

Technolinguistics: Computer and Internet Terms

Learning the computer vernacular is important if you hope to understand what the heck a lot of people are talking about these days. Not just that, it also would be nice if you could toss out a few choice morsels of technical terminology here and there your-self. Experienced globetrotters maintain that you'll be greeted more warmly and treated more kindly by the locals if you learn a few key words and phrases in the language of the country you're visiting. This could easily be applied to the computing world as well, so that jargon becomes a kind of lingua franca ("common language") for the wired set. The chapters in this section help you along by focusing on the words and phrases native to computers (including buying a computer), the Internet, and communications technologies such as e-mail, chat, and newsgroups.

Chapter 19

A Glossary for Computer Buyers

In This Chapter

➤ Words related to microprocessors

➤ Words about computer memory

➤ Words for various types of disk drives

➤ Words for computer video and monitors

➤ Words for sounds cards, modems, notebooks, and more

"Hardware (noun): The collective term for any computer-related object that can be kicked or battered when inclined to do so."

—Anonymous

Anyone who has shopped for a computer has come across ads like this one:

```
Intel Pentium III 733 Mhz
128 MB 133 Mhz SDRAM
10 GB 7200RPM Ultra ATA HD
17" (15.9" v.i.s.) Monitor
32 MB AGP Video Card
8×4×32 CD-RW Drive
Sound Blaster-compatible with Subwoofer
56 Kbps V.90 Modem
10/100 Network Card
```

The specifics may differ from ad to ad, but the sense of reading some ancient and long-forgotten Martian language hangs over every computer ad ever made. Who could possibly make sense of this GOBBLEDYGOOK? Believe it or not, almost every word in this ad is explainable in layman's terms, and that's exactly what I propose to do in this chapter. I'll take you through all the terms that appear in the preceding ad, and lots of others that you're likely to furrow your brow over when looking to purchase a computer. I've divided the terms into four main categories—the microprocessor, memory, disks, and video—and I close with a mixed bag of terms to round things out.

It's What's Inside That Counts:
The Microprocessor

The **microprocessor** (*my·kroh·PROS·uh·sor*) is a CHIP inside the computer that controls most of the computer's functions and performs most of its calculations. Many people liken the microprocessor to the computer's "brain," and that's as good an analogy as you're likely to hear. The microprocessor is often referred to as just the *processor* or, more rarely nowadays, as the *central processing unit* (or *CPU*).

Most ads will tell you three things about the microprocessor:

The company that manufactures the processor—The processors on most machines are made by *Intel*. For Windows machines, you'll also see *AMD*. Macintosh processors are made by *Motorola*.

The type of processor—For Intel, this will be some flavor of *Pentium* (in general, a Pentium III is faster than a Pentium II) or possibly *Celeron* (which is usually found on lower-cost, lower-powered computers). For AMD, it will be a brand name such as Athlon or K6.

Parts Dept.

The prefix *micro–* means "small." It comes from the Greek word *mikros*, "small." *Micro–* also means "one-millionth." For example, a micrometer is one-millionth of a meter.

The speed of the processor—This is measured in *megahertz,* which is usually abbreviated as **MHz.** This value is important because it determines to a large extent how fast the computer operates. For example, an 800 MHz machine will run approximately twice as fast as a 400 MHz machine. (As you'll see, however, there are other factors involved.)

Some ads also refer to a **cache** (pronounced *cash*), which is a small chunk of computer MEMORY that's used to store frequently used bits of data. An *L1 cache* (or *level1 cache*) is better than an *L2 cache* (or *level2 cache*). Finally, if you're looking for a NOTEBOOK computer, the ad may say that the machine's processor supports *SpeedStep*, a technology that reduces the speed of the processor to save battery life.

Getting Through the Memory Maze

The computer's **memory** is a collection of CHIPS that enable information to be stored and retrieved and that act as a work area for the computer. When you launch a program, for example, the MICROPROCESSOR finds the program's files on the computer's HARD DISK and then loads those files into memory. Similarly, when you open and create documents, they're stored in memory. This memory is often called *main memory* to differentiate it from some of the computer's other memory components (such as the CACHE mentioned earlier).

Although there are various types of memory, the type that most people are talking about when they use the word "memory" is **random access memory**, or *RAM* (pronounced *ram,* like the male sheep) for short. When you're buying a computer, the ad will tell you how much main memory the system has, and the unit used is almost always the **megabyte** (*MEG·uh·bite*), or *MB*, which is equal to one approximately million BYTES. The amount of memory is just as important, and possibly even more important, than the microprocessor speed. That's because the more memory you have, the more programs and files you'll be able to work with at once.

You'll also see various acronyms associated with the memory size, including *SDRAM* (synchronous dynamic RAM) and *RDRAM* (Rambus dynamic RAM). The specifics of these technologies are too geeky to go into here. Just remember that the presence of either one in a system is a good thing. If you see references to *PC100* or *PC133*, it means the system comes with a type of SDRAM. The numbers 100 and 133 are in MHz, and they basically tell you how fast the memory is.

The Dope on Disk Drives

After the MICROPROCESSOR and the amount of MEMORY, the next most important consideration when purchasing a computer is the size of the **hard drive**, which acts as the system's permanent storage area. The size of the hard drive is almost always measured in **gigabytes** (*GIG·uh·bites;* abbreviated as *GB*), and one gigabyte equals approximately one billion BYTES.

Some ads will abbreviate "hard drive" as *HD* or *HDD;* the latter is actually short for *hard disk drive,* which is the full name for the drive, but it's rarely used. Instead, you'll hear people use "hard drive" and "hard disk" interchangeably.

You may occasionally see hard drive statistics that include an *RPM* (*ar·pee·em*) number. This is short for *revolutions per minute,* and since the hard drive

Idiom Savant

When deciding on the size of the hard drive you want, remember *Parkinson's Law of Data:* Data expands to fill the storage space available. (This comes from the original Parkinson's Law: Work expands to fill the time available.)

has to spin to get data from different parts, the higher the RPM rating the faster the hard drive.

If the ad boasts about the hard drive supporting *Ultra ATA* or *Ultra DMA,* don't worry too much about it except to know that it means the hard drive will operate a bit faster than one that uses plain ATA.

Most computers nowadays come with a **CD-ROM drive**, which you use to work with a disc called a *CD-ROM* (*see·dee·ROHM*). CD-ROM stands for "compact disc–read-only memory." The "compact disc" part tells you that the CD-ROM looks exactly like an audio compact disc (and, in fact, a CD-ROM drive can play audio CDs); the "read-only memory" part tells you that a computer can only read data on a CD-ROM, it can't add new data to the CD-ROM (like it can to, say, a hard drive).

The specifications for a CD-ROM drive usually give you a number followed by an "X": 24X, 48X, and so on. This number tells you approximately how many times faster the CD-ROM drive is than the first generation drives that came out many years ago. This doesn't mean much to the average bear in absolute terms, but it's useful for comparing existing drives. (For example, you can say that a 48X drive is about twice as fast as a 24X drive.)

The computer ad may tell you both the maximum speed and the minimum speed of the CD-ROM drive, as in "24X max/10X min" or "24X–10X." Knowing the maximum speed seems reasonable, but specifying a minimum speed seems a bit strange. The short answer is that all CD-ROMs are created to run at a specific speed or faster. The minimum speed of a CD-ROM drive tells you the slowest CD-ROM that it can run. So, for example, a CD-ROM drive with a minimum speed of 10X wouldn't be able to run an 8X CD-ROM.

CD-ROM drives are great, but their "read-only" heritage means that you can't use them to, say, create your own audio CD or make a backup copy of a CD-ROM. If you're interested in doing these things, you should consider getting a system that has a **CD-R drive.** Unlike a CD-ROM, a *CD-R* (*see·dee·ar*) disc can accept new data (the "R" stands for "recordable").

The problem with a CD-R disc is that you can only write to it once. So even though the disc is capable of holding about 600 MB of data, if you write just 1 MB and stop, that's all you'll be able to write to the disc. A better system is the newer **CD-RW** (*see·dee·ar·double-u*) **drive.** The "RW" is short for "rewritable," and it means that you can write to a *CD-RW* disc, stop, and then come back later and write some more. This makes CD-RW drives great for making backups of your work. The specifications of CD-RW drives are usually shown as "8×4×32," which you read as follows: CD-R×CD-RW×CD-ROM. In other words, the first number tells you the speed at which the drive can write to a CD-R disc, the second number tells you the speed at which it can write to a CD-RW disc, and the third number tells you the speed at which it can read a CD-ROM disc. Note, however, that most CD-ROM and CD-R drives can't understand CD-RW discs.

Many computers are now shipping with **DVD drives.** A **DVD** (*dee·vee·dee*; short for "digital versatile disc" or "digital video disc") holds about eight times as much information as a CD-ROM (4.7 GB) and can store a feature film (133 minutes' worth) as well as the usual data and music. A DVD drive can also read a CD-ROM and play an audio CD.

Word Wonders

You'd think computers would have taken us away from counting things using our fingers. However, that's not the case, at least from an etymological point of view. That's because the word *digital* (*DIJ·uh·tul,* adj.), "having to do with numbers," goes back to the Latin word *digitus,* "finger." The story here seems to be that the Roman numerals (I, III, III, and so on) were called "digits" because they resembled human fingers, and we've used "digit" to refer to numbers ever since.

Graphics Cards, Monitors, and Other Video Jargon

Your computer's display is what you look at all day long, so you need to be comfortable with what you see. This is especially important for MULTIMEDIA programs and for Web sites that are heavy on graphics and other bells and whistles. To avoid getting bogged down, you need graphics hardware that can handle the blizzard of data produced by the images, videos, and animations that are part of modern MULTIMEDIA. The attractiveness and performance of your computer's display is a function of two components: the graphics card and the monitor.

The **graphics card** (also known as the *video adapter, graphics adapter,* or *video card*) is the internal component in your system that generates the output you see on your monitor. Your main concern with a graphics card is the amount of **video memory** that it comes with. With more video memory (also called *video RAM*), you can operate your computer at a higher RESOLUTION and COLOR DEPTH, and you can open more and bigger graphics files. You'll probably see most graphics cards described as *AGP* (*ay·gee·pee*), which stands for "accelerated graphics port." This gives you faster video performance than the old standard, which was *PCI* (*pee·see·eye*; "peripheral component interconnect").

The **monitor** (also called the *display*) shows the end result of all the PIXEL pushing done by the graphics card, so it's no less an important component. There are two things you need to watch out for in the monitor you purchase with your system: the size and the "dot pitch."

The size of a monitor is measured diagonally from corner to corner. Sounds simple enough, but posted monitor sizes are actually a bit confusing. For example, an ad might say you'll be getting a "17" monitor (16.0" v.i.s.)." What this means is that, although the monitor has a full 17 inches of glass, only 16 inches of that glass are actually used to display the image. (The **v.i.s.** designation stands for "viewable image size.")

To create an image onscreen, most monitors use a beam that sends out electrons to activate phosphors in the back of the screen. The distance between each of these phosphors is called the **dot pitch;** it's a measure of the clarity of a monitor's image: the smaller the dot pitch, the sharper the image. Look for a monitor with a dot pitch of .26 millimeters (mm) or less.

If you're in the market for a NOTEBOOK computer, your monitor choice will usually be between an **active-matrix** display and a **passive-matrix** display. The active-matrix display is far superior because it's easier on the eyes, shows a clearer image, and can be viewed from an angle. Active-matrix displays are made from *thin-film transistors* (*TFT*), so you'll often see "active-matrix display" and "TFT" used interchangeably.

Notebook displays are also classified as follows:

> *Super VGA* (or *SVGA;* VGA stands for "video graphics array")—Supports a RESOLUTION of up to 800×600.

> *XGA* (extended graphics array)—Supports a RESOLUTION of up to 1,024×768.

> *Super XGA*—Supports a RESOLUTION of up to 1,280×1,024.

The last thing to note about notebook displays is that, unlike regular monitors, the advertised size is the actual image size. So if an ad says that a notebook display is 14.1 inches, then you know the screen images will use the full 14.1 inches.

Sound Cards, Modems, and More

To complete our look at computer buying terminology, this section explains words in five other categories: sound cards, modems, the system case, network cards, and notebook computers.

A **sound card** is an internal CIRCUIT BOARD that processes the sounds made by the computer and plays them back through external speakers plugged in to the sound card. It's also called a *sound board* or an *audio card. Sound Blaster* (sometimes abbreviated as *SB*) is currently one of the most popular models, and it's common to see systems advertised with sound cards that are *Sound Blaster–compatible* (which means they work much like the Sound Blaster does). Some computer sound systems come with a

subwoofer, which is a separate amplifier that helps play low-frequency (bass) sounds, giving the normally tinny computer audio a deeper, richer sound.

A **modem** (*MOH·dum*) is a device used to transmit data between computers via telephone lines. These days, a modem is most often used to connect to the INTERNET. The key stat for a modem is the speed with which it can transmit and receive data. This is usually measured in **kilobits per second** (approximately one thousand BITS per second; see KILO-), or *Kbps*. These days, you shouldn't settle for anything less than 56 Kbps (which is sometimes written as *56K* or *V.90*). Most modern modems are *fax modems,* which means they can also send and receive faxes (as long as you have some kind of faxing software installed on the computer).

The **system case** holds the guts of the computer, including the MICROPROCESSOR, the HARD DRIVE, the CD-ROM DRIVE, the MEMORY, the power supply, and more. There are five basic styles:

> *desktop*—A case designed to sit on top of a desk with the monitor on top of the case.

> *full tower*—A case designed to sit on the floor under or beside the desk. This style is also called just a *tower.*

> *midtower*—A case that's six to eight inches shorter than a full tower.

> *minitower*—A case that's two or three inches shorter than a midtower.

> *microtower*—A case that's two or three inches shorter than a minitower (approximately half the height of a full tower).

Some computers come with a **network card** installed. This is an internal CIRCUIT BOARD that enables your computer to connect to a NETWORK. However, they're also required if you want to set up the computer to use a BROADBAND CONNECTION to the INTERNET. A network card is also called an *Ethernet card,* a *network interface card,* or a *NIC* (*nik*). If you see a network card described as *10/100,* it means the card can operate on networks designed to run at either 10 MBPS or 100 MBPS.

A **notebook computer** is a portable computer that combines the SYSTEM CASE, DISPLAY, keyboard, and other PERIPHERALS into a single package weighing five or six pounds or less. It's also called a *laptop* or a *portable.* A *subnotebook* is a computer that's slightly smaller and weights slightly less (two to five

You Don't Say

The word "desktop" has multiple duties in the computing world. Besides being a type of system case, it's also used generically to refer to any personal computer that isn't portable (that isn't a NOTEBOOK COMPUTER). It's also used in Windows and the Macintosh as a metaphor for the way you work with these operating systems.

pounds) than a notebook computer. Here are some other notebook terms you need to know:

lithium-ion battery (sometimes abbreviated as *Li-Ion*)—A rechargeable battery that offers approximately twice the energy storage capacity as older battery technologies such as *nickel cadmium* (*Ni-Cad*) and *nickel–metal hydride* (*Ni-MH*).

docking station—A separate component into which the notebook slides and connects. The docking station has connectors that enable you to attach a normal MONITOR, keyboard, mouse, and other PERIPHERALS, thus turning the notebook into a desktop computer.

PC card—A small, credit-card–size component that's used to expand the capability of the notebook. For example, you can get PC cards for MODEMS, NETWORK CARDS, and even HARD DRIVES. The PC card slips into a *PC card slot* on the side of the notebook. Most notebooks come with one or two of these slots, and a DOCKING STATION might have two to four more.

pointing device—A device that performs the function of a mouse and that's built into the notebook, usually within or near the keyboard. There are three kinds: a *touch pad* is a smooth area along which you run your finger to simulate the moving of a mouse, a *trackball* is a ball that you rotate to move the mouse pointer, and a *pointing stick* is a small knob with a rubber tip that looks much like a pencil eraser and that you push to and fro to move the pointer.

modular (*MAWD·yoo·lur,* adj.)—Describes components that can be removed from the notebook. For example, it's common for notebooks to have modular CD-ROM DRIVES and floppy disk drives. This enables you to swap one for the other as needed.

Questions and Exercises to Help Everything Sink In

Here's a list of the main words you learned in this chapter:

active-matrix	cache	CD-R drive	CD-ROM drive
CD-RW drive	dot pitch	DVD drive	gigabyte
graphics card	hard drive	kilobits per second	megabyte
megahertz	memory	microprocessor	modem
monitor	network card	notebook computer	passive-matrix
RAM	sound card	subwoofer	system case
v.i.s.	video memory		

1. Choose the measurement normally associated with the *hard drive:*
   a. kilobits per second
   b. megahertz
   c. megabyte
   d. gigabyte
2. Fill in the blank: "They tell you the monitor is 15 inches, but it's really 13.8 inches _____."
3. Choose the type of drive that can be written to more than once:
   a. CD-ROM
   b. CD-RW
   c. DVD
   d. CD-R

Match the word on the left with the short definition on the right:

4. subwoofer   a. a component that stores frequently used data
5. memory   b. the computer's container
6. cache   c. a measure of a monitor's image clarity
7. system case   d. amplifier for bass sounds
8. dot pitch   e. chips that store data
9. Choose the word that's a type of *microprocessor:*
   a. Motorola
   b. Pentium
   c. SpeedStep
   d. PC100
10. Choose the term that's not related to a *modem:*
    a. fax modem
    b. modular
    c. V.90
    d. 56K

Chapter 20

More Computer Words

In This Chapter

➤ Some general computer words

➤ Words about software

➤ Words about hardware

"Science and technology multiply around us. To an increasing extent they dictate the languages in which we speak and think. Either we use those languages, or we remain mute."

—J. G. Ballard, British novelist

If computers are intimidating and difficult to use, only part of the blame can fall on the fact that they were designed and created by geeks and nerds who forgot what it was like to be a beginner (or never knew in the first place). However, I'm convinced that the main reason why computers give some people the willies is that there's just so much jargon and technical terminology that can't be avoided. Computerspeak redefines the word arcane, and listening to two computer experts talk shop is about as incomprehensible as hearing the Dead Sea Scrolls recited backward.

My goal here is to improve upon what you learned in the preceding chapter and increase your computer word power with a catalog of the most common technical terms. I've divided them into three sections: general terms, software terms, and hardware terms.

"Bit to WYSIWYG": General Computer Terms

The **bit** is the fundamental unit of computer storage. Computers store data using tiny electronic devices called *gates,* which are either open (electricity flows through) or closed (no electricity flows through). These two states are represented using the *binary number system,* where 1 means open and 0 means closed. Each state represents a single bit, and this explains the origin of the word "bit": it's a blend of "binary" and "digit."

To **boot** (verb) is to turn on or restart a computer. One of the things that happens during the boot process is the *Power-On Self Test* (*POST*), which is the process that detects and tests MEMORY, PORTS, and basic devices such as the GRAPHICS CARD, keyboard, and HARD DISK. If everything passes, your system emits a single beep. To *cold boot* is to restart the computer by turning the power on or by pressing the restart button; to *warm boot* is to restart a running computer, usually by pressing the Ctrl + Alt + Delete key combination. The warm boot skips the POST.

A **byte** is eight BITS, and it represents a single character of information. For example, the letter M is represented by the following byte: 01001101. File sizes, MEMORY capacity, and HARD DRIVE capacity are all usually measured in hundreds, thousands, millions, or billions of bytes. Note, however, that these are only approximate. To understand why, you first have to know that using the BINARY NUMBER SYSTEM means that everything on a computer happens in powers of two: 2, 4, 8, 16, 32, and so on. 2 to the power of 10 is 1,024, which is close enough to 1,000 that computer types feel comfortable using the prefix *kilo-,* which means "thousand." Therefore, a *kilobyte* is 1,024 bytes. Similarly, 1,024 multiplied by 1,024 equals 1,048,576, which is close enough to a million to use the prefix *mega-,* "million." Therefore, a *megabyte* is 1,048,576 bytes. The following table presents the basic computer size prefixes, their meanings, and their sizes.

Word Wonders

The verb "to boot" comes from the phrase *pulling oneself up by one's own bootstraps,* which refers to the fact that the computer can launch its own startup code.

Prefix	Meaning	Size	Size in Bytes
kilo-	"thousand"	1,024 bytes	
mega-	"million"	1,024 kilobytes	1,048,576 bytes
giga-	"billion"	1,024 megabytes	1,073,741,824 bytes
tera-	"trillion"	1,024 gigabytes	1,099,511,627,776 bytes
peta-	"quadrillion"	1,024 terabytes	1,125,899,906,842,624 bytes

To put this in some perspective, the entire contents of the Library of Congress would consume a mere 10 terabytes.

The **color depth** determines the number of colors available to your PROGRAMS and graphics. (This is sometimes called the *color palette.*) Color depth is expressed in either BITS or total colors. For example, a color depth called *High Color* uses 16 bits or 65,536 colors (2 to the power of 16), and a color depth called *True Color* uses 24 bits or 16,777,216 colors (2 to the power of 24). Note that unless your GRAPHICS CARD has a lot of VIDEO MEMORY, you may have to trade off color depth and RESOLUTION.

The **cursor** is usually a blinking, vertical bar that tells you where the next character you type will appear. Its more formal name is the *insertion point cursor.*

Multimedia is the computer-based presentation of data using multiple *media* ("modes of communication") including text, graphics, sound, animation, and video. A *multimediocrity* is a bit of multimedia that's dull or poorly made.

Multitasking refers to a computer's capability to perform more than one operation at one time. For example, you can be working in your WORD PROCESSOR, have your E-MAIL PROGRAM checking for new messages, and have your SPREADSHEET program printing a file, all at the same time.

A **network** is a collection of computers connected via special cables to share files, disks, PROGRAMS, PRINTERS, and other PERIPHERALS. Most networks are *local area networks* (or *LANs*), which means all the computers occupy a relatively small geographical area such as a department, office, home, or building.

The **operating system** is the PROGRAM that controls every aspect of the computer's operation, including the following:

➤ Input from the keyboard and mouse

➤ Output to the MONITOR or a PRINTER

➤ The launching of other programs

➤ The management of files

➤ The allocation and management of MEMORY

➤ The interaction with and management of all hardware including the MICROPROCESSOR, the HARD DISK, and the GRAPHICS CARD

Word Wonders

The word *multitasking* has broken free of its computing shackles and taken up residence in the mainstream world where it means "to perform two or more actions at the same time." So if you find yourself reading a magazine while eating a meal with the TV turned on, you're officially multitasking.

The operating system almost always runs automatically when the computer is started, and you only deal with it via the *interface,* which is composed of the elements you interact with onscreen, including icons and dialog boxes. (The latter are picture oriented, so an interface that uses such devices is called a *graphical user interface,* or *GUI* [GOO *ee*].) The most popular operating system in use today is Microsoft Windows, which comes in various flavors including Windows 98, Windows Me, Windows 2000, and Windows XP. Macintosh computers come with their own operating system called Mac OS.

A **pixel** (*PIKS·ul*) is a tiny monitor element that displays the individual dots that make up the screen image. (The word "pixel" combines the words "picture" and "element.") Each pixel consists of three components—red, green, and blue—and these are manipulated to produce a specific color. All the colors you see on the screen are the result of thousands of these pixels being activated on your monitor and set to display a specific hue.

Programming is the craft of designing and building computer software PROGRAMS. The *programmer* begins with an *algorithm* (*AL·guh·rith·um,* "th" as in "the"), a logical sequence of steps for solving a problem. She then converts these steps into a series of statements written in a particular *programming language*. These statements are then *compiled* (translated into a language the computer can understand) into a working program, which the programmer then checks for BUGS (this is called *debugging*). This process is repeated many times until the program is complete. (A program that isn't yet finished is called a *beta program*.)

Word Wonders

The word algorithm comes from the last name of one of the greatest mathematicians in history: Abu Abdullah Muhammad Ibn Musa al-Khwarizmi. Working in the ninth century, al-Khwarizmi developed a systematic approach to decimal numbers that influenced all of medieval mathematics. This approach was named *algorizm* after him, which eventually became our word *algorithm*. He was also the inventor of *algebra* (now you know who to blame!), a term that comes from *al-jabr*, part of the title of a book that al-Khwarizmi wrote on the subject: *Al-Kitab Almukhtamar fi Hisab Al-Jabr wa'l-Muqabala.* (This translates roughly as *The Compendious Book on Calculation by Completion and Balancing.*)

The **resolution** is a measure of how many PIXELS are used to display the screen image. Pixels are arranged on the screen in a row-and-column grid. The lowest resolution is 640×480. This means that the pixels are arranged in a grid that has 640 columns and 480 rows. A higher resolution enables you to display more things on the screen, but each of those things appears a bit smaller.

WYSIWYG (*WIZ·ee·wig*) is an acronym that stands for What You See Is What You Get, and it means that the what you see when you open a document within a program is what you'll see when you print it out. (This doesn't always work, so some folks say that WYSIWYG must really stand far When You See It Won't You Gag.)

"Program" to "Virus": Software Terms

Despite all the MICROPROCESSOR brainpower under the hood, computers are actually as dumb as posts and will just sit there uselessly unless someone comes along and tells them what to do next. For the average user, the easiest way to tell a computer where to go is to launch a **program**, a sequence of instructions that can be understood and executed by a computer and that is designed to perform (or to let the user perform) a specific task. (Note, however, that even the simplest program is a complex creation consisting of probably thousands of instructions. The biggest programs contain tens of millions of instructions and are among the most complex constructions ever created.)

Parts Dept.

The suffix *–ware* means "things of the same general type or made of the same material." It comes from the Old English word *waru,* "goods." Software, of course, isn't really soft, so how did "soft" and "ware" get together? The short version of the story is that the word *hardware*—the physical components of a computer system—already existed when programs were invented. Since these programs could be viewed as the nonphysical components of the computer, somebody thought the opposite of hardware—*soft*ware—would be the appropriate name.

You can also call a program an *application.* **Software** is the general name for all programs, although an individual program is often called a *software package.* There are many different types of programs, but here's a list of the types most commonly used:

word processor—A program used for typing, editing, and formatting text documents such as memos, letters, and resumés.

spreadsheet (*SPRED·sheet*)—A program that uses a row-and-column format to construct numerical tables and perform calculations.

201

graphics (GRAF·iks)—A program used for drawing or painting images.

desktop publishing—A program used for designing, creating (using text and graphics), and laying out publications such as newsletters, brochures, and flyers. This phrase is sometimes abbreviated as *DTP*.

database—A program used for storing data in a structured format.

file management—A program used for copying, moving, renaming, and deleting files.

utility—A program that performs some kind of maintenance or repair function.

See also: WEB BROWSER, E-MAIL PROGRAM, NEWSREADER.

Word Wonders

There's a popular and appealing tale of how the word *bug* came about. Apparently, an early computer pioneer named Grace Hopper was working on a machine called the Mark II in 1947. While investigating a glitch, she found a moth among the vacuum tubes, so from then on glitches were called bugs. Appealing, yes, but true? Not quite. In fact, engineers had already been referring to mechanical defects as "bugs" for at least 60 years before Ms. Hopper's discovery. As proof, the *Oxford English Dictionary* offers the following quotation from an 1889 edition of the Pall Mall Gazette:

"Mr. Edison, I was informed, had been up the two previous nights discovering 'a bug' in his phonograph—an expression for solving a difficulty, and implying that some imaginary insect has secreted itself inside and is causing all the trouble."

Most software is available from computer and electronics stores, and the price ranges vary considerably: from a simple $10 utility program to massive *suites* (collections of programs) costing hundreds of dollars. You can also obtain programs by DOWNLOADING them from the Internet. However you get it, any program that you pay for in advance is called *commercial software*. However, there are two varieties of downloadable software that don't require an up-front payment:

shareware—This type of software is free to download and install on your computer so that you can give it a test run. If you don't like the program, you can delete it and that's the end of it. However, if you like the program and believe you'll use it regularly, then you're expected to pay for it. If they're not paid for, some shareware programs will quit working after a set time, while others offer only limited functionality (the latter type is called *crippleware*).

freeware—This type of software is totally free to download, install, and use as you see fit. It's usually crippleware, but you'll occasionally find a freeware program that's fully functional. Some freeware authors ask only that you perform a good deed or donate money to charity, in which case the software is called *careware*.

Although most programs work just fine most of the time, it's an unfortunate fact of computing life that a program will occasionally act flaky or even seize up entirely. (In the latter case, the program is said to be *hung* or to have *crashed*.) The most common cause of this frustrating behavior is a **bug**, a flaw in the logic or *syntax* ("construction rules") of the program. Bugs apply to software, so if you need a word for a software *or* hardware problem, use *glitch*.

Speaking of bugs, another possible cause of strange computer behavior is a **virus**, a rogue program that infects your system and then displays annoying messages at best or deletes files at worst. Viruses are crafted by modern-day MISCREANTS, *hackers* ("programming wizards") who've succumbed to the dark side of The Force. These amoral programmers like to muddy the waters by describing their nasty creations as "self-propagating, autonomous computer programs" and giving them innocent-sounding names such as Michelangelo and Christmas. However, most viruses have names that more directly reflect their intentions: Armageddon, Beast, Black Monday, Dark Avenger, and Darth Vader.

You Don't Say

Technically, a *hacker* is someone who enjoys programming at a high level and who likes to explore the limits of both hardware and software. On the other hand, a *cracker* is a malicious hacker who uses his talents to break into systems and create viruses. Unfortunately, the mainstream media have seized on "hacker" as the word of choice for bad-apple programmers, so the good sense of hacker may soon be lost. (An excellent indication of this is that hackers who do positive things are now often called *white-hat hackers* or *ethical hackers*.)

"Bus" to "Printer": Hardware Terms

The **bus** is a pathway along which electrical signals are sent as a way of transferring data from one computer component to another. There are three types of buses in common use today: *ISA* (Industry Standard Architecture), *PCI* (Peripheral Component Interconnect), and *USB* (Universal Serial Bus). From a user's standpoint, the important thing about the bus is that it determines to a certain extent the types of CIRCUIT BOARDS that can be added to the computer. See also EXPANSION SLOT.

A **chip** is an electronic device that consists of numerous (sometimes millions of) connected components such as transistors embedded on a silicon wafer. Chip is short for *microchip,* and its more technical name is *integrated circuit* (*IC*). For examples, see MICROPROCESSOR and MEMORY.

A **circuit board** is a thin, plastic plate that has been specially coated so that CHIPS and other electrical components can be attached to the surface of the plate and connections can be made between the components. See also EXPANSION BOARD. This is also called a *printed circuit board*, *adapter*, or *card*. For examples, see GRAPHICS CARD, NETWORK CARD, SOUND CARD, and MOTHERBOARD.

A **device driver** is a small software program that serves as an intermediary between a hardware device and the OPERATING SYSTEM. Device drivers encode software instructions into signals that the device understands, and conversely, the drivers interpret device signals and report them to the operating system.

An **expansion board** is a CIRCUIT BOARD that attaches to the BUS to expand the capabilities of the computer. See also EXPANSION SLOT. For examples, see GRAPHICS CARD, NETWORK CARD, and SOUND CARD.

An **expansion slot** is an internal socket into which an EXPANSION BOARD is inserted to attach it to the BUS. ISA and PCI buses use slots that are different lengths (PCI slots are shorter). Note, however, that USB devices don't use expansion slots. Instead, they plug into special PORTS in the back of the computer.

The **motherboard** is the computer's main CIRCUIT BOARD containing major system components such as the MICROPROCESSOR, the MEMORY CHIPS, PORTS for the keyboard and mouse, and connectors for the HARD DRIVE and CD-ROM DRIVE.

A **peripheral** is a device that's attached to the computer. Common peripherals include a HARD DRIVE, MONITOR, CD-ROM DRIVE, MODEM, keyboard, and mouse.

Plug and Play is a standard that enables hardware and software to communicate with each other to recognize devices and configure them automatically. For Plug and Play (sometimes abbreviated as PnP) to work for a particular device, that device must be Plug and Play–compatible (it will tell you on the box), you need to have a Plug and Play OPERATING SYSTEM (such as Windows 95, 98, Me, 2000, or XP), and you must have a Plug and Play computer. Most computers manufactured since about 1996 support Plug and Play, but ask the manufacturer if you're not sure.

A **port** is a connector that usually appears on the back of the computer and is used to connect external PERIPHERAL devices. This connection is made by attaching a *cable* to the back of the device and then attaching the other end of the cable to the appropriate port. Most computers have several ports, but they each have a unique shape, and the cable's plug has a shape that matches one of those ports. So there's usually only one possible place into which any cable can be plugged.

A **printer** is an external PERIPHERAL that transfers the text and graphics from a document on the computer to one or more pieces of paper. There are three main types:

dot matrix—With this type of printer, text and images are created using tiny dots, each of which is transferred to the paper by striking a pin against an ink ribbon. These printers are fast, but they're noisy and the quality isn't very good.

ink-jet—This type transfers the text and images by heating liquid ink into a mist that's sprayed through tiny holes onto the paper. The quality of most ink-jet printers is excellent and color printers are within most budgets, but they print slowly and the ink can smudge if proper ink-jet paper isn't used.

laser—This type transfers text and images by using a laser beam to draw an image of the paper on a photosensitive drum, which is then charged so that it attracts *toner,* a dry, powdery ink. The toner is then transferred to the paper, and heat is applied to seal the toner on the page. (This is the same process that a photocopier uses.) Laser printers produce high-quality pages and are quiet and fast, but they tend to be expensive, especially color laser printers.

Questions and Exercises to Help Everything Sink In

Here's a list of the main words you learned in this chapter:

bit	boot	bug	bus
byte	chip	circuit board	color depth
cursor	device driver	expansion board	expansion slot
freeware	motherboard	multimedia	multitasking
network	operating system	peripheral	pixel
Plug and Play	port	printer	program
programming	resolution	shareware	software
virus	WYSIWYG		

1. How many *bits* are in a *byte?*

2. Choose the term that's most closely related to *resolution:*
   a. color depth
   b. bit
   c. WYSIWYG
   d. pixel

3. Choose the term whose functionality does not include having computer components connected to it:
   a. device driver
   b. port
   c. expansion slot
   d. motherboard

Match the word on the left with the short definition on the right:

4. peripheral   a. a sequence of instructions
5. virus   b. running more than one program at once
6. program   c. a connector for a device
7. port   d. a device attached to a computer
8. multitasking   e. a malicious application

9. Choose the word that's a synonym for *chip:*
   a. circuit board
   b. integrated circuit
   c. card
   d. gate

10. Choose the abbreviation that's not related to *bus:*
    a. USB
    b. PCI
    c. LAN
    d. ISA

Chapter 21

Internetese: The Internet and Its Jargon

"Jargon: any technical language we do not understand."

—Mason Cooley, American aphorist

As you'd expect with anything that boasts millions of participants, the Internet is home to a wide variety of characters. In particular, the Net seems to attract more than its fair share of three kinds of folks: neologists, jargonauts, and nymrods.

A *neologist* (*nee·OL·uh·jist,* noun) is a person who coins new words and phrases by making them up, by enlisting existing words to perform new duties, or by combining two or more words into a new creation.

A *jargonaut* (*JAR·guh·not,* noun) is a person who seeks out new words and new phrases and who boldly tries to get these coinages into general circulation by using them as often as possible.

A *nymrod* (*NIM·rod,* noun) is a person who, without even the slightest sting of conscience or pang of doubt, insists on turning every multiword computer term into an acronym or abbreviation.

As you work with the Internet, you're bound to run into many examples of each kind of Internet word hound, which means you'll be exposed to all kinds of new jargon and acronyms. To help you decipher this *Internetese,* this chapter presents translations of some common terms.

Wired Words: Getting on the Internet

Although the Internet *seems* like it's everywhere these days, it isn't like, say, radio signals, where all you have to do is plug in a radio and start listening. Instead, you have to find an **Internet service provider** (ISP; *eye·ess·pee*), a business that has negotiated a deal with (usually) the local telephone company to get a direct connection to the Internet and then offers subscribers a link to this connection.

Once you've paid your money (which is usually a monthly fee), the ISP provides you (or asks you for) a **username**, a handle that uniquely identifies you among the ISP's customers. You also get (or supply) a **password** so that no one else can use your connection. You then use both the user name and password to **log on** to the ISP's system each time you want to access the Internet.

Most ISPs offer a **dial-up connection**, an Internet connection that's initiated by having your computer's MODEM dial the ISP's phone number. However, dial-up connections are slowly falling out of favor because of two limitations:

➤ They tie up a phone line, which means that either you miss calls while connected or you have to pay for a second phone line.

➤ They offer low **bandwidth**, which is a measure of how much data can be sent through a transmission medium such as a phone line.

On the dial-up level, bandwidth is measured in KILOBITS PER SECOND (KBPS; see also BIT), with most modems (and most ISPs) offering connections at 56 Kbps. However, **broadband** (*BRAWD·band*) connections are much faster and offer speeds measured in the hundreds of kilobits per second or even over one **megabit per second** (*Mbps*), which means approximately one million bits per second (see MEGA-). There are two technologies competing to be the broadband provider-of-choice among consumers:

cable modem—This is a special type of MODEM that attaches to a cable TV line. The theoretical bandwidth is 1.5 Mbps, but since the connection is shared with people in your neighborhood, the speed decreases as more people go online.

digital subscriber Line (DSL)—This technology adds some enhancements to your existing telephone line to speed data transmissions up to, in theory, about 1.5 Mbps. However, line conditions and distance from the central phone office usually mean that "real-world" bandwidth is between 500 Kbps and 1 Mbps. In any case, you can still use your phone line for voice calls when you're on the Internet.

Once you're connected to the Internet, you can describe yourself as being **online**, which has the general meaning "connected to a computer NETWORK." Things available on the Internet can also be described as *online,* which in this case means "accessible via a computer network." When you're disconnected, you're **offline**.

When you're online, you're said to be in **cyberspace** (*SYE·bur·space*), the *virtual* ("non-physical") terrain created by computers connected to the Internet. Cyberspace is a metaphor that's used to describe the "place" where E-MAIL and CHAT conversations are held, where WORLD WIDE WEB–based stores and libraries are located, and along which you "travel" to visit WEB SITES from other parts of the (real) world.

The *cyber-* prefix comes from the Greek word KUBERMAN, "a person who steers a ship." If you read Chapter 17, "Weasel Words from Politics and Government," then you'll recognize this is as the word that was also the source of GOVERNOR. *Cyber-* came into English in the 1940s when mathematician Norbert Weiner used *cybernetics* as the name for his theories related to communication and control in machines and animals.

Word Wonders

The word cyberspace was coined by the writer William Gibson in his 1984 novel *Neuro-mancer.* He envisioned a future *dystopia* ("an imaginary world where life is extremely bad") that contained a virtual world (sometimes called the "matrix") where people could "jack in" to communicate with each other and manipulate data as though they were physical objects. He defined cyberspace as a "consensual hallucination experienced daily by billions of legitimate operators" and as a "graphic representation of data abstracted from the banks of every computer in the human system."

A World Wide Web of Words

The **World Wide Web** is a collection of documents accessible via the Internet and containing text, images, audio, video, and HYPERLINKS. To speed things up and avoid all those syllables, most people shorten "the World Wide Web" to just *the Web.* Each of the documents is called a **Web page**, or just a *page.* The collection of documents found at a single location is called a **Web site**. A person who creates or runs a Web site is called a **Webmaster**.

The defining feature of the Web is the concept of **hypertext** (*HY·pur·tekst*), which refers to pieces of information that are associated with each other to form a complex, interconnected structure (that is, a *web*). The association is created by setting up one or more **hyperlinks** (*HY·pur·links*), connections between one Web page and another. Each *link* (the more common short form) is either a specially formatted word or phrase or an image that, when clicked with a mouse, automatically loads the other Web page.

The software that enables you to view and interact with Web pages is called a **Web browser.** The two most popular browsers are Microsoft's Internet Explorer and Netscape's Navigator.

To **surf** (verb) is to view Web pages and click links to jump to other pages. A related word is *egosurfing,* scouring the Internet's sites and SEARCH ENGINES for mentions of your own name or your business name.

Here's a quick list of some types of pages and sites you should know about:

home page—The main or starting page of a Web site. The home page usually gives you an overview of the site as well as links to other parts of the site.

cobweb page—A Web page that hasn't been updated in a long time.

Macarena page—A Web page capitalizing on a current fad. Such a page is usually full of fluff and (like the fad it follows) tends to have a short life expectancy. Also called a *Barney page* (after the Barney the Dinosaur fad from a few years ago).

guru site—A Web site, put together by an expert on a particular subject, that contains a large amount of useful, accurate information on that subject.

stalker site—A site devoted to a celebrity, the content of which clearly indicates that the fan who created the site is obsessed with his subject.

portal site—A Web site that combines a wide array of content and services in an effort to convince users to make the site their home page. There are many different flavors of portals:

corporate portal—An internal Web site on a corporate network that offers content and services aimed at the company's employees.

horizontal portal—A portal that offers a broad range of content and services.

personal portal—A portal that offers content and services customized for an individual.

vertical portal—A portal that offers content and services aimed at a specific type of user. Also called a *vortal* or a *vertical community.*

A **bookmark** is a Web site pointer that's stored in a Web browser. When the user selects a bookmark (usually from a menu), the browser loads the associated page automatically. Note that this word can also be used as a verb. (Note, too, that the Internet Explorer Web browser uses the term *favorite* instead of bookmark.)

Link rot is the gradual obsolescence of the links on a Web page as the sites they point to become unavailable. A link that no longer points to a valid site is called a *dead link*. This can lead to **Web rage**, anger caused by Web frustrations such as slow downloads, nonexistent links, and information that is difficult to find.

Can I Get Here from There?
Internet Address Terms

Every resource (and just about every person) on the Internet has an **address** that provides a unique location that people can use to locate that resource. Although these addresses take many forms, there are two types—e-mail and the Web—that come up 99 percent of the time, so I'll focus on them here.

An **e-mail address** is a unique Internet address for receiving E-MAIL MESSAGES. To help you understand the structure of these addresses, consider this generic e-mail address:

    username@domain

This address has three parts:

> *username*—This is the recipient's USER NAME, as previously discussed.

> *@*—This symbol (it's pronounced *at*) separates the "who" part of the address (the part to the left of the @ sign) and the "where" part (the part to the right of the @ sign).

> *domain*—This is the **domain name**, which identifies a specific network or computer connected to the Internet. (For most e-mail addresses, the domain name identifies the network of the user's ISP.)

The domain name can take various forms, with the simplest being the following:

    name.type

Here, the *name* part is a word that varies with each network or organization, and it's usually either the name of the associated company or the name of an individual. The *type* part tells you what type of organization you're dealing with, and it's called the **top-level domain** (or *TLD*). The most common type is *com,* which is theoretically only used by commercial businesses but has seen much broader use over the past few years. For example, my own domain name is mcfedries.com.

Notice, too, how the name and type are separated by a period. You pronounce this as "dot," so the entire domain name reads as "mcfedries dot com." Because of this, a domain name that uses the *com* type is called a **dot com**.

Here is a list of the main TLDs.

TLD	What It Represents
com	Commercial businesses
edu	Educational institutions
gov	Governments
int	International organizations
mil	The military
net	Networking organizations
org	Nonprofit organizations

In addition to these top-level domains, there are also **geographical domains** that are two-letter codes for specific countries. For example, ca is for Canada, jp is for Japan, and us is for the United States. In late 2000, the Internet powers-that-be announced seven new top-level domains. The following list explains these new domains.

TLD	What It Represents
aero	Airlines
biz	Businesses
coop	Cooperatives
info	General sites
museum	Museums
name	Individuals
pro	Professionals

A **Web address** is a unique address that identifies a specific WEB PAGE. The format is a bit different than an e-mail address. Here's an example:

http://www.mcfedries.com/books/index.html

http://	This part identifies that this as a Web address. (If you're curious, the abbreviation *HTTP* is short for *Hypertext Transfer Protocol*.)
www.mcfedries.com	This is the *host name* of the computer where the Web page resides. A **host** is an individual computer connected to the Internet. Each host is part of a domain and is identified by tacking a prefix onto the domain name. The most common prefix is www, which is used for a host that acts as a **Web server**, a computer that stores and displays Web pages.

| /books/ | This is the directory that contains the Web page. |
| index.html | This is the filename of the Web page. |

A Web address is also known as a *Uniform Resource Locator,* or *URL* (*yoo·ar·ell* or *erl*).

More Net Words You Should Know

This section presents a list of Internet terms that you're likely to stumble upon during your surfing safaris.

A **cookie** (noun) is small piece of data that a Web site stores on your computer as a way of remembering information about your visit to the site. For example, an online shopping site would use a cookie to preserve your *shopping cart,* the list of items you've ordered.

To **download** (verb) is to request that a file be sent to your computer. (The file requested is also called a download.) See also UPLOAD.

A **FAQ** (*FAK,* noun) is a list of frequently asked questions. Many Web sites offer a FAQ so you can get quick answers to the most common questions (and to save the site's operators from having to answer the questions a thousand times).

A **firewall** (noun) is a security PROGRAM that prevents unauthorized access to a computer or network that's connected to the Internet. Although most firewalls are designed to protect corporate sites (and thus are hideously expensive), there are now *personal firewalls* that are designed for individuals, especially those who have BROADBAND connections.

An **MP3** (*em·pee·three,* noun) is a type of music file that you DOWNLOAD and then play either on your computer or on a special device that can handle such files.

Netiquette (*NET·uh·kuht* or *NET·uh·kit,* noun) is a combination of "Net" and "etiquette" and is the set of practices and conventions that are prescribed by the generally accepted social norms of the Internet.

Script kiddies (noun) are inexperienced and unskilled CRACKERS who attempt to infiltrate or disrupt computer systems merely by running programs designed to crack those systems. They're looked down upon by true crackers because they lack the skills to create these programs themselves.

A **search engine** (noun) is a Web site that enables you to search the Web for information by entering one or more keywords that identify the type of information you want to view.

Streaming (noun) is the Internet-based broadcast of a multimedia file that plays as it is sent rather than having to wait for the entire file to be DOWNLOADED. People who listen to such broadcasts are called *streamies.*

To **upload** (verb) is to send a file from your computer to another computer. See also DOWNLOAD.

From Newbie to Netizen: Internet People

I close this chapter with a list of just a few of the many words that exist to describe the various types of people who populate the Internet:

A **knowbie** (*NO·bee*) is a knowledgeable and experienced Internet user. See also NEWBIE.

A **lamer** (*LAY·mur*) is a computer user who pretends to great knowledge but who in fact lacks fundamental skills and can only parrot the ideas and techniques of other people. Also known as a *poser*.

A **luser** (*LOO·zur*) is an Internet user who doesn't have the faintest idea what he's doing and who, more importantly, refuses to do anything about it. This word is a blend of "loser" and "user."

A **netizen** (*NET·i·zun*) is a person who actively participates in Internet culture. This word combines "Net" and "citizen."

A **newbie** (*NOO·bee*) is a new or inexperienced user, especially one who is ignorant of NETIQUETTE and other online proprieties. Newbie is a variation of *new boy,* which the *Oxford English Dictionary* defines as a "schoolboy during his first term at a school, esp. one at a preparatory school or English public school."

A **power newbie** is a NEWBIE who actively seeks knowledge in an effort to become a KNOWBIE.

A **read-only user** is a person who uses the Internet exclusively for reading Web pages and e-mail and doesn't create his own original content. (See also LURKER.)

Questions and Exercises to Help Everything Sink In

Here's a list of the main words you learned in this chapter:

@	address	bandwidth	bookmark
broadband	cable modem	cookie	cyberspace
dial-up connection	digital subscriber line	domain name	dot com
download	e-mail address	FAQ	firewall
geographical domain	host	hyperlink	Internet service provider
knowbie	lamer	link rot	luser
megabits per second	MP3	netiquette	netizen

newbie	offline	online	password
power newbie	read-only user	script kiddies	search engine
streaming	surf	top-level domain	upload
user name	Web address	Web browser	Web page
Web rage	Web server	Web site	Webmaster
World Wide Web			

1. Choose the word that means "connected to a computer network":
   a. online
   b. surf
   c. cyberspace
   d. host

2. Choose the phrase of which "com" is an example:
   a. geographical domain
   b. top-level domain
   c. Web address
   d. Web server

3. Choose the word that's not an insulting term:
   a. lamer
   b. script kiddies
   c. knowbie
   d. luser

4. What is the correction pronunciation of @:
   a. ah
   b. at
   c. ay
   d. achoo

Match the word on the left with the short definition on the right:

5. hyperlink   a. a security program
6. surf   b. a computer that stores and displays pages
7. bandwidth   c. to view Web pages
8. firewall   d. a connection from one Web page to another
9. Web server   e. data-carrying capacity

215

10. Choose the word that means "nonphysical":
    a. link
    b. vortal
    c. virtual
    d. dystopia

Chapter 22

Talking the "Talk" Talk: E-Mail, Chat, and More

In This Chapter

➤ Words from the e-mail world

➤ Chat and instant-messaging terminology

➤ Words related to Usenet newsgroups

➤ A long list of acronyms and abbreviations

"While modern technology has given people powerful new communication tools, it apparently can do nothing to alter the fact that many people have nothing useful to say."

—Lee Gomes, American journalist

All human communities, large and small, develop unique behavior patterns, arts, beliefs, and institutions. In other words, they develop a culture they can call their own. This is certainly true of the Internet as well. However, "culture shock" is *way* too mild a term for what most people feel when they first get online. I mean, let's face facts: The Internet is often just plain weird. People on the Net use unfathomable buzzwords unashamedly, unintelligible abbreviations unreservedly, and undecipherable symbols unblushingly. New Net recruits can be forgiven for thinking the inmates are running the asylum because, well, they often are!

This chapter is designed to help you overcome the inevitable Internet culture-shock-and-then-some. It introduces you to the jargon, abbreviations, and acronyms you'll encounter most often when using the Internet's main communications technologies: e-mail, chat, instant messaging, and Usenet newsgroups.

"Have Your People E-Mail My People"

Now that the twenty-first century is in full swing, it's starting to seem, well, *strange* to come across people who don't have any access to e-mail. In just a few short years, e-mail has gone from a relatively obscure, geeks-only technology to a *ubiquitous* ("seemingly everywhere") and essential communications tool. However, the success of e-mail doesn't necessarily mean that its terminology is understood by all who use it (to say nothing of those brave souls who have thus far resisted the call to e-mail arms). To help, this section runs through a few useful e-mail terms.

Although most corporations have their own internal e-mail systems, I'm discussing Internet e-mail in particular in this section. (That said, most of the words here will apply to any e-mail system). So to get in on the e-mail fun, you first need an account with an INTERNET SERVICE PROVIDER, which almost always includes at least one e-mail **mailbox**, your own personal e-mail storage location on the ISP's **e-mail server.** The latter is a computer that processes incoming and outgoing e-mail messages. (Note, too, that there are third-party companies that will provide you with an e-mail account that you access on the WORLD WIDE WEB. This is called *Webmail*.)

To do the e-mail thing, you need the services of an **e-mail program** (sometimes called an *e-mail client*). You use this program to retrieve from your mailbox any messages sent to you and to ship messages out to anyone who'll listen. (Speaking of sending messages, note that it's perfectly acceptable to use *e-mail* as a verb.)

When you receive or send e-mail, you'll notice that each message has three more or less distinct parts. The first part is called the **header,** and it consists of some or all of the following fields:

> **To**—This field specifies the E-MAIL ADDRESS for the recipient of the message.
>
> **Cc**—This field specifies the addresses of one or more "courtesy copy" recipients. These are people who might be interested in getting a copy of the e-mail but who don't necessarily have to do anything about it (such as respond).
>
> **Bcc**—This field specifies the addresses of one or more "blind courtesy copy" recipients. This is similar to a courtesy copy except that the addresses in the Bcc field are not shown to any of the other recipients.
>
> **Subject**—This field is used to enter a brief title or description of the message.

Note that, when you're composing an e-mail message, you can usually fill in the To, Cc, and Bcc fields by selecting names from an **address book**, which is a list of people and their e-mail addresses.

The second part of the message is called the **body**, which appears below the header and holds the main text of the message.

The third part is the **signature**, a few lines of text at the end of the body that identify the sender and include her contact information (such as her company name, e-mail address, and fax number). Some people also include snappy quotations or other tidbits.

Some messages come with a fourth part called an **attachment**, a separate file that's linked to the e-mail message and that hitches a ride to the recipient when the message is sent.

Besides replying to a message you've received, you can also **forward** (verb) it, which means you pass it along to another e-mail address.

After sending an e-mail, you may receive a **bounce message**, which is an error message returned by an e-mail system if a message can't be delivered (because, say, the address is wrong).

Not all the e-mails that come your way will be pleasant. The worst kind (at least in my opinion) is **spam**, unsolicited commercial e-mail messages advertising everything from get-rich-quick schemes (or their online equivalent: *get-rich-click* schemes) to pornographic Web sites.

Word Wonders

Spam originally meant "flooding a Usenet newsgroup with irrelevant or inappropriate messages." This original sense derived from the overuse of the word "spam" in a sketch performed by the comedy troupe Monty Python's Flying Circus. The sketch begins as follows:

Mr. Bun: Morning.

Waitress: Morning.

Mr. Bun: Well, what you got?

Waitress: Well, there's egg and bacon; egg, sausage and bacon; egg and spam; egg, bacon and spam; egg, bacon, sausage and spam; spam, bacon, sausage and spam; spam, egg, spam, spam, bacon and spam; spam, sausage, spam, spam, spam, bacon, spam, tomato and spam; spam, spam, spam, egg and spam; spam, spam, spam, spam, spam, spam, baked beans, spam, spam, spam and spam ...

In recent years, the meaning of "spam" was extended to include unsolicited e-mail ads. In case you don't know, Spam is a luncheon meat consisting of compressed pork shoulder with a bit of ham tossed in.

Another scourge upon your mailbox is **chain mail**, e-mail chain letters that promise dire consequences if you don't forward the message to some specified number of people. This type of scam is similar to the e-mail **virus hoax**, which purports to warn you of a dangerous e-mail–based virus that's making the rounds and that, if read, will wipe out your data or perform some other nasty act.

Real-Time Talk: Words from Chat and Instant Messaging

Some impatient types didn't like the fact that it might take several minutes or even several *hours* to get an answer to an e-mail message. So they satisfied their need for communication speed by inventing **chat**, a system that enables users to conduct real-time conversations by sending simple text messages that are immediately delivered to all participants.

Chat started out as a component of online services (such as America Online) that set up various **chat rooms**, VIRTUAL spaces where chat participants gather to discuss a specific topic.

On the Internet, however, chat is mostly done through the **Internet relay chat** (**IRC**) service, which maintains various **channels.** Each channel is a kind of communications link that users can join to talk about the channel's designated topic.

Although most chat rooms and channels are text-only, there are some that use limited graphics. In these cases, each participant selects an **avatar,** a graphical representation of the user (which might be a caricature, a cartoon, an animal, or some other image).

Chat rooms and channels tend to be chaotic and confusing, and the discussions (when you can figure them out) seem to only rarely deal with the appropriate topic. Some folks find this exhilarating, but everyone else just wants to have a quick conversation with a friend or colleague. For these people, there is **instant messaging,** a system that enables users to have real-time, text-based conversations without joining a chat room or channel. Instead, all the participants need only be connected to the Internet and be running the same instant messaging software. The list of people you regularly send instant messages to is called your **buddy list.**

Usenet Lingo for Newsgroupies

Usenet is essentially a collection of topics available for discussion. These discussions are organized into various **newsgroups** (or *groups,* for short), each of which covers a single topic area.

Usenet divides its newsgroups into several classifications, or **hierarchies.** There are seven so-called *mainstream hierarchies:*

comp—Computer hardware and software.

misc—Miscellaneous stuff that doesn't really fit anywhere else.

news—Usenet-related topics.

rec—Entertainment, hobbies, sports, and more.

sci—Science and technology.

soc—Sex, culture, religion, and politics.

talk—Debates about controversial political and cultural topics.

Parts Dept.

Why are they called *newsgroups*? Usenet began its life back in 1979 at Duke University, where a couple of resident computer whizzes (James Elliot and Tom Truscott) invented it as a way to easily share research, knowledge, and smart-aleck opinions among the Duke students and faculty. Someone would use this system if he had some "news" to share with his colleagues. The name stuck, and now you'll often hear Usenet referred to as *Netnews* or simply *News*.

Most Usenet-equipped Internet service providers will give you access to all the mainstream hierarchies. There's also a huge *alt* (alternative) hierarchy that covers just about anything that either doesn't belong in a mainstream hierarchy or is too whacked out to be included with the mainstream stuff.

A newsgroup name has three parts: the hierarchy to which it belongs, followed by a dot, followed by the newsgroup's topic. Here's an example:

    rec.boats

The hierarchy is *rec* (recreation), and the topic is *boats*. (To be hip, you'd pronounce this name as *reck dot boats*). Sounds simple enough so far. But many newsgroups were too broad for some people, so they started breaking them down into subgroups. For example, the *rec.boats* people who were into canoeing got sick of speedboat discussions, so they created their own "paddle" newsgroup. Here's how its official name looks:

    rec.boats.paddle

To participate in Usenet, you need a **newsreader**, a program that enables you to manage newsgroups and read and send messages.

The first thing you need to do is **subscribe** (verb), which means you add a newsgroup to the list of groups you want to participate in. (Later, if you no longer want to read the group, you *unsubscribe* from the group.) Subscribing enables you to DOWNLOAD the messages that have been sent to the newsgroup, each of which is called an **article.**

To **post** (verb) means to send an article to a newsgroup. (A similar verb, *cross-post,* means to post an article to multiple newsgroups.) The way a newsgroup works is that a person posts an article, and then if someone else wants to respond to that article, they post a **follow-up.** Other people respond to the follow-up, and soon a full-fledged conversation is going. A conversation on a specific topic is called a **thread.**

Not everyone who is subscribed to a newsgroup will necessarily post articles to that group. In fact, a large percentage of any newsgroup's audience is said to **lurk** (verb), which means they read articles without posting anything. Such a person is called a *lurker* (see also READ-ONLY USER). If a lurker finally decides to post something, he is said to **delurk** (verb).

To **troll** (verb) is to post a purposely facetious, flippant, or aggressively dumb article. Its purpose is to dupe the gullible or the self-important into responding with follow-ups that make them look foolish. (See also FLAME BAIT and YHBT.)

A **holy war** is a never-ending, unchanging (and *very* boring for the rest of us) argument in which the opinions of combatants on both sides of the issue never budge an inch. Common holy war topics include religion, abortion, which OPERATING SYSTEM is superior, and the optimum way to dispense toilet paper.

Holy wars can affect a group's **signal-to-noise ratio,** an electronics term used ironically to compare the amount of good, useful info ("signal") in a newsgroup to the amount of bad, useless junk ("noise"). The best groups have a high signal-to-noise ratio, while groups that have lots of FLAME WARS and SPAM rate low on the signal-to-noise ratio totem pole.

A good way to get a high signal-to-noise ratio is to select a newsgroup that uses a **moderator,** a volunteer who reads all submissions to a particular newsgroup and selects only the best (or most relevant) for posting.

If you see the prefix **ob-** in a post, it means "obligatory." For example, it's traditional that each post to rec.humor contain a joke. If someone writes in with some nonjoke material, they'll usually finish with an *objoke,* or *obligatory joke.*

Word Wonders

Many *spammers* (companies or individuals who send out spam) get their victims' e-mail addresses from Usenet postings. Therefore, a smart Usenet participant performs *address munging,* altering her return E-MAIL ADDRESS in her NEWSREADER so that the address is invalid. For example, some people insert the word "NOSPAM" at a random spot in the address.

The Incendiary Internet: Playing the Flame Game

Everyone—even the calmest and most level-headed among us—has a particular bugaboo or bête noire that gets under his skin and makes his blood boil. In the real world, it could be people who drive too slow in the fast lane, discourteous types who butt in ahead of you in line, or those annoying, late-night infomercials. In the online world, it could be a thoughtless remark, a misunderstood attempt at humor, or an annoying CHAIN MAIL message.

Whatever the reason, the immediate reaction usually is to pull out the electronic version of your poison pen and compose an emotionally charged, scathing reply dripping with sarcasm and venomous abuse. Such a message is called a **flame**. Firing off a particularly inventive flame may make *you* feel better, but it's likely effect will be to make the recipient madder than a hoot owl. The person will, almost certainly, flame your flame, and before you know it, a full-bore **flame war** will have broken out.

Flaming has become such an integral part of Internet culture that it's developed its own subgenre of colorful lingo and phrases. Here's a brief primer on flame jargon:

asbestos longjohns—What a person puts on (metaphorically speaking, of course) before sending a message she expects will get flamed. Other popular flame-retardant garments are the *asbestos overcoat* and *asbestos underwear*.

burble—Similar to a flame except that the burbler is considered to be dumb, incompetent, or ignorant.

dictionary flame—A flame that criticizes someone for spelling or grammatical gaffes.

firefighter—A person who attempts to put out flame wars before they get out of hand.

flamage—The content of a flame. This word seems to be a blend of the words flame and *verbiage* ("an excess of words").

flame bait—Provocative material in a message that will likely elicit flames in response. See also TROLL.

flame warrior—A person who surfs the Net looking for flame bait. Someone who tries to start flame wars intentionally.

flamer—A person who flames regularly.

rave—A particularly irritating type of flame in which the writer rambles on *ad nauseam*, even after a flame war has ended.

You Don't Say

Don't confuse an abbreviation and an acronym. An *abbreviation* is any shortened form of a phrase. In particular, if the abbreviation is formed by taking the first letters of all or most of the words in the phrase, and those letters are pronounced separately, then the result is called an *initialism*. An acronym is similar to an initialism except that the resulting initials are pronounced as a word. So while CIA (*see·eye·ay*) is an initialism, RAM (*ram*) is an acronym. All of the abbreviations in this list are initialisms.

An Initial Look at Internet Abbreviations

For most new users, abbreviations are the bugbears and hobgoblins of computer life. They imply a hidden world of meaning that only the COGNOSCENTI and those "in the know" are privy to. The Internet, in particular, is a maddeningly rich source of abbreviations and other ciphers. To help you survive, here's a list of the most commonly used abbreviations in Net discourse:

AAMOF	As a matter of fact
AFAIK	As far as I know
AFK	Away from keyboard
B4N	Bye for now
BAK	Back at keyboard
BBL	Be back later
BTW	By the way
CU	See you
CUL	See you later
DIIK	Darned if I know
F2F	Face-to-face
FAWOMPT	Frequently argued waste of my precious time

FOAF	Friend of a friend (implies that information was obtained third-hand or worse)
FOTCL	Falling off the chair laughing
FWIW	For what it's worth
FYA	For your amusement
FYI	For your information
GMTA	Great minds think alike
HHOK	Ha ha only kidding
HHOJ	Ha ha only joking
HHOS	Ha ha only serious (used with ironic jokes and satire that contain some truth)
HTH	Hope this helps
IANAL	I am not a lawyer
IC	I see
IIRC	If I remember correctly
IMCO	In my considered opinion
IMHO	In my humble opinion (although, in practice, opinions prefaced by IMHO are rarely humble; see IMNSHO)
IMO	In my opinion
IMNSHO	In my not so humble opinion
IOW	In other words
IRL	In real life
IWBNI	It would be nice if
IYFEG	Insert your favorite ethnic group (used in off-color and offensive jokes and stories to avoid insulting any particular ethnic group, race, religion, or sex)
IYSWIM	If you see what I mean
JAM	Just a minute
JOOTT	Just one of those things (usually in reference to an unexplained computer problem that resolves itself over time or by just rebooting the machine)

225

KISS	Keep it simple, stupid
L8R	Later
LOL	Laughing out loud
MEGO	My eyes glaze over
MORF	Male or female
MOTAS	Member of the appropriate sex
MOTOS	Member of the opposite sex
MOTSS	Member of the same sex
MYOB	Mind your own business
NRN	No response necessary
OBO	Or best offer
OBTW	Oh, by the way
OIC	Oh, I see
OTOH	On the other hand
OTT	Over the top
PMJI	Pardon my jumping in
ROTF	Rolling on the floor
ROTFL	Rolling on the floor laughing
ROTFLOL	Rolling on the floor laughing out loud
ROTFLMAO	Rolling on the floor laughing my ass off
RSN	Real soon now (read: never)
RTFF	Read the freaking FAQ (see RTFM)
RTFM	Read the freaking manual (an admonition to users—usually NEWBIES—that they should try to answer a question themselves before asking for help)
RYFM	Read your freaking manual
SO	Significant other
TANSTAAFL	There ain't no such thing as a free lunch
TFS	Thanks for sharing

TIA	Thanks in advance (also ADVthanksANCE)
TIC	Tongue in cheek
TNX	Thanks
TNXE6	Thanks a million (E6 means "million" in scientific notation—think of 10 raised to the power of 6)
TPTB	The powers that be
TTFN	Ta-ta for now
TTYL	Talk to you later
WRT	With respect to (or with regard to)
WTB	Want to buy
WTH	What the heck?
YHBT	You have been TROLLED
YMMV	Your mileage may vary (the advice/info/instructions just given may not work for you exactly as described)
YWIA	You're welcome in advance

Internet Hieroglyphics: Smileys

Flame wars ignite for a variety of reasons: derogatory material, the skewering of one sacred cow or another, or just for the heck of it (see FLAME WARRIOR). One of the most common reasons is someone misinterpreting a wryly humorous, sarcastic, or ironic remark as insulting or offensive. The problem is that the nuances and subtleties of wry humor and sarcasm are difficult to convey in print. *You* know your intent, but someone else (especially someone for whom English isn't his first language) may see things completely differently.

To help prevent such misunderstandings and to grease the wheels of Net social interaction, cute little symbols called **smileys** (or, more rarely, *emoticons*) have been developed. The name comes from the following combination of symbols: :-). If you rotate this page a quarter-turn clockwise, you'll see that this combination looks like a smiling face. You'd use it to indicate to your readers that the previous statement was intended to be humorous or, at least, unserious.

The basic smiley is the one you'll encounter most often, but there are all kinds of others to tilt your head over (some of which are useful, most of which are downright silly). The following list presents a sampling.

Smiley	What It Means
:-)	Ha ha, just kidding.
:-D	(Laughing) That's hilarious; I break myself up.
;-)	(Winking) Nudge, nudge, wink, wink; I'm flirting.
:-(	I'm unhappy.
;-(	I'm crying.
:-|	I'm indifferent; well whatever, never mind.
:-#	My lips are sealed.
:-/	I'm skeptical.
:->	I'm being sarcastic.
:-V	I'm shouting.
;^)	I'm smirking.
%-)	I've been staring at this screen for too long.

Smileys are a handy way to make sure your messages aren't misunderstood. However, many people find those little faces to be insufferably cute and wouldn't be caught dead using them. Instead, they use the following *nonsmileys:*

Nonsmiley	What It Means
<g>	Grinning, smiling
<l>	Laughing
<I>	Irony
<s>	Sighing
<jk>	Just kidding
<>	No comment

Questions and Exercises to Help Everything Sink In

Here's a list of the main words you learned in this chapter:

address book	article	attachment	avatar
Bcc	body	bounce message	buddy list
Cc	chain mail	channels	chat
chat room	e-mail program	e-mail server	flame
flame war	follow-up	forward	header
hierarchy	holy war	instant messaging	Internet relay chat

lurk	mailbox	moderator	newsgroup
newsreader	ob-	post	signal-to-noise ratio
signature	smiley	spam	Subject
subscribe	thread	To	troll
virus hoax			

1. Choose the e-mail message section that contains the text of the message:
    a. attachment
    b. header
    c. body
    d. signature

2. Choose the word that means "a newsgroup response":
    a. post
    b. follow-up
    c. thread
    d. troll

3. Choose the program you need to participate in Usenet:
    a. mailbox
    b. e-mail program
    c. address book
    d. newsreader

4. Choose the e-mail message type that wouldn't be considered junk mail:
    a. bounce message
    b. virus hoax
    c. spam
    d. chain mail

5. Choose the word that means "to read without posting":
    a. lurk
    b. chat
    c. troll
    d. forward

Match the word on the left with the short definition on the right:

6.	avatar	**a.**	a collection of related articles
7.	flame	**b.**	possible instant message recipients
8.	buddy list	**c.**	a never-ending debate
9.	thread	**d.**	a graphical representation of a user
10.	holy war	**e.**	an emotionally charged message

Vocabucopia: An Abundance of Miscellaneous Word Treats

A cornucopia (korn·yoo·KOH·pee·uh, noun) is a goat's horn overflowing with fruits, vegetables, and other food, and it's used to signify prosperity and abundance. (It's also called the horn of plenty.) My goal in Part 6 is to create a kind of linguistic cornucopia and fill it with a varied and tasty selection of word treats for you to munch on.

This "food for thought" includes an exotic appetizer of foreign words, a hearty helping of names of things that you may not know have names, new words fresh off the lexical vine, and some fun words to finish off with a kind of dictionary dessert.

Hey, Que sera sera!

Chapter 23

Speaking in Tongues: Words from Foreign Languages

In This Chapter

➤ Latin words and phrases

➤ French words and phrases

➤ German words and phrases

➤ Words from Spanish, Italian, and Yiddish

"Not only does the English Language borrow words from other languages, it sometimes chases them down dark alleys, hits them over the head, and goes through their pockets."

—Eddy Peters

If English is the most dominant language on the planet today (and there are few who would doubt that it is), one of the main reasons is that it's the most welcoming language in the world. No other tongue is so ready and eager to incorporate words from other languages. The linguist David Crystal calls English "a kind of vacuum cleaner of language" because it "sucks in vocabulary from any language it can get."

Not only that, English tends to assimilate words quickly, so words often don't stay "foreignisms" for very long. Latin words such as *ergo* and *opus*, French words such as *debut* and *negligee*, and German words such as *angst* and *kitsch* are all full English citizens now, their foreign pasts forgotten by most speakers.

However, many foreign words that are part of the English lexicon still have a foreign aura about them. They're familiar but not quite familiar enough to be used comfortably or to be understood precisely when other people use them. This chapter is devoted to these *loanwords,* as they're called. Here you'll find a number of words and phrases from Latin, French, German, Spanish, Italian, and Yiddish. In most cases, I give you not only their English meaning but also their literal meaning in their native language, so you can see what you're getting for your money.

Ad Hoc to Sine Qua Non: Latin Words

It has been estimated that some 60 percent of English words have Latin as their root. That's not surprising when you consider that Latin is the source for French, Italian, and Spanish, to name just three languages that have had a big influence on English. So far in this book, you've seen dozens of words that have a Latin root, as well as a few pure Latin words and phrases (see, for example, HABEAS CORPUS and MEA CULPA). Here are a few more to help expand your Latin vocabulary:

The phrase **ad hoc** (*ad HAWK,* adj.) means formed for a specific purpose or situation; improvised. Literal meaning: "for this."

> ➤ The **ad hoc** Committee for the Chastisement of Pedants Who Complain About Split Infinitives planned to disband once it was no longer needed.

You can also use ad hoc as an adverb, in which case it means "for a specific purpose or situation."

Ad nauseam (*ad NAW·zee·um,* adv.) means to a disgusting or sickening degree; to the point of nausea. Literal meaning: "to sickness."

> ➤ Augustus dreaded going over to her brother's house because he always showed his family's home movies **ad nauseam.**

A similar phrase is *ad infinitum* (*ad in·fuh·NYE·tum,* adj. and adv.), which means "endlessly; to infinity."

Caveat emptor (*KAY·vee·ut EMP·tor,* noun) is the principle that the buyer is solely responsible for checking the quality of a product before buying it. Literal meaning: "let the buyer beware."

> ➤ If you feel you *must* purchase a robotic hedgehog, remember that the quality varies widely, so **caveat emptor** applies.

Note, too, that the word *caveat* is often used by itself to mean "a caution."

College grads may (or may not) recognize **cum laude** (*koom LOWD·uh* or *koom LOWD·ee,* adj. and adv.), which means with honor; with distinction. Literal meaning: "with praise."

➤ Despite never having left Delta Tau Chi for four years, Claudius managed to graduate **cum laude** from Faber College.

There's also *magna cum laude,* "with great honor," and *summa (SOO·muh) cum laude,* "with the highest honor."

Use **ipso facto** (*IP·soh FAK·toh,* adv.) to mean by that very fact. Literal meaning: "by the fact itself."

➤ A man named Jack who works all the time is, **ipso facto,** a dull boy.

This phrase has the same basic meaning as "by definition."

A **modus operandi** (*MOH·dus awp·uh·RAN·dye* or *awp·uh·RAN·dee,* noun) is a method of operating or working (often abbreviated as *m.o.* or *M.O.* and pronounced *EM·oh*). Literal meaning: "mode of working."

➤ Not wanting to be seen as a "common" criminal, Marcus' **modus operandi** included vacuuming up the glass shards from the windows he smashed when breaking into houses.

A close phrase is *modus vivendi* (*vi·VEN·dye* or *vi·VEN·dee*), which means "a manner of living; a way of life."

A **non sequitur** (*non SEK·wuh·tur,* noun) is a conclusion or statement that does not follow logically from what was said before it. Literal meaning: "it doesn't follow."

➤ When, during a discussion of the Electoral College, Pontius asked what Twinkies were made of, he cemented his reputation as the master of the **non sequitur.**

Quid pro quo (*KWID pro KWOH,* noun) refers to something given in return for something else. Literal meaning: "this for that."

➤ "Okay, I might be willing to give you my painting of Elvis on black velvet, but what's the **quid pro quo?**"

The word **sic** (*sik,* adv.) means it is thus in the original. This word is almost always seen in square brackets ([]) within a copied text and is used to mean that the apparent spelling or grammatical error that comes before it is what was in the original text, so don't blame me! Literal meaning: "thus."

➤ "It's a lovely house with a nice derangement [**sic**] of flowers as you come in the front door."

If something is a **sine qua non** (*SIN·i kwah NON* or *SYE·nuh kway NON,* noun), it means it's an essential condition or element; a prerequisite. Literal meaning: "without which not."

➤ "Breathing is certainly a **sine qua non** of life, but must you do it so noisily?"

Here are some quick definitions of other common Latin terms you should know:

a priori (*ah pree·OH·ree* or *ay pry·OH·rye*)—Reasoning from cause to effect or from the general to the particular. Literal meaning: "from the former."

carpe diem (*car·pee·DEE·em,* noun)—Enjoy the pleasures of the moment without regard for the future. Literal meaning: "seize the day."

deus ex machina (*DAY·oos eks MAH·kuh·nuh,* noun)—In a work of fiction or drama, an unexpected and contrived solution to a seemingly intractable problem. Literal meaning: "the god from the machine." This phrase comes from the practice of the ancient Greek and Roman dramatists of having a god arrive on the scene (often lowered by stage machinery) to resolve a plot difficulty.

e pluribus unum (*ay PLOO·ruh·boos OO·num*)—One out of many. Literal meaning: "from many, one." This motto appears on the back of the U.S. dollar bill, on the banner that the eagle holds in its mouth. It refers to the original 13 states (represented by the stars above the eagle's head) becoming one nation.

pace (*PAY·see* or *PAH·kuh* or *PAH·chay,* preposition)—With deference to; contrary to the opinion of. Literal meaning: "permission."

Word Wonders

The dollar bill's eagle is one side of the great seal of the United States. The other side of the seal is on the left half of the bill, and it includes two Latin phrases: *Annuit coeptis* (*AW·noo·it koh·AYP·tis*) means "God has smiled on our undertakings," and *novus ordo seclorum* (*NOH·voos OR·doh suh·KLOR·oom*) means "a new order of the ages (has begun)".

pax (*paks,* noun)—A period of peace and stability in international affairs dominated by a single military power. Most often used with the Latinized named of the power, for example *Pax Romana* or *Pax Americana.* Literal meaning: "peace."

semper fidelis (*SEM·pur fuh·DAY·lus*)—Always faithful. This is the motto of the U.S. Marine Corps, and it means they're faithful to honor, country, and the Marines. Most often abbreviated to *semper fi* (*SEM·pur FYE*).

sui generis (*soo·ee JEN·uh·ris,* adj.)—One of a kind; unique. Literal meaning: "of its own kind."

tabula rasa (*TAB·yuh·luh RA·zuh,* noun)—A clean slate; a mind without preconceived notions. Literal meaning: "erased tablet."

The following table presents some common Latin abbreviations, the phrases they stand for, and their meanings.

Abbreviation	Phrase	Meaning
A.D.	Anno Domini	In the year of the Lord
cf.	confer	Compare
e.g.	exempli gratia	For example
et al.	et alia	And others
etc.	et cetera	And so on
i.e.	id est	That is
ibid.	ibidem	In the same place
n.b.	nota bene	Note well
p.s.	postscriptum	Marks additional text in a letter or note ("written after")

Au Contraire to *Nouveau Riche:* **French Words**

French was the language of politics, law, and the upper classes for several hundred years, so its influence on English is second only to Latin. I've already covered quite a few French terms in this book (see, for example, ARBITRAGEUR and PRIX FIXE), but there are plenty more where they came from:

The phrase **au contraire** (*OH kon·TRAYR*) means on the contrary (which is also the literal meaning).

➤ "I mangled the milk carton while trying to open it, now the spout is useless." "**Au contraire**, you can use the 'illegal' side, instead."

Carte blanche (*kart BLAHNSH,* noun) is unrestricted authority; full discretionary power. Literal meaning: "white card."

➤ In an unprecedented move, Bouchard decided to give Marcel **carte blanche** to manage the photocopier.

C'est la vie (*say la VEE*) means that's the way things happen sometimes. Literal meaning: "that's life."

➤ "I slashed my tire running over a milk bottle. I would have steered around it, but the darn kid had it hidden under his jacket, so **c'est la vie**, I guess."

You Don't Say

One of the most common errors people make is to confuse *e.g.* and *i.e.* One way to keep them separate in your head is to remember that the word "example" is pronounced *eg·ZAM·pul*. The first two letters of that pronunciation are "eg," which is easily associated with "e.g."

237

Use **comme ci, comme ça** (*kum SEE kum SAH*) to mean so-so; neither one way nor the other. Literal meaning: "like this, like that."

> ➤ "I see you've had the operation to separate you and your Siamese twin. How do you feel?" "Oh, **comme ci, comme ça.**"

A **coup d'etat** (*koo day·TAH,* noun) is the sudden overthrow of a government, especially by a small group. Literal meaning: "blow against the state."

> ➤ "In Grzyncsky today, members of President Klymkw's inner circle staged a **coup d'etat** after riots had broken out over the lack of vowels in the country's names."

A near relative of this phrase is *coup de grâce* (*koo duh GRAHS,* noun), "a final blow given to end the suffering of a mortally wounded opponent."

Parts Dept.

The little squiggle (ç) under the letter "c" in the word *ça* is called a *cedilla* (*si·DIL·uh,* noun), and it's used to indicate that the "c" is to be pronounced as an "s." The cute hat (ˆ) over the letter "a" in *grâce* is called a *circumflex* (*SUR·kum·fleks,* noun) and is used to mark the pitch or quality of a vowel. (In *grâce,* for example, the circumflex tells you to pronounce the word as *GRAHS* instead of *GRAS.*)

If something is described as **de rigueur** (*duh ree·GUR,* adj.), it means that it's required by social convention or current fashion. Literal meaning: "of rigor."

> ➤ Forcing bridesmaids to wear the most hideous dress imaginable is **de rigueur** at any modern wedding.

A **faux pas** (*foh PAH*) is a social blunder. Literal meaning: "false step."

> ➤ Antoine's hopes of impressing his dinner companion were dashed after he made the inexcusable **faux pas** of using the big fork to eat his salad.

Use the phrase **je ne sais quoi** (*zhuh nuh SAY kwah*) to refer to a quality or characteristic that's difficult to describe. Literal meaning: "I don't know what."

➤ The aftertaste of this Chateau du Rotgut wine has—how should I put it?—a certain **je ne sais quoi** that won't go away.

Le mot juste (*luh moh ZHOOST,* noun) is exactly the right word for a given situation or occasion. Many writers drop the "le" and replace it with the English "the." Literal meaning: "the right word."

➤ Celine had the annoying habit of pausing for 10 or 20 seconds at a time while she tried to summon up **le mot juste**.

A similar phrase is *bon mot* (*bonh MOH,* noun; literally, "good word"), "a clever remark; a witticism."

Nouveau riche (*noo·voh REESH,* noun) refers to the class of people who have recently become rich. (You can also use this word to apply to an individual is newly wealthy.) Literal meaning: "new rich."

➤ The dot-com boom of the late 1990s created thousands of **nouveau riche** for old money types to sneer at.

This is a slightly insulting term, and it's most often used by someone who has been wealthy for a long time (*old money*) and who looks down upon a person newly arrived on the money scene. This idea of looking down upon a new arrival is captured perfectly by another French word, *arriviste* (*ah·ree·VEEST,* noun), "a person who has recently risen to a high position of wealth or power." There's also *parvenue* (*PAR·vuh·noo,* noun), "a person who has recently risen to a higher social or economic status but who doesn't have the prestige or dignity normally associated with that status."

Here are some quick definitions of a few more common French terms:

déjà vu (*day·zhah VOO,* noun)—The feeling that you have previously experienced something that you are in fact experiencing for the first time. The most famous use (or, I guess, misuse) of this common phrase is a statement attributed to Yogi Berra: "It was déjà vu all over again." Literal meaning: "already seen."

enfant terrible (*ahn·FAHN tuh·REE·bluh,* noun)—A person known for making shocking remarks or for outrageous behavior. Literal meaning: "frightful child."

haute couture (*ote koo·TOOR,* noun)—The leading fashion designers as well as the fashions they create. Literal meaning: "High sewing." See also HAUTE CUISINE.

née or *nee* (*nay,* adj.)—Born as; formerly known as. Literal meaning: "born." This word is used to indicate the family name of a woman before she was married. So "Mrs. Griselda Longstocking, *née* Griswald" means "Mrs. Griselda Longstocking, born as Griselda Griswald." If a man has changed his name, use the masculine form *né* instead of the feminine *née*.

joie de vivre (*zhwa duh VEEV·ruh,* noun)—The intense or carefree enjoyment of life. Literal meaning: "joy of life."

239

noblesse oblige (*noh·BLES oh·bleezh,* noun)—The obligation people of high rank or birth have to act in an honorable, responsible, and BENEVOLENT manner. Literal meaning: "nobility obligates."

nom de plume (*nom duh PLOOM,* noun)—A fictitious name (a *pseudonym*) used by a writer. Literal meaning: "pen name." Two close phrases are *nom de guerre* (*nom duh GAYR*), "an undercover identity; a pseudonym taken for a specific situation" (literal meaning: "war name"), and *nom du théâtre* (*nom duh tay·AT·ruh*), "a stage name."

plus ça change (*ploo sa SHANZH*)—The more that some things change around us, the more we realize that life at its core remains basically the same. Literal meaning: "the more things change." This is actually a shortened form of a longer phrase: *plus ça change, plus c'est la même chose* (*ploo say la MEM SHOHZ*), which means literally "the more things change, the more they are the same thing."

prêt-à-porter (*pret·a·por·TAY,* noun)—Clothing that can be worn off-the-rack. Literal meaning: "ready-to-wear."

raison d'être (*RAY·zon DET·ruh,* noun)—The reason or justification for something's existence. Literal meaning: "reason to be."

roman à cléf (*roh·mah·na CLAY,* noun)—A novel in which real people or events are disguised with fictional names. Literal meaning: "a key novel." See also BILDUNGSROMAN.

Autobahn to *Zeitgest:* German Words

Approximately one third of the world's languages came from a single language that scholars now call "Indo-European." Some four to six thousand years ago, the Indo-Europeans (no one knows for sure who they were or where they lived) began branching out, and so did their language. One linguistic branch eventually turned into Latin, which then gave rise to the Romance languages (such as French, Italian, and Spanish). Other branches eventually generated language families such as Slavic (Czech, Polish, Russian, and others), Indo-Iranian (Sanskrit, Persian, and others), Greek, and Celtic. A major branch led to the Germanic languages, including Dutch and German.

It was in this latter family that English was raised, so German has had a huge effect on English. However, the German influence is so old (it dates back to the times when the Angles, Saxons, and Jutes invaded England in the fifth century) that the English words derived from it have long since been fully incorporated into the language (see NOSH and WAR, for example). However, there are still plenty of more modern German words that are used in everyday English, and I take you through a few of them in this section (see also BLITZKRIEG).

An **autobahn** (*AW·toh·bahn,* noun) is a highway or expressway. Literal meaning: "automobile road."

➤ People who detest the overused phrase "information superhighway" can instead use "infobahn," a shortened form of "information **autobahn.**"

Use **dummkopf** (*DOOM·kof*) to refer to a stupid person. Literal meaning: "dumb head."

➤ "Watch out, Helmut. The **dummkopf** in the car ahead of us thinks he can drive and talk on his cell phone at the same time."

My other favorite German insult is *schweinhund* (*SHVYN·hoont,* noun), "a BLACKGUARD or SCOUNDREL." The literal meaning is "pig dog"!

Parts Dept.

The mark represented by the two dots over the "a" in fräulein is called an *umlaut* (*OOM·lout,* noun). It's used to indicate that the vowel under it isn't pronounced in the usual way the same two dots are also known as a *dieresis* (*dye·UR·uh·sis,* noun), but in this case the mark is placed over the second of two consecutive vowels to indicate that the two vowels should be pronounced separately. For example, *coördinate* (*koh·OR·duh·nayt* or *koh·OR·duh·nut*). The dieresis is also used to indicate when a particular vowel shouldn't be silent. For example, *Brontë* (*BRAWN·tee*).

A **fräulein** (*FROY·lyne* or *FROW·lyne,* noun) is an unmarried woman. Literal meaning: "young woman."

➤ Friedrich went to the Oktoberfest celebration hoping to meet a cute **fräulein.**

Fräulein is also used as a courtesy title for an unmarried woman, which makes it the German equivalent of the English "Miss." A married woman is called a *frau* (*frow*), which can also be used as a courtesy title equivalent to our "Mrs." A similar word is *hausfrau* (*HOWS·frow*), "housewife."

Schadenfreude (*shah·dun·FROY·duh,* noun) is pleasure derived from the misfortune of others. Literal meaning: "hurtful joy."

➤ Simmons felt a tinge of **schadenfreude** as he watched Wainwright miss the 7-10 split to fall one pin short of Simmons' all-time high score.

241

Use **verboten** (*vur·BOH·tun* or *vur·BOTE·n,* adj.) to describe something that is prohibited or forbidden. Literal meaning: "forbidden."

➤ "ATTENTION: The use of the photocopy machine to create images of ANY part of the human anatomy is **verboten!**"

A **wunderkind** (*VOON·dur·kint,* noun) is a person who shows extraordinary talent or who has great success at a young age; a child PRODIGY. Literal meaning: "wonder child."

➤ With a concert at Carnegie Hall under her belt at age 10, Heidi was a **wunderkind**, for sure, but that didn't stop the boys from pulling her pigtails.

Kind (*KINT,* noun) is German for "child," and it's where we get the word *kindergarten* (*KIN·dur·gar·dun* or *KIN·dur·gar·tun;* literal meaning: "children's garden").

Zeitgeist (*ZYTE·gyst,* noun) The overall cultural, intellectual, and moral climate of an era or generation. Literal meaning: "the spirit of the time."

➤ With a CAPPUCCINO in one hand, a cell phone in the other, and a stud through his tongue, Gustav was the perfect reflection of the **Zeitgeist**.

Here are some quick definitions of other fun-to-pronounce German words:

bildungsroman (*BIL·doongz·roh·mahn,* noun)—A novel that chronicles the moral and intellectual development of a young person. Literal meaning: "formation novel." See also ROMAN À CLÉF.

doppelgänger (*DOP·ul·gang·ur,* noun)—A ghostly counterpart of a living person, especially one who haunts that person. This word is also occasionally used to refer to a person who looks remarkably like another. Literal meaning: "double goer."

fingerspitzengefühl (*FING·ur·SHPITS·en·guh·FEWL,* noun)—Intuition. Literal meaning: "fingertip feeling."

gesundheit (*guh·ZOONT·hyte*)—Said after a person sneezes. It's similar to the English "Bless you!" Literal meaning: "be restored to good health."

leitmotiv (*LYTE·moh·teef,* noun)—A dominant and recurring theme in a work of art. Literal meaning: "lead motif."

liebchen (*LEEB·chun*)—Sweetheart. Literal meaning: "little love."

lumpenproletariat (*LOOM·pun·pro·luh·TAY·ree·aht,* noun)—The class of society that includes beggars, tramps, and criminals. Literal meaning: "ragamuffin proletariat."

realpolitik (*ray·AL poh·li·TEEK*, noun)—A form of politics that is concerned only with what is possible and practical in a given situation. Literal meaning: "practical politics."

Weltanschauung (*VELT·ahn·SHAW·ung*, noun)—A comprehensive outlook or philosophy of the world or of human life. Literal meaning: "world view."

Weltschmerz (*VELT·shmurts*, noun)—A mood of sentimental sadness or romantic pessimism caused by comparing the apparently poor state of the real world with an idealized view of what the world could or should be. Literal meaning: "world pain."

Casa to *Kvetch:* **Words from Other Languages**

Although Latin, French, and German may have had the most influence on what English is like today, the language is open to any and all influences. This is particularly true in places such as the United States and Canada where waves of immigration have brought millions of non-English dialects into the mix. To celebrate this glorious linguistic diversity, this section closes the chapter with quick looks at words from three languages: Spanish, Italian, and Yiddish.

Here are some Spanish words:

casa (*KAS·uh*, noun)—House, residence, or building. The phrase *mi casa es su casa* means "what's mine is yours" (literally, "my house is your house").

hacienda (*hah·see·EN·duh*, noun)—A large estate, ranch, or plantation; a mansion on such an estate.

hasta la vista (*AHS·tuh lah VEES·tuh*)—See you later. Literal meaning: "until I see you again."

hasta mañana (*AHS·tuh mah·NYAH·nah*)—See you tomorrow.

hombre (*OHM·bray,* noun)—Man.

incommunicado (*in·kuh·myoo·ni·KAH·doh,* adj. and adv.)—Lacking the means or ability to communicate.

mañana (*mah·NYAH·nah*)—Tomorrow; an unspecified time in the future.

que será será (*KAY suh·rah suh·rah,* adv.)—Being resigned to whatever happens in the future. Literal meaning: "what will be, will be."

señor (*sen·YOR* or *see·NYOR,* noun)—A courtesy title used before the full name, surname, or professional title of a man (which makes it the Spanish equivalent of the English "Mr."). Also, a Spanish man.

señora (*sen·YOR·uh* or *see·NYO·ruh*, noun)—A courtesy title used before the full name, surname, or professional title of a married woman (which makes it the Spanish equivalent of the English "Mrs."). Also, a married Spanish woman.

señorita (*sen·yuh·REE·tuh* or *seh·nyo·REE·tuh*, noun)—A courtesy title used before the full name, surname, or professional title of an unmarried woman (which makes it the Spanish equivalent of the English "Miss."). Also, an unmarried Spanish woman.

Word Wonders

The word *paparazzo* became associated with annoying celebrity photographers thanks to Federico Fellini's film *La Dolce Vita* (*The Good Life*), which included a street photographer named Signor Paparazzo. Appropriately, *paparazzo* means "buzzing insect" in dialect Italian.

Here are some Italian words:

a capella (*a kuh·PEL·uh*, adv.)—Without instrumental accompaniment (used to describe singing). Literal meaning: "in the manner of a choir."

aria (*AH·ree·uh*)—A vocal piece sung solo, especially in an opera. Literal meaning: "air."

arrivederci (*ah·ree·vuh·DAYR·chee*)—Goodbye. Literal meaning: "until we meet again."

bambino (*bam·BEE·noh*, noun)—A child or baby. Literal meaning: "Small child."

capo d'i tutti capo (*ka·poh dee TOO·tee ka·poh*, noun)—The boss of bosses, particularly the head of an organized crime syndicate. Literal meaning: "the head of all the heads."

paparazzi (*pah·puh·RAHT·see*, noun)—Freelance photographers who aggressively pursue celebrities to take candid pictures to sell to newspapers and magazines. The singular form is *paparazzo* (*pah·puh·RAHT·soh*).

piazza (*pee·AT·suh*)—An open, public square within a town or city.

prima donna (*PREE·muh DON·uh*, noun)—A leading female singer in an opera company. Also, an extremely vain or temperamental person. Literal meaning: "first lady."

Here are some Yiddish words:

chutzpah (*HOOT·spuh*, "hoot" rhymes with "foot," noun)—Audacity, nerve, or gall in an extreme degree.

kibitz (*KIB·its*, verb)—To look on and offer meddlesome, unwanted advice. Literal meaning: "pewit" (a type of bird).

kosher (*KOH·shur*, adj.)—Fit to eat under Jewish dietary law. Also, proper or legitimate. Literal meaning: "proper."

kvetch (*kvech, verb*)—To complain habitually and whiningly. Literal meaning: "to squeeze or pinch."

mazel tov (*MAH·zul tawf*)—An expression of congratulations used upon the completion of a successful or happy event. Literal meaning: "good luck."

mensch (*mensh,* noun)—An admirable, honorable person, especially one who exhibits integrity and fortitude. Literal meaning: "human being."

meshuga (*muh·SHUG·uh,* "shug" sounds like the first syllable of "sugar," adj.)—Crazy; nonsensical. A person who exhibits such behavior is called a *meshuggener* (*muh·SHUG·uh·nur,* noun).

oy vey (*oy VAY*)—An interjection used to express surprise, despair, horror, pain, or relief. Often shortened to just *oy.* Literal meaning: "woe is me."

schlock (*shlok,* noun)—Something that is of inferior or shoddy quality.

shmatta (*SHMAH·tuh,* noun)—A cheap piece of clothing. Literal meaning: "rag."

tchotchke (*CHAWCH·kuh,* noun)—A cheap knickknack or trinket.

Word Wonders

The classic chutzpah example is the man who murders his mother and father and then asks the judge to have mercy on a poor orphan.

You Don't Say

There are a number of Yiddish words and expressions in common use, but they might be far less common if people knew what they *really* meant. This being a book for the whole family, I can't get too detailed. However, I can tell you to avoid both *putz* and *schmuck,* which are Yiddish slang for a certain part of the male anatomy. Also, avoid *dreck* and *bubkes,* which are related to excrement.

Questions and Exercises to Help Everything Sink In

Here's a list of the main words you learned in this chapter:

ad hoc	ad nauseam	au contraire	autobahn
carte blanche	caveat emptor	c'est la vie	comme ci, comme ça
coup d'etat	cum laude	de rigueur	dummkopf
faux pas	fräulein	ipso facto	le mot juste

modus operandi	non sequitur	nouveau riche	quid pro quo
schadenfreude	sic	sine qua non	verboten
wunderkind	Zeitgeist		

1. Choose the term that means "unrestricted authority":
   a. faux pas
   b. de rigueur
   c. au contraire
   d. carte blanche

2. Choose the term that has the literal meaning "let the buyer beware":
   a. caveat emptor
   b. non sequitur
   c. ad hoc
   d. ipso facto

3. Fill in the blank: "Pulling those all-nighters at exam time helped her to graduate _____."

4. Choose the word that means "forbidden":
   a. sic
   b. verboten
   c. ad nauseam
   d. coup d'etat

Match the term on the left with the literal meaning on the right:

5. schadenfreude   a. spirit of the time
6. quid pro quo   b. without which not
7. c'est la vie   c. this for that
8. Zeitgeist   d. that's life
9. sine qua non   e. hurtful joy

10. Choose the phrase that means "seize the day":
    a. carpe diem
    b. semper fidelis
    c. tabula rasa
    d. sui generis

Aglet

Names of Things You Didn't Know Had Names

"It is a sad truth, but we have lost the faculty of giving lovely names to things. Names are everything."

—Oscar Wilde, Irish playwright and novelist

In Roman times, a noble would often walk around with a *nomenclator* (*NOH·mun·klay·tur,* noun), a slave who would whisper in the noble's ear the names of people that they came upon. Nomenclator combines *nomen,* "name," and *calator,* "caller," and it's the source of the modern word *nomenclature,* "a system of names used within an art or science." Naming things may well be the most fundamental act of language, and there's no doubt we humans have a deep-seated need to name things. I'll tap into that need in this chapter as I play the *nomenclator* and whisper in your ear the names of all kinds of objects and actions that you most likely didn't know even had a name to begin with. Let's begin our walk …

Names for Body Parts

Consisting as it does of hundreds or even thousands of bits and pieces, I could easily devote this entire chapter (perhaps even the entire book) to the names of the body's parts. Instead, I've chosen just a few obscure nooks and crannies.

Let's start with the **glabella** (*gluh·BEL·uh*, noun), the area between the eyebrows just above the nose. This comes from the Latin *glabellus*, "hairless," although I've met a few people for whom that adjective certainly doesn't apply!

The **lunula** (*LOON·yuh·luh*, noun) is the whitish, crescent-shaped area at the base of the human fingernail. This area is moon-shaped, so it makes sense that the Latin word *lunula* means "little moon." This part is also called the *lunule* (*LOON·yool*).

The **nasal columella** (*NAY·zul kol·um·EL·uh*, noun) is the ridge of cartilage that lies at the bottom of the nose and that separates the two nostrils. (*Columella* is Latin for "little column.") The partition that lies behind the nasal columella and serves to separate the two nasal cavities is the **nasal septum.**

Right below the nasal columella is the **philtrum** (*FIL·trum*, noun), the central part of the upper lip. The indentation is called the **philtral dimple,** and the ridges on either side of it are the **philtral columns.**

The **tragus** (*TRAY·gus*, noun) is the pointed flap of cartilage that rises just above the earlobe and partially covers the entrance to the inner ear. This entrance is an example of a **meatus** (*mee·AY·tus*, noun), an opening or passage into the body (technically, it's the *external acoustic meatus*).

Word Wonders

The history of the word *tragus* goes back to the Greek word *tragos*, "a male goat," which is a bit of a brow-furrower. The explanation is that the tragus area is also where ear hairs sprout, so the combination of the hairs and the tragus must have reminded the Greeks of a billy goat and the "beard" of hair that hangs under his chin. (As an aside, the male goat's beard is also the source of the word *goatee* (*goh·TEE*), "a beard that covers only the chin.")

Names for Sleep Things

Discussing sleep-related things may seem like an odd path for this chapter to take, but I've gathered a small collection of sleep words over the years, and this just seemed like a good place to put them.

For instance, a **sleep camel** (noun) is a person who gets little sleep during the week and then attempts to make up for it by sleeping in and napping on the weekend.

(The analogy here, of course, is to a camel and its ability to take in water and then live on that supply for many days in the desert.)

A **microsleep** (*MYE·kro·sleep*, noun) is a brief period (usually only a few seconds) in which the brain enters a sleep state regardless of the activity the person is performing at the time.

Microsleeps happen to people who are tired, but the truly exhausted may fall into a **sleep seizure** (noun), a long period of unexpected sleep.

When they wake up, those people will likely experience **sleep inertia** (*in·UR·shuh*, noun), the grogginess and disorientation that a person feels for a few minutes after a sleep or long nap. (*Inertia,* by the way, is a general resistance or reluctance to move or act.) See also VACATION HANGOVER.

Names for Traffic Things

On a road or highway, a **contraflow lane** (*kawn·truh·FLOH layn*, noun) is a lane that accepts traffic driving in different directions, depending on the time of day.

A **speed hump** (noun) is a low ridge that runs across a street and is designed to slow down cars. A speed hump is a longer, flatter version of a **speed bump.** You can also call a speed hump or speed bump a *sleeping policeman.*

Each of the preceding terms is an example of a **traffic-calming device** (noun), a device installed on or near a roadway to force motorists to slow down. Another example is a **traffic island,** a curbed area that juts out into the road. These usually appear in groups of two or three on opposite sides of the street to force motorists to weave through them rather than traveling in a straight (and faster) line.

Rumble strips (noun) are grooves etched into a highway surface, designed to emit a loud rumble when a car drives over them. Their goal is to wake up a sleepy driver who might be drifting into another lane. Some highways use **lane-divider dots,** the round, puck-like objects that separate lanes. (These are also called *Botts dots* because they were invented by a chemist named Elbert Dysart Botts.)

Spillback (noun) is the full or partial blockage of an intersection by one or more cars that don't make it through before the traffic lights turn red. Many people confuse this term with **gridlock** (noun), but the latter actually occurs when spillback ties up traffic around an entire square block so that traffic can't move in any direction.

Street furniture is the name given to street features such as lampposts, traffic lights, benches, bus shelters, and garbage cans.

Parts Dept.

The prefix *contra–* means "against; opposite."

Miscellaneous Names

An **aglet** (*AG-lit,* noun) is a plastic or metal sheath on the end of a shoelace. The aglet (which is also known as a *tag*) makes it easier to thread the lace through each eyelet (see also GROMMET) it prevents FEAZINGS.

An **anagram** (*AN·uh·gram,* noun) is a word or phrase formed by rearranging the letters of another word or phrase. For example, you can rearrange the letters in NAME to produce MEAN or MANE. However, an **antigram** (*an·tee·GRAM,* noun) is an anagram in which the new word or phrase has the opposite meaning of the original. The following table shows some examples.

Original	Antigram
antagonist	not against
commendation	aim to condemn
conversation	voices rant on
diplomacy	mad policy
funeral	real fun
honestly	on the sly
infection	fine tonic
protectionism	nice to imports
spittoon	it's no pot
violence	nice love

As you might expect, the opposite of an antigram is an anagram in which the new word has a similar meaning to the original. Such a word is called an **aptagram** (*AP·tuh·gram,* noun). This table presents a few aptagram examples.

Original	Aptagram
a shoplifter	has to pilfer
a gentleman	elegant man
astronomers	moon starers
desperation	a rope ends it
dormitory	dirty room
eleven plus two	twelve plus one
endearment	tender name
sunbathe	heat buns
the Morse code	here come dots
Western Union	no wire unsent

A **bar-code hairstyle** (noun) is a style in which a man's last few strands of hair are combed across the top of his head, thus resembling a bar-code pattern.

A **contrail** (*KAWN·trayl,* noun) is the white trail of smoke created by a jet airplane. This word is a shortened form of the phrase *condensation trail.*

A **deskfast** (*DESK·fust,* noun) is a breakfast eaten at a desk in an office. Speaking of "fast" food, **one-handed food** (noun) is food that's small enough to hold in one hand and isn't messy to eat so that it can be consumed while working or driving. Speaking of driving, **dashboard dining** (noun) is eating a meal while driving a car. Watch out for those RUMBLE STRIPS!

Word Wonders

If you have access to the Internet, you can generate anagrams automatically using my Word Arranger page at www.logophilia.com/WordPlay/WordArranger.html.

Dittography (*di·TOG·ruh·fee,* noun) is the accidental repetition of one or more letters when writing or typing a word.

A **dol** (*dole,* noun) is a unit of pain intensity. The root of this word is the Latin *dolor,* "pain," which also provides us with the English word *dolor,* "sorrow; grief."

Door dwell (noun) is the amount of time it takes for the door to close after having boarded an elevator. Think you can reduce door dwell by pressing the "Door Close" button once you're inside the elevator? Probably not because, on most elevators, the Door Close button has been disabled for safety reasons. Why keep the button? Most likely to give people in a hurry something to poke at, which makes them feel better.

An **escutcheon** (*i·SKUCH·un,* noun) is an ornamental plate placed around a keyhole, door lock, or doorknob.

Feazings (*FEE·zings,* noun) are the frayed ends of a shoelace or the unraveled ends of a rope or thread. See also AGLET.

A **ferrule** (*FAYR·ul,* noun) is the metal ring that appears just below the eraser on a lead pencil. It can also refer to any metal cap or ring placed on or around a shaft or pole for reinforcement. An example is the metal cap on the end of an umbrella.

A **grommet** (*GRAWM·it,* noun) is an eyelet that has been reinforced with a plastic or metal ring to enable a lace, rope, or fastener to be passed through it. (It can also refer to the plastic or metal ring itself. Note, too, that this word is also spelled as *grummet.*)

A **harp** (noun) is a pair of metal supports inside a lampshade designed to fit over a light bulb.

A **hawsehole** (*HAWZ·hole,* noun) is the opening in the bow of a ship through which a chain or cable is passed. If the cable is used to tow or moor the ship, it's called a **hawser** (which is where the word hawsehole comes from).

A **keeper** (noun) is the extra loop added to a belt to hold the end of the belt after it has passed through the buckle.

The **kerf** (*kurf,* noun) is the width of the groove made by a saw or other cutting tool.

A **logogram** (*LOH·guh·gram,* noun) is a symbol that represents an entire word (such as $ for "dollar" and @ for "at"). Also called a *logograph, ideograph,* or *grammalogue.*

A **moon-glade** (or moonglade; noun) is the track created by the reflection of moonlight on water.

Oronyms (*OR·oh·nims,* noun) are two phrases that sound the same but have different meanings. Examples are listed in the following table.

Phrase 1	Phrase 2
a notion	an ocean
I scream	ice cream
may cough	make off
some mothers	some others
the stuffy nose	the stuff he knows

An oronym that comes from mishearing the lyrics of a song is most often called a **mondegreen** (*MON·duh·green,* noun). The name comes from a misheard lyric in an old Scottish folk song called *The Earl of Moray.* The line "Oh, they have slain the Earl o' Moray and laid him on the green" was heard as "Oh, they have slain the Earl o' Moray and Lady Mondegreen." Perhaps the most famous mondegreen occurs in the Jimi Hendrix song "Purple Haze"; people regularly mishear "'Scuse me while I kiss the sky" as "'Scuse me while I kiss this guy."

A **prebuttal** (*PREE·but·ul, n*oun) is a rebuttal, inserted into an argument, that refutes an anticipated counter-argument.

A **punt** (noun) is the indentation in the bottom of a wine or champagne bottle. And no, the punt isn't there so the SOMMELIER can grip the bottom of the bottle while pouring. The punt's only purpose in life is to strengthen the bottle.

Spindrift (noun) is sea spray blown by the wind.

A **sprag** (noun) is a wooden block or brick wedged under a wheel (or sometimes between a wheel's spokes) to prevent a vehicle from rolling down an incline.

A **vacation hangover** (noun) is a feeling of sluggishness and disorientation that occurs when you return to work from a particularly long or adventurous vacation.

In a jigsaw puzzle piece, a **void** (noun) is the space into which another piece's rounded end (a **nub**) fits.

A **wall wart** (noun) is the blocky plug/transformer combination used with modems, telephones, and other consumer electronics.

Wildposting (noun) is the poster advertising displayed on construction hoardings, buildings, and other free spaces.

A **windrow** (*WIN·droh,* noun) is the pile of snow that a snowplow leaves at the end of a driveway. This comes from older word *windrow,* "a row of hay raked up to dry before being rolled."

Questions and Exercises to Help Everything Sink In

Here's a list of all the words you learned in this chapter:

aglet	anagram	antigram	aptagram
bar-code hairstyle	Botts dots	contra-	contraflow lane
contrail	dashboard dining	deskfast	dittography
dol	dolor	door dwell	escutcheon
external acoustic meatus	feazings	ferrule	glabella
goatee	grammalogue	gridlock	grommet
harp	hawsehole	hawser	ideograph
inertia	keeper	kerf	lane-divider dots
logogram	logograph	lunula	meatus
microsleep	mondegreen	moon-glade	nasal columella
nasal septum	nomenclator	nomenclature	nub
one-handed food	oronyms	philtral columns	philtral dimple
philtrum	prebuttal	punt	rumble strips
sleep camel	sleep inertia	sleep seizure	sleeping policeman
speed bump	speed hump	spillback	spindrift
sprag	street furniture	tag	traffic island
traffic-calming device	tragus	vacation hangover	void
wall wart	wildposting	windrow	

1. DETOUR and ROUTED illustrate what type of word?

2. Choose the word that's not a body part:

    a. philtrum

    b. lunula

    c. glabella

    d. ferrule

3. Fill in the blank: "Lampposts, traffic lights, and bus shelters are examples of _____."

4. Choose the term that's not a *traffic-calming device:*

    a. contraflow lane

    b. speed hump

    c. sleeping policeman

    d. traffic island

Match the word on the left with the short definition on the right:

5. dittography   a. pile of snow left by a snowplow

6. keeper   b. indentation on the bottom of a wine bottle

7. dol   c. accidental repetition of letters

8. windrow   d. an extra loop attached to a belt

9. punt   e. a unit of pain intensity

10. Choose the word that's a synonym for *aglet:*

    a. freazings

    b. tag

    c. grommet

    d. ferrule

254

Brave New Words

"The English language is like a fleet of juggernaut trucks that goes on regardless. No form of linguistic engineering and no amount of linguistic legislation will prevent the cycles of change that lie ahead."

—Robert Burchfield, lexicographer

Chapter 23, "Speaking in Tongues: Words from Foreign Languages," showed you that English grows and rejuvenates itself by eagerly borrowing words from other languages. English also keeps up a youthful appearance thanks to a steady influx of new words and phrases. Every year, thousands of these *neologisms* (nee·AWL·uh·jiz·ums, noun) spring up from some linguistic nook or cranny. The majority are technical terms of interest only to specialists, and most of the others are either *nonce words* (words invented only for a particular occasion) or *stunt words* (words that display a neat verbal trick—such as a good pun—but aren't useful for everyday conversation). In the end, a small percentage catch on with the general public and are eventually accorded full linguistic status in dictionaries and other mainstream sources.

This chapter is a celebration of the neologism. Here you'll find dozens of words that have appeared only in the last few years. In most cases, no one yet knows whether the words will live on or die a slow lexical death, but that's all part of the fun.

You should know that every word discussed in this chapter was culled from my Word Spy database. The Word Spy is a World Wide Web site and mailing list devoted to new and recently coined words as well as older words that have recently sprouted new meanings. Each weekday, I present a new word, define it, give a citation from a newspaper or magazine to show that people are really using it, and give some background about the word. If you're interested (and have access to the Internet), here's the address:

www.logophilia.com/WordSpy/

If you want to join the free mailing list and receive the new word via e-mail each weekday, send a message to the following address:

listmanager@mcfedries.com

In the subject of the message, include only the following command:

join wordspy

Ad Creep to Casualization

Ad creep (noun) is the gradual expansion of advertising space to nontraditional surfaces such as floors, bathroom walls, cars, and the sides of buildings.

➤ With a big, fat ad staring him right in the face in the men's washroom, Will realized that **ad creep** had gone too far.

Here are a few other new words that demonstrate just how much this ad creep business is getting out of hand:

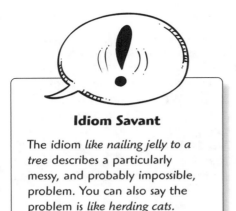

Idiom Savant

The idiom *like nailing jelly to a tree* describes a particularly messy, and probably impossible, problem. You can also say the problem is *like herding cats*.

advertecture (noun)—Advertisements painted on the walls of buildings.

advertorial (noun)—An advertisement designed to resemble editorial content.

live commercial (noun)—A form of advertisement in which participants promote a product in real-world settings.

on-hold advertising (noun)—Telephone-based advertising directed at consumers while they are waiting on hold.

virtual advertising (noun)—Computer-generated ads, logos, and products that are superimposed on a live video feed or are inserted into a completed movie or television show.

Perhaps because of ad creep, we have the relatively recent phenomenon of **affluenza** (*af·loo·EN·zuh*, noun), an extreme form of materialism in which consumers overwork and accumulate high levels of debt in order to purchase more goods.

➤ If she weren't so tired from working two jobs to help pay their huge mortgage, Celeste would have been able to diagnose herself as having **affluenza**.

This word combines AFFLUENCE and *influenza*, "an ACUTE, CONTAGIOUS viral infection" (also known simply as the *flu*). A similar new word is *maffluent* (*MAFF·loo·unt*, noun), "the mass affluent; the relatively large group of people who can now make some claim to affluence because of the increased value of their stock portfolios." This is related to the *wealth effect* (noun), "an increase in consumer spending based on the perceived wealth created by the escalating value of stock market portfolios."

Some folks are immunizing themselves against affluenza by taking the following "cures":

downshifting (noun)—Quitting a high-stress job in an effort to lead a simpler life.

inconspicuous consumption (noun)—Purchasing goods that convey a lower socio-economic status.

voluntary simplicity (noun)—A lifestyle that consciously avoids luxury, flamboyance, and pretense.

work-life balance (noun)—A state of equilibrium in which the demands of both a person's job and personal life are equal.

Branding (*BRAN·ding*, noun) is the marketing of a product or service in such a way as to create a distinctive identity (that is, a BRAND).

➤ The swoosh plays a big part in Nike's **branding** strategy, but Jacob swore that if he saw one more he'd eat his shoes.

The idea of a brand isn't all that new, but branding has been the hottest marketing buzzword over the past five years. It's so hot, in fact, that it has spawned a whole slew of "brand" new words:

brandscape (noun)—The brand landscape; the expanse of brands and brand-related items (logos, ads, and so on) within a culture or market.

brandwagon (noun)—The current fad of using branding concepts and techniques in marketing. This word combines BRAND and *bandwagon* (see JUMP ON THE BANDWAGON).

Word Wonders

Brand in this sense comes from the verb *brand*, which means "to use a hot iron to burn a mark into an object or the hide of an animal."

brandwidth (noun)—The amount of brand recognition enjoyed by a product or service. This is a blend of BRAND and BANDWIDTH.

passion brand (noun)—A brand that resonates intensely with consumers and makes them passionate about the brand's products or services.

single-brand store (noun)—A store that sells only a single brand of merchandise.

Casualization (*ka·zhoo·ul·i·ZAY·shun,* noun) is the trend toward a more casual atmosphere in the workplace, particularly regarding the clothes worn by office workers.

➤ Beryl could live with **casualization**; it was the jeans and T-shirts the kids wore to the office that drove her up the wall.

This trend has caused workers to come up with a *third wardrobe,* a set of clothes with a style that lies between formal business attire and casual wear. Examples would be khaki pants and button-down shirts. Note, too, that in recent years casualization has adopted a second meaning: the trend toward using casual workers (workers who are called in as they are needed) instead of permanent full-time or part-time workers.

Chad to Day Trading

Chad (noun) are the tiny bits of paper left over from punching data cards or election ballots.

➤ After months of campaigning and tens of millions of dollars spent, it was impossible to believe the entire election was decided by a few measly **chad**.

Word Wonders

Nobody is really certain where the word chad came from. One speculation is that it comes from the Scottish word *chad,* "loose stones or gravel."

Against all the odds, the U.S. presidential election of 2000 turned chad into a famous buzzword. Who knew that we would eventually end up with an entire *taxonomy* ("classification scheme") of chad? Apparently, there's chad and then there's *chad:*

pregnant chad (noun)—A chad that's only indented slightly and is still fully attached to the card. This is also called a *dimpled chad.*

hanging chad (noun)—Only one corner remains attached to the card.

swinging chad (or a *swinging-door chad;* noun)—Two corners remain attached to the card.

tri-chad (noun)—Three corners remain attached to the card.

A **coolhunter** (noun) is a person who investigates cutting-edge trends, fashions, and ideas and sells them as market research to companies so they can incorporate them into their latest products.

> ➤ Buffy's job as a **coolhunter** took her into the malls and inner cities of America in search of the soon-to-be-hip.

A **cube farm** (noun) is a collection of cubicles in an office.

> ➤ In the ecology of his company's **cube farm**, Theo fell into the genus of "nesters," employees who "feather" their cubicles with many personal items.

One of my favorite cube farm words is *prairie dogging,* which is when the heads of office workers pop up over cubicle walls in response to a loud voice or noise. This comes from the behavior of the prairie dog, a burrowing rodent that looks for danger by poking its head up out of its hole.

Day trading (noun) is Internet-based stock-market trading in which individual investors quickly buy and sell SHARES to take advantage of short-term trends and then sell most if not all of their holdings before the end of the day.

> ➤ Jenna had lost most of her life savings by **day trading** stocks, but hey, at least she was her own boss.

Many people see day trading as a modern-day get-rich-quick scheme or, more accurately, a *get-rich-click scheme,* "a strategy that attempts to use online investing or the creation of an Internet-related business to amass wealth quickly." Looking at the big picture, this is all part of our society's *casino culture,* "a culture in which low-percentage money-making schemes—such as high-tech stocks, day trading, and lotteries—become mainstream investment vehicles.

Entreprenerd to *Learning a Living*

An **entreprenerd** (*awn·truh·pruh·NURD,* noun) is an entrepreneur, often one with technical skills, who creates an online business.

> ➤ Tired of programming for someone else, Milton decided to become a full-fledged **entreprenerd** and launch *The Coder Caterer,* an online food delivery service for programmers.

This word combines *entrepreneur* (*awn·truh·pruh·NUR,* noun), "a person who creates and runs a business," and *nerd* (*NURD,* noun), "a person who is technically adept but socially inept." If the entreprenerd is a young person, call him a *yettie* (*YET·tee,* noun), which comes from the phrase "young, entrepreneurial, tech-based 20-something." (Compare this with *yuppie,* a "young, urban professional.") If he strikes it rich, call him a *millionerd* (*mil·yuh·NURD,* noun) or a *sneaker millionaire.*

Word Wonders

More than a few people believe the word *nerd* comes from the following lines in *If I Ran the Zoo*, by Dr. Suess (1950):

> And then just to show them, I'll sail to Ka-Troo
> And Bring Back an It-Kutch, a Preep and a Proo,
> A Nerkle, a Nerd, and a Seersucker, too!

The illustration shows the Nerd to be an unpleasant-looking creature, and it was only a few years later that *nerd* came to mean "an uninteresting person; a dud; a square." It was in the computer-literate 1990s that nerd became fully associated with the technically savvy, and the word is now used as a compliment in technical circles. This is in contrast to a *geek*, which is a nerd with extremely poor eating habits and nonexistent hygiene.

A **first-person shooter** (noun) is a type of computer game in which the player assumes the perspective of a gunman.

➤ Eileen took one look at the blood and gore splashed all over the screen of her son's **first-person shooter** game and promptly fainted on the spot.

Here are some other computer game–related words that have recently entered the lexicon:

frag (verb)—To kill a character in a computer game.

killboard (noun)—In a computer game, a list of the enemies that a player has killed.

Nintendo epilepsy (noun)—Epilepsy-like symptoms caused by up-close viewing of video games, television shows, or other events that feature rhythmic, fast-paced flashes of light and bursts of color.

Nintendo thumb (noun)—A repetitive stress injury that causes swelling at the base of the thumb due to overuse of video games. A similar term is *Tetwrist*, a form of repetitive stress injury caused by extended sessions playing computer games such as Tetris.

thumb candy (noun)—A computer game that's all hand-eye coordination with little strategy or thought required.

Flex place (noun) refers to a company policy that enables employees to work either at the office or from home.

➤ Duane appreciated his company's **flex place** policy because he enjoyed working at home on occasion, but he wished he also has a "flex brain" to handle the transition.

Flex place is the spatial equivalent of *flex time,* "a company policy that enables workers to set their own starting and finishing times."

Working from home has become increasingly common over the past couple of years, and of course, the language fully reflects that popularity. Here's a small sampling of new words related to working from home:

flexecutive (noun)—An executive whose hours and place of work are flexible.

homepreneur (noun)—An ENTREPRENEUR who creates and manages a home-based business.

modem cowboy/cowgirl (noun)—A person who lives and works out of a home located in the country.

office-free (adj.)—Describes employees whose jobs do not require them to work inside an office.

telecommuting (noun)—TELEWORK performed at home.

telework (noun)—Computer work, particularly work that requires a DIAL-UP CONNECTION to the INTERNET or a corporate NETWORK, performed from home or any remote location.

Learning a living (noun) means working in a job that requires the constant learning of new knowledge and skills.

➤ Since she seemed to spend more time in courses and reading books than actually working, Constance realized she was no longer earning a living, but **learning a living**.

This phrase comes from media guru Marshall McLuhan: "In the age of electricity and automation, the globe becomes a community of

Idiom Savant

To *wave a dead chicken* is to attempt to resolve a problem by taking steps that one believes to be futile but are nevertheless necessary so that others are satisfied that an appropriate degree of effort has been expended.

261

continuous learning, a single campus in which everybody irrespective of age, is involved in learning a living."

Similarly, *multiskilling* refers to a person being proficient in multiple areas of expertise within an organization or profession. Such a person might be a *portfolio worker*, a worker who holds multiple jobs or contracts in multiple fields with multiple companies. She might also practice *just-in-time learning,* the acquisition of knowledge or skills as they're needed.

Lexus Liberal to Screenager

A **Lexus liberal** (noun) is a person who is liberal in words but not in deeds.

> ➤ Claude would champion the cause of the working poor in one breath and then brag about his fancy new car the next. He was truly a **Lexus liberal.**

(A Lexus is an expensive make of automobile.) A similar creature is a *Kojak liberal,* a liberal who believes that social justice is enhanced through tough-minded anticrime policies. ("Kojak" was the name of a tough cop played by Telly Savalas in a 1970s TV series of the same name.)

Mansionization (*man·shun·eye·ZAY·shun,* noun) refers to the act of tearing down an existing house and replacing it with one that is bigger, especially one that is much larger than the surrounding houses.

> ➤ When the new owners across the street tore down that beautiful old Victorian home and replaced it with a hideous, 5,000-square-foot monster house, Jessie knew the **mansionization** of her neighborhood had begun.

Word Wonders

Big hair refers to a bouffant hairstyle, especially one in which long hair has been sprayed, permed, or teased to make it stand away from the head and give it volume. It was once seen as an emblem of rich, powerful, or glamorous women, but is now mocked as being garish and very "1980s."

Such a house is more often than not a *starter castle,* "a large house built on a relatively small property." A similar species is the *big hair house,* "a house that has a garish style and that is overly large compared to its lot size and to the surrounding houses."

You can also bet that the pretentious owners of the house will install at least one *trophy tree,* "a large, fully mature, tree that has been uprooted and planted in a yard or estate."

It's a rare day when you can pick up a newspaper and not see a story about **road rage** (noun), a form of anger exhibited by motorists in response to a perceived injustice from another driver.

➤ After he had intentionally slammed into the back of the car that had cut him off, Scott knew he needed to do something about his **road rage.**

The recognition of this level of public anger began with road rage, but it didn't take long before we started hearing about other types of rage. So much so, that it seems that rage has become all the, well, rage:

air rage (noun)—An airline passenger's physical or verbal assault of crew members or other passengers.

dot-com rage (noun)—Rage against the perceived commercialization of the Internet.

trade rage (noun)—Anger generated by personal stock market losses.

Web rage (noun)—Anger caused by WORLD WIDE WEB frustrations such slow downloads, nonexistent links, and information that's difficult to find.

work rage (noun)—Workplace anger exhibited by an employee who has been mistreated or fired.

Inevitably, there's also *rage rage,* "anger directed at people who commit acts of road rage, air rage, and so on."

You Don't Say

Go postal is a reference to the stories that pop up occasionally about postal workers going berserk and shooting at their colleagues. Although these stories exist, it's also true that postal workers are no more or less likely to fly off the handle than anyone else, so the stereotype is a bit unfair. Postal workers tend to be a tad defensive about this issue, so it's a good idea to avoid using "go postal" in their presence.

Why all this anger? Some experts think it's because people today have such a large *stress portfolio,* "the collection of events and situations that cause stress in a person's life." At some point, the person may *go postal* (verb), " become stressed out to the point of losing it completely."

A **screenager** (noun) is a young person who has grown up with, and is therefore entirely comfortable with, a world of screens.

> ➤ Ashley grew up watching television, playing with computers, and accessing ATMs, so she was a total **screenager.**

A screenager (a word that combines "screen" and "teenager") is almost certainly part of the *generation lap* (a play on "generation gap"), the tendency for young people to be increasingly more technically savvy than their parents or elders.

Soccer Mom to Zine

A **soccer mom** (noun) is a suburban woman who is married and has children.

> ➤ With the kids loaded into the minivan for soccer practice, Cynthia wondered exactly when it was that she became one of those **soccer moms** that everyone's always talking about.

Soccer moms were the big demographic that every politician wanted to connect with back in the 1996 U.S. elections. In the 1998 elections, the politicians decided instead to chase the vote of the *waitress mom,* a woman who is married, has children, works in a low-income job, and has little formal education. In the 2000 elections, the target was the *WMWM,* the white married working mom.

A **synthespian** (*sin·THES·pee·un,* noun) is a synthetic *thespian* ("actor or actress"); a simulated character who "acts" in animated computer games or movies.

> ➤ The characters Woody and Buzz Lightyear in *Toy Story* proved that **synthespians** can be even more appealing than real actors.

Parts Dept.

The suffix *–plegic* means "paralyzed."

A **technoplegic** (*tek·noh·PLEE·jik,* noun) is a person who feels paralyzed mentally when faced with technology.

> ➤ A true **technoplegic**, Errol's brain would freeze solid as soon as he sat in front of a computer.

You can also use technoplegic as an adjective. The opposite would be a *technomaniac* (*tek·noh·MAY·nee·ak,* noun), a person obsessed with change that is based on technology. In between is the *technorealist* (*tek·noh·REE·uh·list,* noun), a person who has a balanced and realistic view of technology.

A **zine** (*zeen,* noun) is a small magazine that focuses on nonmainstream topics and that is usually written, edited, and published by an individual or a small group of people.

➤ An old computer and a beat-up printer were all that Sid and Nancy needed to publish *Masterpierce Theater,* their body-piercing **zine.**

A person who writes, edits, and publishes a zine is called a *zinester* (*ZEEN·stur,* noun).

Questions and Exercises to Help Everything Sink In

Here's a list of the main words you learned in this chapter:

ad creep	affluenza	branding	casualization
chad	coolhunter	cube farm	day trading
entreprenerd	first-person shooter	flex place	learning a living
Lexus liberal	mansionization	road rage	screenager
soccer mom	synthespian	technoplegic	zine

1. Choose the word that means "a person who investigates cutting-edge trends, fashions, and ideas":
    a. Lexus liberal
    b. coolhunter
    c. screenager
    d. technoplegic
2. Fill in the blank: "_____ is the stock market version of a get-rich-click scheme."

Match the word on the left with the short definition on the right:

3. screenager   a. an actor in an animated show
4. branding   b. a person paralyzed by technology
5. zine   c. marketing that creates a distinctive identity
6. synthespian   d. reform-minded in words but not deeds
7. lexus liberal   e. a young person comfortable with monitors
8. technoplegic   f. a small publication

9. Choose the word that's not related to *flex time:*

    a. third wardrobe

    b. modem cowboy

    c. telecommuting

    d. office-free

10. Choose the type of *chad* that's the same as a *pregnant chad:*

    a. tri

    b. hanging

    c. dimpled

    d. swinging

Chapter 26

Making Word Whoopee: Fun Words

"We have a deep-rooted delight in the comic effect of words in English, and not just in advertising jingles but at the highest level of endeavor."

—Bill Bryson, American writer and journalist

If words had faces, most of the words in this book would come with pursed lips, sober expressions, and creased foreheads. They would look, in other words, like the serious representatives of our lexicon that they are. Not so the words that I feature in this chapter. Here the word faces you'll see would be more likely to come with goofy grins, protruding tongues, and raised eyebrows. That's because this chapter is devoted to fun, so I highlight words that have funny sounds or funny definitions. You'll notice, too, that I like words that are a bit old fashioned and anachronistic, but not so *antediluvian* (*an·tee·duh·LOO·vee·uhn,* adj.) that they're obsolete (antediluvian, "extremely old; before the Biblical Flood," is a good example). Using such words is called *gadzookery* (*gad·ZOOK·uh·ree,* noun), a fun term that comes from the oath "Gadzooks!" the modern equivalent of which would be something like "Oh my gosh!" Now if you'll just take a second to put a silly look on your face, we can begin …

Akimbo to Flibbertigibbet

Akimbo (*uh·KIM·boh,* adv.) describes a position in which the hands are on the hips and the elbows are turned outwards. This usually indicates that the person is feeling angry or impatient.

> ➤ After Jimbo glanced at the bimbo and then saw his wife standing with arms **akimbo**, he knew his love life was now in limbo.

Codswallop (*KODZ·wol·up,* noun) means nonsense, rubbish, or drivel (also *cod's wallop* and *cod's*).

> ➤ The old story about alligators in the sewers of New York City is nothing but a load of **codswallop!**

No one has any idea where this word came from. The tale most often told concerns a gentleman named Hiram C. Codd, who sold bottled lemonade in England in the 1870s. In those days, *wallop* was a slang term for an alcoholic drink, especially beer, so "Codd's wallop" became a sarcastic reference to any weak drink and then to anything of little or no value. Of course, it's entirely possible that this story is itself just a load of codswallop!

If you don't want to use codswallop but you're still in the mood for making IRONIC use of an old-fashioned-sounding word, try *balderdash* (*BAWL·dur·dash*), *flapdoodle* (*FLAP·doo·dul*), or *horsefeathers* (*HORS·feth·urs,* "th" as in "the").

Use **crepuscular** (*kri·PUS·kyuh·lur,* adj.) to describe dim lighting, especially the fading light associated with dusk or twilight.

> ➤ Boris hated the bright glare of the afternoon and wouldn't go out until the light outside was suitably **crepuscular.**

What I love about this word is that its sound is so, well, *ugly.* Just saying it out loud is enough to give one the WILLIES. Strange, then, that its rough exterior gives way to a rather benign meaning. What a waste! With that hard "c" at the beginning and that "pus" in the middle, I can't help thinking this word would be better suited to some revolting medical condition. Even so, it has inspired me to verse:

> When, on an evening crepuscular,
> I met a mugger muscular,
> Who said, "My, you're minuscular,"
> I burst something corpuscular.

Parts Dept.

Words that have a nice sound are described as *euphonious* (*yoo·FOH·nee·us,* adj.), which comes from the ancient Greek word *euphonos,* meaning "sweet-voiced." It combines the prefix *eu-,* "good," and *phonos,* "sound."

A **flibbertigibbet** (*FLIB·ur·tee·jib·it,* noun) is a silly, irresponsible, flighty person, especially one who chatters constantly.

➤ After listening to Muriel jabber mindlessly for 10 minutes, Macon realized he was dealing with a real **flibbertigibbet.**

The origin of this word is obscure, but the Oxford English Dictionary speculates that it's an imitation of the sound of idle, trivial chatter. That makes it *onomatopoeic* (*on·uh·mat·uh·PEE·ik,* adj.), which describes a word formed from the imitation of the sound associated with the thing or action it refers to. This approach has produced dozens of English words, including *splash, buzz, murmur, meow, chirp, hiss, sizzle,* and *cock-a-doodle-do.* Onomatopoeia (the process; pronounced *on·uh·mat·uh·PEE·uh*) is also responsible for two other terms that deal with idle chatter: *babble* and *yadda-yadda-yadda.*

Here are a few other fun words you can use instead of flibbertigibbet: *scatterbrain, birdbrain, featherbrain, dingbat, rattle-head,* and *giddy-head.*

Word Wonders

Flibbertigibbet has an obscure but still noteworthy claim to linguistic fame: It contains four Bs, which is the most of any common word.

Galoot to Hullaballoo

A **galoot** (*guh·LOOT,* noun) is a clumsy, uncouth, and not overly smart person.

➤ "Some big, dumb fool kept knocking into me on the subway this morning. I think they need a 'No **Galoots'** policy during rush hour."

Somewhere back in the shrouded mists of movie history, a leading lady called John Wayne or Clark Gable or some other leading man a "big galoot," and the word stuck. (Actually, the words "big" and "galoot" have been used together so often that it now seems wrong to apply galoot to a small person.) These days, you're more likely to hear people use a dull synonym such as *oaf,* but another fun word that I like is *clodhopper.*

The **heebie-jeebies** (*hee-bee JEE-beez,* noun) are feelings of nervousness and anxiousness.

➤ "If snakes give me the **heebie-jeebies,**" Marian mused to herself, "then why on earth am I working at a serpentarium?"

You can thank the cartoonist Bill DeBeck for the invention of this barrel full of linguistic fun. He used it in the 1920s in his strip *Barney Google,* which was also the source of gems such as *hotsy-totsy* (*hot-see TAWT-see,* adj.), "wonderful; pretentiously fashionable," and HORSEFEATHERS. Synonyms for the heebie-jeebies include the *jitters* and the *willies*.

Highfalutin (*hye·fuh·LOOT·n,* adj.) describes something that is POMPOUS or pretentious.

➤ "The opera is a bit **highfalutin** for my tastes. I'm more of a Bugs Bunny in 'The Rabbit of Seville' kind of person."

Highfalutin (or, if you prefer, *highfaluting,* but that just doesn't sound right to my ear) has been around since the middle of the nineteenth century, but nobody knows how it got started. The SCUTTLEBUTT is that it comes from the image of a person pompously playing high notes on a flute, or "high-fluting." An equally fun adjective to toss out is *hoity-toity* (*hoy·tee TOY·tee,* adj.).

Word Wonders

I mentioned earlier that ONOMATOPOEIA is one of the ways that new words are formed. Another is *reduplication* (*ree·doop·luh·KAY·shun,* noun), the formation of a new word by doubling all or part of an existing word. *Hoity-toity* was formed that way (from the obsolete verb *hoit,* "to romp"), and it is in fact a special case called *rhyming reduplication,* in which two words that rhyme are combined, as in *bow-wow, harum-scarum, super-duper,* and *teeny-weeny.* Regular examples of reduplication *are fiddle-faddle, wishy-washy,* and *riff-raff,* but you'll meet quite a few more before this chapter is done.

A **hullaballoo** (*hul·uh·buh·LOO,* noun) is a great noise or commotion; an uproar.

➤ After hearing the **hullaballoo** that eight kids hopped up on sugar could make, Rupert decided to never again volunteer to help out at a Halloween party.

This is a fun word to use in conversation, and it's perfect if you need an unusual synonym for *noise* or *commotion.* It's just obscure enough that it doesn't get overused, but it's not so obscure that most people won't recognize it and chuckle to themselves. Hullabaloo began its life as the word *halloo,* meaning "to urge or incite with shouts." Then, thanks to our old friend RHYMING REDUPLICATION, the *balloo* part was added to form *halloo-balloo,* which eventually morphed in hullabaloo.

Some synonyms that register about the same on the fun-meter are *brouhaha, hubbub,* and *hurly-burly.*

Kibosh to Nincompoop

A **kibosh** (*KYE·bosh,* noun) is a thing that stops or restrains something else. However, it's always used as part of the phrase *put the kibosh on* something.

> ➤ Fenwick started blaring Wagner's *Siegfried's Death and Funeral March* before firing someone, but his boss quickly put the **kibosh** on that.

The world's linguists have occasional skirmishes over the origin of this word, but the winning theory seems to be that it comes from the Gaelic phrase *cie bas* (pronounced the same as kibosh), which means "cap of death." In ancient Ireland, a judge would slip on this cap before he sentenced a person to death, which is about as stopped or restrained as you can get.

A **lollapalooza** (*lawl·uh·puh·LOO·zuh,* noun) is an outstanding person or thing or something that's an exceptional example of its kind.

> ➤ Any book that could make Johnny "The Sponge" Johanson give up booze had to be a real **lollapalooza** of a read.

In his book *The American Language,* the great writer H. L. Mencken claims that this word (which is also spelled *lallapalooza*) originated with the French phrase *allez-fusil,* "forward the muskets!" After the French landed in Ireland in 1798, the phrase passed into the local language and eventually became *allay-foozee,* "a sturdy fellow," and it somehow morphed into lollapalooza from there.

Unfortunately, this word has been taken over in recent years by a tour of alternative music bands called *Lollapalooza* that runs each summer. So (speaking of alternatives) here are some other words you can use instead: *corker, doozy, humdinger,* and *lulu.*

To **lollygag** (*LAWL·ee·gag,* verb) means to waste time in an IDLE, aimless way.

> ➤ "If only I had a dollar for each time my poor, long-suffering mother told me to stop my infernal **lollygagging**."

This word probably comes from the word *loll* (*lawl,* verb), which means "to move or recline in an INDOLENT way." Note, too, that although none of the dictionaries that I checked included *lollygagger* (*LAWL·ee·ga·gur,* noun), "a person who lollygags," it's a perfectly acceptable word and is, in fact, quite common. Why, it has even appeared in *The New York Times:*

> "Rome was surprisingly serene, tidy and composed. While motor scooters continue to skirl through the tiniest piazzas and tightest defiles, lots of streets are

off-limits to cars, and there's room for **lollygaggers** and cafe loiterers." (From the April 26, 1998 issue)

(To *skirl* [*skurl*, verb], by the by, means "to produce a high-pitched wailing tone." It's most often used with reference to Scottish bagpipes.)

Some chuckle-inducing synonyms are *dawdle* (*DAW·dul* or *DAWD·l*) and two REDUPLI-CATIONS: *dilly-dally* (*DIL·ee dal·ee*) and *shilly-shally* (*SHIL·ee shal·ee*). See also SLUGABED.

A **nincompoop** (*NIN·kum·poop* or *NING·kum·poop*, noun) is a person who is stupid or silly.

> ➤ Mr. Loblolly tried to insult his Grade 3 class by calling them **nincompoops**, but they just giggled because he'd said "poop."

Samuel Johnson once speculated that this word came from the Latin phrase *non compos mentis*, "of unsound mind," which comes up often in the medical and legal professions. Doctors and lawyers often shorten this phrase to *non compos*, so it doesn't seem unreasonable for nonprofessionals to have shaped this into nincompoop. Another theory is that it came from a combination of the French word *nicodême* "a simpleton," and *poop*, "a clown." The *Oxford English Dictionary* pooh-poohs such suggestions and calls nincompoop "a fanciful formation."

The OED also mentions some other rather hilarious forms of the word, including *nincompoopish, nincompoopery, nincompoophood,* and *nincompoopiana*.

Some synonyms: *boob, ninny, noddy*. See also: TOMFOOLERY.

Razzmatazz to *Thingamajig*

Razzmatazz (*RAZ·muh·taz*, noun) is a flashy, GAUDY display designed to impress people and get them excited.

> ➤ She was only trying to add some **razzmatazz**, but the others thought Wanda's fireworks, jugglers, and elephants were a bit much for a budget presentation.

Razzmatazz probably originated as a variation of *razzle-dazzle* (*raz·ul DAZ·ul*, noun), which means "an amazing or bewildering display." It's the "bewildering" component that gives razzle-dazzle an additional meaning of "an action designed to confuse," which is often used in sports ("the old razzle-dazzle play"). This also explains why razzmatazz is sometimes used to mean "double talk; ambiguous or evasive language."

Scuttlebutt (*SKUT·ul·but*, noun) is gossip or rumors.

> ➤ The **scuttlebutt** from the labs is that we'll soon have "smart" refrigerators that will crash just like computers do.

Scuttlebutt brings together the word *scuttle* (noun), "a hole or hatch," and *butt* (noun), "a small cask." In days of yore, this word first referred to a cask that contained a sailing ship's drinking water. The *tars* and *salts* (both informal terms for sailors) would gather around this nautical version of a water cooler and exchange the latest rumors and gossip, which then took on the name of the cask.

A **slugabed** (*SLUG·uh·bed,* noun) is a person who prefers to stay in bed out of laziness.

➤ Most teenagers seem to naturally sleep in until noon, but the fact that Crystal was still doing it at age 35 made her just another **slugabed.**

This is a word that probably needs no commentary (not that *that* will stop me). Slugabed seems to me to be the perfect description for someone too lazy, too slothful, too SLUGGARDLY to drag themselves out of bed. As far as I know, the word was coined by Shakespeare and was first used in *Romeo and Juliet.* In Act V, Scene IV, the nurse comes to wake Juliet from her "unnatural sleep" and says:

"Why lamb!—why lady!—fie, you slugabed!"

At least Juliet had an excuse!

See also: LOLLYGAG.

Thingamajig (*THING·uh·muh·jig,* noun) is a word to use when the proper name for something either isn't known or has been temporarily forgotten.

➤ Pass me the **thingamajig** that's over there beside the dingus. You know, under the whatchamacallit.

This is a kind of nonsense word derived from *thing* and having many other forms including *thingam-abob* and *thingy.* Humans must be awfully forgetful creatures because we've coined many different nonsense words to use as placeholders for the names of things we've temporarily mislaid. Here's a small sampling: *dingus, whatchamacallit, whatsit,* and *whoosit.* For nameless gadgets or trinkets, there are also *doodad, doohickey, gizmo,* and *widget.* In fact, the word *gadget* itself began life as a nonsense word to substitute for a forgotten name.

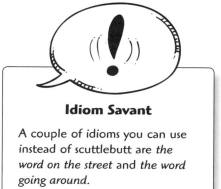

Idiom Savant

A couple of idioms you can use instead of scuttlebutt are *the word on the street* and *the word going around.*

Tomfoolery to Zilch

Tomfoolery (*tom·FOO·luh·ree,* noun) is foolish or silly behavior.

➤ There were spitballs being spat, paper airplanes being flown, and armpits being used to make a variety of unpleasant noises. Baxter had never seen such **tomfoolery** at a BOARD OF DIRECTORS meeting.

Tomfoolery is a perfect representation of the gadzookery species. It's recognizable enough that most people understand what you mean, but it's just out-of-date enough (and silly sounding) to elicit a smile.

Word Wonders

The original spelling of tomfool was *Tom Fool,* and there's written evidence of the latter all the way back to the fourteenth century! Who was this Tom and why was he such a fool? The "Tom" part comes from the long–standing use of "Tom" as a generic name for an unknown person (as in *Tom, Dick, and Harry*). The "Fool" part comes from the strange fact that, in less enlightened times, people were often allowed to visit insane asylums as a form of "entertainment." If the audience saw someone who was deranged in a particularly amusing way, they would nickname him "Tom Fool," and the *epithet* ("term of abuse") was later used in nonasylum settings.

This enjoyable word comes from the noun *tomfool,* "a half-wit; a remarkably foolish person," from which we also get *tomfool idea,* "an extremely stupid or foolish notion."

A **whippersnapper** (*WHIP·ur·snap·ur,* noun) is an insignificant but impertinent person, especially a young person. (In this context, *impertinent* (*im·PUR·tun·unt,* adj.) means "improperly bold or forward.")

➤ "I've been mowing lawns for over 40 years, so how dare that little **whippersnapper** lecture me about my technique!"

The OED describes this word, pleasingly, as "a jingling extension of *whip-snapper.*" A whip-snapper, it turns out, was a seventeenth-century layabout who would pass the time by hanging around on street corners and snapping a whip. (Hey, I don't make this stuff up!) In those days, a *snipper-snapper* was a "young insignificant or conceited fellow," so I'm sure it didn't take long for some wag to merge "whip-snapper" and "snipper-snapper" to make "whipper-snapper."

One of my favorite expressions (I'm quite certain I've used it in every book I've written) is **willy-nilly** (*wil·ee·NIL·ee,* adv.), which means "haphazardly; in a disorganized or unplanned way; whether desired or not."

➤ Roland knew his **willy-nilly** approach to brain surgery would get him in trouble one day.

The like-it-or-not-here-it-comes sense of this word was the original meaning, and it comes from the seventeenth-century phrase *will ye, nill ye,* a shortened form of *be ye willing, be ye unwilling.* Both of these mean "whether you like it or you don't like it" (*ye* is an archaic form of "you"). There's also a Latin version of this that comes up now and again: *nolens volens* (*NOH·lenz VOH·lenz*). The haphazard sense has some particularly jovial synonyms, including *helter-skelter* and the classic *higgledy-piggledy.* (Boy, that REDUPLICATION stuff is coming up a *lot* in this chapter, isn't it?)

In the end, this chapter comes to nothing, literally, because our final bit of linguistic merriment is **zilch** (noun), "zero; nothing."

➤ "I spent six hours waiting for her autograph, but I got **zilch.** I *knew* I shouldn't have worn my "Marry Me, Madonna!" T-shirt."

The world's word detectives have traced zilch back to a 1930s comic strip called *Ballyhoo,* which featured an unseen character named Mr. Zilch. What you *did* see was a bunch of near-naked, suggestively posed young women who would exclaim "Oh, Mr. Zilch" in reaction to something or other our hidden hero had done. Since there was nothing to see of Mr. Zilch, his name came to mean "nothing."

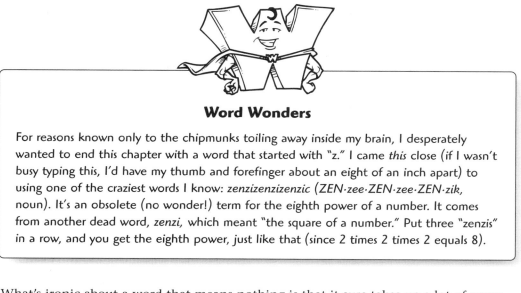

Word Wonders

For reasons known only to the chipmunks toiling away inside my brain, I desperately wanted to end this chapter with a word that started with "z." I came *this* close (if I wasn't busy typing this, I'd have my thumb and forefinger about an eight of an inch apart) to using one of the craziest words I know: *zenzizenzizenzic* (*ZEN·zee·ZEN·zee·ZEN·zik,* noun). It's an obsolete (no wonder!) term for the eighth power of a number. It comes from another dead word, *zenzi,* which meant "the square of a number." Put three "zenzis" in a row, and you get the eighth power, just like that (since 2 times 2 times 2 equals 8).

What's ironic about a word that means nothing is that it sure takes up a lot of room in a thesaurus. Here's a by-no-means-complete listing of zilch synonyms: *aught, bagel, bubkes* (*BUB·kus;* Yiddish), *cipher, donut, goose egg, love* (used in tennis), *nada* (Spanish), *naught, nil, rien* (*ree·ENH;* French), and *zip.*

Questions and Exercises to Help Everything Sink In

Here's a list of the main words you learned in this chapter:

akimbo	codswallop	crepuscular	flibbertigibbet
galoot	heebie-jeebies	highfalutin	hullaballoo
kibosh	lollapalooza	lollygag	nincompoop
razzmatazz	scuttlebutt	slugabed	thingamajig
tomfoolery	whippersnapper	willy-nilly	zilch

1. Choose the word that means "a lazy person who prefers to sleep":
   - **a.** scuttlebutt
   - **b.** slugabed
   - **c.** galoot
   - **d.** lollapalooza

2. Fill in the blank: "I love the time after sunset, when the light is _____."

Match the word on the left with the short definition on the right:

3. heebie-jeebies   **a.** something that stops or restrains
4. tomfoolery   **b.** hands on hips, elbows out
5. akimbo   **c.** flashy, gaudy display
6. razzmatazz   **d.** nervous and anxious feelings
7. kibosh   **e.** silly behavior

8. Name two things you can eat that are also synonyms for *zilch*.

9. Choose the word that's not a synonym for *lollapalooza*:
   - **a.** doozy
   - **b.** corker
   - **c.** humdinger
   - **d.** hoity-toity

10. Choose the word that's a synonym for *galoot*:
    - **a.** clodhopper
    - **b.** dingbat
    - **c.** boob
    - **d.** tomfool

Part 7

Sharpening Your Skills: More Words You Should Know

Each of the first 26 chapters of this book focused on one or more relatively specific topics. This subject-oriented approach is one of the main features of the book, and it has served us well by helping to introduce hundreds of main words and another couple of thousand secondary terms. That's a lot of lexicon, to be sure, but English words don't all fit neatly into convenient compartments. There's a vast number of all-purpose, "subjectless" words that you can wield at the office, at school, at home, or wherever the fancy strikes you. These words are the subject of the three chapters in Part 7. Here you'll find another 300 must-know words, divided precisely into the three main parts of speech: nouns, verbs, and adjectives.

Chapter 27

100 Nouns You Should Know

In This Chapter

➤ Adjunct, advent, and adversity

➤ Cataclysm, catalyst, and catch–22

➤ Prodigy, propensity, and proximity

➤ Transgression, travail, and trepidation

"All men conduct their conversations in metaphors and pertinent and proper nouns."

—Aristotle, Greek philosopher

You probably learned in grade school that a noun is a "person, place, or thing," and this remains about as good (and as simple) a definition as you'll ever need.

The "person" part of this definition I covered throughout the chapters in Part 1, "The Good, the Bad, the Ugly, and More: People Words," and I've mentioned all kinds of people in other chapters, too (for example, see GOURMAND, DEFENDANT, and DIPLOMAT).

The "place" part of the definition hasn't got much coverage in this book mostly because the names of places would fall under the category of general knowledge rather than vocabulary.

That leaves us with the "thing" part of the definition, and although I've defined hundreds of things in previous chapters (for example, see BROADSHEET, INDICTMENT, and MICROPROCESSOR), the world is full of stuff and time's a-wasting. Therefore, this chapter is devoted exclusively to things of all kinds. My approach will be a bit different than in previous chapters because I'm just going to run through the list of 100 nouns, provide definitions for each word's most common meanings, and give you a short sample sentence for each meaning so you can see how the word is used.

Acclaim *to* Catalyst

acclaim (*uh·KLAYM*) Enthusiastic praise or approval given publicly: *With the crowd's thunderous acclaim still ringing in his ears a week later, Toby feared he'd become addicted to adulation.* (This word can also be used as a verb.)

acme (*AK·mee*) The highest point, especially of achievement or perfection: *Upon hearing that she'd reached the acme of her profession with her appointment to the Supreme Court, Hilda thought "Ooh, I am good!"* See also ZENITH.

Word Wonders

Things are always "under" the aegis because the word comes from Greek mythology, where it represented the shield of Zeus himself.

You Don't Say

Don't confuse allusion with *illusion* (*i·LOO·zhun*), an erroneous or misleading perception or belief or something that caused such a perception or belief.

adjunct (*AJ·ungkt*) Something added to something else without forming an essential part of it: *As an adjunct professor, he wasn't considered part of the faculty.*

advent (*AD·vent*) The arrival of something important or long-awaited: *The advent of the computer, with its genius for crashing at exactly the wrong time, has given new life to Murphy's Law.*

adversity (*ad·VUR·si·tee*) Hardship, suffering, or misfortune: *Jake had faced such adversity as a child that now you practically had to use a crowbar to pry money from his hands.*

aegis (*ee·jis*) 1. Protection or support: *They returned to their homes under the aegis of the U.N. peacekeeping force.* 2. Patronage; auspices: *The charity ball was held under the aegis of the Chamber of Commerce.* See also PATRON.

affinity (*uh·FIN·i·tee*) 1. A natural attraction to or liking for something: *He has a strong affinity for old-fashioned words.* 2. A similarity or likeness between persons or things: *There are many affinities between American and Canadian cultures.*

allusion (*uh·LOO·zhun*) An indirect or implied reference to something: *The "road less traveled" is an allusion to Robert Frost's poem* The Road Not Taken.

analogy (*uh·NAL·uh·jee*) A comparison between two things that have some features in common but are otherwise different from each other: *When things start* *to pile up at work, the analogy I like to use is "I'm as busy as a one-legged man in a bum-kicking contest!"* See also METAPHOR.

annotation (*ann·uh·TAY·shun*) An explanatory note or commentary added to a document: *Put your annotations on the fax and then send it back to me.*

antithesis (*an·TITH·uh·sis,* "th" as in "thin") The direct or exact opposite of something: *Your shoddy grammar and ill-formed ideas are the antithesis of good writing.*

archetype (*AR·kuh·type*) 1. The original model or pattern for other things of the same type: *There are three archetypes that have defined horror stories: Frankenstein, Dr. Jekyll and Mr. Hyde, and Dracula.* 2. An ideal or typical example of something: *Bill Gates is the archetype of the successful computer geek.* See also EPITOME, PARADIGM, QUINTESSENTIAL.

artifact (*AR·tuh·fakt*) An object created by a human, especially something used as a tool or for some other practical purpose and that has archaeological, historical, or cultural interest: *The Italian town of Fiesole has a museum that contains Etruscan artifacts of great beauty.*

avant-garde (*a·vahnt GARD*) The leading edge of a trend or movement, especially in the arts; the vanguard: *In any art form, the avant-garde innovate and the old guard consolidate.*

bathos (*BAY·thaws* or *BAY·thohs,* "th" as in thin) 1. Insincere or excessive *pathos* ("feelings of pity or compassion"): *The movie was okay until it starting getting soppy and sentimental, which was the start of the descent in mere bathos.* 2. A sudden change in style from the sublime to the commonplace; an anticlimax: *He's a director willing to use bathos to good effect, like the time the hero dons his suit or armor to stirring music and then asks "Okay, how do I look?"*

behemoth (*buh·HEE·muth*) Something that is monstrously big or powerful: *At 6'5" and 350 pounds, the new lineman was a true behemoth.*

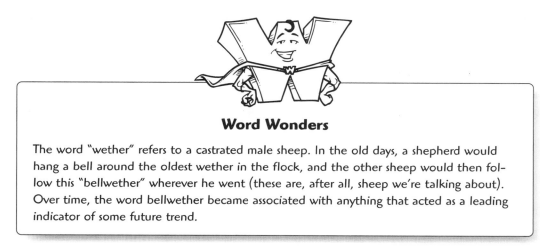

Word Wonders

The word "wether" refers to a castrated male sheep. In the old days, a shepherd would hang a bell around the oldest wether in the flock, and the other sheep would then follow this "bellwether" wherever he went (these are, after all, sheep we're talking about). Over time, the word bellwether became associated with anything that acted as a leading indicator of some future trend.

You Don't Say

The "bully" in bully pulpit has nothing to do with the cruel thugs who terrorize schoolyard playgrounds. Instead, this bully is an archaic word that means "wonderful; splendid." Bully pulpit was coined by former U.S. President Teddy Roosevelt, who used the phrase to describe the presidency.

bellwether (*BEL·weth·ur*, "th" as in "the") Something that acts as an indicator of a future trend: *New Mexico voters supported the winner in nearly every U.S. presidential election of the twentieth century, making it a true bellwether state.* See also PRECURSOR.

bully pulpit (*BULL·ee PUL·pit*) A public position of prominence, such as political office, that gives the holder a large audience: *He was determined to use the bully pulpit of the presidency to pitch his ideas directly to the people.*

cataclysm (*KAT·uh·kliz·um*) A sudden and violent disaster or upheaval that causes tremendous destruction or fundamental changes to society: *The cataclysm of the Reformation changed Christianity forever.* See also: DEBACLE.

catalyst (*KAT·uh·list*) Somebody or something that causes change to occur or brings about an action or event: *The new player really make things happen out there; he's a real catalyst for the offence.*

Catch-22 to Embargo

catch-22 (*kach twen·tee·TOO*) A situation in which the desired outcome is impossible to achieve because the rules that govern the situation always work against the solution: *The catch-22 of young workers is that you can't get a job unless you have experience, but you can't get experience unless you get a job.*

chagrin (*shuh·GRIN*) A feeling of annoyance or humiliation caused by a failure or disappointment: *I had them put "Will you marry me, Sheena?" on the scoreboard at the game, but much to my chagrin, she said "No."*

chronology (*kruh·NAWL·uh·jee*) 1. The order in which events occur: *The chronology of the Dark Ages is unknown.* 2. A list of events in order of occurrence: *Any chronology of the twentieth century must include the fall of the Berlin Wall.*

cliché (*klee·SHAY*) A word or phrase that has lost its original effectiveness due to long-term overuse: *Her writing was riddled with clichés such as "food for thought" and "rags to riches."*

collusion (*kuh·LOO·zhun*) Secret cooperation or a secret agreement between two or more parties for illegal or deceitful purposes: *The players union accused the owners of using collusion to keep salaries artificially low.*

compendium (*kum·PEN·dee·um*) 1. A brief but complete summary of a larger work or subject: *Not wanting to get too bogged down in the entire history of the war, he decided to* *look for a good compendium instead.* See also SYNOPSIS. 2. A list or collection of items: *The* Random House Historical Dictionary of American Slang *is one of the greatest slang compendiums ever produced.*

Word Wonders

Catch-22 comes from Joseph Heller's novel *Catch–22*, which covers the antics of bomber pilots in World War II. Heller explains catch-22 in the following passage:

> "There was only one catch and that was Catch-22, which specified that a concern for one's safety in the face of dangers that were real and immediate was the process of a rational mind. Orr was crazy and could be grounded. All he had to do was ask; and as soon as he did, he would no longer be crazy and would have to fly more missions. Orr would be crazy to fly more missions and sane if he didn't, but if he was sane he had to fly them. If he flew them he was crazy and didn't have to; but if he didn't want to he was sane and had to."

complement (*KOM·pluh·munt*) 1. Something that completes or perfects another thing: *A good Chianti is a complement to pasta.* 2. The quantity of things required to make something complete: *The old codger still had his complement of 32 teeth.*

conduit (*KON·doo·it*) 1. A pipe or channel that conveys a liquid: *During bypass surgery, doctors construct a conduit so that blood can flow around a blocked artery.* 2. A pipe or tube that encloses and protects electrical wires or other cables: *We need to run these wires outside for about 20 feet, so we'll have to put up some conduit to protect them from the weather.* 3. A person or thing that conveys information or goods: *During the negotiations, her assistant acted as a conduit between the two sides.*

correlation (*kor·uh·LAY·shun*) A relationship between two or more things that tend to change or occur together: *There is a high correlation between smoking and lung disease.*

You Don't Say

Complement is only one letter away from *compliment*, "an expression of praise or admiration," so be careful. Speaking of compliment, the word "uncomplimentary" is famous in word trivia circles for having all five vowels in reverse order.

283

dearth (*durth*) A scarcity or shortage of something; a famine: *The reason we seem to be running the same articles month after month is that we have a dearth of new ideas.*

debacle (*duh·BAH·kul* or *duh·BAK·ul*) A disaster, defeat, or total and humiliating failure: *They lost 10 to 0 in the championship game, so the coach figured the right thing to do was to resign after such a debacle.* See also CATACLYSM and FIASCO.

decadence (*DEK·uh·duns*) The state or process of decline or decay in standards or morals; degeneration: *Before it became more family-oriented, rampant gambling and prostitution made Las Vegas the center of American decadence.*

You Don't Say

Don't mix up deprivation and *depravation*, "moral debasement or corruption."

demeanor (*duh·MEE·nur*) A person's behavior or manner; bearing; deportment: *His restless, fidgety demeanor during the interview said more about him than his resumé did.*

deprivation (*dep·ruh·VAY·shun*) The condition of being without something, especially food and shelter: *Her donation ensured that many families would never suffer the same deprivation that she had as a child.* See also DEARTH and POVERTY.

deterrent (*dee·TUR·unt*) Something that prevents or discourages an action, especially by using fear or doubt: *The warships in the area served as a deterrent for anyone thinking of trying to get around the embargo.*

dichotomy (*dye·KOT·uh·mee*) A separation into two contradictory or fundamentally different parts: *There is always a dichotomy between theory and practice.*

disparity (*di·SPAIR·i·tee*) 1. A lack of equality between people or things: *The disparity between the incomes of men and women has been shrinking.* 2. A dissimilarity: *The debate served to highlight the disparities between the two candidates' economic plans.* See also DISPARATE.

dynasty (*DYE·nuh·stee*) 1. A series of rulers from the same family: *The Ming dynasty ruled China for nearly 300 years.* 2. A family or group that holds power and influence through several generations: *The Daley family is a Chicago political dynasty.*

effect (*i·FEKT*) 1. The result of some action or cause: *Does this drug have any side effects?* 2. The ability to influence something or someone: *The pain had lessened, so he knew the drug was having some effect.* See also AFFECT.

embargo (*em·BAR·goh*) 1. A government order that prohibits some or all trade with a foreign nation: *Many governments prefer to discipline a rogue nation by imposing an embargo rather than by using military force.* 2. A prohibition: *The results of many scientific studies are embargoed, which means news organizations can view the findings but they can't publish anything until a certain date.*

Enigma to *Juxtaposition*

enigma (*i·NIG·muh*) Something that is not easy to understand or explain; a mystery: *Winston Churchill famously described Russia as "a riddle wrapped in a mystery inside an enigma."*

epitome (*i·PIT·uh·mee*) A representative or ideal example of a class or type: *Mother Teresa was the epitome of compassion.* See also ARCHETYPE, PARADIGM, QUINTESSENTIAL.

euphemism (*YOO·fuh·miz·um*) A word or phrase substituted for another word or phrase that is considered to be too blunt, harsh, or offensive: *She always used "powder room" as a euphemism for "toilet."*

exodus (*EKS·uh·dus*) A departure that involves a large number of people: *In most northern retirement communities, there is an exodus to Florida every fall.*

fiasco (*fee·AS·koh*) A total failure: *After all the name-calling in the morning, when lunch degenerated into a food fight, Webster officially declared the conference a fiasco.* See also DEBACLE.

foresight (*FOR·syte*) The ability to imagine or provide for possible future consequences or problems; anticipation; forethought; providence: *They were snowed in, so she was glad her husband had the foresight to buy a supply of canned goods and water before the storm.* See also HINDSIGHT.

gambit (*GAM·bit*) 1. A maneuver or ploy, especially one used in the beginning; a stratagem: *Her debate-opening gambit was to thrust a "No New Taxes" pledge at her opponent and ask him to sign it.* 2. A remark used to begin a conversation: *His "Hey, baby, what's your sign?" gambit was just corny enough to be successful.* 3. An opening chess move that sacrifices a minor piece such as a pawn to gain a positional advantage: *She opened the game with the classic "Queen's Gambit."*

gamut (*GAM·ut*) A complete range or series: *In their brief affair, he experienced a gamut of emotions, from intense joy to deep despair.* (This word is most commonly seen as part of the verb phrase *run the gamut*: *His emotions ran the gamut from intense joy to deep despair.*)

gusto (*GUS·toh*) Lively and vigorous enjoyment; relish; zest: *She loved food and could always be counted on to tuck into her dinner with gusto.*

hiatus (*hye·AY·tus*) A gap or break in an otherwise continuous object or schedule; an interruption: *Our show will be on hiatus through the summer and will return in September.*

hindsight (*HINED·syte*) The ability to judge or understand the significance of an event after it has happened: *In hindsight, he realized that "I like a woman with some meat on her bones" was not a good answer to her "Am I fat?" question.* See also FORESIGHT.

horde (*hord*) A large group; a throng (usually of people); a swarm (usually of insects): *She loved Christmas, but she hated fighting the hordes at the mall.*

You Don't Say

Horde sounds just the same as *hoard*, "a hidden supply or fund put aside for future use." (Hoard can also be used as a verb.)

impasse (*IM·pas*) A situation in which no further progress can be made; a deadlock; a logjam; a stalemate: *When it was clear that the two sides had reached an impasse, the judge decided to call in a mediator.*

inception (*in·SEP·shun*) The beginning of something; a commencement: *He was the old-timer of the group, having been a member since its inception.*

inverse (*IN·vurs*) The opposite of something: *Division is the inverse of multiplication.* (This word can also be used as an adjective, in which case it's pronounced *in·VURSE.*)

iota (*eye·OH·tuh*) An extremely small amount of something; a jot; a tad; a whit: *There is not an iota of evidence to support the accusations made against my client.*

irony (*EYE·ruh·nee* or *EYE·ur·nee*) 1. The use of words to express something different from and usually opposite to their literal meaning: *Since he knew of the charges against the incumbent, it's clear he was using irony when he mentioned "my honorable opponent" during his opening remarks.* 2. An absurd or humorous incompatibility between what actually happens and what might have been expected to happen: *The irony of it all was that her house burned to the ground the same day she paid off her mortgage.* See also SARCASM.

itinerary (*eye·TIN·uh·rair·ee*) A route for a journey that lists different places in the order they are to be visited: *Our itinerary has us visiting no fewer than five castles today.*

juxtaposition (*juk·stuh·puh·ZISH·un*) The placement of two or more things side by side to compare or contrast them: *The juxtaposition of the older, savvy George Bush and the younger, inexperienced Dan Quayle fascinated political junkies.*

Labyrinth to Recourse

labyrinth (*LAB·uh·rinth*, "th" as in "thin") 1. A place that contains an interconnected and complicated set of tunnels, passageways, or paths in which it would easy to become lost; a maze; a warren: *The bus was delayed because several tourists got lost in the estate's massive hedge labyrinth.* 2. Something with an extremely complex or intricate structure or composition: *The local zoning laws were a labyrinth of rules and regulations.*

longevity (*lon·JEV·i·tee*) 1. The long duration of a life; the length of a life: *Most people can increase their longevity by eating well, exercising often, and drinking in moderation.* 2. The length of a career: *His longevity as a Hollywood star was remarkable.*

metaphor (*MET·uh·for*) A word or phrase that ordinarily designates one thing but is applied to another to suggest a likeness or make a comparison: *One of her favorite metaphors came from Miguel de Cervantes, who described the eyes as "those silent tongues of love."* See also ANALOGY.

mettle (*MET·ul*) Courage, spirit, or strength of character; fortitude: *The hardships they ordered him to go through were designed to prove his mettle.*

miscellany (*MIS·uh·lay·nee*) A diverse collection of things; an assortment; a mixed bag: *Their basement had become a miscellany of unused, broken, and neglected objects.* 2. A diverse collection of writings from various authors, on various subjects, and in various genres; an anthology; a potpourri (*poh·puh·REE* or *poh·poo·REE*): *For her birthday, he gave her a miscellany of nineteenth-century Romantic poets.*

misnomer (*mis·NOH·mur*) A wrong or unsuitable name for a person or object: *Calling a dolphin a fish is a misnomer because it's really a mammal.*

morale (*muh·RAL*) The overall level of optimism or confidence felt by a person or group, especially as it affects discipline and loyalty; esprit de corps (*es·PREE duh KOR*): *After the second round of layoffs, morale at the company hit an all-time low.*

onus (*OH·nus*) A necessity or responsibility, especially a disagreeable one; a burden: *"Innocent until proven guilty" means the onus is on the prosecution to prove that the accused is guilty beyond a reasonable doubt.*

oxymoron (*awk·see·MOR·on*) A phrase that combines two words that have contradictory meanings: *The phrases "pretty ugly" and "deafening silence" are oxymorons.*

paradigm (*PAIR·uh·dime* or *PAIR·uh·dim*) A typical example, especially one that serves as a model or pattern: *Canada is a paradigm of tolerant multiculturalism.* See also ARCHETYPE, EPITOME, PARADIGM SHIFT, QUINTESSENTIAL.

paraphernalia (*pair·uh·fur·NAYL·yuh* or *pair·uh·fuh·NAYL·yuh*) 1. Equipment or gear used in a particular activity; accessories: *The wedding was over, so the photographer gathered up his lights, lenses, and other paraphernalia* 2. Personal belongings: *There was no future with him, so she packed her paraphernalia into her car and took off without looking back.* 3. Assorted objects or items; odds and ends: *There is enough paraphernalia at a flea market to please even the most dedicated of pack rats.*

penchant (*PEN·chunt*) A strong liking or taste for something; a partiality: *He has a penchant for chocolate ice cream and the waistline to prove it.*

You Don't Say

Mettle is pronounced identically to *metal*, but the latter means "a type of chemical element, such as copper or iron." Also, both derive from the Greek *metallon*, "mine, mineral, metal," so confusing them is understandable.

Word Wonders

The word *oxymoron* is itself an oxymoron! It comes from the Greek *oxumoros*, "pointedly foolish." However, the roots of the word are *oxus*, "sharp," and *moros*, "dull."

plethora (*PLETH·ur·uh*) A large or excessive amount; an overabundance: *The ad in the paper resulted in a plethora of applications and resumés.*

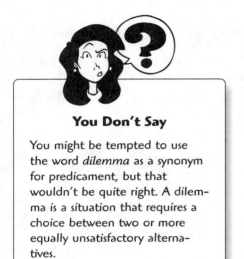

You Don't Say

You might be tempted to use the word *dilemma* as a synonym for predicament, but that wouldn't be quite right. A dilemma is a situation that requires a choice between two or more equally unsatisfactory alternatives.

plight (*plyte*) A bad or unfortunate situation; a pickle: *The plight of the homeless touched her heart.* See also PREDICAMENT.

precursor (*pri·KUR·sur* or *PREE·kur·sur*) 1. A person or thing that comes before and leads to the development of another person or thing: *The year-long drought was the precursor of the famine.* See also BELLWETHER. 2. A person who has held a particular position before someone else; a forerunner; a predecessor: *She was pleased to see that her precursor as president had installed a washroom just outside the office.*

predicament (*pri·DIK·uh·munt*) An unpleasant, troublesome, or embarrassing situation from which there is no easy way out; a fix; a jam: *With bears behind them and a steep gorge in front of them, she wondered how they would ever get themselves out of this predicament.* See also PLIGHT.

prelude (*PRAY·lood, PREE·lood, or PREL·yood*) An event or action that precedes or serves to introduce something else, especially something longer or more important: *The toast to the bride served as the prelude to the evening's speeches.*

prodigy (*PROD·uh·jee*) A wondrous act or event, especially a young person who demonstrates extraordinary talent: *Ever since his appearance on* The Mike Douglas Show *at age 2, the world has known that Tiger Woods was a golf prodigy.* See also WUNDERKIND.

propensity (*pruh·PEN·si·tee*) A natural inclination; a proclivity; a tendency: *He has a propensity for punning that drives his wife up the wall.* See also PENCHANT.

proximity (*prok·SIM·uh·tee*) Nearness in space or in time; closeness: *When she was looking for a house, she resolved not to get one in proximity to a school.*

ramification (*ram·uh·fi·KAY·shun*) A consequence of an action or decision that may complicate the situation: *The financial ramifications of quitting his job to return to school were only just now starting to sink in.*

recourse (*REE·kors* or *ri·KORS*) 1. The act of turning to a person or thing for assistance: *She knew that, if all else failed, she's still have recourse to the courts.* 2. A person, thing, or course of action to which a person turns for assistance: *"I'm sorry to bother you, but I had no other recourse."*

Repertoire to *Zenith*

repertoire (*REP·ur·twahr*) 1. The collection of musical or dramatic material that a player or troupe knows and can perform: *The band played every song in their repertoire.* 2. The complete body of works available in a particular segment of the arts: *She had mastered the entire repertoire of Johann Sebastian Bach.* 3. The range of skills, abilities, and techniques of a person or troupe: *Baking bread was not in his cooking repertoire.*

respite (*RES·pit*) A short period of rest or relief, especially one that comes after a period of exertion: *With the campaign over, the victorious candidate vowed to enjoy a brief respite before starting the transition.*

rift (*rift*) 1. A break in relations caused by a disagreement: *The usual "musical differences" was cited as the cause of the rift between the two band members.* 2. A narrow fissure; a cleft; a crevice: *The climber used a rift in the rock face to get a toehold.*

sarcasm (*SAR·kaz·um*) The use of words that mean the opposite of their literal meaning and that are intended to ridicule, mock, or deride a person or thing: *When she asked him if he wanted to go to the crafts show, she figured he was using sarcasm when he said "Yeah, right."*

satire (*SAT·ire*) 1. The use of wit, especially IRONY or SARCASM, to attack human vice and folly: Saturday Night Live *uses satire to have fun with current political and cultural themes.* 2. A work of art that uses satire: Gulliver's Travels *is one of the greatest works of satire in the English language.*

scourge (*skurj*) 1. A source of widespread affliction and devastation: *A fungus called late blight is the scourge that caused the Irish potato famine.* See also EPIDEMIC. 2. A person or thing that inflicts punishment, suffering, or severe criticism: *Rush Limbaugh is the scourge of liberals.*

serendipity (*sair·un·DIP·i·tee*) A fortunate or useful discovery made by accident; the faculty or gift for making such discoveries: *Christopher Columbus was looking for the West Indies, so it was pure serendipity that he discovered the Americas.*

solecism (*SAWL·uh·siz·um* or *SOLE·uh·siz·um*) 1. An ungrammatical combination of words or a nonstandard usage; a malapropism; a misusage: *When she said "What are this all about?" he decided to ignore the solecism.* 2. Something inappropriate or incorrect: *The referee committed the solecism of changing the rules while the game was still on.* 3. A violation of etiquette or good manners: *Failing to curtsy to the queen is a solecism of the highest order.*

Word Wonders

The word serendipity was coined by the author Horace Walpole in the mid-eighteenth century. It comes from an old Persian fairy tale called *The Three Princes of Serendip.* The tale's heroes were always making accidental discoveries as they traveled, so Walpole coined serendipity in their honor. (Serendip, by the way, is the country we now know as Sri Lanka.)

sophistry (*SOFE·is·tree*) Argumentation that seems plausible but is actually flawed, especially in a dishonest or fallacious way: *To argue that the Earth is the center of the universe because the sun and stars appear to rotate around it is pure sophistry.*

spate (*spayt*) A sudden and strong flood or outpouring of something: *The snowy conditions have caused a spate of accidents.*

status quo (*STAY·tus kwoh* or *STAT·us kwo*) The current condition or state of affairs: *She knew something in their relationship had to change; they just couldn't go on with the status quo.*

surrogate (*SUR·uh·git* or *SUR·uh·gayt*) 1. A person or thing that takes the place of another person or thing: *The vice president often attends funerals as the surrogate of the president.* 2. A woman who bears a child for another couple: *Her friend couldn't have a baby, so she agreed to be the surrogate mother and have her friend's fertilized egg implanted in her.*

synopsis (*si·NOP·sis*) 1. A condensed version of a text; an abstract; a summary; a concise outline of a subject: *I don't have time to read the whole report, so just give me a synopsis.* See also COMPENDIUM.

transcript (*TRAN·skript*) 1. A written record of an event such as a court session or a television or radio broadcast: *The show's subject fascinated him, so he phoned to ask for a transcript.* 2. The record of a student's academic history: *The graduate school required a transcript of her undergraduate courses.*

transgression (*tranz·GRESH·un*) 1. An act that violates a law, command, duty, or moral code; a breach; an infraction: *His transgressions at the office Christmas party were probably serious enough to get him fired.* 2. An act that oversteps a limit or bound; an encroachment; a trespass: *Although he was just being friendly, he realized immediately that touching his colleague's shoulder was a transgression of her personal space.*

Word Wonders

Verisimilitude is one of the few (relatively) common English words that alternates consonants and vowels. Another one is *unimaginatively* (counting "y" as a vowel, in this case).

travail (*truh·VAYL* or *TRAV·ayl*) Hard work, especially work that requires painful effort or hard physical labor over a long period; toil: *After much travail, he succeeded in building his own cottage.*

trepidation (*trep·i·DAY·shun*) 1. Fear or uneasiness about the future: *Her imminent departure for college filled her with trepidation.* See also APPREHENSION.

verisimilitude (*VAIR·uh·suh·MIL·uh·tood*) The quality of being or appearing to be true or real: *He threw in details such as the color and feel of the fish to lend verisimilitude to his tale.*

zenith (*ZEE·nith*, "th" as in "thin") 1. The high point or climax of something; the culmination; the peak: *Nobody could understand why the player would retire at the zenith of his career.* See also ACME. 2. The point on the celestial sphere that is directly overhead of the observer (the celestial sphere is the imaginary sphere on which the stars and planets appear to lie): *You know it's noon when the sun is on the zenith.*

Questions and Exercises to Help Everything Sink In

Here's a list of the 100 nouns you learned in this chapter:

acclaim	acme	adjunct	advent
adversity	aegis	affinity	allusion
analogy	annotation	antithesis	archetype
artifact	avant-garde	bathos	behemoth
bellwether	bully pulpit	cataclysm	catalyst
catch-22	chagrin	chronology	cliché
collusion	compendium	complement	conduit
correlation	dearth	debacle	decadence
demeanor	deprivation	deterrent	dichotomy
disparity	dynasty	effect	embargo
enigma	epitome	euphemism	exodus
fiasco	foresight	gambit	gamut
gusto	hiatus	hindsight	horde
impasse	inception	inverse	iota
irony	itinerary	juxtaposition	labyrinth
longevity	metaphor	mettle	miscellany
misnomer	morale	onus	oxymoron
paradigm	paraphernalia	penchant	plethora
plight	precursor	predicament	prelude
prodigy	propensity	proximity	ramification
recourse	repertoire	respite	rift
sarcasm	satire	scourge	serendipity
solecism	sophistry	spate	status quo
surrogate	synopsis	transcript	transgression
travail	trepidation	verisimilitude	zenith

Match the noun on the left with the short definition on the right:

1. onus		**a.** a fortunate but accidental discovery
2. deterrent		**b.** something that prevents an action
3. serendipity		**c.** the opposite of something
4. inverse		**d.** something that is monstrously big
5. behemoth		**e.** a necessity or responsibility

In the following lists, I've supplied two meanings for each of the following five nouns. Match the meaning on the left (the list a to e) with the related meaning on the right (the list f to j):

6. aegis   **7.** disparity   **8.** gambit   **9.** paraphernalia   **10.** solecism

a. a maneuver or ploy	**f.** a dissimilarity
b. protection or support	**g.** a violation of etiquette
c. ungrammatical usage	**h.** personal belongings
d. a lack of equality	**i.** patronage
e. equipment or gear	**j.** an opening remark

Match the noun on the left with the synonym on the right:

11. mettle	**a.** relish
12. dearth	**b.** fortitude
13. synopsis	**c.** misfortune
14. gusto	**d.** famine
15. adversity	**e.** abstract

Match the noun on the left with the related noun on the right:

16. sarcasm	**a.** debacle
17. archetype	**b.** irony
18. metaphor	**c.** precursor
19. cataclysm	**d.** paradigm
20. bellwether	**e.** analogy

Chapter 28

100 Verbs You Should Know

In This Chapter

➤ Alienate, allay, and allocate

➤ Condone, convene, and converge

➤ Dismantle, dispel, and dissuade

➤ Permeate, perpetrate, and persevere

➤ Rebuke, reiterate, and repudiate

"Social institutions are what they do, not necessarily what we say they do. It is the verb that matters, not the noun."

—Aneurin Bevan, British statesman

Many writers love verbs above all other types of words. For example, in his classic book *On Writing Well*, William Zinsser says that verbs "are the most important of all your tools. They push the sentence forward and give it momentum." Lewis Carroll called verbs the "proudest" of the words. But even if you're not writing for publication, you'll still need a good stock of verbs. This chapter helps in that regard by supplying you with 100 ready-to-roll verbs that you can use as the engines of your sentences.

Abstain to Censure

abstain (*ab-STAYN*) 1. To deliberately refrain from doing something: *I'm going to abstain from alcohol for a month.* 2. To not cast a vote: *The mayor abstained because of a conflict of interest.*

adhere (*ad·HEER* or *ud·HEER*) 1. To stick firmly to something else: *Don't lick cold metal or your tongue will adhere to it.* 2. To hold firmly to a belief or idea: *She adhered to the teachings of her church.* See also ADHERENT. 3. To follow a set of instructions or a plan exactly: *We'll all be rich tomorrow if we just adhere to the plan.*

Idiom Savant

An *advocate* (*AD·vuh·kut*, noun) is a person who advocates. A *Devil's advocate* is a person who criticizes or argues against something purely for the sake of argument or to provoke a discussion. (This comes from the name given to the Roman Catholic official who is appointed to argue against someone's beatification or canonization.)

advocate (*AD·vuh·KAYT*) To speak or argue in favor of something; to plead: *Martin Luther King advocated non-violent resistance.*

affect (*uh·FEKT*) 1. To act upon or change something; to influence: *The quality of your soil affects your plants.* 2. To move a person emotionally: *His eulogy affected the crowd deeply.* 3. To pretend: *She affected an air of sophistication.* See also EFFECT.

aggregate (*AG·ruh·gayt*) To gather into a mass, sum, or whole; to unite: *Aggregate your costs to get the total expenses.*

alienate (*AYL·yuh·nayt* or *AY·lee·uh·nayt*) 1. To cause a person or group to become unfriendly or unsympathetic; to estrange: *She alienated her friends with her constant carping.* 2. To make a person feel disaffected or isolated: *Nerds often feel alienated from society.* 3. To cause something, especially a person's affections, to be directed elsewhere: *My neglect has succeeded only in alienating her affections.*

allay (*uh·LAY*) 1. To calm or pacify a strong emotion: *The counselor tried to allay her fears.* See also APPEASE, PLACATE. 2. To reduce or relieve physical or mental discomfort or pain; to alleviate: *Take this to allay your headache.*

allocate (*AL·uh·kayt*) 1. To distribute according to a plan; to allot: *Each member of the group was allocated a certain amount of water.* 2. To set aside for a specific purpose; to designate: *Each month they would allocate a portion of their salaries for the kids' education.*

annex (*AN·eks* or *uh·NEKS*) 1. To attach something to a larger or more significant thing; to append: *The new clinic will be annexed to the east wing of the hospital.* 2. To take over a territory and incorporate it into an existing political unit such as a country or city: *The Gulf War began when Iraq annexed Kuwait.*

appease (*uh·PEEZ*) 1. To satisfy or relieve something, especially a physical appetite: *He wolfed down a couple of cookies to appease his hunger.* 2. To pacify a person or group by granting concessions or acceding to demands: *She appeased the strikers by promising to return to the bargaining table.* See also ALLAY.

ascend (*uh·SEND*) 1. To move upward; to rise: *Please remain seated until we ascend to cruising altitude.* 2. To slope upward: *The path ascends at a 20-degree angle.* 3. To climb something: *His goal was to ascend the Matterhorn.* 4. To move up to a position of importance, especially a monarch to a throne: *Tomorrow the new king ascends to the throne.*

ascertain (*as·ur·TAYN*) To find out something with certainty: *He needed to ascertain whether his wife really was having an affair.*

aspire (*uh·SPYR*) To have a lofty ambition, goal, or desire: *She aspires to become a writer of vocabulary books.*

assert (*uh·SURT*) 1. To state something to be true; to affirm: *He asserted his innocence all through the interrogation.* 2. To maintain or exercise your rights: *To avoid incriminating herself, she asserted her Fifth Amendment rights.* 3. To put yourself forward boldly or forcefully, especially to state an opinion or demonstrate authority: *I had to assert myself at the meeting to get my proposal accepted.*

attest (*uh·TEST*) 1. To supply or be evidence that something exists or is true: *His low golf handicap attests to the fact that he spends little time at work.* 2. To confirm that something is true: *She was there; I can attest to that.* 3. To certify something is true or valid using a signature, oath, or some other official capacity: *This form requires a signature attested by two witnesses.*

augment (*awg·MENT*) To make something grow or increase in quantity, strength, or intensity: *He augments his income by working at the car wash on the weekends.*

avert (*uh·VURT*) 1. To turn your eyes away from something: *I'll avert my eyes while you change into these pants.* 2. To prevent something from happening: *She got off her cell phone just in time to avert an accident.* See also OBVIATE.

bristle (*BRIS·ul*) 1. To react angrily or indignantly to someone or something: *The player bristled at the suggestion of cheating.* 2. To make the hair or fur stand on end in response to anger or fear: *Your average cat will bristle at the sight of a dog.* 3. To be covered or thick with something, like the bristles on a brush: *The warship bristled with cannons and guns.*

cede (*seed*) 1. To surrender something to another, especially land, rights, or power by treaty: *The treaty required them to cede some of their territory.* 2. To yield something to another: *The angry politician refused to cede the floor when his time was up.*

censure (*SEN·shur*) 1. To criticize someone or something severely: *His plan to ban all Harry Potter books from the school was censured by the parents.* See also REBUKE. 2. To express official condemnation or disapproval of someone or something: *Congress threatened to censure the president.*

Circumvent to Ensue

circumvent (*sur·kum·VENT*) 1. To get around or avoid something, especially by using craftiness or ingenuity: *Her lawyer came up with an ingenious plan to circumvent the bylaw.* 2. To go around something; to bypass: *I've planned my route so that I circumvent the city.*

collaborate (*kuh·LAB·uh·rayt*) 1. To work together with another person or group to achieve something: *John and Paul collaborated on a new song.* 2. To cooperate in a treasonous way with an enemy, especially an occupying force: *As the tanks rolled down his street, he decided to collaborate with the enemy to survive.*

compel (*kum·PEL*) 1. To force a person to do something: *The author's deathless prose compelled her to keep reading.* 2. To make something happen by force or necessity: *Drought compels water conservation.*

comprise (*kum·PRYZ*) 1. To consist of something: *America is comprised of 50 states and the District of Columbia.* 2. To include or contain: *Our neighborhood comprises people of many different ethic backgrounds.*

condone (*kun·DOHN*) To overlook, forgive, or regard in a tolerant way some misbehavior or impropriety: *The teacher condoned sloppy handwriting but not sloppy spelling.*

convene (*kun·VEEN*) To come together for an official meeting or assembly; to arrange such a meeting: *The user's group will convene on Saturday.*

You Don't Say

Some people confuse comprise with *compose*, "to make up the parts of; to constitute." The basic rule is this: The whole *comprises* the parts, and the parts *compose* the whole.

You Don't Say

Elicit is perilously close to, and is pronounced the same as, *illicit*, "not allowed by law."

converge (*kun·VERJ*) 1. To meet at a single point coming from different directions: *The roads converge at the town square.* 2. To gradually become the same: *Car designs seem to be converging on a single style.* 3. To gather or arrive at a common destination: *The demonstrators converged on the embassy.*

covet (*KUV·it*) To strongly or longingly desire something owned by someone else: *He coveted his neighbor's table saw.* 2. To yearn to have something: *She coveted the new Volkswagen Beetle.*

decry (*di·KRY*) To openly condemn or disapprove of something: *The coach's critics decried his lack of leadership.*

delve (*delv*) To research or investigate something thoroughly: *I need to delve into his background to make sure he's a suitable candidate.*

detract (*di·TRAKT*) To reduce the value, importance, or quality of something; to derogate: *The cigarette dangling from her mouth detracted from her beauty.*

dismantle (*dis·MAN·tul*) To take something apart; to disassemble; to tear down; to sunder: *I've got to dismantle the old porch before I can build a new one.* 2. To destroy something gradually by removing key components: *The new owner dismantled the team by trading away the best players.*

dispel (*di·SPEL*) 1. To rid a person's mind of an idea, especially a wrong idea: *Her reassurances were enough to dispel my doubts.* 2. To scatter or drive off; to disperse: *The sun rose and dispelled the morning fog.*

dissuade (*di·SWAYD*) To persuade a person to not do something: *I must dissuade him from putting his life savings into pork belly futures.*

divest (*di·VEST* or *dye·VEST*) 1. To take something away from a person or thing, especially status or authority: *The board voted to divest the president of his title.* 2. To sell off a subsidiary, division, or other holdings: *The company will divest itself of its foreign operations.*

divulge (*di·VULJ*) To reveal something, especially something private or secret: *The actress will use her memoir to divulge the names of her lovers.*

elicit (*i·LIS·it*) To draw out something hidden; to educe: *The prosecutor's questions were designed to elicit a confession from the accused.* 2. To cause a reaction; to evoke: *His puns never failed to elicit a chuckle from his wife.*

embellish (*em·BEL·ish*) 1. To make something more beautiful by adding ornaments or decorations: *Use lots of candy canes to embellish your Christmas tree.* 2. To add fictitious, exaggerated, or ornamental details in an attempt to make a story more interesting; to enhance: *Granddad would embellish his yarns with stories of kings and queens.*

embody (*em·BAWD·ee*) 1. To represent or exemplify an abstract thing in bodily form: *The five-term senator embodies the old-school style of politics.* 2. To organize a number of things into a whole; to incorporate: *The latest cell phones embody many Internet features.*

ensue (*en·SOO*) 1. To take place shortly after something: *After her lottery win was announced, she knew the calls from "relatives" would ensue.* 2. To be a result or consequence of something: *With two marching bands accidentally on the field at the same time, chaos ensued.*

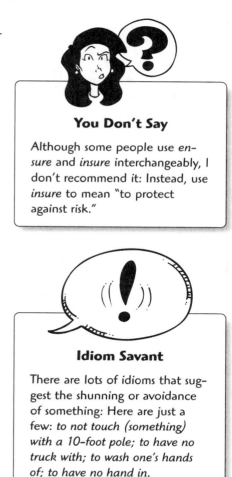

You Don't Say

Although some people use *ensure* and *insure* interchangeably, I don't recommend it: Instead, use *insure* to mean "to protect against risk."

Idiom Savant

There are lots of idioms that suggest the shunning or avoidance of something: Here are just a few: *to not touch (something) with a 10-foot pole; to have no truck with; to wash one's hands of; to have no hand in.*

Ensure to Jeopardize

ensure (*en·SHOOR*) To make certain that something happens: *To ensure that your package gets there tomorrow, use a reputable courier.*

eschew (*es·CHOO*) To avoid as a matter of course, especially on principle; to shun: *The writer vowed to eschew* CLICHÉS *like the plague.*

exacerbate (*eg·ZAS·ur·bayt*) To make a bad situation worse; to aggravate: *The threat of legal action only served to exacerbate the problem.*

expedite (*eks·puh·DYTE*) To deal with something quickly and efficiently; to see to it that something happens or is dealt with faster than usual: *The city councilor promised to expedite his friend's zoning request.*

exploit (*ek·SPLOYT*) 1. To use something selfishly or unethically, especially for personal gain: *His co-workers took advantage of him by exploiting his good nature.* 2. To make the most out of something: *To get ahead, she knew she had to exploit all of her talents.*

facilitate (*fuh·SIL·uh·tayt*) To make something easy or easier: *To facilitate processing your application, please fill in all the fields.*

You Don't Say

Don't mix up flaunt and *flout*, "to show contempt for; to scorn."

flaunt (*flawnt*) 1. To display something shamelessly or ostentatiously: *He married into money, so now he flaunts his wealth at every turn.* 2. To parade yourself shamelessly or ostentatiously: *She flaunts herself around town in flimsy outfits.*

foist (*foyst*) 1. To impose something unwanted on another person by force or by trickery: *Her inability to stand up for herself meant that she was always getting projects foisted on her.* 2. To give a person something inferior while claiming that it is valuable or genuine: *He tried to foist cheap costume jewelry on his wife.* 3. To insert something surreptitiously or fraudulently: *The senator managed to foist some* PORK *into the budget bill.*

foment (*foh·MENT*) To cause or stir up trouble; to incite: *He hoped his pamphlets would foment rebellion.* See also GALVANIZE.

galvanize (*GAL·vuh·nyze*) To stimulate a person or thing into action; to spur: *The perceived threats of globalization have galvanized today's youth.* See also FOMENT.

gesticulate (*jeh·STIK·yuh·layt*) To move the arms or hands, especially for emphasis when speaking; to say something using gestures: *She'll have more impact if she learns to gesticulate during her speeches.*

glean (*gleen*) To gather information bit by bit over a period of time: *I was able to glean these facts from the archives.*

impede (*im·PEED*) To slow down or obstruct the movement or progress of a person or thing; to hinder; to hamper: *The strikers formed a human chain to impede the trucks entering and leaving the plant.*

imply (*im·PLY*) 1. To express something indirectly; to suggest: *Her arched eyebrows implied surprise.* 2. To signify or suggest as a logical consequence of something: *His good grades imply a lot of studying.*

inculcate (*in·KUL·kayt* or *IN·kul·kayt*) To impress something firmly into the mind of another, especially by frequent repetition: *Their goal was to inculcate a sense of duty and responsibility in their children.*

incur (*in·KUR*) 1. To acquire or become burdened with something, especially something unpleasant; to sustain: *I incurred major losses during the stock market downturn.* 2. To suffer or be subjected to something as a result of your actions: *Being late yet again meant she would incur the wrath of her boss.*

ingratiate (*in·GRAY·shee·ayt*) To bring (or try to bring) oneself into favor with someone, especially to gain some advantage: *The new guy has been trying to ingratiate himself with the boss since the day he started.*

interject (*in·tur·JEKT*) To insert a comment or question abruptly into an ongoing discussion; to interpose: *"Don't go there!" she interjected as I was about to tell the room my favorite Raquel Welch joke.*

jeopardize (*JEP·ur·dyze*) To put a person or thing at risk of being lost or injured; to endanger; to imperil: *Your stupidity is going to jeopardize the entire mission!*

Jettison to Purport

jettison (*JET·uh·sun*) 1. To throw something from a plane, ship, or vehicle: *The pilot jettisoned some excess fuel before landing.* 2. To discard or abandon something: *We need to jettison the entire ad campaign and start from scratch.*

loathe (*lohth*, "th" as in "the") To dislike intensely; to abhor; to detest: *He worked in retail despite the fact that he loathed dealing with the public.*

mitigate (*MIT·uh·gayt*) 1. To make something milder or less harsh: *Her smile mitigated his anger.* 2. To make a crime less serious or more easily excused: *The fact that the victim was threatening him with a knife mitigates his assault.*

mollify (*MAWL·uh·fy*) To calm a person who is angry or emotionally upset; to pacify; to soothe: *The therapist's reassuring tone helped to mollify the patient.* See also APPEASE, PLACATE.

negate (*nuh·GAYT*) 1. To declare something to be invalid or ineffective; to nullify: *Falsifying information automatically negates the contract.* 2. To prove that something is false or that it can be ruled out; to deny: *The new findings negate the current theory.*

You Don't Say

Be careful not to confuse loathe with *loath* (*lohth*, "th" as in "thin"), "unwilling to do something; reluctant."

neutralize (*NOO·truh·lyze* or *NYOO·truh·lyze*) To render something ineffective, either by counteracting it or by removing its ability to act as a threat: *The weeklong bombing runs were designed to neutralize the enemy's ability to retaliate.*

obviate (*OB·vee·ayt*) To render something unnecessary or to avoid something by anticipating it and taking steps to dispose of it or prevent it from happening: *Save for retirement to obviate future financial problems.* See also AVERT.

oscillate (*AWS·uh·layt*) 1. To swing between two points with a steady, rhythmic motion: *The pendulum on the grandfather clock oscillates soothingly.* 2. To waver between two conflicting positions, points of view, or courses of action; to vacillate: *When she read the paper, she would oscillate between hope and despair.*

paraphrase (*PAIR·uh·frayz*) 1. To restate something using different words, usually in a shortened form: *He said, and I'm paraphrasing here, that we all need to get along.* 2. To rephrase something to use it creatively or in a different context: *To paraphrase Andy Warhol, everyone gets his or her 15 minutes of shame.*

permeate (*PUR·mee·ayt*) 1. To spread or flow throughout something; to pervade: *The Internet has permeated our everyday lives.* 2. To pass through tiny openings in a porous substance: *In the next stage, the liquid permeates the cell membrane.*

perpetrate (*PUR·puh·trayt*) To be responsible for something, especially a crime or other wrongdoing; to commit: *Who could perpetrate such a heinous crime?*

persevere (*pur·suh·VEER*) To persist determinedly in an action or belief, especially one that presents difficulties or obstacles: *Despite financial difficulties and exhausting work, she vowed to persevere through medical school.*

peruse (*puh·ROOZ*) To read or examine something thoroughly or carefully: *I spent the morning perusing the want ads.* (Note that this verb is often used to mean "to read something leisurely.") See also SCRUTINIZE.

placate (*PLAY·kayt* or *PLAK·ayt*) To make a person less angry or upset, especially by doing or saying things that please the person: *He tried to placate her with flowers and candies.* See also ALLAY, APPEASE, MOLLIFY.

pontificate (*pawn·TIF·i·kayt*) To express opinions or judgments in a dogmatic or self-important manner; to speak pompously: *After dinner, she would pontificate on the news of the day.*

preclude (*pri·KLOOD*) 1. To prevent something or to make something impossible: *The poor turnout precludes us from reaching a decision.* 2. To exclude a person from something; to bar: *A conflict of interest precludes him from taking the case.*

prevaricate (*pri·VAIR·uh·kayt*) To avoid telling the truth by quibbling or by being deliberately ambiguous or misleading: *The judge could always tell when a witness prevaricated on the stand.*

procrastinate (*proh·KRAS·tuh·nayt* or *pruh·KRAS·tuh·nayt*) 1. To put off doing something, especially out of habit or laziness: *She found it remarkably easy to procrastinate doing her household chores.* 2. To postpone or delay needlessly: *If you procrastinate, you'll just make things worse for yourself in the long run.*

procure (*proh·KYOOR* or *pruh·KYOOR*) To obtain something, especially by effort; to acquire: *I managed to procure two tickets to tonight's hockey game.*

purport (*pur·PORT*) To claim or seem to be something: *This painting is purported to have been done by Van Gogh.*

Raze to Yearn

raze (*rayz*) To level a building or group of structures to the ground; to demolish. *The tornado razed entire neighborhoods.*

rebuke (*ri·BYOOK*) To criticize someone, especially sharply; to reprimand; to reprove: *The judge rebuked the defense attorney for berating the witness.* See also CENSURE.

rebut (*ri·BUT*) To argue against something, especially by presenting opposing evidence or reasoning; to refute: *For each question in the debate, a candidate will be given 60 seconds to rebut the position of his opponent.*

reiterate (*ree·IT·uh·rayt*) To say or do something again, especially in an insistent or tiresome way: *The mayor reiterated that there just wasn't enough money in the budget.*

renege (*ri·NEG*) 1. To break a promise or commitment: *The player reneged on his contract.* 2. To fail to follow suit in a game of cards when required to do so: *When I saw her play the Jack of Clubs to end the game, I knew right away she'd reneged earlier.*

repudiate (*ri·PYOO·dee·ayt*) 1. To disown a person or thing: *He repudiated the child he had out of wedlock.* 2. To reject something emphatically: *She held a press conference to repudiate the charges against her.*

rescind (*ri·SIND*) To cancel or make void; to annul; to repeal: *When I take office, I will rescind this terrible legislation.*

scrutinize (*SCROO·tun·ize*) To examine something critically or with great care: *The lawyer needed to scrutinize the Supreme Court's decision before deciding what to do next.* See also PERUSE.

segregate (*SEG·ruh·gayt*) 1. To separate a person or group from a larger group or to keep people or groups separate: *In some schools, the students are segregated according to ability.* 2. To impose the separation of groups along lines of race, ethnicity, religion, gender, or class: *Racial segregation is still practiced in some countries.*

stanch (*stanch* or *stawnch*) To stop the flow of a liquid, especially blood from a wound: *He needed to stanch the bleeding to avoid going into shock.*

You Don't Say

It's easy to confuse stanch with *staunch* (*stawnch*, adj.), "loyal, steadfast, and dependable; solidly built."

stigmatize (*STIG·muh·tyze*) To characterize or label a person or thing as socially undesirable or disgraceful: *It's unfair to stigmatize someone based on where they were born.*

subjugate (*SUB·juh·gayt*) To bring a thing, person, group, or nation under the control of another; to conquer; to enslave: *The tyrant planned to* ANNEX *the neighboring country and subjugate its citizens.*

supersede (*soo·pur·SEED*) 1. To take the place of a person or thing: *These rules supersede all previous rules.* 2. To replace something with another that is better or more modern: *Television long ago superseded radio as the average family's evening entertainment.*

tantalize (*TAN·tuh·lyze*) To torment people by allowing them to see something they strongly desire but can't have; to tease: *She had no time off left to take a vacation this winter, but her friend would tantalize her with brochures of Caribbean hot spots.*

Word Wonders

Tantalize comes from the Greek myth of Tantalus, a mortal son of Zeus who was allowed to eat with the gods. When Tantalus took some of the gods' forbidden food and drink to earth, Zeus condemned him cruelly but appropriately. Stricken with a constant thirst and hunger, Tantalus was placed neck–deep in water and with fruit hanging just overhead. But when he bent down to drink, the water drained away, only to return again when he straightened up. And when he reached for the fruit, the wind would always blow it just out of reach. A tantalizing fate indeed.

transcend (*tran·SEND*) 1. To go beyond a limit: *The Internet transcends national boundaries.* 2. To surpass something: *The idea of infinity transcends human understanding.*

truncate (*TRUNG·kayt*) To shorten something by removing or cutting off part of it: *I'll truncate the story to save time.*

usurp (*yoo·SURP* or *yoo·ZURP*) To seize or take over something without the right or authority to do so; to appropriate (*uh·PROH·pree·ayt*); to commandeer: *The courts cannot usurp the authority of the legislature.*

vie (*vye*) To strive for superiority or victory; to contend: *Coke and Pepsi vie for a bigger share of the soft drink market.*

vilify (*VIL·uh·fye*) To make vicious and abusive statements about a person; to malign: *He was ahead in the polls until he started to vilify his opponent.*

wrest (*rest*) 1. To gain control of something in the face of opposition: *The people finally wrested power from the monarchy.* 2. To take something away by force, especially using the hands: *He wrested the gun out of her hands.*

yearn (*yurn*) 1. To long for a person or thing, especially in a sad, melancholy way because the object of desire is lost or beyond reach: *He was married, but she yearned for him still.* 2. To feel pity, tenderness, or compassion: *She yearned over the fate of the city's homeless.*

Questions and Exercises to Help Everything Sink In

Here's a list of the 100 verbs you learned in this chapter:

abstain	adhere	advocate	affect
aggregate	alienate	allay	allocate
annex	appease	ascend	ascertain
aspire	assert	attest	augment
avert	bristle	cede	censure
circumvent	collaborate	compel	comprise
condone	convene	converge	covet
decry	delve	detract	dismantle
dispel	dissuade	divest	divulge
elicit	embellish	embody	ensue
ensure	eschew	exacerbate	expedite
exploit	facilitate	flaunt	foist
foment	galvanize	gesticulate	glean
impede	imply	inculcate	incur
ingratiate	interject	jeopardize	jettison
loathe	mitigate	mollify	negate
neutralize	obviate	oscillate	paraphrase
permeate	perpetrate	persevere	peruse
placate	pontificate	preclude	prevaricate
procrastinate	procure	purport	raze
rebuke	rebut	reiterate	renege
repudiate	rescind	scrutinize	segregate

stanch	stigmatize	subjugate	supersede
tantalize	transcend	truncate	usurp
vie	vilify	wrest	yearn

Match the verb on the left with the short definition on the right:

1. delve
2. facilitate
3. neutralize
4. ascertain
5. stanch

a. stop the flow of a liquid
b. find out with certainty
c. research thoroughly
d. make easier
e. render ineffective

In the following lists, I've supplied two meanings for each of the following five nouns. Match the meaning on the left (the list a to e) with the related meaning on the right (the list f to j):

6. adhere   7. collaborate   8. exploit   9. preclude   10. yearn

a. use selfishly
b. stick firmly
c. prevent something
d. work together
e. to long for

f. cooperate treasonously
g. exclude a person
h. to feel pity
i. follow instructions exactly
j. make the most of

Match the verb on the left with the synonym on the right:

11. permeate
12. eschew
13. vie
14. procure
15. rescind

a. acquire
b. annul
c. shun
d. pervade
e. contend

Match the verb on the left with the related verb on the right:

16. censure
17. allay
18. peruse
19. avert
20. galvanize

a. obviate
b. scrutinize
c. foment
d. placate
e. rebuke

304

Chapter 29

100 Adjectives You Should Know

"Abrasive"   "Wry"

In This Chapter

➤ Ambiguous, ambivalent, and amicable

➤ Concerted, conducive, and consummate

➤ Disgruntled, disingenuous, and disparate

➤ Imminent, impeccable, and impromptu

➤ Procrustean, prodigious, and prone

"Adjective salad is delicious, with each element contributing its individual and unique flavor; but a puree of adjective soup tastes yecchy."

—William Safire, American journalist

As much as verbs have an exalted status among professional writers, adjectives are often seen as the low members of the lexical totem pole. For example, the editor Clifton Fadiman once described the adjective as "the banana peel of the parts of speech," and poet Carl Sandburg once declared himself to be "more suspicious of adjectives than at any other time in all my born days."

Despite these misgivings, adjectives *do* have a place in everyone's writing and conversations. The key, as hinted in the William Safire quotation that opened this chapter, is to use adjectives as though you were making a salad. That is, use ingredients (adjectives) that are high quality (the right word for the right situation), fresh (new and different words), and varied (don't use the same word over and over).

This chapter helps you make a tasty adjective salad by presenting 100 words that you should find useful when describing things when writing or talking.

Abrasive to Concerted

abrasive (*uh·BRAY·siv* or *uh·BRAY·ziv*) 1. That grinds or polishes using friction and a rough texture: *You'll need an abrasive cleanser to take care of that grime.* 2. Rough, irritating, or harsh, especially in manner: *How does a guy with such an abrasive personality get his own radio show?*

adamant (*AD·uh·munt* or *AD·uh·mant*) Determined not to be influenced by pleas or appeals to reconsider an opinion or belief; unyielding: *The prime minister is adamant that this legislation cannot be changed in any way.*

adept (*uh·DEPT*) Highly skilled; expert (*eks·PERT*); proficient: *She's adept at manipulating the corporate bureaucracy to get what she wants.*

ambiguous (*am·BIG·yoo·us*) 1. Having more than one meaning or interpretation: *Not wanting to alienate anyone, the candidate became a master of the ambiguous response.* See also DISINGENUOUS. 2. Uncertain or confusing: *With his term coming to an end, his place in history remains ambiguous.*

ambivalent (*am·BIV·uh·lunt*) Having mixed or conflicting feelings about something: *She has some good qualities and some bad qualities; I'm ambivalent about her.*

amicable (*AM·i·kuh·bul*) Characterized by friendliness and goodwill: *There were no hard feelings at all; it was one of those rare amicable divorces.*

antiquated (*AN·tuh·kway·tud*) Extremely out of date or outmoded; old-fashioned; quaint: *His antiquated ideas seemed out of place in the twenty-first century.*

auspicious (*aw·SPISH·us*) Characterized by good omens or lucky signs that promise future success or happiness: *The bright sun and warm temperature made them feel this was an auspicious day to begin their trek.*

austere (*aw·STEER*) 1. Self-disciplined; ascetic: *He desired to live the austere life of a monk.* 2. Plain in style or design; bare; undecorated: *I grew up in an austere household with few treats for the senses.* 3. Humorless and stern in appearance or manner; grave; somber: *Her blind date had the austere figure of a funeral director, which, in fact, he was.*

averse (*uh·VURS*) Strongly opposed or disinclined to something: *When it comes to my retirement account, I'm averse to taking risks.*

banal (*BAY·nul* or *buh·NAWL*) Drearily ordinary and dull; commonplace; unoriginal: *We were expecting something fresh and different, but the new CEO's remarks were simply banal.*

You Don't Say

Averse is very close to *adverse* (*ad·VURS* or *AD·vurs*), but the latter means "antagonistic; harmful." To keep them straight, think of "having an *aversion* to something" versus "having an *adversary*."

beleaguered (*bi·LEE·gurd*) 1. Harassed or under severe pressure; beset: *When the holidays come, I pity the beleaguered store clerks.* 2. Surrounded by troops; besieged: *The citizens of the beleaguered city didn't know if they could hold out through the winter.*

biennial (*bye·EN·ee·ul*) 1. Happening every two years: *Our state's senate seats have biennial elections.* 2. Living or lasting for two years: *This plant is biennial, which means it produces flowers in the second year and then it's done.*

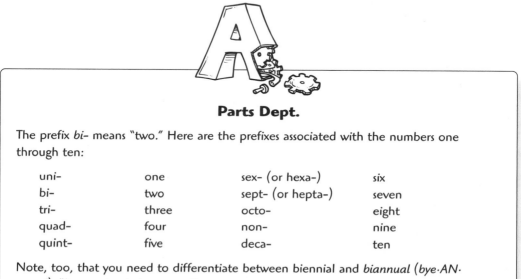

Parts Dept.

The prefix *bi–* means "two." Here are the prefixes associated with the numbers one through ten:

uni–	one	sex– (or hexa–)	six
bi–	two	sept– (or hepta–)	seven
tri–	three	octo–	eight
quad–	four	non–	nine
quint–	five	deca–	ten

Note, too, that you need to differentiate between biennial and *biannual* (*bye·AN·yoo·ul*), "happening twice a year."

blatant (*BLAY·tunt*) Very obvious or conspicuous, especially in an offensive way: *That's a blatant lie and you know it!*

bogus (*BOH·gus*) 1. Counterfeit; fake: *They caught him trying to use a bogus $20 bill.* 2. Useless, bad, or incorrect (slang): *That board is totally bogus.*

bombastic (*bom·BAS·tik*) Characterized by lofty phrases and pretentious words; grandiloquent; pompous: *Her speech was supposed to impress us, but it was so bombastic that we didn't understand much of it.*

circuitous (*sur·KYOO·uh·tus*) Lengthy and indirect; roundabout: *Those directions you gave me took me on quite a circuitous route.*

coherent (*koh·HEER·unt* or *koh·HAIR·unt*) 1. Holding together in a harmonious or credible way due to a logical or aesthetic consistency: *The professor enjoyed reading the student's coherent essay.* 2. Logical and intelligible speech: *I can't put together a coherent sentence before I've had my first cup of coffee.* 3. Sticking together to form an inseparable whole: *A solid is a more coherent substance than a liquid.*

colloquial (*kuh·LOH·kwee·ul*) Characterized by informal language: *He peppered his story with colloquial expressions such as "gotta" and "two bits."*

concerted (*kun·SUR·tid*) Planned or carried out together; combined: *The Human Genome Project was a concerted effort by many different laboratories, organizations, and agencies.*

Conducive to Esoteric

conducive (*kun·DOO·siv* or *kun·DYOO·siv*) Tending to encourage or make happen, especially a positive or intended result: *The silence of the library is conducive to studying.*

consummate (*KON·sum·it*) 1. Perfect or supreme: *She played the concerto with consummate skill.* 2. Complete or utter, especially with respect to a bad quality: *His father is the consummate bore.*

contiguous (*kun·TIG·yoo·us*) 1. Sharing a border or boundary: *Canada and the United States are contiguous.* 2. Touching physically; neighboring; adjacent: *She's been to every one of the 48 contiguous states.* 3. Continuous in time or space: *The senator served five contiguous terms in office.*

continual (*kun·TIN·yoo·ul*) Recurring regularly or frequently: *I can't work with these continual interruptions!* See also INCESSANT.

You Don't Say

The words *continual* and *continuous* (*kun·TIN·yoo·us*, adj.) are easy to confuse. The latter means "occurring without interruption or change." Although both words describe something that goes on for a long time, *continual* implies that there are breaks in the action, while *continuous* does not.

credible (*KRED·uh·bul*) Believable; plausible: *She's crucial to our defense because she's the only credible witness we've got.*

cryptic (*KRIP·tik*) 1. Obscure or mysterious, especially with a hidden meaning; mystifying: *People have been trying for centuries to figure out the Mona Lisa's cryptic smile.* 2. Secret or encoded: *The agents exchanged cryptic messages.*

cumbersome (*KUM·bur·sum*) 1. Awkward to handle because of size, shape, or weight; unwieldy: *Movers hate pianos because they're so cumbersome.* 2. Difficult to deal with, especially because of complexity or length; troublesome: *We're not reacting fast enough because our chain of command is too cumbersome.*

didactic (*dye·DAK·tik*) 1. Containing moral advice or instruction: *Didactic books are dominating the bestseller lists.* 2. Fond of giving advice or instruction: *Tell your didactic husband that if I want his advice I'll ask for it.*

disgruntled (*dis·GRUN·tuld*) Displeased and resentful: *The disgruntled shareholders asked the chairman why he received a bonus when the company lost money.*

disingenuous (*dis·in·JEN·yoo·us*) Not candid, sincere, or straightforward; crafty: *The minister's disingenuous reply was that she couldn't remember the events of just two days ago.* See also AMBIGUOUS.

disparate (*DIS·pur·it* or *dis·PAIR·it*) Fundamentally different or distinct; totally dissimilar: *With their disparate personalities, I'm surprised they get along so well.* See also DISPARITY.

divisive (*di·VYE·siv*) Capable of causing deep divisions or disagreements, especially within a group: *Politics can be a divisive subject, so it should be avoided at the dinner table.*

draconian (*dra·KOH·nee·un* or *druh·KOH·nee·un*) Excessively or unjustly harsh or severe: *We must work to reverse these draconian budget cuts.*

dubious (*DOO·bee·us*) 1. Uncertain; doubtful; mistrustful: *I'm dubious about his claims of religious persecution in his homeland.* 2. Possibly dishonest or immoral; of questionable character: *Rumors of dubious business practices continue to swirl around the company.*

eclectic (*i·KLEK·tik*) Drawing or drawn from a variety of sources: *She has eclectic taste in music.*

egregious (*i·GREE·jus* or *i·GREE·gee·us*) Conspicuously or outrageously bad: *Paying $1,000 for a toilet seat is the most egregious example of wasteful spending that I've ever seen.*

Word Wonders

Egregious comes from the Latin *egregius*, "outstanding," which combines *e–*, "out of" and *gregis*, "the herd." That is, the original meaning of this word described a person or thing that was of superior quality, that was literally chosen from the herd. This is totally opposite to what the word means now, which shows you that the paths taken by words aren't always straight lines!

elusive (*i·LOO·siv*) 1. Difficult to find, catch, or remember: *The elusive arch-criminal has frustrated authorities for years.* 2. Difficult to describe, define, or understand: *The idea of four-dimensional space is an elusive concept to say the least.* See also ESOTERIC.

eminent (*EM·uh·nunt*) 1. Standing above others; superior in position or achievement; exalted; prominent: *We're here tonight to honor a few eminent members of our community.* 2. Distinguished; notable: *Everyone wanted to read the new book by the eminent historian.*

ersatz (*AIR·zahts*) Characterized by being an imitation of or a substitute for something of superior quality: *He insisted that margarine was nothing but ersatz butter.*

esoteric (*es·uh·TAIR·ik*) 1. Intended for or understood by only a few, especially an initiated group: *The esoteric practices of the cult remained a mystery to outsiders.* 2. Difficult to understand; abstruse; recondite: *She liked to look at the esoteric symbols that remained on the blackboard from the previous calculus class.* See also ELUSIVE.

Ethical to Innocuous

ethical (*ETH·i·cul*) Consistent with or conforming to accepted standards of right and wrong conduct, especially those within a profession: *Violating attorney-client privilege is one of the most serious breaches of ethical legal conduct.*

exorbitant (*ig·ZOR·buh·tunt*) Exceeding what is reasonable, fair, or manageable; excessive; inordinate; unreasonable: *I refuse to pay such exorbitant prices!*

fulsome (*FULL·sum*) Offensively flattering or insincere; unctuous: *The fulsome praise offered by these toadies is enough to make one ill.*

gaudy (*GAW·dee*) Tastelessly or vulgarly showy; flashy; garish; tawdry: *She liked him but wished he would stop buying her these gaudy trinkets.*

generic (*juh·NAIR·ik*) 1. Applicable to or descriptive of an entire group or class; general: *The separate numeric keypad is a generic feature of modern computer keyboards.* 2. Lacking a brand name or trademark: *Many supermarkets are starting to carry generic goods, the so-called "no-name" products.*

germane (*jur·MAYN*) Suitably related; relevant; pertinent: *I don't see how the size of your outboard motor is at all germane to a discussion of early childhood education.*

glamorous (*GLAM·ur·us*) Desirable or alluring in a stylish, exciting, or romantic way: *She enjoyed reading about the glamorous lifestyles of Hollywood stars.* See also LUMINARY.

gratuitous (*gruh·TOO·i·tus* or *gruh·TYOO·i·tus*) Unnecessary and unjustified; uncalled-for; unwarranted: *I like an action flick but not one that contains gratuitous violence.*

halcyon (*HAL·see·un*) Calm and peaceful; tranquil: *How well I remember the halcyon days of my youth.*

hapless (*HAP·lis*) Unlucky or unfortunate: *Our hapless home team just can't catch a break.*

ignoble (*ig·NOH·bul*) Not noble in character or quality; dishonorable; shameful: *It's sad to see such a once-great man come to such an ignoble end.*

imminent (*IM·uh·nunt*) About to occur; likely to happen soon without any warning: *The jury's return is imminent.*

impeccable (*im·PEK·uh·bul*) Without errors or flaws; perfect: *She has impeccable taste.*

impractical (*im·PRAK·ti·kul*) 1. Unworkable, unfeasible, or not sensible in practice: *Critics of a space-based defense system dismiss the idea as impractical.* See also VIABLE. 2. Incapable of dealing with everyday matters: *He created corporate budgets but was impractical with household finances.*

impromptu (*im·PROMP·too* or *im·PROMP·tyoo*) Not planned in advance; done on the spur of the moment; extemporaneous; spontaneous: *The bride's impromptu remarks turned out to be the best speech of the entire reception.*

incessant (*in·SES·unt*) Unceasing or uninterrupted, especially to the point of annoyance: *Will you kids stop that incessant chatter!* See also CONTINUAL.

inchoate (*in·KOH·it*) 1. Just starting to develop; incipient: *The inchoate forces of anticonsumerism have been buoyed by their successes.* 2. Imperfectly or partially formed: *So far my essay is nothing but a collection of inchoate ideas.*

You Don't Say

Impractical and *impracticable* (*im·PRAK·ti·kuh·bul,* adj.) aren't the same thing. The latter means "impossible."

incognito (*in·KOG·NEE·toh*) With a concealed or disguised identity: *The starlet would often travel incognito to avoid being mobbed by her fans.*

inherent (*in·HAIR·unt* or *in·HEER·unt*) Existing as an inborn or essential characteristic; innate; intrinsic: *He believed in the inherent goodness of human nature.*

innocuous (*i·NOK·yoo·us*) 1. Having no negative effect; harmless: *Tell the props department that we need an innocuous white powder to substitute for cocaine in the next scene.* 2. Unlikely to offend or cause a strong reaction; insipid: *Her innocuous prose is best read just before going to sleep.*

Insidious to *Procrustean*

insidious (*in·SID·ee·us*) Harmful in a gradual, subtle, or stealthy manner: *AIDS is an insidious disease because the HIV virus can lie dormant for many years.*

integral (*IN·tuh·grul* or *in·TEG·rul*) Essential for completeness; constituent: *Fruit is an integral part of a balanced breakfast.* 2. Without missing anything essential; complete; entire: *You have to admire his integral personality.*

intrepid (*in·TREP·id*) Resolutely fearless and persistent, particularly in pursuit of the unknown; undaunted: *The intrepid adventurer forged ahead into the jungle.*

jingoistic (*JING·goh·is·tik*) Zealously patriotic, especially as expressed by hostility toward other countries: *The government's jingoistic foreign policy has the neighboring countries worried.*

lackluster (*LAK·lus·tur*) Lacking excitement, enthusiasm, or vitality; dull; drab; humdrum; pedestrian: *The play was marred by the lackluster performance of the star.*

laudable (*LAW·duh·bul*) Worthy of admiration; praiseworthy: *Raising money for the children's hospital is a laudable goal.*

lucid (*LOO·sid*) 1. Easy to understand; clear; intelligible: *The professor's lucid explanations helped her to understand general relativity for the first time.* 2. Rational; mentally sound; clear-headed: *Are we sure he was lucid when he changed his will?*

macabre (*muh·KAW·bruh* or *muh·KAWB* or *muh·KAW·bur*) Dealing with the gruesome and horrific elements of death and decay: *His macabre sense of humor meant that he was only fun to be around at Halloween.*

mediocre (*mee·dee·OH·kur*) Of average or ordinary quality; merely adequate; relatively inferior: *Although she didn't fail anything, her marks were only mediocre, which she blamed on excessive partying.*

meticulous (*muh·TIK·yuh·lus*) Extremely careful and precise; painstaking: *His meticulous attention to detail ensured that the show went off without a hitch.*

mundane (*mun·DAYN*) 1. Commonplace; everyday; ordinary: *It was all the little mundane chores that she could no longer stand.* See also QUOTIDIAN. 2. Relating to this world instead of the spiritual world; secular: *After his calling he was no longer concerned with mundane existence.*

oblivious (*uh·BLIV·ee·us*) 1. Unaware; unmindful: *My boss seems oblivious to the chaos her new rules are causing.* 2. Forgetful: *During a good play or movie, we're oblivious to the passage of time.* See also VIGILANT.

onerous (*OWN·ur·us*) Troublesome, oppressive, or laborious; burdensome: *The onerous demands of his new job were becoming too much to bear.*

optimum (*AWP·tuh·mum*) The most favorable or desirable; the best: *In summer, the optimum time to run a marathon is early in the morning.*

Word Wonders

Procrustean comes from Procrustes, a mythical Greek giant who would capture people and tie them to his bed. If they were too long for the bed, he chopped off part of their legs; if they were too short, he stretched them until they fit.

ostensible (*aw·STEN·suh·bul*) Professed or seeming, but especially hiding an ulterior motive: *The ostensible purpose behind his donation was to help the poor, but his real goal was to get people to like him.*

overt (*oh·VURT*) Performed or manifested openly; unconcealed: *I was taken aback by her overt hostility.*

posthumous (*POS·choo·mus*) 1. Occurring after one's death: *Her posthumous award will be accepted by her widower.* 2. Published after a writer's death: *His posthumous book hits the shelves today.*

preoccupied (*pree·AWK·yuh·pyed*) Totally absorbed in doing or thinking about something; engrossed: *There's no point bothering her now; she's preoccupied with the business plan.*

pristine (*PRIS·teen* or *pris·TEEN*) 1. Looking like new; immaculate: *This apartment is in pristine condition.* 2. Unspoiled; uncorrupted; pure: *Antarctica remains one of the few pristine places left on earth.*

procrustean (*proh·KRUS·tee·un*) Characterized by a ruthless disregard for individual differences or special circumstances; enforcing a merciless conformity: *As a free sprit, he hated the private school's procrustean rules and regulations.* See also STRINGENT.

Prodigious to Wry

prodigious (*pruh·DIJ·us*) 1. Impressively great in amount, size, or force: *I can't believe the facts she knows; she must have a prodigious memory.* 2. Extraordinary; marvelous: *People must surely have been in awe of the young Mozart's prodigious talents.*

prone (*prone*) 1. Inclined; liable; disposed: *The supervisor was prone to fits of rage.* 2. Lying face down: *After the client was prone on the table, the chiropractor began his ministrations.*

quintessential (*kwin·tuh·SEN·shul*) Being the best, purest, or most perfect example: *Donald Trump is the quintessential real estate tycoon.* See also: ARCHETYPE, EPITOME, PARADIGM.

quotidian (*kwoh·TID·ee·un*) 1. Performed or experienced daily: *She began to dread the quotidian commute.* 2. Everyday; commonplace: *I need a vacation to get away from these quotidian concerns.* See also MUNDANE.

You Don't Say

Prone and *prostrate* (*PRAWS·trayt*) both mean "lying face down." However, the latter has an extra meaning that conveys that the person is lying face down out of humility or worship. While we're down here, I should also mention that *supine* (*SOO·pyne* or *soo·PYNE*) means "lying face up."

rampant (*RAM·punt*) Happening in an unrestrained manner; unchecked: *The rampant growth of the weeds next door is starting to cause problems in our garden.*

redundant (*ri·DUN·dunt*) 1. Not necessary; superfluous: *The two public schools in the area are half full, so one of them must be redundant.* 2. Included as a backup component: *All airplanes come with a redundant power supply.* 3. Needlessly repetitive: *The phrase "hollow tube" is redundant since, by definition, a tube is hollow.*

regardless (*ri·GARD·lis*) In spite of everything; anyway: *He'd lost two men already, but he was determined to go ahead with the mission regardless.*

requisite (*REK·wuh·zit*) Necessary or indispensable; required: *Her resumé showed that she had the requisite skills for the job.*

retroactive (*ret·troh·AK·tiv*) Applying to a time or to things that happened in the past: *The union won a pay increase retroactive to the start of the year.*

stationary (*STAY·shuh·nair·ee*) Not moving; fixed; unchanging: *She bought herself a stationary bike so she could exercise during the winter.*

strident (*STRY·dunt*) Loud in a harsh, grating, or shrill manner; discordant: *The strident protests of the mob were giving him a headache.*

You Don't Say

Many grammarians and linguists get their shirts in a knot when confronted with the word *irregardless* and will dismiss it out of hand by claiming that the word simply doesn't exist. They can stick their heads in the lexical sand all they want, but irregardless *does* exist, and people—even professional writers—use it all the time. Having said all that, I'm certainly not claiming that *you* should use it. After all, it means exactly the same thing as *regardless*, and it has those two extra letters up front to complicate matters.

stringent (*STRIN·junt*) Strictly or severely controlled or enforced; rigorous: *Stringent regulations are discouraging people from constructing new apartments.* See also PROCRUSTEAN.

tangible (*TAN·juh·bul*) 1. Able to be touched; palpable: *Her new house was tangible proof of her success.* 2. Real or definite; concrete: *The low unemployment rate is tangible evidence that our economic policies are working.*

tenuous (*TEN·yoo·us*) 1. Weak and unconvincing; without substance; flimsy: *He could think of a half dozen ways to refute his opponent's tenuous argument.* 2. Slender, delicate, and fine: *She loved to gaze at the tenuous strands of a spider's web.*

uncanny (*un·KAN·ee*) 1. Too strange or mysterious to be of human origin or nature; eerie: *Each time I go into that house, I get an uncanny feeling that something terrible is about to happen.* 2. Surprisingly accurate or keen: *She bore an uncanny resemblance to Zsa Zsa Gabor.*

viable (*VYE·uh·bul*) 1. Capable of being done; feasible: *A bridge across the river is definitely a viable proposition.* 2. Capable of surviving: *Democracy is not viable if the people are not free.* See also IMPRACTICAL.

vicarious (*vye·KAIR·ee·us*) Experienced or felt through the actions or feelings of another person rather than firsthand: *He was married now, so he could only live a vicarious bachelor life by listening to the stories of his single buddies.*

vigilant (*VIJ·uh·lunt*) On the alert, especially for danger; watchful: *While the others slept, I remained vigilant for bears and other night wanderers.* See also OBLIVIOUS.

volatile (*VAWL·uh·tyle*) 1. Characterized by or subject to sudden change; inconstant: *You need a strong stomach to invest in this volatile market.* 2. Tending to become suddenly violent; explosive: *The police and strikers faced off in what had become a volatile situation.*

wry (*rye*) 1. Dryly and ironically amusing: *His wry remark set the room to chuckling.* 2. Twisted temporarily, especially a face into an expression of distaste: *She made a wry face at his off-color joke.*

Questions and Exercises to Help Everything Sink In

Here's a list of the 100 adjectives you learned in this chapter:

abrasive	adamant	adept	ambiguous
ambivalent	amicable	antiquated	auspicious
austere	averse	banal	beleaguered
biennial	blatant	bogus	bombastic
circuitous	coherent	colloquial	concerted
conducive	consummate	contiguous	continual
credible	cryptic	cumbersome	didactic
disgruntled	disingenuous	disparate	divisive
draconian	dubious	eclectic	egregious
elusive	eminent	ersatz	esoteric
ethical	exorbitant	fulsome	gaudy
generic	germane	glamorous	gratuitous
halcyon	hapless	ignoble	imminent
impeccable	impractical	impromptu	incessant
inchoate	incognito	inherent	innocuous
insidious	integral	intrepid	jingoistic
lackluster	laudable	lucid	macabre
mediocre	meticulous	mundane	oblivious
onerous	optimum	ostensible	overt
posthumous	preoccupied	pristine	procrustean
prodigious	prone	quintessential	quotidian
rampant	redundant	regardless	requisite
retroactive	stationary	strident	stringent
tangible	tenuous	uncanny	viable
vicarious	vigilant	volatile	wry

Match the adjective on the left with the short definition on the right:

1. exorbitant
2. disparate
3. requisite
4. adamant
5. jingoistic

a. fundamentally different
b. zealously patriotic
c. determined not to be influenced
d. exceeding what is reasonable
e. necessary or indispensable

In the following lists, I've supplied two meanings for each of the following five nouns. Match the meaning on the left (the list a to e) with the related meaning on the right (the list f to j):

6. beleaguered   7. consummate   8. inchoate   9. lucid   10. uncanny

a. perfect or supreme
b. inhumanly strange
c. harassed
d. easy to understand
e. starting to develop

f. mentally sound
g. imperfectly formed
h. surprisingly accurate
i. complete or utter
j. surrounded by troops

Match the adjective on the left with the synonym on the right:

11. laudable
12. antiquated
13. redundant
14. dubious
15. gaudy

a. superfluous
b. doubtful
c. tawdry
d. praiseworthy
e. old-fashioned

Match the adjective on the left with the related adjective on the right:

16. vigilant
17. mundane
18. procrustean
19. disingenuous
20. continual

a. quotidian
b. ambiguous
c. oblivious
d. incessant
e. stringent

Answers to End-of-Chapter Exercises

Here are the answers to the exercises found at the end of each chapter.

Chapter 1
1. confidant; 2. nemesis; 3. charlatan; 4. b; 5. c; 6. b; 7. e; 8. d; 9. c; 10. a

Chapter 2
1. cognoscenti; 2. d; 3. agnostic; 4. a; 5. iconoclast; 6. b; 7. e; 8. a; 9. c; 10. d; 12. c; 13. b; 14. d; 15. a; 16. b; 17. c; 18. gyno; 19. d; 20. a

Chapter 3
1. arrogant; 2. gracious; 3. a; 4. c; 5. c; 6. e; 7. d; 8. b; 9. a; 10. b

Chapter 4
1. c; 2. b; 3. a; 4. facetious; 5. c; 6. e; 7. d; 8. b; 9. a; 10. d

Chapter 5
1. a; 2. c; 3. speculate; 4. d; 5. c; 6. e; 7. a; 8. b; 9. d; 10. a

Chapter 6
1. b; 2. a; 3. hideous; 4. d; 5. e; 6. a; 7. b; 8. c; 9. d; 10. a; 11. c; 12. d; 13. c; 14. d; 15. e; 16. a; 17. b; 18. petty; 19. c; 20. b

Chapter 7
1. c; 2. du jour; 3. a; 4. e; 5. c; 6. a; 7. b; 8. d; 9. c; 10. a

Chapter 8
1. b; 2. a; 3. nose; 4. c; 5. e; 6. d; 7. a; 8. b; 9. d; 10. b

Chapter 9
1. interlaced scanning; 2. b; 3. digital TV; 4. b; 5. c; 6. d; 7. a; 8. e; 9. b; 10. a

Chapter 10
1. front matter; 2. b; 3. advance; 4. d; 5. b; 6. e; 7. a; 8. c; 9. d; 10. a

Chapter 11
1. column inch; 2. c; 3. retraction; 4. a; 5. d; 6. a; 7. e; 8. b; 9. c; 10. a

Chapter 12

1. b; 2. a; 3. rainmaker; 4. b; 5. d; 6. e; 7. b; 8. a; 9. c; 10. b

Chapter 13

1. c; 2. b; 3. supply-side economics; 4. c; 5. e; 6. d; 7. a; 8. b; 9. c; 10. c

Chapter 14

1. mission-critical; 2. b; 3. action item; 4. b; 5. c; 6. d; 7. e; 8. a; 9. b; 10. b

Chapter 15

1. b; 2. c; 3. sell short; 4. d; 5. c; 6. d; 7. e; 8. a; 9. b; 10. d

Chapter 16

1. jury; 2. c; 3. indictment; 4. a; 5. e; 6. d; 7. a; 8. b; 9. c; 10. c

Chapter 17

1. spin; 2. a; 3. barnstorm; 4. d; 5. d; 6. c; 7. e; 8. a; 9. b; 10. c

Chapter 18

1. d; 2. b; 3. front line; 4. a; 5. d; 6. e; 7. a; 8. c; 9. b; 10. d

Chapter 19

1. d; 2. v.i.s.; 3. b; 4. d; 5. e; 6. a; 7. b; 8. c; 9. b; 10. b

Chapter 20

1. 8; 2. d; 3. a; 4. d; 5. e; 6. a; 7. c; 8. b; 9. b; 10. c

Chapter 21

1. a; 2. b; 3. c; 4. b; 5. d; 6. c; 7. e; 8. a; 9. b; 10. c

Chapter 22

1. c; 2. b; 3. d; 4. a; 5. a; 6. d; 7. e; 8. b; 9. a; 10. c

Chapter 23

1. d; 2. a; 3. cum laude; 4. b; 5. e; 6. c; 7. d; 8. a; 9. b; 10. a

Chapter 24

1. aptagram; 2. d; 3. street furniture; 4. a; 5. c; 6. d; 7. e; 8. a; 9. b; 10. b

Chapter 25

1. b; 2. day trading; 3. e; 4. c; 5. f; 6. a; 7. d; 8. b; 9. a; 10. c

Chapter 26

1. b; 2. crepuscular; 3. d; 4. e; 5. b; 6. c; 7. a; 8. bagel, donut; 9. d; 10. a

Chapter 27

1. e; 2. b; 3. a; 4. c; 5. d; 6. b and i; 7. d and f; 8. a and j; 9. e and h; 10. c and g; 11. b; 12. d; 13. e; 14. a; 15. c; 16. b; 17. d; 18. e; 19. a; 20. c

Chapter 28

1. c; 2. d; 3. e; 4. b; 5. a; 6. b and i; 7. d and f; 8. a and j; 9. c and g; 10. e and h; 11. d; 12. c; 13. e; 14. a; 15. b; 16. e; 17. d; 18. b; 19. a; 20. c

Chapter 29

1. d; 2. a; 3. e; 4. c; 5. b; 6. c and j; 7. a and i; 8. e and g; 9. d and f; 10. b and h; 11. d; 12. e; 13. a; 14. b; 15. c; 16. c; 17. a; 18. e; 19. b; 20. d

Prefixes and Suffixes

This appendix lists dozens of the most commonly stumbled-upon prefixes (word beginnings) and suffixes (word endings). I know it can seem a bit silly to study word fragments instead of entire words, but there's method lurking behind this apparent madness. If you come across an unfamiliar word but you know what the word's beginning or ending means, you stand a good chance of figuring out what the whole word means. For example, if you know that the prefix *bio-* means "life," then it becomes easier to tackle a previously daunting word such as *biodiversity,* "the diversity or variety of life within a specific area."

Sometimes you get lucky and a new word will consist of just a prefix welded to a suffix. For example, knowing that the prefix *homo-* means "same" and the suffix *-phone* means "sound," it will come as no surprise that the word *homophone* means "a word that sounds the same as another word."

Note, too, that prefixes and suffixes are part of a general class of word chunks called *affixes* and that this class also includes a third member, the *infix.* This is an element that's inserted into the body of a word instead of at the beginning or end. Many infixes are just prefixes and suffixes working overtime. For example, consider this brain-bender of a medical term: *otorhinolaryngology.* It's looks like an undecipherable mess, but let's see what we can figure out:

➤ The prefix *oto-* means "ear."

➤ The infix *-rhino-* is the same as the prefix *rhino-*, "nose."

➤ The infix *-laryngo-* is the same as the prefix *laryngo-*, "throat."

➤ The suffix *-logy* means "the study of."

Putting it all together, we can surmise that the word means the study of the ear, nose, and throat and its associated diseases.

Some Common Prefixes

The following table presents a list of common prefixes and provides a definition and example words for each.

Prefix	Definition	Examples
a-	Not, without	Agnostic, anemia, arrythmia, asymptomatic, atheist
ab-	Away from	Abjure, abnegate, abstain, abstemious
abdomino-	Abdomen	Abdominal, abdominous
acro-	Top, height, tip, beginning	Acrobat, acronym, acrophobia
ad-	Toward, to	Adaptation, adhere, advent, adversity
adeno-	Gland	Adenoid, adenoma
agri-	Farming	Agriculture, agribusiness
ambi-	Both	Ambiguous, ambivalent
an-	Not, without	Analgesic, anarchy, anesthesia, anodyne
andro-	Male, masculine	Androphobia, androgen
ante-	Before	Antediluvian, antedate
anthropo-	Human	Anthropology, anthropomorphism
anti-	Against, opposite	Antagonist, antihistamine, antisocial, antithesis
arthro-	Joint	Arthroscopy, arthritis
astro-	Star	Astronomy, astrophysics
audio-	Hearing	Audiologist
auto-	Self, same	Autobiography, autocracy, autocrat, autograph
avi-	Bird	Aviary, aviation, aviculture
be-	Completely, on, around, make	Bemuse, besmear, beleaguered, bequeath
bene-	Good	benediction, benefactor
bi-	Two	Biennial, bilateral, bipartisan
biblio-	Book	Bibiolography, bibliolatry, bibliophile
bio-	Life	Biography, biology, biopsy, biotechnology
brachio-	Arm	Brachial, brachiopod
calli-	Beautiful	Calligraphy, callipygian
carcino-	Cancer	Carcinogen, carcinoma
cardio-	Heart	Cardiologist, cardiovascular
centi-	Hundred	Centigrade, centimeter, centipede

Prefix	Definition	Examples
centri-	Center	Central, centrifigal
cerebro-	Brain	Cerebral, cerebrospinal, cerebrum
chiro-	Hand	Chriomancy, chiropractor, chiropodist
circum-	Around	Circumference, circumvent
co-	Together, with, jointly	Cogitate, cognition, coherent, cohort
col-	Together, with, jointly	Collaborate, collusion, colloquial
com-	Together, with, jointly	Complement, complicity, comprise, computer
con-	Together, with, jointly	Condone, confide, congenital, consummate
contra-	Against	Contraflow, contraception, contradict
counter-	Contrary, opposite	Counterintelligence, counter-programming
cranio-	Skull	Craniology, cranium
crypto-	Hidden, secret	Cryptic, cryptography
de-	Reverse, remove, out of, reduce	Deflation, debug, defector, detract
dec-	Ten	Decathlon, December
deci-	One tenth	Deciliter, decimate
denti-	Tooth	Dentist, dental, denture
dermato-	Skin	Dermatologist
di-	Two, twice	Dichotomy
dia-	Through, between	Diagnosis, dialectic, dialogue, diastole
dis-	Not, absence of, undo, free from	Disorder, disease, dismantle, dispel
dys-	Abnormal, bad	Dyspepsia, dystopia
em-	Into, cover with, cause	Empathy, embody, empower
en-	Into, cover with, cause	Ensue, enrobe, engorge
endo-	Within	Endoscopy
entero-	Intestine	Enteritis, enteron
epi-	On, upon	Epidemic, epilogue, epitome
equi-	Equal, equally	Equilibrium, equity, equivalent
ergo-	Work	Ergonomics
ethno-	Race, people	Ethnocentric, ethnology
eu-	Good, well	Euphemism, euphonious
ex-	Outside, without, former	Expurgate, expurgate, ex-wife
extra-	Outside, beyond	Extroverted, extravagant

continues

continued

Prefix	Definition	Examples
for-	Completely	Forswear
fore-	Before, in front of	Foreclose, foresight, foreword
gastro-	Stomach	Gastroenterologist, gastroscopy, gastritis
geo-	Earth	Geocentric, geography
geronto-	Old age	Gerontocracy, gerontologist
gyno-	Woman	Gynecologist, gynephobia
hemi-	Half	Hemiplegic, hemisphere
hemo-	Blood	Hemorrhage
hepato-	Liver	Hepatitis, hepatoma
hetero-	Different	Heterogeneous, heterosexual
hexa-	Six	Hexagon, hexameter, hexapod
histo-	Tissue	Histology
homeo-	Like, similar	Homeopath, homeostasis
homo-	Same	Homophone, homosexual
hydro-	Water	Hydraulic, hydrophobia, hydroplane
hygro-	Wet	Hygrometer
hyper-	Over	Hyperbole, hyperglycemia, hyperinflation, hyperthermia
hypo-	Under	Hypochondriac, hypoglycemia, hypothermia, hypothesize
hystero-	Uterus	Hysterectomy, hysterotomy
il-	Not	Illegal, illegible, illicit
im-	Not	Impertinent, impecunious, impractical
immuno-	Immune system	Immunology, immunoreaction
in-	Into, cover with, cause	Ingest, inculcate, incur
in-	Not	Incessant, inert, infirm
infra-	Beneath, below	Infrared, infrastructure
inter-	Between, within, mutual	Interface, interject, internecine
intra-	Within	Intramural, intrastate, intravenous
intro-	In, inward	Internist, introspection, introverted
ir-	Not	Irredeemable, irreformable
iso-	Equal	Isobar, isometric
kilo-	Thousand	Kilobyte, kilometer

Prefix	Definition	Examples
lacto-	Milk	Lactate, lactose
laryngo-	Larynx	Laryngologist, laryngoscope
lympho-	Lymph	Lymphatic, lymphocyte
macro-	Large	Macroevolution, macromolecule, macroeconomics
mal-	Bad, abnormal	Malcontent, malignant
matri-	Mother, maternal	Matriarch, matricide, matron
mega-	Million	Megabyte, megahertz
micro-	Small	Microchip, microprocessor, microsleep
milli-	One thousandth	Millimeter, millibar
mini-	Small, miniature	Miniskirt, minitower
mis-	Bad, wrong,	Miscreant, misnomer
miso-	Hatred	Misanthrope, misogynist
mono-	Single, one	Monochrome, monologue
multi-	Many, multiple	Mulitimedia, multiskilling, multitasking
myo-	Muscle	Myocardial
nephro-	Kidney	Nephritis, nephrotomy
neuro-	Nerve	Neuralgia, neurologist
non-	Not	Nonchalant, nonpartisan, nonsense
ob-	Against, toward	Obdurate, obsequious, obstinate
omni-	All	Omnipotent, omnivorous, omniscient
ophthalmo-	Eye	Ophthalmologist
ortho-	Straight	Orthodontist, orthopedic
osteo-	Bone	Osteoarthritis, osteopath
oto-	Ear	Otolaryngologist
out-	Surpasses, exceeds, goes beyond	Outdoing, outflanking
over-	Excessive	Overconfident, overstock
oxy-	Sharp	Oxymoron
pan-	All	Panacea, pandemic
para-	Beside, abnormal	Paramilitary, paraphernalia, paraphrase, paraplegia
patri-	Father, paternal	Patriarch, patricide, patron
penta-	Five	Pentagon, pentameter, pentateuch
per-	Through	Permeate, perpetrate, persevere
peri-	Around, enclosing	Peripheral, periodontist

continues

continued

Prefix	Definition	Examples
peta-	Quadrillion	Petabyte
philo-	Love	Philanthropist, philology
phlebo-	Vein	Phlebitis, phlebology
photo-	Light	Photocell, photograph, photosynthesis
post-	After	Postdate, posthumous, postscript
pre-	Before	Prebuttal, preface, prelude
pro-	Favoring, before	Propensity, proactive
pseud-	False, sham	Pseudonym, pseudoscience
psycho-	Mind, mental	Psychoanalysis, psychology, psychosis
quadri-	Four	Quadrilateral, quadriplegic
radio-	Radiation	Radioactive, radiologist
re-	Back, again	Recede, receive
retro-	Backward	Retroactive
rhino-	Nose	Rhinoplasty
semi-	Half, partial, resembling occurring twice	Semicircle, semiconductor, semiofficial, semiannual
septi-	Seven	September, septet
sero-	Serum	Serology, serotonin
sex-	Six	Sextet, sextillion
sub-	Under	Subhead, subordinate, subversion, subwoofer
super-	Upon, above, superior	Superficial, supersede, superstar
sym-	Together, with	Symmetry, symptom
syn-	Together, with	Synergy, synopsis, synthesis
tachy-	Rapid	Tachycardia, tachyon, tachypnea
techno-	Technique, skill	Technology, technocracy, technoplegic
tele-	Distant	Telecommuting, telework
tera-	Trillion	Terabyte
tetra-	Four	Tetrahedron, tetrapod, tetrarchy
theo-	God	Theocracy, theology
tri-	Three	Triarchy, tri-chad, tricycle
un-	Not	Uncanny, ungovernable, unkempt, unruly
under-	Inferior, beneath	Underling, underwater
uni-	One, single	Unicorn, unicycle, unilateral
xeno-	Foreign	Xenophobe

Some Common Suffixes

The following table presents a list of common suffixes, along with definitions and example words for each.

Suffix	Definition	Examples
-able	Capable of; inclined	Portable, transmittable; insufferable, sociable
-ac	Pertaining to	Cardiac, hypochondriac
-acity	Quality of	Perspicacity, sagacity
-age	Collection; action	Verbiage; coinage
-aholic	One with an obsession for	Chocaholic, workaholic
-al	Relating to	Celestial, perihperal, skeletal, venal
-algia	Pain	Neuralgia
-an	Relating to	Bipartisan, protean, spartan
-ance	State; action	Alliance; continuance
-ant	State or condition; one who causes	Arrogant, incessant; litigant, tyrant
-ar	Related to; resembling	Crepuscular, modular; avatar, scholar
-ard	One who is habitually or excessively	Dullard, sluggard
-arium	Place containing or associated with	Aquarium, planetarium, serpentarium
-ary	Relating to; connected with	Monetary, pecuniary; military
-ate	Characterized by; act upon	Articulate, innate; abnegate, mutate
-ation	Action; result; state	Fermentation; ramification; deprivation
-ative	Relating to	Sedative, talkative
-centesis	Puncture	Amniocentesis
-cide	Act of killing	Genocide, homicide, suicide
-cule	Diminutive	Miniscule, molecule
-dom	State; realm	Boredom, stardom; dukedom, fiefdom
-derm	Skin	Epiderm
-ectomy	Surgical removal of	Appendectomy, hysterectomy
-ee	Possessor; receiver; performer	Mortgagee; nominee; devotee
-eer	Associated with or engaged in	Engineer, volunteer
-emia	Blood condition	Anemia, hypoglycemia
-en	Cause to be; cause to have	Widen, redden; lengthen, strengthen
-ence	State or condition; action	Affluence, decadence; munificence

continues

continued

Suffix	Definition	Examples
-ency	Condition or quality	Clemency, dependency
-ent	Performing or causing	Absorbent
-ent	One who performs or causes	Adherent, correspondent
-ent	Condition or state	Acquiescent, coherent
-er	Something that; one who	Filler, printer; cabinetmaker, dabbler;
-escence	State or process	Adolescence, convalescence
-ese	People or language	Chinese, Japanese, Internetese
-esque	In the style of	Kafkaesque, statuesque
-ess	Female	Actress, lioness, waitress
-est	Most	Biggest, farthest, warmest
-ette	Diminutive	Cigarette, diskette, kitchenette
-ful	Full of	Careful, scornful, slothful, willful
-fy	Make; cause	Mollify, vilify; horrify, certify
-gen	Producer	Carcinogen, pathogen
-genesis	Origin	Biogenesis, psychogenesis
-genic	Causing	Allergenic, hallucinogenic
-gram	Tracing; something written	Electrocardiogram; anagram, logogram
-hood	Condition or quality	Brotherhood, likelihood, sisterhood
-ial	Relating to	Celestial, editorial, judicial, martial
-ian	Relating to; one relating to	Authoritarian, utopian; pediatrician, thespian
-iasis	Diseased condition	Elephantiasis, psoriasis
-iatric	Healing practice	Pediatric, psychiatric
-ible	Capable of; inclined	Tangible, ostensible; incorrigible, irascible
-ic	Relating to; one relating to	Eclectic, lethargic; fanatic, skeptic
-ical	Relating to	Juridical, whimsical
-ine	Relating to; made of	Asinine, pristine; saline
-ion	Action or result; state or condition	Annotation, donation; remission, affliction
-ish	Relating to; similar to	Peevish, selfish; bullish, sluggish
-ism	Action; characteristic; doctrine	Nepotism; sensualism; conservatism
-ist	One who acts; a specialist	Lobbyist; dermatologist
-ist	A follower; one characterized by	Monetarist; egoist
-ite	Resident of; follower; product	Suburbanite; luddite; dynamite

Suffix	Definition	Examples
-itis	Inflammation; preoccupation	Appendicitis, tonsillitis; frontrunneritis
-ity	State; quality	Adversity, prosperity; generosity, vitality
-ive	Quality of; that which performs	Diminutive, elusive; operative, purgative
-ize	Cause; treat; become; perform	Galvanize; bowdlerize; militarize; visualize
-less	Without	Brainless, penniless, selfless
-let	Smaller version of	Booklet, droplet
-like	Resembling	Reedlike, warlike
-ling	Younger or inferior	Duckling, underling
-loger	One who does	Astrologer, chronologer
-logist	One who does	Cardiologist, neologist
-logue	Speech; speaker	Dialogue, monologue; ideologue
-logy	The study of	Biotechnology, psychology
-ly	Like or resembling	Homely, miserly, shapely, surly
-ment	Action; result	Indictment, reapportionment; ailment, enlightenment
-ness	State; quality	Sadness, happiness; articulateness, fickleness
-oid	Resembling	Humanoid, tabloid
-oma	Tumor	Carcinoma, osteoma
-opia	Eye defect	Myopia
-opsy	Examination	Biopsy
-or	One who performs an action	Agitator, counselor, defector, facilitator
-ory	Relating to; used for	Dilatory, savory; lavatory, observatory
-osis	Process; Diseased condition	Diagnosis, prognosis; neurosis, psychosis
-ostomy	Surgical opening	Colostomy, tracheostomy
-otomy	Surgical incision	Craniotomy, lobotomy
-ous	Possessing; full of	Curvaceous, infectious; poisonous, ubiquitous
-path	Practitioner	Homeopath, naturopath
-pathy	Feeling; diseased condition	Apathy, empathy; neuropathy, osteopathy
-phile	One who loves	Bibliophile, logophile

continues

continued

Suffix	Definition	Examples
-phobe	One who fears	Bibliophobe, hydrophobe
-phone	Sound	Homophone, microphone, telephone
-plasty	Surgical reconstruction	Rhinoplasty
-plegia	Paralysis	Paraplegia, quadriplegia
-plegic	One who is paralyzed	Paraplegic, quadriplegic, technoplegic
-pole	Seller or dealer	Bibliopole
-scopy	Visual exam	Arthroscopy, gastroscopy
-ship	Quality; rank; skill; collection	Ownership; kingship; penmanship; readership
-some	Characterized by; group of	Cumbersome, quarrelsome; foursome
-sophy	Wisdom or knowledge	Philosophy, theosophy
-tion	Act of; the thing done	Correction, fermentation; juxtaposition, retraction
-trophy	Growth	Atrophy, hypertrophy
-tude	State or quality	Lassitude, verisimilitude
-ty	State; quality	Amnesty; crotchety, pasty
-ure	Act; something that acts	Censure, procure; legislature
-ward	In the direction of	Forward, homeward
-ware	Things of the same type or material	Hardware, software, kitchenware
-wise	In a the specified manner	Clockwise, lengthwise
-y	Characterized by; like	Brawny; oaky

Index of Vocabulary Words

331

333

General Index

341

343

F

345

G

347

I

353

359

X–Y

Z

Check Out These
Best-Selling
COMPLETE IDIOT'S GUIDES

A Little Knowledge Goes a Long Way ...

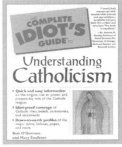

Understanding Catholicism

0-02-863639-2
$16.95

Learning Spanish on Your Own
SECOND EDITION

0-02-862743-1
$16.95

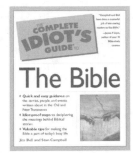

The Bible

0-02-862728-8
$16.95

Feng Shui
SECOND EDITION

0-02-864339-9
$18.95

Playing the Guitar
SECOND EDITION

0-02-864244-9
$21.95 w/CD-ROM

Personal Finance in Your 20s & 30s

0-02-862415-7
$18.95

Creating a Web Page
FIFTH EDITION

0-02-864316-X
$24.95 w/CD-ROM

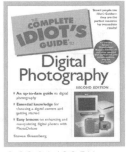

Digital Photography
SECOND EDITION

0-02-864235-X
$24.95 w/CD-ROM

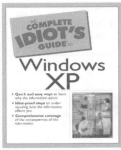

Windows XP

0-02-864232-5
$19.95

More than *400* titles in *26* different categories
Available at booksellers everywhere